No Country for Old Age

MISCHA HONECK

No Country for Old Age

America's War on Aging from Valley Forge to Silicon Valley

The University of North Carolina Press *Chapel Hill*

This book was published with the assistance of the Thornton H. Brooks Fund of the University of North Carolina Press.

Set in Arno Pro by Westchester Publishing Services
Manufactured in the United States of America

Complete Cataloging-in-Publication Data for this title is available from the
Library of Congress at https://lccn.loc.gov/2024034314

ISBN 978-1-4696-8096-5 (cloth: alk. paper)
ISBN 978-1-4696-8097-2 (pbk.: alk. paper)
ISBN 978-1-4696-8098-9 (epub)
ISBN 978-1-4696-8099-6 (pdf)

Cover art: Glass negative of Boy Scouts in Gettysburg, 1913, George Grantham Bain
Collection, Library of Congress, via Wikimedia Commons.

For Elena, Nikita, and Vera,

again, and always

Contents

Illustrations

Acknowledgments

Here is an obvious irony: embark on a book about rejuvenation, and you don't end up younger writing it. For someone moving into midlife-crisis territory, this may ring an alarm bell or two. Fortunately for me and the people around me, I continue to age gracefully (at least I try most of the time). I owe this in no small measure to the valuable contributions of colleagues, friends, and loved ones who have made this book a privilege to research and a pleasure to finish. I cherish the conversations I had with Kristine Alexander and Isabel Richter. They provided the spark I needed to get this project off the ground. I am indebted to Gabriele Metzler for giving me an office after my research position at the German Historical Institute in Washington, D.C., ended in 2017. Josef Ehmer, who passed away too soon, kindly lent his time and expertise as one of Europe's eminent historians of age and aging. Josef invited me to work at the Humboldt University's humming re:work Institute, where my ideas continued to ripen. Thanks to all the fellow scholars there who pushed me in ways too numerous and productive to mention.

I received valuable input at different venues at which I got the opportunity to speak about rejuvenation's place in US history. I am grateful to the German Historical Institute's director, Simone Lässig, for backing me early on, and for allowing me to host an international workshop on age and antiaging as categories of historical analysis. Hartmut Berghoff, Paul Nolte, Ute Frevert, Britta Waldschmidt-Nelson, Jürgen Martschukat, and Friederike Kind-Kovács generously invited me to present my research at their respective colloquiums. The bulk of the research poured into this book was made possible by a substantial grant from the German Research Foundation. I want to thank the selection committee and the anonymous reviewers for giving the application two thumbs-up. Without their approval, financing the trips to archival collections located in the United States would have remained a distant dream.

The COVID-19 pandemic put a temporary dent in my research and writing plans, and I am fully aware that I tested the patience of the good people at The University of North Carolina (UNC) Press. Had it not been for the magnanimity of Debbie Gershenowitz and her team, I doubt I would be typing these words today. Debbie's enthusiasm for the project never wavered, even when I thought I could never write my way into the twentieth century (yes, the nineteenth century can be excruciatingly long!). Working with Debbie, JessieAnne D'Amico, Erin Granville, Dino Battista, Lindsay Starr, and Liz Orange Lane has been beyond rewarding. I am happy to acknowledge the outside readers who weighed in on the manuscript at different stages, and I appreciate that they struck a healthy balance between constructive criticism and heartening reassurance. Fred Kameny, a true master of his craft, wrote the index. Thanks also to Nick Syrett, who encouraged me to reach out to UNC Press as I was looking for a publisher. Another shout-out goes to my student assistant Jonas Dittmann for helping me string together the bibliography.

I hope all are pleased with the fruits of my labor, which in significant parts also belong to them. There are trade-offs to condensing two-and-a-half centuries over roughly 300 pages. Some episodes are more richly developed than others. Other aspects of America's ongoing war on aging may not have gotten the coverage they warrant. I am aware of these imperfections. But I am content with the decisions I made, knowing full well that in any scholarly discipline, history included, we need both sharp and blunt instruments—the scalpel as well as the broad brush. This is where I want to tip my hat to all the long-term thinkers in the field. History is the study of change over time, but sometimes it also has to be the study of how little some things change over a very long time.

Rejuvenation lends itself to nostalgia, and its darker sides are on full display in our troubled times. In my somber moments, I find myself trembling at the thought of what the world will look like when the book goes to press. Are we incapable of averting climate disaster? Will our democracies disappear? Are aging autocrats, filled with resentment and vanity in their pursuit of political immortality, on the cusp of sealing a new international order? What good would it do to extend youth to those who deserve it the least? Then I snap out of it, and I look into the loving eyes of my two children and my wife. They keep me going, despite the headlines that are bound to drive sane people mad. This is their book as much as it is mine.

Abbreviations

AI	Artificial Intelligence
BSA	Boy Scouts of America
CCC	Civilian Conservation Corps
CIE	Civil Information and Education Division
CRLE	Coalition for Radical Life Extension
ERA	Equal Rights Amendment
FDA	Food and Drug Administration (US)
GSA	Girl Scouts of America
GYA	German Youth Activities
LEI	Life Extension Institute
LSD	lysergic acid diethylamide
NAACP	National Association for the Advancement of Colored People
SDS	Students for a Democratic Society
WPA	Works Progress Administration
WTA	World Transhumanist Association
YMCA	Young Men's Christian Association
YWCA	Young Women's Christian Association

No Country for Old Age

Prologue
To Begin the World Over Again

The youth of America is their oldest tradition.
—Oscar Wilde, *A Woman of No Importance* (1893)

A giant coffin on wheels. This is how the journalist Mark O'Connell chris-
tened the oddity parked in front of the United States Capitol on December 14, 2015. The man behind the steering wheel of the redesigned 1978 Blue
Bird Wanderlodge RV was Zoltan Istvan, the forty-two-year-old leader and
presidential candidate of the Transhumanist Party. Driving his "Immortality
Bus" across the United States, Istvan campaigned for his vision of a society in
which aging could be reversed and death conquered. To get there with the
help of modern science and technology, Istvan stated, "would be the greatest,
most positive revolution in the history of America and of the world." His
choice of the word *revolution* was intentional. Istvan walked up to the Capitol,
holding a document that he wanted to post on the building. But the paper
kept falling off the sandstone wall, and police officers armed with M16 rifles
began threatening him with arrest. Before he left, Istvan read out the "Transhumanist Bill of Rights" to a small group of journalists and supporters and
hastily taped it to the wall one last time. Its six articles, among other things,
labeled aging a "disease" and stated that all modified and nonmodified human
beings had the right to achieve "an indefinite lifespan."[1]

Istvan's publicity stunt may seem quixotic. His premise, though, that growing old is a malady in search of a cure resonates back in time. In declaring war
on aging, the transhumanists have joined one of the longest struggles ever
waged. Skip back to the year 1772, and we can hear the poet Philip Freneau
yearning for "America" to be a "Paradise anew" where, absent illness and
death, "future years of bliss alone remain." Fast-forward to the present, and
we find the two oldest presidents ever to run for office, eager to prove that
they are still young enough to serve. We also find futurists proclaiming aging
a code on the verge of being cracked, and tech billionaires turning Silicon
Valley into the mecca of antiaging science. Facebook's Mark Zuckerberg and
Amazon's Jeff Bezos are investing enormous sums of money to stop their biological clocks from ticking. The work of elevating humanity into a higher

state of existence is entering a new phase, and rejuvenation's portfolio—from uploading minds into supercomputers to upgrading bodies with cyber-enhancements—keeps on expanding.[2]

Money and technology are two reasons why the Bay Area has become the world's laboratory for cutting-edge research on how to turn back the life clock. A third one is history. Ever since the signers of the Declaration of Independence placed the right to life at the apex of the nation's revolutionary ideals, Americans have made undeniable advances toward securing the blessings of longevity. But the question must be asked: Whose lives exactly are we talking about? Our enchantment with spectacular antiaging schemes funded by the superrich cloaks a more troubling history, one that rejuvenation's wealthy backers are loath to address. Statistically, the United States is getting older each year, with the nation's median age approaching a record 40 years. Yet, the graying of America has barely disrupted the notion that youth is the true destiny of this country. Marginalized racial and ethnic groups have long been at a health care disadvantage compared to the privileged classes. The COVID-19 crisis has thrown such disparities into sharp relief. Simultaneously, the increase of mortalities from so-called deaths of despair among low-income adults addicted to alcohol or opioids has led to alarming forecasts. Ghastly pandemics, rising suicide rates, political violence, and shrinking life expectancies—not indefinite lifespans—are poised to become the new normal for many twenty-first-century Americans. The Istvans and Zuckerbergs may well be barking up the wrong tree.[3]

What is rejuvenation anyway? People from all cultures have striven to perpetuate youth and stave off old age, a desire probably as ubiquitous as falling in love, caring for children, dreading illness, or fearing death. But while the dream of eternal youth has deep roots, like those of an ancient oak, rejuvenation as an evolving set of biocultural mechanisms of regeneration and repair is younger historically. Modern concepts of rejuvenation, which have revolved around attempts to maintain youthful, healthy, and productive bodies, first emerged during the Age of Revolutions. The exaltation of youth, and with it the language of development, provided the soundtrack for a host of new nations, most notably for the United States. In a republic said to be uniquely wedded to the ideals of growth and perfectibility, the image of America as "the land of youth" would harden over time.[4]

So far, the question of how the centuries-long obsession with ageless youth spun itself into major threads of the American experience has escaped serious investigation. *No Country for Old Age* changes that. It reveals how the currents of rejuvenation have merged with the larger social, political, and cultural streams that run through the history of the United States, from its late eighteenth-century birth pangs to its twenty-first-century fractures. This widened lens has two advantages. First, it allows measuring continuity and change over the longue durée. Second, this book goes beyond accounts in which rejuvenation is mainly about sex and an upshot of the early twentieth century, forged at a time when doctors became famous for allegedly making flaccid men potent again.[5]

Breakthroughs in the fields of biochemistry, pharmacology, endocrinology, and plastic surgery spawned a dazzling array of new and at times highly popular and frequently contentious antiaging techniques. However, to say that the story commenced with these scientific revolutions is misleading. Manifestations of rejuvenation started interfacing with specific cultural and political contexts much earlier. Rejuvenation may not have become a catchword before the 1900s, yet key characteristics associated with it—regenerative growth, fears of untimely decay, the human capacity for starting over—already existed long before, from the time when George Washington's troops struggled to survive the winter at Valley Forge. Americans in the late eighteenth century peddled restorative balms, teeth-whitening lotions, and youth tinctures of various kinds. The replacement body parts grown in today's laboratories have their antecedents in the wooden arms and peg legs sold by nineteenth-century prosthetic vendors. The formation of distinct age-related categories could predate explicit recognition through naming. As Harvey Graff put it, "Formal naming often follows rather than precedes basic social change."[6]

When it comes to defining rejuvenation, conceptual boundaries can be as elusive as temporal ones, as the triad of rejuvenation, longevity, and youth illustrates. Defying cyclical models of growth and decline, longevity and rejuvenation are both expressions of the effort to combat the deterioration of bodies and minds over time. Still, they do not always overlap. Longevity advocates have been chiefly interested in extending lives, even if that goal involves easing the physical burdens of old age. Rejuvenationists, in contrast, have painted old age in much bleaker colors, as a place of irredeemable yet preventable doom. They seek health but rarely do so without trying to turn back the clocks of biology or history. Revitalization, not mere prolongation, has been the rallying cry of rejuvenationists across generations.

The connection between rejuvenation and youth is more intricate, ranging from the symbiotic to the confrontational. Their spheres commonly touch in youth's upper echelons where, according to Nicholas Syrett and David Pomfret, "youth was something 'mid-lifers' strove to recapture, floating relatively free of its chrono-biological markers."[7] Ideally, rejuvenationists seek to unite the best of two worlds: the delight of possessing at once the privileges of maturity and the dynamism of youth. Rejuvenation mixes the ages not only technically but socially: although endeavors to regain youth are mostly spearheaded by middle-aged adults and older people, they never fully own them. Their designs often depend on some form of participation, or at least acquiescence, by younger people, sometimes even by children. Youth can be quite antagonistic toward old age, and not every youth culture is an affirmation of rejuvenation. The annals of American rejuvenation are filled with examples of young people attacking the old, which made it harder for the elderly to age backward. The struggle over what youth is, and to whom youth belongs, is central to all rejuvenation projects and thus one of the main themes of this book.

Making the old seem young is the main ambition behind rejuvenationist schemes of age engineering. Age has multiple layers that unfold in different patterns and at a different pace. It is a biological fact: living organisms grow old until they die. It is a legal category: whether one has the right to vote, collects an old-age pension, or has to join the army, all depends to a substantial part on one's date of birth. It is a cultural construct: age not only historically draws and redraws the boundaries between one life stage (youth) and the next (adulthood); it also imbues these life stages with meaning, which itself is subject to change as semantic boundaries shift over time. Lastly, age is social performance. Similar to concepts coming out of the fields of critical race and gender studies, I want to emphasize the importance of "doing age" as a mode of passing. Adolescents seeking maturity or elders seeking vitality "do age" because they want to be accepted as members of an age segment other than their own.[8]

Bodies, like age, consist of different layers. From medieval Europe to the modern era, individual bodies have served as metaphors for the imagined bodies of kingdoms, empires, and nation-states. Conversely, these larger entities have been pictured as susceptible to the same forces of degeneration and decay that human bodies have to endure. This duality framed historical understandings of rejuvenation, which promised not just to erase the stamp of time from biological bodies. An equally important task is to identify the junctures at which rejuvenationists wielded their tools on behalf of repairing and regenerating the body politic. Rejuvenation's body projects, with the prospect of better health, potency, and joy, have always moved up and down an uneven ladder, stretching from the smallest living cells up to entire populations. Debates over birth rates, life expectancies, or migration evolved in complex ways; yet behind trepidations about demographic change, a fundamental question often lurked: Are we too old or too young?[9]

Oscillating between the collective and the individual, rejuvenation comprises soft as well as hard elements. "Pay your surgeon very well to break the spell of aging" is a line from the Red Hot Chili Peppers' 1999 song *Californication*. Histories focusing on invasive procedures from plastic surgery to blood transfusions, however, sometimes falsely imply that softer practices such as cosmetics and skin care take place in a different universe. On the contrary, these practices promised similar results with different methods and constituted moving parts on a wider antiaging spectrum. A useful analytical framework needs to take into account that different rejuvenationist practices had different temporalities and destinations. Backward-looking aspirations to be young again coexisted with forward-looking efforts to stay young. Some chose iterative modes of escaping the liabilities of aging, like middle-aged men who sought to recapture boyhood through forays into the worlds of play and make-believe. Others wanted to extend their youthfulness with one decisive intervention, be it through modes of surgical restoration or by joining mass movements that strove to renew society.[10]

No Country for Old Age looks at America's long war on aging from all these angles. It takes rejuvenation seriously as a form of nation-making, not just as an instrument for self-improvement. This recalibration away from narrower medical definitions requires telling a broader story. Both a product and driver of historical change, the scramble for youth branched out in many directions, and following these branches can uncover connections between people and movements from different eras that have long gone unrecognized. Is it a coincidence that Americans of the 1840s and 1850s began trusting the recuperative powers of the water cure at the same time that they exhibited a greater distrust of aging elites at home and abroad; that camping became one of the nation's favorite recreational pursuits in the years following the official closing of the frontier in 1890; that the experiments of rejuvenation doctors in the 1920s to resexualize white men hit the front pages in the heyday of racist demography; or that the hippie revolutionaries of the 1960s advertised the use of lysergic acid diethylamide (LSD) as a way to return to their inner childhoods while the country was losing its innocence in the jungles of Vietnam? This book answers with a resounding no.

BEFORE CHARTING REJUVENATION'S SERPENTINE PATHS through US history, it may be prudent to recall that youth has always stood tall in the national mythology. "In the beginning, all the world was America," penned John Locke in 1689. During the English philosopher's lifetime, stories that likened the New World to a Garden of Eden, and its Indigenous peoples (who were already being slaughtered by the thousands) to childlike "noble savages" had started circulating in Europe. "We found the people most gentle, loving, and faithful, void of all guile and treason and such as lived after the manner of the Golden Age," noted a survivor of the lost English colony of Roanoke in what is now North Carolina. No proof exists of whether the Roanoke colonists knew about another ill-fated venture that had taken place farther south about seventy years earlier, which gave birth to the most enduring rejuvenation legend of the second millennium. What drove the Spanish conquistador Ponce de León around 1513 to set foot on what later became Florida, according to lore, were no material riches or military exploits. He wished to bathe in the waters of a fabulous spring said to make people young again.[11]

The Spaniard never found the "Fountain of Youth," yet its imaginary waters would fill the well of American exceptionalism. From Ponce de León's expedition to current transhumanist schemes, such myths have irrigated the belief that the land was destined for greatness because it enabled its people to start afresh. Thomas Paine, the English-born pamphleteer, gave classic expression to this idea when he tried to mobilize support for independence in the spring of 1776. "We have it in our power to begin the world over again," Paine implored, predicting that "the birthday of a new world is at hand."[12] Already at the nation's inception, contemporaries linked the birth of the United States to the rejuvenation of the entire globe.

Paine's revolutionary rhetoric offers a glimpse of the first of rejuvenation's many faces. Rejuvenationist thought and practice have repeatedly clustered around utopian ideas, conjuring up worlds where youth is readily available to those who seek it. It is hard to miss the messianic glow radiating from refusals to succumb to the aging process. Rejuvenation shares with religion the wish to overcome the limitations of human bodies and temporalities, even as its promise of transcendence could serve decidedly nonreligious ends. Americans of all ages, genders, classes, and colors have found strength and purpose in trying to make older legacies assume younger forms, whether this meant mending themselves or reforming the communities to which they belonged. Age-to-youth engineering promised the liberties associated with infinite growth and expansion, but it also held out the possibility of liberation from corrosive pasts. The renovation of bodies, individual or collective, often contained an element of moral hygiene. That element bubbled to the surface when the struggle to reclaim youth melded with the aspiration to wash off the unyouthful stains of fatigue, cynicism, and despair. In rejuvenation's most utopian guise, empowerment was redemptive, and redemption was empowering.[13]

At no point, however, were the roads to ageless youth broad enough to accommodate everybody. They appeared wide to the privileged few but could turn out very narrow for the unprivileged many. Which persons and groups constructed these roads, and which were licensed to travel them? Who sat in the front seats and who in the rear? And which people were denied permission to use them at all? No critical history can afford to ignore these questions. Rejuvenation comes with a price tag, and this book is every bit as devoted to calculating the economic, political, and cultural costs inflicted by different antiaging fads as it is to explaining their appeal. Another fallacy would be to assume that only because youth as a purifying force could be harnessed to all kinds of purposes, all inevitably craved it. As we turn to various youth crazes, we must also examine their limitations, contradictions, and, above all, their divisive effects.

Consider class. To the extent that rejuvenation became commodified and tied to consumer choices, buying power emerged as a crucial marker of difference. In an increasingly urban and commercialized society, where the products of rejuvenation—from invigorating elixirs sold on the streets of Civil War–era America to the rise of recreational tourism after 1900 and the invention of Viagra in 1989—were available to those who could afford them, including the knowledge of how to apply them, poverty became ever more entangled with the visible signs of premature aging (weary eyes, saggy skin, missing teeth). Capitalism itself was celebrated in rejuvenationist terms. Rendering all that was sluggish outdated, the captains of industry held that in an economy valuing innovation and constantly overturning customs, youth was always in the making. Labor activists pushed back, developing their own youth-themed recipes of reform and revolution. Critics on the left, mainly within the framework of organized labor, posited that fighting a decadent bourgeoisie required a muscular working-class masculinity, akin to the aestheticized brawny bodies that dominate much of the public artwork created during the New Deal.

Consider gender. As the mention of masculinity indicates, efforts to manage and engineer bodies are rarely ungendered, and apprehensions over the loss of youthfulness have affected the sexes differently. The philosopher and activist Susan Sontag made this point in 1972 when she assailed the "double standard of aging" in Western culture that had placed an extra burden on women to conform to hegemonic beauty ideals. Often blamed by feminists for making attractiveness the prime measure of female social capital, with significant exchange value on the marriage and employment markets, the rise of the cosmetics industry seems to bear out Sontag's thesis. Such a reading, however, glides over the playful and emancipatory aspects built into cosmetic practices of rejuvenation. I intend to leave more room for ambivalence. This includes showing where lipsticks and face powder aligned with the reproductive body of the mother who was to secure the biological survival of the nation. But it also means stressing how Americans accessed beauty markets to carve out alternative femininities and queer identities. These have ranged all the way from the glitzy flapper and confident business girl of the 1920s to drag queens and the middle-aged millennial women who reject conventional looks by dyeing their hair gray or silver.[14]

By no means mutually exclusive, feminine and masculine body projects often fed off one another. This is true for the relationship between reproduction and state-building, but no less so for the materiality of rejuvenation. When talking about soaps, creams, and mascaras, one must not pass over the imperial infrastructures that facilitated the import of raw materials needed for the manufacture and consumption of cosmetic products in the metropole. From the mid-nineteenth century onward, palm kernel nuts harvested in West Africa became ever more indispensable for their high-quality oils and thus a central part of colonial economies. As early as the 1830s, when searching for an export good to replace slaves, British and US merchants began investing in the palm and coconut oil trade. Indigenous workers extracted "youth fluids" under the harshest of conditions for the enjoyment of middle-class homes in Europe and North America. Long before the pioneering businesswomen Helena Rubinstein and Elizabeth Arden opened their beauty parlors in early twentieth-century New York, men who perceived colonial conquest as youthfully rejuvenating had laid the material foundations for the beauty industry to flourish.[15]

Consider therefore race. If rejuvenation was complicit in stabilizing hierarchies of class and gender, it was also remarkably white. Skin color has been a critical factor in defining the boundaries of socially acceptable body enhancement. Still, the historical relationship of rejuvenation and race was far from monolithic. The prevalence of whiteness in Western efforts to inject a healthy dose of youthfulness in aging organisms begs the question of whether participating in such endeavors ever constituted a viable option for people of color. The long history of infantilizing rather than rejuvenating the non-whites—of keeping them locked in a state of immaturity—added insult to injury. From demeaning grown Black men with the epithet "boy" to portraying colonized peoples in Southeast Asia or the Caribbean as childlike wards, white America tended to deny any significant role to racial others in pursuing rejuvenation for themselves. In the logic of empire, non-whites stood outside dominant notions of progressive as well as deep historical time. Nonetheless, counterhegemonic critiques were possible. Antiracist and anticolonial activists turned the racist view on its head that healthy encounters with the primitive were needed to cure Anglo-Saxon culture of "civilization fatigue." The vocabulary of youth, they hoped, would further their causes, too.[16]

Finally, consider political ideology. Americans who lived through the founding era adopted a youthful image for their nascent republic with relative ease since the United States was formed in explicit opposition to the old monarchies of Europe. The challenge to this exceptionalist binary arrived in the form of distant revolutions with their own distinct notions of newness. In the nineteenth-century world of competing nationalisms, and perhaps even more so in Eric Hobsbawm's twentieth-century world of ideological extremes, age became a crucial tool of self-making and othering. Much ink has been spilled over how fascists and communists embraced youth-led action to fight the remnants of the old order and to enforce alternative modernities built on militarized concepts of class and race. But "new men" and "new women" were not just in high demand in Rome, Moscow, or Berlin. Policymakers from white middle-class America, too, championed revitalization treatments for their time-honored republic, if only to refute allegations that liberal democracies were like doddering elders staring into their own graves. Such demands for rejuvenating the state often concealed a strong conservative, if not reactionary, streak. This is another sobering lesson this book aims to impart: the prime reason America's political elites sought to shed old skins was, in many cases, the fear that youthful alternatives from foreign shores might overtake them, rather than a sincere wish to start over again.[17]

HISTORY HAS A BAD HABIT of overwhelming those who study it. The deeper one digs, the greater the risk of drowning in information. Rejuvenation, too, may appear as a many-headed hydra. Slash off one head without cauterizing its stump, and two new ones will grow in its place. The mission at hand, though, is not to slay a monster. I see my role as that of a cartographer who tracks directions, locates intersections, assesses dead ends, and gauges distances. In rejuvenation's grid system, we find uncharted paths that expand into busy highways alongside roads that fizzle out and lead nowhere. Each body project that left a mark in the annals of the United States had its own lifespan, geographic reach, social constituency, degrees of acceptance and rejection, and ideas about what constitutes the perfect age. A set of rejuvenationist practices that chimed with one group might have struck another as misguided. Others rejected the scramble for youth wholesale, sensing an assault on the virtues of old age (such as wisdom and dignity) or, more disturbingly, a wolf in sheep's clothing: a perfidious scheme to disguise the legacies of misogyny, racism, and war.

And yet, rejuvenation's contested pasts add specificity to the human longing to bridge two conflicting desires. On the one hand, rejuvenation fascinates us because it conjures up a horizon of unfading physical and mental powers where the linearity of time is suspended and subjected to human control. In a future in which crossing the threshold from vitality to exhaustion is indefinitely delayed, holding on to youth is seen as tantamount to realizing fantasies of seemingly boundless improvement. On the other hand, rejuvenation is tangled up in idealized pasts waiting to be rebooted, a nostalgic yearning to return to a place where one finds relief from a vexing present. Precisely because it swings between the dynamism of youth and the innocence of childhood, this pendulum has served reactionary as well as revolutionary causes, as a means of preserving society as well as changing it.

The chapters of this book revolve around some of the more momentous pendulum swings in America's past. They focus on examples from different periods but are tied together by the same analytical matrix: Where and when did enterprises dedicated to repairing individual and collective bodies reinforce one another? Where did they clash and collide or simply go separate ways? How inclusive was the circle of we in such circumstances? Which actors voiced criticism, and which were deemed unworthy of rejuvenation and left out? What difference did it make when adult rejuvenators sought alliances with actual youths, and when did the latter sense identity theft and push back? What was the historical fallout of failed rejuvenation attempts? Did the wreckage they left behind give birth to cautionary tales? Or did disaster simply initiate the next round of rejuvenation?

The episodes highlighted here cover all these questions, tracing the evolution of a dauntingly vast obsession that has attached itself to different causes over two-and-a-half centuries. This story does not move along a straight path, and reading the following nine chapters may feel a little like tracking the famous baseball in Don DeLillo's novel *Underworld* as it passes from one owner to the next. Emphasizing that rejuvenation is a highly malleable concept, at times even a jarring shape-shifter, is exactly the point. Hardly ever pursued as an end in itself, the desire to fend off old age was woven into a grand historical tapestry of biopolitical struggle in which diverse groups believed they needed younger selves to better their status in society. Open to redefinition, rejuvenation could pop up in unexpected places as a frequently unspoken yet powerful concern.

Chapter 1 revisits the nation's founding, detailing how its architects tried to convince themselves that the new United States was both the most youthful and most mature nation ever established. This consensus was shaken in the 1840s and 1850s, when the country was gripped by water cures, revolutionary movements, and generational strife. These connections are the subject of chapter 2. In chapter 3, the story turns to the rejuvenationist effects that Americans ascribed to various frontier crossings, from fin de siècle expeditions to the advent of mass tourism in places like Florida and California. Chapter 4 addresses the fraught relationship between cosmetics and colonialism, before chapter 5 reassesses surgical attempts to boost Euro-American potency in the interwar years against the triple backdrops of the Harlem Renaissance, the Great Depression, and eugenic concerns about the fading vitality of the nation.

Chapter 6 moves on to discuss rejuvenation as a tool in US foreign relations, using the reeducation of defeated Germany and Japan after 1945 as the two main examples. The long 1960s serve as the backdrop to chapter 7, which examines the ways in which countercultural activists eager to take on the establishment idealized youth and childhood as redemptive spaces. Chapter 8 expounds how youthfully fit and slim bodies became fixations for disoriented and predominantly suburban middle-agers in the 1970s. The book ends with an appraisal in chapter 9 of the antiaging schemes hatched by Silicon Valley's tech elite, demonstrating how fantasies of everlasting youth have both animated transhumanists and alarmed their critics.

Dreams of returning to purer forms spanned oceans and continents, and my interest in the United States is not meant to minimize rejuvenation's global reach. There is nothing inherently American about the desire to dodge the jaws of old age. Yet, when it came to believing that it can prosper in power and prestige without having to pay the price of aging, the United States has had few rivals. At home and abroad, images of America's perennial youth have endured the passage of time. That sense of unfading newness has shored up claims about the nation's special destiny compared to the rest of the world. For some, the country has never stopped coming of age, despite the fact that it has existed for almost 250 years. Youth and innocence have been remarkably resilient symbols throughout US history, even as they have caused more harm than good. I want to resist the temptation of a narrative in which withered creeds survive countless winters only to regreen more lavishly the following spring. Writing about rejuvenation that way would amount to a refusal to listen—a failure to heed the experiences of people who, excluded from the refurbishing powers of a fresh start, have groaned under history's agonizing burdens far too long. More than ever, we need stories about ourselves that teach us humility instead of hubris, empathy instead of self-enhancement.

As I tell the unfamiliar story of America's war on aging, I want to retell the story of America in refreshing new ways. Nations thrive on fictions of unity, and nationalisms of various origins recoil at the diversities and fragmentations of modern life. Similarly, concepts of youth fluctuate between clarity and chaos as the transgressions of young people often arouse anxiety in adults. Those craving immunity from disintegration have found solace in youth's apparent wholeness, which lies at the bottom of countless quests for rejuvenation. Grasping these quests may bring us a little closer to unraveling the mystery of the green light at the end of F. Scott Fitzgerald's *The Great Gatsby*—"that orgiastic future that year by year recedes before" American go-getters of the Gatsby type.[18] But it also provides some of the strongest criticisms that history has to offer, compelling us to pause in front of humanity's greatest ash heaps and the vices that caused them: rapacity, chauvinism, and a narcissistic sense of entitlement. This story is bigger than the United States, but it is not one from which Americans can claim exemption.

CHAPTER ONE

Phoenix Rising

New Lives in the New Nation

All hail, thou western world! By heaven design'd
Th' example bright, to renovate mankind.
Soon shall thy sons across the mainland roam;
And claim, on far Pacific shores, their home.
—Timothy Dwight, *Greenfield Hill* (1794)

Before the eagle, there was the phoenix. On July 4, 1776, the day of the signing of the Declaration of Independence, the Continental Congress tasked a committee with proposing a Great Seal for the thirteen states. Six years and two committees later, the country was still without a national emblem. Enter William Barton. Looking for an adviser, the congressmen settled on the young Pennsylvanian. Barton was only twenty-eight years old but confident to the point of cockiness. The War of Independence had just broken out when Barton sailed for England to study heraldry. It was there, Barton told George Washington, that he gained an understanding of heraldry as science and of himself as its envoy in a country where blazonry was still seen as "a matter of amusement." Heraldry was serious work, Barton insisted, one that should give pride and purpose to "this infant nation, now rising into greatness."[1]

The design Barton submitted to Congress on May 9, 1782, was an iconographic spectacle (see figure 1.1). The back featured the radiant Eye of Providence hovering above a pyramid of thirteen strata, which, to Barton, was a sign of "strength and duration." The front contained a stack of elements, most notably a big shield supported by a soldier on its right side, a maiden on its left, and an eagle perching at the top and holding the American flag with one claw and a sword balancing a wreath of laurel with the other. A different kind of bird held sway in the centerpiece. On the pillar in the shield Barton placed a "Phoenix in Flames, with wings expanded," signifying, as he explained, the "expiring Liberty of Britain, revived by her Descendants, in America." Revolutionary Americans could relate to the phoenix, the mythical animal that was consumed by fire after living a long life only to ascend in renewed glory. The bird appeared on vases, plates, engravings, even on South Carolina's new paper money. For Barton, the phoenix best symbolized what was to become

FIGURE 1.1 Design for the Great Seal of the United States, 1782. William Barton's proposal expressed the belief that the birth of the United States marked the revival of liberty. Courtesy of the National Archives, College Park, Maryland.

the hallmark of the new nation: the union of tradition and innovation, of experience and everlasting youth.[2]

To Barton's dismay, the committee rejected his design, and the bald eagle eventually replaced the phoenix in the final version of the Great Seal. Barton's belief in renewal from the ashes of tyranny, however, endured. Nine years later, Barton returned to the theme of the nascent republic as uniquely durable and regenerative in an essay he presented to the American Philosophical Society in Philadelphia. Demography, like the United States, was a fledgling enterprise. Barton was keen on joining the ranks of the country's leading scholars by treading on barely charted ground. His intellectual sales pitch? The new nation deserved to live long because it promised longer lives to its citizens than humans in other parts of the globe had thus far enjoyed. "This country possesses, to a superior degree, an inherent, radical, and lasting source of national vigor and greatness," wrote Barton. He predicted that a favorable climate, abundant natural resources, early marriages, and the "virtuous and simple manners" of the nation's citizens would result in "unparalleled" growth.

To prove that Americans stayed young longer, Barton compiled a list of men and women from Massachusetts to Georgia who reached ages up to 125 years. Barton's essay was as data laden as any late eighteenth-century demographic tract. Buried under the onslaught of numbers, however, lay a tantalizing message: the United States was not only liberty's surest guardian; more than any other nation, it shielded its people from the tyranny of an early death.[3]

Barton's interventions—first allegorical, then statistical—open a revealing window onto the politics of age in the founding era. Examining that politics poses a conceptual challenge. Neither rejuvenation nor antiaging was common parlance at the time. If Americans before and around 1800 spoke about how to make old bodies assume younger forms, they used expressions such as "renovation," "restoration," or "regeneration." English-speakers coming of age in the Age of Revolutions understood these words, which they often used interchangeably, as encompassing various ways of warding off degeneration and decay. As with capitalism or racism, it is important to remind ourselves that phenomena existed long before the terms we now use to describe them.

All this played out in larger arenas. Barton and his contemporaries were part of the Atlantic networks of trade and consumption in which the seeds of an emerging antiaging market had generated little more than tender sprouts. Poor oral health was the norm then, even as the use of tooth-whitening lotions and artificial teeth became more extensive. George Washington was known to have bad teeth. The dentures he wore consisted of ivory, brass, lead-tin and silver alloy, and horse and human teeth. An entry in one of Mount Vernon's ledgers suggests that the first president bought them from enslaved workers.[4]

Hair restoration products, more so than dentures, were a regular staple in newspaper advertisements during the revolutionary era. Men worrying about balding could (at their own peril) purchase at their local apothecary shops or from traveling hucksters lotions made out of bear grease, sulfur, borax, bone marrow, and lead acetate. The boundaries between the medical practice and quackery were porous. On occasion, the period's transgressions provoked satirical commentary. One such case was "Ramrod's Tincture of Gridiron," an invigorating fluid that was supposedly first sold on the streets of Baltimore in 1805. Advertisements of this fake essence included testimonials from aging customers who claimed that applying the tincture had supplied them with rock-hard muscles, sharp minds, even "as fine a pair of ears" as they could boast the days they had been born.[5]

Hilarious as they may sound, these testimonials were fringe expressions of a much broader conversation about the improvability of all forms of life that swept the revolutionary Atlantic. Vitalism, the idea that an undying vital force stirred the tiniest particles of matter, captivated the same salons and clubs of Paris, London, Weimar, and Philadelphia that were debating the meaning of liberty and equality. Some theories were meant to amuse. One traveling joke at the time—set in motion by the personal doctor of the Bishop of Münster, Johann Heinrich Cohausen—was that young girls could revitalize old men by letting them inhale their breath. Other postulations were no laughing matter. Prior to inventing an intricate system of how to group different peoples into distinct races, Johann Friedrich Blumenbach had discovered the *Bildungstrieb* (formative force). Experiments with plants led Blumenbach to conclude that all living organisms had regenerative capabilities. For Christoph Wilhelm Hufeland, another German physician, the key to life extension lay in nutrition. In *The Art of Prolonging Life* (1797), which introduced the concept of macrobiotics, Hufeland advocated dietary therapies that were conspicuously gendered and reeked of bourgeois morality. To avoid gluttony, impotence, and an early death, men needed to eat in moderation, preferably bread and vegetables. More examples could be added, but the lowest common denominator would be the same: if Enlightenment optimism spurred the period's interest in vitalist research, so did the conviction that privileged white men should be its main beneficiaries.[6]

Revolutionary Americans took a lively interest in these debates. Their fascination with rejuvenation, however, was rooted in state-building rather than in personal concerns about aging. At a time when patriarchs ruled households, oversaw churches, and governed countries, reaching old age tended to shore up masculine authority. According to most historians who have studied the subject, criticism of the elderly as out-of-touch and prone to corruption grew louder in the Age of Revolutions. At the same time, invectives against the old were reined in by an intergenerational consensus that seniority deserved to be valued. In much of the educational literature of the period, the young were admonished to honor their elders even as they were told that they were carrying inside them the seeds of a bright future. This dovetailed with the demographic realities on the ground. North America was teeming with children. In Boston alone, the 1765 census counted 8,119 white minors younger than sixteen among its 15,520 inhabitants—roughly 52 percent. These youngsters did not stay silent as their elders demanded no taxation without representation. Although school-age boys were sometimes scolded for staging their own protests against the British, adults welcomed their involvement. In most cases, local commentators interpreted joint father-and-son actions on behalf of American liberties as a sign of unity between the generations.[7]

Positing that rejuvenation in US history was collective before it was personal must not be confused with a search for origins. Making this argument means expanding our sense of the range of ideas about age available to men and women in the Early Republic and how they employed these ideas to shape their nation's image and its place in a world at once riveted by novel forms of government. The American Revolution has been called many things: democratic and republican, moderate and violent, conservative and radical. But neotenic? The first to do so in a sweeping fashion was the literary scholar Robert Pogue Harrison, who portrayed American Independence as a simultaneous act of departure and retrieval, a collective struggle in which "rupture . . . takes the form of continuity" and vice versa. In evolutionary biology, neoteny describes the retention of juvenile traits in aging bodies. Translated into culture, it can also include the reverse: a revolutionary force that carries over "into its youth a number of older elements from the heritage of nations." Anyone loosely familiar with the founders will recall how they kept insisting that their infant nation was founded not in opposition to wisdom and maturity but as their latest incarnation.[8]

This chapter elaborates on Harrison's musings in two ways. The neotenic story gained traction in elite circles but had little to offer to those who did not find themselves empowered by the revolution. Women were denied the equal station of property-holding white men and thus the rights of republican citizenship that were bounded as much by age as by race, class, and gender. Farther removed from the blessings of liberty were the African Americans, who felt slavery's dehumanizing sting ever more intensely. If their age mattered at all, it was for estimating the value of Black bodies on the auction block. Demeaned as either infantile or beastly, they remained politically and culturally ageless in the eyes of most white Americans. This logic extended to Native Americans as well, although in a more ambivalent manner. Treating Indigenous groups as domestic others, some founders nonetheless defended America's native inhabitants against Europeans, who viewed the former as living proof that life in the New World was inferior.

The transatlantic war of words over the alleged degeneracy of New World ecosystems points to a second important dimension in the neotenic moments of 1776 and 1787. Debates about the relative age of the young United States took place on an international stage. To neglect the multiplicity of actors—domestic as well as foreign—involved in these debates is to miss an important pillar in the edifice of American exceptionalism. Indeed, boisterous proclamations about the country's superior fertility and youthfulness were often preceded by outrage over Europeans stating the opposite. As an instrument of state-building, rejuvenation amounted to boosterism, seeping into histories, geographies, and travel accounts published for audiences on both sides of the Atlantic that praised the advantages of the early United States for investment and immigration. The founders congratulated themselves on their good fortune of living in an expansive settler empire that would become the envy of the civilized world. A closer look, however, shows that their exaltations were dampened by deep-seated insecurities about its longevity.

EMPIRES, LIKE HUMANS, live in cycles. They are fragile and weak at birth, full of energy in their youth, reach the pinnacle of strength and maturity in adulthood, decline as old age sets in, and ultimately perish. Of this a young John Adams was convinced. Two years into the French and Indian War, the twenty-one-year-old Adams recorded in his diary: "History . . . can settle in our minds a clear and a comprehensive View . . . of the growth of several Kingdoms and Empires, of their Wealth and Commerce, Wars and Politics, of the Characters of their principal Leading Men, of their Grandeur and Power, of their Virtues and Vices, and of their insensible Decays at first, and of their swift Destruction at last." Was there a way to break this fatal cycle? Maybe in America, Adams mused, where "after the Reformation a few people came over . . . for Conscience sake. Perhaps this (apparently) trivial incident, may transfer the great seat of Empire into America. It looks likely to me."[9]

The notion that the laws of aging provided a template for understanding the laws of history goes back to antiquity, but it gained greater urgency for a generation of British American settlers trying to impose meaning onto a world that was changing rapidly and violently before their eyes. In an age of revolutionary turmoil, men like Adams and Jefferson made repeated references to the historical cycle of the rise and fall of empires. They were not alone. As they were declaring their independence, Edward Gibbon published the first volume of *The History of the Decline and Fall of the Roman Empire,* copies of which soon landed on bookshelves across North America. Yet the founders also believed, or at least hoped, that the new nation born in war might prove to the world that its demise was not inevitable, that it could be delayed or averted altogether.[10]

Supporters of American independence certainly appreciated the irony of an English historian writing about the downfall of Rome at the same time that British might was receding in North America. To patriots of various stripes, it confirmed the vision that Adams had jotted down twenty years earlier: the vibrant colonies were destined to inherit the position of a doddering British Empire, now only a shadow of its former self. This modern version of the medieval idea of *translatio imperii*, which held that the seats of empire moved westward as older ones imploded and younger ones took their place, found countless adherents. By the late 1780s, the view that the newly formed United States was the final piece in the chain of empire, following Greece, Rome, and Great Britain, had become so commonplace that the Congregationalist minister Jedidiah Morse stated laconically in 1789: "Besides, it is well known that empire has been traveling from east to west. Probably her last and broadest seat will be America." If history was destiny, geography rejuvenated history.[11]

Morse felt qualified to make that equation. A best-selling geographer who authored several popular works and schoolbooks, the Massachusetts pastor was in the vanguard of a "geographic revolution" that aided the white colonists in their quest for self-definition. Prior accounts have stressed the importance of maps, surveys, and census reports for molding a national identity, which was predicated on rejecting Eurocentric models of mapping. The spatial expansiveness of early American cartography fostered myths of boundless mobility. Travel writing, often embellished with small maps, rose into a popular genre that coupled narratives of heroic discovery with the overarching message that progress unfolded in open geographical space. Exploring America, be it on horseback or with a finger on the map, meant youthful movement, the best antidote to the sclerosis that had brought down the great civilizations of the past. Thomas Jefferson turned this doctrine into a hallmark of his presidency. After completing the Louisiana Purchase and sending Meriwether Lewis and William Clark on their transcontinental expedition, Jefferson gave a rationale for expansion that seemed all about self-preservation. "By enlarging the empire of liberty," he noted in 1805, "we . . . provide new sources of renovation, should its principles, in any time, degenerate, in those portions of our country, which gave them birth."[12]

Modern-day readers will probably recoil at pairing the words *empire* and *liberty*, although it is not news to historians that revolutionary republicanism nurtured a definition of empire suitable for a fledgling settler nation. Jefferson's phrase, sanguine as it may sound, gave license to trample over those who stood in the way of "progress." But rather than evoke despotic rule, the imperial visions circulating among Euro-American settlers envisaged a sprawling yet inclusive community animated by a shared belief that land ownership drove human development. What has garnered less attention is Jefferson's ominous mention of possible degeneracy in a sentence rife with the optimism of future rejuvenation. To get to the root of this dichotomy, we have to travel back in time and meet a younger Jefferson in 1784, during his stint as minister to France.[13]

As soon as the Virginian arrived in Paris, he was ready for battle. This time the enemy was not British redcoats but an accomplished French scientist whose theories about North America had insulted Jefferson. Like most European scholars of his day, Georges-Louis Leclerc, Comte de Buffon never visited the New World, but that did not keep the nobleman from judging it. His monumental *Histoire Naturelle*, which spanned thirty-six volumes published between 1749 and 1789, contains scathing passages on what he regarded as the flawed constitution of America's flora and fauna. American plants and animals, Buffon claimed, were undersized and underdeveloped. More troubling, he saw the same forces of degeneration wreak havoc on Indigenous bodies. Native Americans, according to Buffon, were "a kind of weak automaton" with no "vivacity and activity of mind." He called their sexual organs "small and feeble," which Buffon believed was the reason the natives had not procreated in greater numbers.[14]

Buffon later walked back some of his derogatory statements. His theory of New World degeneracy, however, had started to assume a life of its own. Buffon stopped short of applying his claims to European settlers, yet other writers stepped over that line with relish. Pehr Kalm, the Finnish-Swedish explorer who spent three years in parts of French and British North America from 1748 to 1751, made a couple of disturbing observations. His tour of the Eastern Seaboard left him convinced that the descendants of European migrants had deteriorated physically and mentally. They "grow sooner old" and were "far less hardy" than their Old World relatives. The Dutch scholar Cornelius de Pauw, who never left Europe, passed a similar verdict. De Pauw's descriptions of Native Americans were as vitriolic as Buffon's. But his remarks about the crippling effects of the environment sounded scary enough to fill prospective settlers with alarm. Europeans born in America might start life with an advantage because they "come to a maturity of intellect . . . earlier than the children born in Europe." However, degeneration would set in around puberty. After that, de Pauw writes, "vivacity deserts [the Creole], his powers grow dull, and he ceases to think at the very time he might think to some purpose." De Pauw boasted of his close relationship with Frederick the Great, which has fueled conjecture over whether de Pauw's diatribes had an impact on the Prussian king's efforts to discourage transatlantic migration. Surely, it is hard to imagine how anybody would want to settle in a part of the world where the staircase of life pointed downward after the first few steps.[15]

In 1798, the founders' optimism took another blow from the founding father of modern demography, the British economist Thomas Malthus. Not a degenerationist in the strict sense of the word, Malthus mocked the idea that the United States could escape the laws of overpopulation. His critics on the other side of the Atlantic disagreed. They were convinced that the "Malthusian trap," which holds that more mouths to feed would inevitably result in food shortages and starvation, would not apply to a land blessed with natural bounties unobtainable in crowded Europe. For Malthus, it amounted to a fool's errand to believe that the United States could maintain "perpetual youth" simply by virtue of its young age. One could just "as reasonably expect to prevent a wife or mistress from growing old by never exposing her to the sun or air," Malthus commented with a whiff of sarcasm.[16]

Seeing the degenerationists smother any expectation that colonizing the New World might rejuvenate the old one begs the question of how they justified their assertions, let alone what caused them in the first place. Climate theory saw its first heyday in the 1700s, especially in the slipstream of European overseas expansion. Much of the period's theorizing about the climate seemed inchoate and arbitrary. Montesquieu argued that civilization had flourished in Western Europe because of its cooler climes. Conversely, Buffon and de Pauw claimed that America and its peoples had been degenerating because the continent, with its vast forests and wetlands, lacked the relative warmth and dryness of the Old World. In both scenarios, environmental differences determined differences of culture and vitality, with countries like France, Britain, and Italy coming out on top. Buffon left a loophole, though. The count surmised that North America was a sickly place because the continent was younger geologically and needed more time to "mature"—that is, dry up. De Pauw disagreed. For him, the differences were carved in stone, ruling out any possibility of regenerative growth.[17]

There is no definitive answer to why Buffon, de Pauw, Kalm, and a few more European writers wedded their reputation to the degeneration thesis. Anti-English sentiments (though their criticism did not exempt settlers of other nationalities), fear of European depopulation, and the desire to debunk the myth of the noble savage are some of the reasons cited by historians. For Jefferson, the science was dangerously bad. He fired his opening salvo on the degenerationists with the publication of his *Notes on the State of Virginia,* which first appeared in 1785 when Jefferson was living within walking distance of the French luminaries who scoffed at American pretensions to future greatness. *Notes* was one big rehabilitation effort. Officially conceived as a response to a French diplomat who sought information about Virginia, Jefferson's work covers a broad range of subjects, stretching from the state's geography and geology to its commerce, politics, population, schools, laws, and religion. The longest section titled "Productions Mineral, Vegetable and

Animal" processed vast amounts of zoological and botanical data to highlight the country's ecological splendor and prove Buffon wrong. Jefferson predicted that Virginia's population would multiply on a scale unattainable in the Old World, aided by the fertile land, healthy climate, and bustling commerce. Jefferson's obsession with American fecundity famously peaked in his decision to send Buffon a dead moose, a creature so big and bulky that it towered over its European relatives.[18]

The founders were a quarrelsome lot, but when it came to defending their country, differences were quickly set aside. Benjamin Franklin shared an anecdote in which he disarmed his opponents with wit. At a dinner party in Paris in the early 1780s, where he met the Abbé Raynal, one of the *philosophes* who sided with Buffon and de Pauw, Franklin asked all Americans and Frenchmen seated at the table to stand up. Raynal, Franklin chuckled afterward, was "a mere shrimp," and no other French guest could match the height of his American counterparts. Alexander Hamilton regarded such theatrics as insufficient: "Men admired as profound philosophers . . . have gravely asserted that all animals, and with them the human species, degenerate in America—that even dogs cease to bark after having breathed awhile in our atmosphere. Facts have too long supported these arrogant pretensions of the European. It belongs to us to vindicate the honor of the human race, and to teach that assuming brother moderation." John Adams shared Hamilton's anger. Reflecting on his European sojourn in the late 1770s, Adams confessed that his "Indignation was roused, at the Shameless Falsehoods which were continually propagated, and I took a great deal of Pains to have them contradicted but I have long Since found it an Augean Stable." A clear pattern formed in Adams's mind: behind degenerationism stood a sinister plan to "discourage Emigrations" to North America. Leaving that plan intact, Adams warned, would imperil national security.[19]

In an age rife with conspiracy theories, many Americans believed that the survival of their infant nation depended on patriotic citizens foiling the plots of powerful enemies. In that regard, the degeneracy controversy was not that different from other founding-era paranoias. Consider the transatlantic tit-for-tat over the need for more migrants. Some followed Jefferson's example by trying to disprove the degenerationists' claims. In an essay discussing circumstances that favored longevity, the Philadelphia physician Benjamin Rush identified migration as a key factor. "I have observed many instances of Europeans who have arrived in America in the decline of life, who have acquired fresh vigor from the impression of our climate . . . and whose lives, in consequence thereof, appeared to have been prolonged for many years." The idea that migration rejuvenated the migrant as much as it rejuvenated the

United States found classic expression in J. Hector St. John de Crèvecoeur's *Letters from an American Farmer* (1782). Crèvecoeur's boosterism becomes palpable in his description of the transatlantic passage as a metamorphosis, not just a mere journey. His America was a myth-turned-reality, a magical place that brought forth a breed of new men (120 years before communism and fascism crafted their own versions). "Everything has tended to regenerate them," writes Crèvecoeur, "new laws, a new mode of living, a new social system. Here they are become men: in Europe they were as so many useless plants, wanting vegetative mold, and refreshing showers." That a naturalized French-American proved capable of producing such glowing prose made it all the more precious in the eyes of early US nationalists.[20]

Based on what we know about life expectancies in the late eighteenth century, Rush or Crèvecoeur were hardly more reliable sources than Buffon or de Pauw. There is not one scientific model that suggests that mortality rates in the early United States were significantly lower than in most European countries. Around 1800, white Americans who saw their twentieth birthdays lived to be forty-five on average. The first waves of urbanization and industrialization brought new health risks. The yellow fever epidemic that struck Philadelphia in 1793 killed more than 5,000 people, and countless more succumbed to cholera outbreaks the following century. Economic slumps, wars, pollution, and the appearance of new diseases were common to modernizing societies across the globe. In the transatlantic row over which continent was more hazardous, shared mortality risks gradually disappeared behind nationalist invocations of age as a tool of othering.[21]

Those making such invocations had various bodies at their disposal—real and imagined, human and animal, degenerated and revitalized. Youth was more than a floating metaphor in all this. It entwined the political task of preserving the liberties won by a young nation with the cultural task of renewing tradition. This rejuvenationist theme suffused the public sphere in letters and image. A case in point is Edward Savage's 1796 engraving *Liberty*, which was reproduced on pottery, needlework, and behind-glass paintings (see figure 1.2). At first glance, it features a triumphant Lady Columbia as a symbol of the young nation treading on the broken vestiges of tyranny. Importantly, however, Savage chose to conflate Columbia with the Greek goddess Hebe, who nourishes the bald eagle out of the chalice of everlasting youth. The artist ascribed neotenic powers to America. It breathed new life into the old while elevating the young to higher levels of maturity.[22]

Religious leaders, too, associated the United States with youthfulness. This equation was not new in the spiritual realm. The Protestant revivals that

FIGURE 1.2 Edward Savage, *Liberty in the Form of the Goddess of Youth*, 1796. The engraving became one of the most popular nationalist images of the Early Republic. It shows Hebe feeding the American eagle from the chalice of youth. Courtesy of the Library of Congress Prints and Photographs Division.

had swept British America in the 1730s and 1740s were youth-centered events. Young people responded most enthusiastically to a culture of faith based on personal commitment and emotional involvement. Some have argued that the "Old Lights" versus "New Lights" distinction that divided supporters and opponents of the Great Awakening fostered a mild antiauthoritarianism that energized resistance against Britain's colonial policies after 1763. Recent scholarship has questioned this assumption, stressing that it rests on thin evidence. Historians now tend to depict Jonathan Edwards, George Whitefield, and other Awakening preachers as engaged in giving their movement a youthful veneer, not as fanning intergenerational discord. The revivalist language of rejuvenation proved adaptable to the independence struggle in the second half of the century. Oliver Hart, a clergyman from New Jersey, likened the thirteen colonies to Jacob in the Old Testament, "the youngest, yet most favored child of an indulgent Providence." Beneath such messages lay a reassuring tautology. America was the infant nation, and those who cared for it could reap the blessings of youth's vast possibilities.[23]

However, as Jefferson's vision of a growing empire of liberty implied, age did not offer easy answers, and even the most optimistic expressions were punctuated by doubt and uncertainty. Matricide seemed justified when Great Britain, in the words of the Connecticut pastor John Cleaveland, behaved crueler "than Sea-Monsters towards their loved ones." But who could say that the children thus threatened would not one day be devoured by their own offspring? There was a fundamental instability at the core of early American nationalism, which aspired to childhood and manhood at the same time. Few said it better than the poet and historian Mercy Otis Warren. Writing in the wake of Shays's Rebellion, an armed uprising in her home state against the new Massachusetts government during 1786 and 1787 that had attracted many disaffected young men, Warren did not see a country ripening into true independence, only a "child just learning to walk . . . afraid of [its] own movements." She compared the fledgling republic to an inexperienced "young heir." Newly acquired wealth, Warren surmised, "had intoxicated him so far as to render him incapable of weighing the intrinsic value of his estate, and had left him without discretion or judgment to improve it to the best advantage of his family." Though almost twenty years apart, Warren's and Jefferson's forebodings met at a crucial point: the real threat to American rejuvenation might not come from the outside after all.[24]

GENDER CIRCUMSCRIBED Warren's skepticism as much as partisan politics. As one of the few women in the Early Republic who published political works under her own name, she never fully subscribed to the masculine vision of regenerative growth. Although Warren did not speak out in favor of equality between the sexes, she too had to endure male chauvinism. A staunch opponent of centralized power, Warren famously broke with her former mentor John Adams, who bristled at how Warren had criticized him in her three-volume study of the American Revolution. "History is not the Province of the Ladies," Adams shot back.[25]

It would be a stretch to posit a direct connection between Adams's misogyny and Warren's characterization of the new nation as a vulnerable and overwhelmed child, but the historian Corinne T. Field suggests how both might be related. Surveying the areas where antebellum African American and white female activists shared common ground, Field introduced the concept of equal adulthood. Her purpose was twofold: to highlight the centrality of age in the efforts of social reformers to widen the circle of citizenship, and to show where and how the idea that passing a certain age threshold should entitle all Americans to the same rights and responsibilities gained currency. Critics might object that equal adulthood lumps together highly specific and, for some, even incomparable experiences of oppression and disenfranchisement. Still, the concept provides a useful frame for understanding how dominant articulations of rejuvenation were embedded in complex hierarchies of power and privilege. Whenever white men infantilized people of a different sex or color, they were also implying that the latter had not accomplished anything of civilizational value worth conserving.[26]

For the founders, granting women a role in keeping the body politic young meant one thing above all: reproduction. In the colonial period, nine or ten births per family were no rarity. Neither were assertions that high birth rates would result in prosperity. Popular representations of women echoed this belief, turning fertility into a measure of female beauty and worth. Exuberant adjectives were commonly attached to seventeenth- and eighteenth-century pregnant bodies; they were "teeming," "flourishing," "fruitful," or "lusty," to name a few. Contemporary portraits of white woman bearing cornucopias out of which poured an abundance of fruits linked productivity and youth. Benjamin Franklin had his Poor Richard rhapsodize in 1737: "A Ship under sail and a Big-Bellied Woman/Are the Handsomest two things that can be seen common." Aphorisms such as this one reflected the belief that bearing as many children as possible was both the destiny of women and the foundation of plentiful communities.[27]

Early American demography furthered the notion that American women possessed superior procreational capabilities. Statistically, the colonists were younger than the Europeans, married at an earlier age, and had children in shorter intervals. Between 1720 and 1770, the population in British America quadrupled from 620,000 to almost 2.5 million, mostly through domestic increase rather than through forced or free migration. Some British American leaders used high fertility rates to argue against unwanted immigration. When Franklin forecast in 1751 that the colonial population would double every twenty years, he also wished to see the influx of "tawny" Africans and "swarthy" Germans limited. Jefferson's nativist sentiments were as much motivated by ideology as by race. Mulling over the future of his home state, Jefferson saw no regeneration in the prospect of receiving the greatest number of migrants from Europe's absolutist monarchies. Untrained in republican principles, these new arrivals would "infuse" into the laws of Virginia "their spirit, warp and bias [their] direction, and render [them] a heterogeneous, incoherent, distracted mass." James Madison's outlook on migration was less anxious. His thoughts in *Federalist No. 10* on how to avoid destructive factionalism in a republic rested on a vigorous defense of a philosophy of growth. For Madison, the best safeguard of American independence, as well as the best insurance against preventing its early demise, was achieving a healthy equilibrium between geographical *and* demographic expansion. In all these projections, regardless of whether they supported or opposed non-Anglo-Saxon migration, the precept to be fruitful and multiply remained the essence of womanhood.[28]

Multiply they did, but with increasing moderation. As white men of property and standing were (re)creating the American body politic in broad daylight, many of their wives started to become more conscious of their own bodies. The decade-long reduction of crude birth rates that began in colonial North America continued to drop during and after the War of Independence. Circumstantial evidence suggests that the revolutionary rhetoric of self-government animated more women to push back the notion that their contributions to the general welfare should be confined to a lifetime of childbearing. Susan E. Klepp was one of the first to take issue with interpretations that attributed the transition from birth-centered to child-centered motherhood to macroeconomic factors such as land availability, industrial development, or the cost of childrearing. The missing link here is the agency of individual women. In lieu of modern methods of contraception, women used other means to limit the number of pregnancies: they married later, breastfed their babies longer, practiced sexual abstinence, and passed on knowledge on how to apply certain herbs to regulate the menstrual cycle. Giving birth held little romance in an era when stillbirths and women dying in childbirth were extremely common. Because of this, expectant mothers began pushing back against the exuberant language used by Franklin and others. From the standpoint of women's health, the pregnant body was not a cornucopia but could quickly turn into a lethal hazard.[29]

How, then, were women to exercise their independence from the politics of procreation? Demands for participation of women in public matters already surfaced in the period of the nation's founding—from Abigail Adams's memorable admonition in 1776 to "Remember the Ladies" to the lesser-known complaint of an anonymous "lady" from Connecticut who in 1801 mocked the idea that women should forever be "destined solely to the distaff and the needle, and never expand an idea beyond the walls of her house." Such protofeminist statements, however, were soon hedged in by another concept that defined female duties in relation to the state. Women were to become republican mothers: the expectation was that they would use their intelligence and God-given moral sentiment to prepare their sons for their future role as citizens (and, if need be, reprimand their husbands for straying from the paths of virtue).[30]

Crucially, republican motherhood was at odds with equal adulthood. One might even argue that espousing the former furthered associations of women with childrearing and thus childhood. It almost seemed as if founding-era Americans imagined femininity as inherently non-adolescent, which only strengthened the bond of manhood and youth. Whether as educators or wives, republican mothers were the real-life corollaries of Savage's Hebe: they would dispense youth to the nation's boys and men but barely claim it for themselves.

This, to be sure, was an uneven development. Birth rates were falling across the board, but the decrease was greatest in New England, and there especially among educated white Protestant women. Although working-class families and rural communities kept having more children, infant mortality rates remained higher in areas where people lacked medical care. Republican motherhood smacked of elitism, unattainable for a majority of women who took care of family farms or worked for wages to help sustain their families. African American women faced an even more existential struggle. Black babies died about twice as often as white babies, while the pressure on African American women to procreate was high. This was largely an upshot of slavery, which dictated that young healthy Black bodies were, literally, capital. In the words of Wilma A. Dunaway, the plantation was a place of "reproductive exploitation," and white masters resorted to all kinds of brutal measures, including rape, to drive up the number of babies born into slavery. The only thing that enslaved Blacks were supposed to prevent from aging was a system in which slaveholders wielded near absolute power over them.[31]

Slavery's manifold oppressions manifested themselves not just in practices that denied Black people control over their bodies. They involved calculations designed to make the enslaved look younger or older against their will. By forcing slaves to adhere to the temporal rhythms of the plantation—when to rise, to work, to worship, and to rest—slaveholders convinced themselves that they owned the biographical time of the enslaved. Age became a tool of white supremacy: the more rigorously slaveholders recorded their slaves' birthdays in account books, decided when they had attained the physical strength needed for field work, or assessed when they had reached sexual maturity, the harder it became for enslaved African Americans to claim age and assert their individuality. Keeping the enslaved in the dark about their date of birth was widespread. "The white children could tell their ages," Frederick Douglass recalled. "I could not tell why I ought to be deprived of the same privilege."[32]

Chattel slavery also engendered various forms of age fraud that intensified African American distrust of white practices of age making. Racial capitalism dictated that enslaved workers were young as long as they were productive. Old age set in once Black bodies were cast as incapable of supplying menial labor to their masters. The late eighteenth-century plantation economy invented the label "superannuated" as a designation for slaves whose productivity had sunk to the level of "no value." Elderly, sick, and disabled African Americans, who, according to the white enslavers' accounting logic, had grown old to the point of uselessness, had to pursue rejuvenation out of naked self-preservation. To avoid the precarious position of superannuation, the old would feign proficiency in a wide range of occupations that were physically less taxing than fieldwork. Such performances usually depended on the kindness and cooperation of younger bondspeople, but even then, older slaves lived under the constant threat of abandonment or being sold off. To squeeze the last drops of profit from aging workers, white masters looking for potential buyers showed few qualms when it came to making their slaves appear younger than they were. In some cases, elderly slaves resisted by counteracting the complimentary descriptions of their relative youth on the auction block, only to risk additional punishment.[33]

To this day, the apologists of racial slavery continue to wrap the institution in the self-serving ideology of paternalism, which cast slaveholders as caring masters and Blacks as obedient children. Rationales for withholding from African Americans the rights of adulthood are easy to find. In his *Notes*, Jefferson famously denied that Blacks had "faculties of memory, reason, and imagination" analogous to whites, emphasizing that they were childlike in their "want of forethought" and in the fleeting nature of their grief. Questioning Black people's capacity for rational autonomy, Jefferson compared freeing enslaved Africans to deserting children. Keeping the white body politic healthy and youthful, however, meant more than withholding equal adulthood from Blacks. For Jefferson, it involved policing Black sexuality. He supported deporting emancipated Blacks to Africa out of fear of interracial mixing (something he paradoxically practiced himself). Despite such glaring inconsistencies, Jefferson advocated successful race management as a tool to avoid white degeneration.[34]

The racist trope of Black immaturity was also foundational to white abolitionism. Much to the dismay of revolutionary-era Black abolitionists, white Americans sympathetic to antislavery, who were quick to liken colonial resistance to British rule to an impatient young man casting off the shackles of undue guardianship, were reluctant to make a similar case for the enslaved aspiring to freedom. Paternalism continued to aggravate relations between Blacks and whites in the movement until the Civil War. Slave narratives produced by former slaves often contained prefaces written by white abolitionists that minimized Black authorship. Frederick Douglass was one such author who broke with his mentor William Lloyd Garrison over political differences in the late 1840s. "I was growing, and needed room," Douglass wrote in retrospect, implying that he was just as unwilling to subject himself to the tutelage of white benefactors as he had been to endure the humiliations of slavery.[35]

Before African Americans could even start situating themselves within revolutionary-era narratives of rejuvenation, they had to grapple with a bifurcated lexicon of childhood—one that excluded them from the radical potentiality associated with white children and consigned them to a state of permanent inferiority. Black people thus denigrated tried their best to rip this lexicon apart. The tipping point came in 1791 when news of a major slave uprising on France's wealthiest colony made every slaveholder in the Western Hemisphere shudder. For its supporters, the Haitian Revolution had the label righteous rebellion written all over it. Black Haitians drew inspiration from the same revolutionary script that their French and American counterparts had already enacted—in which youths being unfairly infantilized and insulted rose up against their tyrannical parents. Moreover, the former colony's push for independence provided a model of assertive Black manhood that fired the African American imagination.[36]

Several slave revolts that took place in the southern United States after 1791 (or foiled plots that could have resulted in one) bear the fingerprints of Haiti. In 1800, some African Americans found their Toussaint in Gabriel, an enslaved Virginian blacksmith who almost succeeded in mobilizing a small army of enslaved and free Blacks under the motto "Death or Liberty." Eleven years after Gabriel's Rebellion had been crushed, a group of Louisiana slaves led by Charles Deslondes followed the example of Haitian insurgents and burned down plantations on their way to New Orleans. Many were brutally tortured and killed, including Deslondes. Black abolitionists in the North penned fiery vindications of the Haitian Revolution and drank toasts to the "liberty of our African brothers in St. Domingo, and elsewhere." According to William Watkins, a respected leader in Baltimore's free Black community, France's recognition of Haiti as an independent nation in 1824 gave proof to the world "that the descendants of Africa were never designed by their Creator to sustain an inferiority, or even a mediocrity, in the chain of being."[37]

To the men holding the reins of government in the early United States, this was pure anathema. Among the most shocking counterrevolutionary images to crisscross the Atlantic was that of a white child impaled on the bayonet of a Haitian insurgent. Blacks-as-savages who spared neither the young nor the old took the place of Blacks-as-children. Race and age operated in tandem to justify US efforts to boycott the fledgling Black nation. A people capable of monstrous cruelties such as ripping up pregnant women and throwing their babies to the hogs were beasts, not human beings that ought to be welcomed in the family of revolutionary nations. Jefferson consumed and multiplied such vicious anti-Black propaganda. He warned his white neighbors in 1797 that failing to shield the country from the kind of violence occurring in the Caribbean would make them "murderers of [their] own children."[38]

The political embargo of Haiti that began during Jefferson's presidency and lasted until 1862, after the slaveholding South had seceded from the Union, corroborates a point made by the historian Karen Kupperman more than a decade ago. As white Americans celebrated the youth and maturity of their nascent body politic, they sought to erase both in other nascent nations that, like the United States, were in the process of taking shape. If the revolutionary legacy of slave uprisings in the Americas predated the white colonists' struggle for independence, so did the Indigenous polities that Europeans had encountered when they first crossed the Atlantic. Among them were the great chiefdoms chronicled by the Spanish explorer Hernando de Soto, who from 1539 to 1543 journeyed through the southeastern region all the way to the Mississippi River. Before the American Revolution, the Iroquois Confederacy in upper New York was a political force to be reckoned with: it helped six Native nations maintain their autonomy against the French and the British. Those who claim that the British colonists borrowed from the Iroquois when drafting their own plans for greater union usually cite the words spoken by the Onondaga chief Canasatego at the Lancaster Treaty of 1744. Addressing representatives from Maryland, Pennsylvania, and Virginia, Canasatego advised the colonists to follow the Iroquois example. "By observing the same methods our wise Forefathers have taken, you will acquire fresh Strength and Power," the chief reportedly said.[39]

Any influence the Iroquois might have had on British American constitutional thought was implicit at best. If this influence existed, the founders were careful not to mention it. They did not celebrate Native Americans for their cultural achievements. Positive remarks about Indigenous peoples were part of a broader defense of the American ecosystem. It is telling that Jefferson's attempt to convince readers just how wrong it was to think of Indians as degenerate was embedded in the sixth chapter of his *Notes,* which dealt with Virginia's earthly riches and wildlife. Similarly, occasional reports about Native American longevity that appeared in American newspapers around 1800 cannot be divorced from the larger effort to boost the notion of New World regeneracy. Standing up for Native Americans was a self-serving patriotic pose, and when white caricaturists were looking for a symbol to convey the new nation's natural lushness, quite a few settled on idealized Indians. Speaking of Indian vitality, thus, became a coded way of saying that America was indeed the place where "the great Seat of Empire" might rejuvenate itself.[40]

"IT IS A COUNTRY in flux; that which is true today as regards its population, its establishments; its prices; its commerce will not be true six months from now." The French count Frédéric de la Rochefoucauld-Liancourt made that observation after staying thirty-three months in the United States between 1795 and 1797. Thirty years before his compatriot Alexis de Tocqueville would write similar prose, Liancourt was already struck by the energy and enthusiasm coming from ordinary settlers. Already in the first decade after the ratification of the US Constitution, there was a general sense that the country was bursting out of its early limitations. Everything seemed to expand—people, knowledge, profits, territory. A continuous churning of men and women settling and starting over again, all happening at a dizzying speed, ignited optimism in thousands of Americans coming of age in the new nation. Not all growth was considered a blessing. Liberty might spread, but so might other growing pains of the young republic that, as the founders feared, could cause it to mutate beyond repair.[41]

Considering the boiling agitation that accompanied their nation's birth, Americans in the founding era had reason to dread all sorts of degenerating influences. More than once, they stared into the abyss of civil war, unable to rule out the possibility of the country committing suicide at a young age. Federalists raised the specter of France, where revolution had descended into terror. As the partisan rancor over how to deal with the French Republic intensified, they responded with passing the nation's first anti-immigrant laws: the Alien and Sedition Acts of 1798. Slaveholders worried about Haiti and the menace of a race war that would ravage everything if abolitionists got their way. Anti-Federalists maligned big cities as breeding grounds for corruption, vice, and disease, convinced that urban workers not only lacked the virtue of independent citizen-farmers but were also likely to find an early grave. Jefferson's condemnation of city life was relentless. Voicing apprehensions over unlicensed social mixing—including the breakdown of racial and gender barriers—that defined much of modern anti-urbanism, he compared the damage done to public morality by the "mobs of great cities" to what "sores do to the strength of the human body."[42]

Disenfranchised groups, on the other hand, saw no growing pains but colossal birth defects. In the Age of Revolutions, the number of women willing to speak out against those who measured their worth in terms of their reproductive capacity was still small. That chorus would swell over the next century. Resisting a regime in which they toiled for the prosperity of their masters was immeasurably harder for the hundreds and thousands of enslaved African Americans. For the white men who kept them in bondage, reaching adulthood was synonymous with independence; for the enslaved, it meant an increase in value in the master's ledger. And yet, a question must have fermented more intensely in the minds of the oppressed: Why maintain a social machinery that was not running properly to begin with?

The generation that had broken away from one empire to create another left behind a muddled picture. The state appeared capable of perpetual improvement but also lived under the constant threat of premature decline. Was there a way out of this impasse? At the ripe old age of eighty-one and with only two more years to live, Jefferson once more found comfort in the fantasy of a self-rejuvenating American empire. A wanderer crossing the continent from west to east, he pictured, would travel through space *and* time, conducting a survey of the "progress of man from the infancy of nation to the present day." He would start with "the savages of the Rocky Mountains," move eastward to pass "our frontiers in the pastoral state," next meet "our own semibarbarous citizens, the pioneers of the advance of civilization" until he would reach "his, as yet, most improved state in our seaport towns." But then, just perhaps, the wanderer would realize that "this advance has brought on too complicated a state of society, and that we should gain in happiness by treading back our steps a little way."[43]

Jefferson's desire for his successors not to rush blindly into an uncertain future betrayed nostalgia for earlier, simpler times. We expect such wistful musings from the elderly. But it also reflected the parting hope of a cohort of men who believed that the antiaging formula for their nation consisted of striking the right balance between progress and preservation. What these men could not or did not want to admit was that in treading back and forth over a vast continent in search of the perfect age, they were treading over bodies they thought were unlike their own. In due course, their descendants would also start treading over each other.

CHAPTER TWO

Young America

From Water Cures to the Wide Awakes

Go bathe within the woodland fount
And in the singing rills.
Go forth, ye pale-brow'd, care-worn ones,
Weary of woe and pain,
Until upon your wasted cheeks
The red rose blooms again.

—Fidelia W. Gillette, *Water* (1852)

Sojourner Truth was chronically ill when she arrived in Northampton, Massachusetts. Two years earlier, in 1843, the forty-plus-year-old African American abolitionist, women's rights activist, and survivor of slavery had made a point of starting over. She dropped her slave name Isabella Baumfree and changed it to Sojourner Truth—God's chosen warrior in the crusade for emancipation. Her bodily ailments, though, would not go away that easily. Years of living in slavery's shadow had taken a toll on Truth's health. Bowel problems, muscle pain, and abscesses on her legs were a constant source of misery. The man who promised relief was the head of the local water cure clinic, David Ruggles. Like Truth, Ruggles was Black and an abolitionist. With Ruggles by her side, Truth subjected herself to a treatment that initially made her cringe. More than once, she cursed at the daily cold baths, the constant drinking of water, the vegetarian diet, and the chilling wet towels in which she had to wrap herself. Ruggles told her not to quit. A few weeks later, Truth felt better. Gone were her digestive issues and leg pain. After ten weeks, she considered herself not just cured but rejuvenated. Never before, she stated, had she felt more alive.[1]

Before making Truth a believer in the water cure, or hydropathy, Ruggles had experienced a similar conversion in early 1843. He had worked to the point of exhaustion as an agent in the Underground Railroad, aiding countless fugitive slaves—Frederick Douglass among them—in their escape to freedom. Nearing blindness, and with physicians giving him only a few more weeks to live, Ruggles received care and comfort in the abolitionist community of Northampton. Founded in 1842, the Northampton Association of

Education and Industry was one of several short-lived utopian experiments that sought to build an egalitarian economy independent of slave labor. It was there that Ruggles started dabbling with alternative therapies. Noting the positive results prompted by cold water treatments, Ruggles sought the advice of an émigré doctor who had set up shop in Brattleboro, Vermont. A comradeship ensued between the foreign-born medic and the ailing Black activist. For two years, visits were made and letters were exchanged, in the course of which Ruggles honed his hydropathic skills. Aided by wealthy abolitionists, he eventually opened his own infirmary in Northampton.[2]

Ruggles's mentor, Robert Wesselhöft, was an authority in America's budding water cure scene. His Brattleboro Hydropathic Institution welcomed patients from all walks of life, but members of the country's social and political elites who flocked to Vermont soon turned the center into a more exclusive affair. Harriet Beecher Stowe and Henry Wadsworth Longfellow were among the luminaries who hoped that Wesselhöft's methods would restore them to health and vigor. To boost his credentials, Wesselhöft claimed to be a disciple of Vincenz Priessnitz, the Silesian peasant credited with inventing the water cure. In addition to bringing hydropathy to America, Wesselhöft was also the ambassador of another kind of rejuvenationist enterprise. As a young man in the German state of Thuringia, he had joined the Jünglingsbund, a secret association of former students who had become radical nationalists after the defeat of Napoleon Bonaparte. State authorities exposed the Jünglingsbund in 1824 and sentenced its ringleaders to long prison terms. Pardoned in 1831, Wesselhöft continued to champion an energetic nationalism under the banner of Young Germany, a revolutionary movement dominated by middle-aged literati who sought to replace monarchy with democracy. When Wesselhöft joined his brother Wilhelm in America nine years later, he came to a country where the idea of revitalizing entire societies, not just individuals, was finding fertile soil.[3]

The intertwined lives of Truth, Ruggles, and Wesselhöft are remarkable for three reasons. First, they hint at the possibility of interracial camaraderie under the roof of alternative medicine at a time when such contacts tested the boundaries of acceptable social intercourse. Second, they reveal how water cure enthusiasts wove together different threads of transatlantic reform, most prominently abolitionism, temperance, women's rights, and liberal nationalism. Third, they exemplify that cleanliness and fitness were not just regarded as keys to repairing bodies but, more broadly, to generating a physically and morally rejuvenated citizenry devoted to expanding the realm of democracy.

Democracy was an organism as embattled as it was inchoate. In the mid-nineteenth century, Americans disagreed sharply over which parts of that budding organism they wanted to keep from withering. Water cure reformers, Young Americans, and Wide Awakes were all committed to preventing bodies from disintegrating, but they envisioned very different body politics to emerge from their procedures. When examined together, these three movements sensitize us to changing rites of passage and evolving concepts of anti-aging in the rambunctious 1840s and 1850s. In antebellum America, youth became the rallying cry of men in power as well as those trying to unseat them. Out of the clash of generations and ideologies that jolted societies on both sides of the Atlantic, a tacit consensus emerged: failure to keep up with the youthful tempo of the times, regardless of age, was the gateway to irrelevance.

FAITH IN THE WATER CURE connected nations and bridged continents. But it was in the mid-century United States that hydropathy first gained a mass followership. On the eve of the Civil War, one journalist counted more than 200 water cure centers in the country. Renegade doctors and self-taught healers offered cold water treatments in places as far apart as Biloxi, Mississippi, and Salem, Oregon. Networks of print and sociability spurred the growth of hydropathy. Newspapers carried advertisements listing new establishments. Manuals touted miraculous recoveries. Lecturers promoted the newest methods, and friends and family members shared information about how to harness the recuperative force of water. Water cure entrepreneurs merged reform with business. Some dove deep into their pockets to furnish their establishments—often located in picturesque rural settings with access to pure water—with restaurants, dance halls, and other comforts to attract wealthy patrons. A few water cure devotees even traveled all the way to central Europe to meet Priessnitz, who enjoyed a sage-like reputation. Those seeking a low-budget alternative were encouraged to practice hydropathy at home. Instructions could be gleaned from the pages of the *Water-Cure Journal and Herald of Reform*, the movement's chief organ in the United States. At the peak of its popularity in the early 1850s, the journal had a monthly circulation of more than half a million.[4]

The dramatic expansion of hydropathy in antebellum America owed much to the high percentage of women who decided to live by the doctrine "Wash and Be Healed." About two-thirds of Wesselhöft's patients at Brattleboro were female. Women authored many of the glowing testimonials for hydropathic facilities that catered to both sexes. The movement found one of its most prolific lecturers in Mary Gove Nichols, a social reformer and pioneering feminist who opened her own water cure clinic with her husband in New York City in 1851. Activists like Nichols touted these establishments as places where women could experience a degree of physical and social freedom that polite Victorian society, with its rigid dress codes and sexual mores, did not provide. At the same time, conservative women embraced hydropathy because they viewed it as an extension of their caretaking role as housewives and mothers. In a somewhat curious fashion, the imperative to keep female bodies healthy and clean linked ideals of middle-class domesticity with the emancipatory aspirations of the women's rights movement.[5]

From a medical standpoint, the growing popularity of the water cure mirrored a rising distrust of the procedures recommended by professional physicians. Mainstream doctors before the Civil War favored bloodletting, leeching, and other invasive procedures to fight even the most banal illnesses. These treatments rarely expedited the healing process. When combined with toxic drugs, they tended to weaken patients instead. Morphine became a highly addictive painkiller, and pills consisting of large doses of mercury were commonly prescribed to reduce fever. Women hoped to find in alternative medicine an escape from the hazards of conventional gynecology—its lack of hygiene and overreliance on medication. In addition to encouraging women in labor to relax with massage and warm baths, hydropaths sought to ease the strains of childbearing by promoting exercise during pregnancy and a swift return to routine activities after delivery.[6]

Calling the water cure a health reform movement, however, leaves half the story untold. A more fitting label would be that of a movement promising recovery *and* rejuvenation. The seemingly boundless capacity of water to promote happiness and youth corresponded with the rise of a participatory democratic culture in which attacks on traditional authorities extended to the medical realm. Hydropathy appealed to those who believed that they had a right to choose the kind of medical care they wanted. To the faithful, cold water offered a trustworthy resource for achieving bodily renewal without the dangers associated with invasive treatments. Through subjecting themselves to their regimens, hydropaths claimed, individual patients might not only gain expertise over their own bodies but also on how to delay or even revert the aging process in particular.

More than advertising unorthodox therapies, the *Water-Cure Journal* made it clear that the aim of hydropathy was to "rescue mankind from the jaws of a premature grave . . . and prolong . . . life to a green old age." This pledge must have struck a chord in a society that had not seen life expectancies rise since the 1800s. In some places they were even shrinking. Living in rapidly growing, polluted, and odor-infested cities in the nineteenth century came with a significant mortality penalty. While the urban poor were more likely to fall victim to crime and illness, affluent city dwellers were notorious for their voracious appetites. Gout became known in this period as the "rich man's disease" for a reason. The standard diet in middle- and upper-class households consisted of greasy foods, an overabundance of meat, and very little fruits or vegetables. One of the biggest gluttons of all was President Martin Van Buren. During his term in the White House from 1837 to 1841, he feasted on oysters, doughnuts, pork, and imported French wine. Van Buren paid a price for his lavish cuisine later in life, suffering from arthritis and dystrophy. Countless others with similar eating habits met a harsher fate. They indeed fell into a premature grave.[7]

For Ruggles, Wesselhöft, and other water cure pioneers, the question of what to eat was inseparable from the question of how and where to bathe. Without healthy food, rehabilitation was impossible. Vegetarians and hydropaths pushed overlapping agendas. Their alliance was strongest in the Northeast, where water cure establishments offered diets based on the teachings of the Presbyterian minister Sylvester Graham, who believed that eating animals enfeebled body and spirit alike. Hydropaths and Grahamites spoke the same language of regeneration. "[My] bodily pains are gone, and my sight is perfectly restored," jubilated one elderly scholar after sticking to diet made up of cool water, whole wheat bread, and two small vegetarian meals per day. Taking the form of confessional writings, such reports carried strong religious overtones. Those that appeared in the group's main outlet, the *Graham Journal of Health and Longevity*, recounted journeys from darkness to light that resembled the born-again narratives of the Second Great Awakening. Physical improvement depended on moral improvement, and vice versa. That was the central message running through nearly all conversion stories disseminated by antebellum vegetarians and hydropaths.[8]

Tighter still was hydropathy's association with one of the shrillest moral crusades of the nineteenth century. In terms of ascribing to pure water a divine, otherworldly quality, water cure practitioners found their fervor matched by the men and women who opposed the consumption of alcohol. By 1835, the Protestant-led American Temperance Society, the largest organization of its kind, boasted a membership of 1.5 million, which equaled about 12 percent of the United States' free population. Hydropaths and temperance activists shared a strong belief in water's intrinsic powers of self-cleansing and self-repair. Water figured prominently as both a life-saving elixir and a symbol of virtue in the public initiation rites devised by temperance groups during the

1830s and 1840s. People who signed pledges of abstinence, swearing to never again touch hard liquor, wine, and in some cases beer and tobacco, celebrated their rebirth with a glass of water.[9]

Temperance advocates enlisted children to convey that abstinence could restore seasoned drunkards to their immaculate younger selves. This theme was on full display in the "Cold Water Army," which became the movement's largest juvenile support group in the early 1840s. Guided by adults, underage boys and girls touted the virtues of sobriety in carefully choreographed parades replete with songs, banners, and theatrical performances. Besides warning fellow youths of the dangers of intoxication, the young activists sought to shame drinkers into quitting through the power of their example. Casting children as agents of redemption, one story published in a New York temperance periodical in 1842 begins with a boy on his deathbed. His father, "an intemperate man," inquired how he was doing. Not well, said the boy. "I have been thinking, father, whether or not you thought you had a soul." The question "was an arrow to the heart of the father, who resolved never to drink anymore." Admonished by his dying son, the father reformed himself, attended church, and was elected president of a temperance society.[10]

Temperance was one of the first instances in US history where organized rejuvenation took the form of a cross-generational partnership. In the movement's logic, all age groups had to be mobilized because "King Alcohol" threatened to contaminate even the youngest bodies. Underage drinking was a common nuisance—the first laws establishing a minimum legal drinking age were not enacted until the 1870s. Activists worried that the nation was literally drowning its most precious resource: youth. Consuming alcohol, some claimed, accelerated the aging process. A broadsheet distributed by the New Jersey Juvenile Temperance Band, a local branch of the Cold Water Army, contained a dramatic before-and-after illustration to show the disastrous effects of liquor on a handsome young man. Though barely eighteen in the first image, the youth, once he starts drinking, deteriorates into an ugly forty-year-old in the second image.[11]

By the time this broadsheet was being distributed, mid-century Americans had become accustomed to thinking of aging in terms of a life course. The image of a rising and falling staircase, which had its roots in early modern Europe, was firmly entrenched in the visual culture of the antebellum United States. Echoing the gender ideals of white middle-class Americans, these representations located the prime of life in the middle years, with men priding themselves on their commercial, military, or political exploits and women gaining recognition for their care work in marriage and motherhood. In a

FIGURE 2.1 Round Hill Water Cure Clinic in Northampton, Massachusetts, 1856. Prior to the US Civil War, hydropathy attracted abolitionists and other reformers in pursuit of health and rejuvenation. Courtesy of the New York Public Library, Digital Collections.

parody created by the artist Nathaniel Currier in 1846, intemperance upended the natural order of the ages and sexes. Rather than portray the arc of a long, happy life, Currier's lithograph *The Drunkard's Progress* narrates the early demise of a young alcoholic. Nine steps are depicted during which the man degenerates under the influence of his addiction, wreaking havoc on his wife and baby child, until he ends his miserable life by putting a bullet through his head.[12]

In "All Hail to Pure Cold Water," reformers of various molds found a hymn they could sing in unison, including the ones who embraced a cause that polarized the country like no other. Abolitionists took a particular liking to the water cure. Ruggles's clinic in Northampton evolved into the movement's unofficial spa, with Black and white activists streaming in and out in quick succession (see figure 2.1). When William Lloyd Garrison suffered from weak nerves and muscle problems in 1848, he spent several weeks in Northampton to give himself "to the work of physical regeneration." Friends persuaded a hesitant Wendell Phillips to try the cure on himself and his ailing wife Ann. Some even took up permanent residence in Ruggles's vicinity. By the mid-1840s, Northampton had become home to a small Black community, a large portion of which consisted of former slaves who undoubtedly felt protected living so close to a veteran of the Underground Railroad. Pleased by what he saw during his stay with Ruggles, Douglass saw the microcosm of a possible future society where "there was no high, no low, no masters, no servants, no white, no black."[13]

While Douglass rejoiced at the miniature utopia he saw developing in the hills of western Massachusetts, Henry Clarke Wright discovered his fountain of youth in the mountains of Upper Silesia. Espousing views that were too uncompromising for many of his companions (he was at one point expelled from the American Anti-Slavery Society), Wright was somewhat of an outlier in the movement. However, the book he wrote about his pilgrimage to Priessnitz's establishment in the winter of 1843 and 1844 fired the abolitionist imagination. Wright was traveling to central Europe from Great Britain, where he had contracted a bad cough. Under Priessnitz's ministration, Wright's ailment first got worse, not better, approaching the moment of crisis that hydropaths considered crucial before any real recovery could occur. After five months of climbing in icy baths, swallowing gallons of water, eating meager diets, and going on long hikes over snow-decked landscapes, the forty-six-year-old Wright reported a miraculous change. Not only did his lungs work again with the ease of a young man, but his body had also learned to turn every feeling of torment caused by cold water showers into bursts of energy. Every woman and man, "when the dreaded moment has passed, and the shock is over, finds himself alive, and not only alive, but exceedingly invigorated; every nerve and muscle is braced up, every joint is supple and ready for prompt action." Priessnitz's method, Wright's account seemed to imply, was exactly the kind of elixir needed to fortify a beleaguered minority.[14]

Middle-aged abolitionists had good reasons to care about developing strong physical constitutions. Many led strenuous public lives with grueling lecture tours that spanned immense distances. In the fall of 1847, Garrison and Douglass crisscrossed the western states to speak to an estimated 20,000 people in one month alone. Addressing mixed crowds on the issue of immediate abolition was not a picnic. Abolitionists were interrupted, heckled, pelted with eggs, and sometimes beaten. The most shocking assault happened in 1837, when an angry proslavery mob murdered the Illinois editor Elijah Lovejoy, an outspoken advocate of Black emancipation. Abolitionists were divided on how to respond to the growing hostility that enveloped them. Black activists were most inclined to fight fire with fire, their militancy rooted in a tradition of self-liberation that included risky escapes and armed insurrections. A significant faction of white reformers begged to differ. They held that violence, even if defensive in nature, was impracticable at best. The relationship of abolitionism with pacifism was complex. Activists who pledged regeneration through peaceful means continued to admire manly slaves who resisted their oppressors. In theory, those who sided with Garrison and Wright identified wholly with the religiously inspired principle of "nonresistance"—the idea that taking up arms to defeat an evil practice was as sinful as the practice itself.[15]

Turning the other cheek in the face of violent opposition, whether it seemed ethically correct or politically expedient, asked much of those ready to follow that rule. At the very least, it required bodies robust enough to absorb blows and withstand exhaustion. Garrisonians have often been described as embracing a feminized style of protest, choosing emotional appeals over blaring demonstrations and moral respectability over revolutionary violence. Their belief in the enlivening effects of cold water suggests more complicated gender identities. While disagreeing over how martial the struggle against slavery should be, most abolitionists wanted their movement to be a muscular one. You may hit a rejuvenated abolitionist, but you cannot punch him into retirement. Wendell Phillips from Boston emerged as a perfect role model. One of the most gifted orators of his age, Phillips called tireless antislavery agitation the "daily cold water and simple bread" of a free people. His associates rhapsodized at length about the "manly avowal of his convictions" and his projection of bodily strength. As Phillips's companion George Lowell Austin reminisced in 1890: "He had a fine physique, and his mind was as brilliant as his body was vigorous."[16]

Exercise was a key component in most nineteenth-century water cure therapies. Ruggles, whom one assistant described as a man "with an athletic form," earned a reputation for scolding his abolitionist friends who skipped the workout routines at Northampton. "We are either in the woods or in the water," Garrison recounted. Gymnastic drills were followed by long walks, after which patients relaxed in small groups. Ideally, bodies were toughened up, and bonds of friendship were strengthened. Some patients, quite possibly, engaged in intimacies. The question of sex is shrouded in uncertainty. In keeping with middle-class sensibilities, rooms and bathing facilities at water cure centers were segregated by gender, but in congregations of adults (children were not permitted) who were either naked or lightly dressed most of the time and enjoyed dancing after sunset, a few patrons hinted at the idea of reaping rejuvenation from romance. One of Wright's English acquaintances, for example, noted in a moment of candor how the cure had aroused "his languid animal powers." Judge Adam Shook from Ohio, who apparently enjoyed flirting with younger women during his stay in Brattleboro, did not mince words in a letter he wrote home: "The ladies play with us. What would our town say to all this? But here, in this 'land of steady habits', no one cares, troubles himself about it. At night, we dance till 10 o' clock. I dance every night, as I am only 27 years old!—set back to that!!"[17]

Fusing sex and hydropathy was a delicate issue, and potentially scandalous if women played a leading role. When Mary Gove Nichols and her husband Thomas demanded for women the right to choose their sexual partners in 1853, they were practically ousted from the nation's water cure community. Hydropathic journals refused to print any more advertisements and articles from the Nicholses. Although there are no eyewitness reports of patients disappearing behind bushes, proponents of the water cure felt that they had to dispel any impression that hydropathic institutions were enclaves of free love.[18]

The scent of radicalism that surrounded hydropathy, especially as it was practiced by Northern reformers, helps to explain its limited appeal in the slaveholding states. Shunning cold water cures and the politics associated with them, Southern planters sought relaxation at mineral spas where they indulged, in the words of one historian, "in huge meals, caffeinated beverages, pipes and chewing tobacco, and daily libations." No love was lost between spa advocates and hydropaths, one of whom denounced warm-water retreats as places "where persons in health . . . 'go to debauch.'" But the water cure had its share of critics outside the South as well. Members of the medical establishment fought back, contending that hydropathy was ineffective or, worse, could result in death if applied improperly. Clean water was hard to get in settlements without proper sanitation, and cholera outbreaks were a constant menace.[19]

David Ruggles, for one, did not live to see his fortieth birthday. He succumbed to a bowel infection in 1849. Arguably more tragic (and grossly negligent as it seemed) was the death of Garrison's six-year-old son Charles Follen Garrison that same year. Instead of seeing a doctor, his parents decided to wrap the boy in wet sheets to fight off his flu-like symptoms. When his condition worsened, they exposed him to a steaming vapor bath. The boy started screaming, and after they took him out, the Garrisons understood why: the hot steam had caused horrible skin burns. This was too much for the weakened child. He died a few days later, leaving behind his heartbroken and guilt-stricken parents.[20]

The writer Nathaniel Hawthorne leveled some of the most stinging accusations of quackery against the hydropaths. Literary scholars see in Hawthorne's short story "Rappaccini's Daughter" (1844) and his short novel *The Blithedale Romance* (1852) biting satires of New England's reform movements. "Rappaccini's Daughter" fictionalizes the rivalry between Wesselhöft and the physician and writer Oliver Wendell Holmes, who decried the German-born hydropath as a charlatan and declared him persona non grata in Boston's medical circles. An aversion to all things homeopathic permeates *Blithedale Romance,* which relates how a utopian rural community not unlike the one in Northampton (although Hawthorne's real-life inspiration came from Brook Farm to the west of Boston) falls apart because of the selfish actions of its members. The role of the villain is played by a pernicious doctor with the name of "Professor Westervelt"—a clear swipe directed at Wesselhöft and his brother Wilhelm.[21]

There is speculation that Hawthorne held a grudge against the German-born brothers because his sick wife had sought them out for treatment over her husband's objections. But Hawthorne had always been plagued by a deeper unease over the rise of countless social schemes in his lifetime that rested on the belief in human perfectibility. On that point, he might have been ahead of his time. "Dr. Heidegger's Experiment" (1837), another of Hawthorne's stories, is a cautionary tale about the hubris of trying to turn back the biological clock. It revolves around a "singular doctor" who lures four old friends into drinking water claimed to be from the Fountain of Youth. The fluid takes immediate effect, and the elders feel restored to their younger selves. Wild merrymaking ensues, during which the friends drink glass after glass only to mock the infirmities of old age they had to endure just a while ago. However, their youthfulness is just an illusion. A tall mirror in the back of the room shows the reflection of "three old, gray, withered grandsires, ridiculously contending for the skinny ugliness of a shriveled grandam." The illusion fades, but sanity does not return. Rather, the friends decide to travel to Florida to "quaff at morning, noon, and night" from the actual fountain.[22]

If Hawthorne meant to issue a warning to a nation that, as he sensed, was starting to fetishize youth instead of seeking the maturity that comes with accepting one's imperfections, he was swimming against the current. More nineteenth-century Americans, not just those invested in the water cure, began to regard acquiescence in the irreversibility of aging as unbefitting a people destined for greatness. Bursts of rejuvenation were needed, if only to prevent intemperance and false compromise from turning Americans into "the most unhealthy, sickly, and, in some respects, effeminate people in the world," as one hydropath exclaimed in 1848. Antebellum Americans liked to think of themselves as the youngest among the nations. But as they were cherishing their youth, they were also afraid of losing it.[23]

THE TROUBLE WITH simple slogans is that they tend to be nonpartisan and divisive at the same time. In the antebellum United States, "Keep America

Young" would have fallen under that rubric. Where abolitionists discerned a need for repair, their adversaries saw an obligation to grow. The essayist Edwin de Leon made this point emphatically in his commencement speech at South Carolina College in 1845. Looking into the beaming faces of the sons of local slaveholders seated in the auditorium, de Leon probably recalled his own student days in Columbia. Yet his address did not traffic in nostalgia. With much bombast, de Leon declared that, like the young United States, the graduates were approaching the threshold of "exulting manhood" at a point in history when men and nations were struggling to get ahead with fiercer urgency than ever before. Not just donning but relishing the mantle of leadership was the "duty" of every "Young American," lest he wanted to stand by and watch his country descend from "manly vigor" to "decrepitude"—the path that had spelled doom to great civilizations in the past.[24]

De Leon's college address sharpened the contours of a nationwide movement that went by the moniker "Young America." Calling Young America a movement, to be sure, creates a false image of uniformity. Most political historians associate the name with a group of aspiring East Coast intellectuals who gave the Democratic Party of Andrew Jackson—founded as a reservoir of white rural values—a more urban-cosmopolitan veneer. Their mouthpiece was the *United States Magazine and Democratic Review*. John O'Sullivan, a New York lawyer of Irish descent, edited the paper from 1837 to 1846. Under his stewardship, the *Democratic Review* embraced aggressive westward expansion and a more interventionist foreign policy. O'Sullivan championed the annexation of Texas, applauded the advance of US troops in the war with Mexico, and faulted the administration of President Franklin Pierce for failing to purchase Cuba. With a rhetorical brashness that roused cheers in his quarters, O'Sullivan was one of the first to articulate that it was the "manifest destiny" of the United States to take possession of an entire continent.[25]

A partisan faction, Young America was also much more, seesawing between a close-knit political fraternity and a contagious mood that pervaded a far broader segment of US society in the 1840s and 1850s. Of course, newness and youthfulness were not recent additions to the rhetorical arsenal of antebellum public commentary. Even the people in O'Sullivan's inner circle were a little troubled by the wooliness of the term, admitting that it could be "adopted as a cover for every loose suggestion in religion, politics, and literature." They were not mistaken. Young Americans made their presence felt in the literary marketplace, where a new generation of writers eagerly declared their independence from European models of art and poetry. Ralph Waldo Emerson, the dean of New England transcendentalism, broadcast this theme in his seminal lectures *The American Scholar* (1837) and, tellingly, *The Young American* (1844). Working-class radicals, too, identified as Young Americans, especially those who demanded free land in the western territories for the urban poor. Before long, advertisers discovered the term's commercial value. Young Americans figured as mascots—mostly in the guise of boyish white men—for products as diverse as denim pants, cigarettes, and transoceanic cruises.[26]

Since it contained multitudes, one may be tempted to judge the Young America movement as little more than a glittering generality that commanded attention but no real loyalty. On narrow political grounds, historians rarely grant Young America a lenient verdict. After all, its adherents failed to deliver one of their central promises: the healing of sectional tensions through the saving grace of a youthful nationalism. Yet, it is remarkable that a shared passion for rejuvenating American culture through a feisty confidence in the new could, for a brief period, spawn tacit alliances between polar opposites, such as the antislavery New Englander Emerson and the slaveholding South Carolinian Edwin de Leon. What if the lasting significance of Young America—and the many branches thereof—does not lie in its stated intentions but in its collateral effects? From this vantage point, a set of commonalities comes into view.

One overarching trend was that youth hardened into a form of political currency wielded for domestic as well as international gain. Young America was not a youth movement in the twentieth-century sense of the word. Its standard bearers in the 1840s were educated white men in their late twenties and early thirties. Relatively young for men knocking at the doors of government, they were nonetheless almost twice the country's median age at the time. Generational awareness surely played a role as many of the upstart politicians who gathered around the *Democratic Review* had a common age range. Born between 1812 and 1815, Senator Stephen Douglas, the banker August Belmont, the publicist and diplomat George Nicholas Sanders, the legislator John Wentworth, and other members of the new Democratic guard grew up in a nation that had weathered another war with Great Britain and entered into an era of furious economic growth, a rapidly expanding electorate, and technological revolutions that produced the railroad and the telegraph.

More than the proximity of their dates of birth, it was the shared experience of a specific birthday that made these Young Americans locate the prime of youth in young and middle-aged manhood. In a move that Corinne Field and Nicholas Syrett called "arbitrary but necessary," Jacksonian reformers striving to decouple white male suffrage from property qualifications settled on age twenty-one as the entry point to full citizenship. A new rite of passage took shape that did not merely redraw the boundaries between the dependencies of childhood and the independence of adulthood. Altering this threshold also meshed with the Jacksonian push toward weakening class bias and enfranchising the "common man." For the young white men who celebrated their virgin vote after turning twenty-one, youth did not end with reaching the age of majority; it was yet to reach full bloom.[27]

The type of youth that Young Americans placed the highest premium on was bound only loosely to chronological age. Rather, it was a state of mind, a way of acting and being in the world. Performance, at times even downright posturing, determined who was truly young. Definitions remained elusive, but many regarded displaying an insatiable appetite for widening America's footprint in the world as the signature of youth. Nearly half a century before the United States acquired a transoceanic empire, the New York writer George William Curtis identified the Young American with some hyperbole as one who "prowls about Cuba...seeking how he could devour it, and sends Commodore Perry to Japan, with the very pleasant message that he is the sun, that the moon is his wife, and the earth his heritage." It is unclear whether Curtis modeled his caricature after a real person. George Francis Train certainly came close. A merchant from Boston whose business ventures stretched all the way to Melbourne, Australia, Train garnered literary fame in the late 1850s with a string of semi-autobiographical books in which he cast himself as Young America's global ambassador. Hiding a steely imperialism behind a facade of pure youthful intentions, Train declared: "Young America is the vanguard of change—the coming age.... He dives deeper, swims longer, and comes up drier. He thinks quicker, accomplishes more, and lives faster than any other party."[28]

The boisterous masculinity of Train's "spread-eagleism" was not confined to the printed page. Thousands of American men who enlisted in private armies bent on conquering territory in Central America in the years before the Civil War turned boasts into bloodshed. A significant portion of these filibusters—not to be confused with today's senators engaging in endless speeches to delay legislation—liked to think of themselves as the military wing of Young America. References of that nature multiplied, especially in the wake of William Walker's invasion of Nicaragua in 1855. Although the Tennessean Walker received the loudest cheers from white Southerners looking to enlarge the empire of slavery, Walker's filibuster army could count on support from pockets in the North (Garrison, meanwhile, called Walker a "great scoundrel"). Ready to fight and kill for Walker, a company of fresh recruits out of New York formed the "Young America Pioneer Club" en route to Nicaragua. The streets of Granada, one of the mercenaries proudly noted in the fall of 1855, were now "thronging with the representatives of 'Young America.'" Facing defeat at the hands of Central American coalition forces the following winter, Walker's men and their local allies razed the city to the ground, ending their regime in a final act of cruelty.[29]

Filibustering's popularity cannot be boiled down to a single reason. Still, its wide appeal in the mid-1850s reflected a mounting frustration with the gentlemanly politics of compromise. Embodied by grizzled leaders with long careers in government, compromise had aimed to appease the sections but left neither the North nor the South satisfied. Why should youth bow to experience when the consensual approach of aging senators had fallen short of repairing the country's strained fabric? Perhaps the last hope for national regeneration lay in the foreign adventurism of plucky Anglo-Saxons unfettered by staid decorum.

While this hope did not prevail, the rhetoric of generational revolt accompanying it did. Young America accommodated few dissenters on issues of race and gender. To most expansionists, the question of women's rights was a distraction at best and an abomination at worst. Women were all but absent from the iconography of erect white males carrying the Stars and Stripes into "uncivilized" lands (John Gast painted his famous female allegory for manifest destiny in 1872). Margaret Fuller, one of the most accomplished female writers of the nineteenth century, stood outside the cult of young manhood, even as she appreciated the cultural nationalism of her fellow male authors. Both Whig and Democratic campaigns of the 1840s offered white middle-class women modest means to shape public opinion, currying their favor and inviting women to point out the moral failings of government in poems, pamphlets, and petitions. Party leaders, in turn, did everything they could to prevent women's suffrage from becoming an acceptable demand within their political platforms.[30]

Young Americans pioneered a mode of democratic combat that relied heavily on ageist tropes. With its rise, a new defamation entered the American political lexicon: the country's senior elites, whom Young Americans blamed for almost every conceivable ill under the sun, were maligned as "old fogies." The label stuck, and gray-haired veterans shuddered at the thought of being perceived as bumbling gerontocrats. Take the case of Daniel Webster and John C. Calhoun, two of the three statesmen who, together with Henry Clay, were a dominant force in US politics during the first half of the nineteenth century. In September 1849, Webster and Calhoun, both sixty-eight, opened their respective estates in Massachusetts and South Carolina to correspondents assigned to writing endearing behind-the-scenes stories. Putting the two senators in the best possible light, they presented them as vigorous warhorses, capable of as much physical and intellectual labor as when they were fifty. The main takeaway from these dispatches was unmistakable: no old fogies here.[31]

The word's etymology is murky. According to an English dictionary entry from 1811, old fogy derived from the French *fougueux* (fiery or spirited) and stood for an invalid soldier. Some thirty years later, the idiom seeped into US politics as an insult for party elders who refused to pass the torch to a new generation of Democrats. This was largely the work of O'Sullivan, who was shrewd enough to challenge the party establishment without putting his own motives in the limelight. Flouting the old regulars who "crust themselves over the party . . . until at last they ruin by corrupting it" was about ensuring its "rejuvenescence," asserted the editor of the *Democratic Review* in November 1839. Though he supported Van Buren, O'Sullivan doubted that Andrew Jackson's successor had inherited Old Hickory's feistiness. To beat the Whigs in the upcoming presidential election, "gallant and unsophisticated youth" needed to "come forward on the stage, and take up and carry on the great mission of the party, which is that of unresting democratic reform."[32]

Over time, fogydom assumed a more capacious meaning, evolving into a shorthand for lethargy, timidity, and a misplaced reverence for the past. It came to stand for a growing disrespect of the elderly that emanated from other quarters as well. A variation of the old fogy theme surfaced in the Deep South in 1846, when a group of junior legislators who had adopted the name "Young Carolina" conspired to dethrone the aging Calhoun, whom they viewed as the ultimate "Old Hunker." Ageism reared its head in the Whig Party as well. At the party's 1850 national convention, younger antislavery politicians staged a revolt against the "Silver Gray Whigs," older party leaders whom they derided as out of touch and overly conciliatory toward slaveholders. Literary critics aligned with Young America trashed books that did not breathe their values as "fogy literature." "Give us ungrammatical manhood, before the most polished meanness," one reviewer exclaimed in 1852 in response to a publication that he felt was sycophantic in its imitation of British tastes. This was not the last time that the rejuvenationist defense of youth encouraged anti-intellectual attitudes. When attacked, some Young Americans backpedaled, claiming that they hated old ideas, not old people. Others, like Henry David Thoreau, would not compromise: "Age is no better, hardly so well, qualified for an instructor as youth, for it has not profited so much as it has lost. . . . Practically, the old have no very important advice to give the young, their own experience has been so partial, and their lives have been such miserable failures . . . they are only less young than they were." A more relentless invective against old age as the one included in Thoreau's *Walden* was hard to find.[33]

In sounding Walt Whitman's "barbaric yawp" to chase away the specters of political and cultural sclerosis, Young Americans were playing a transatlantic tune, not just a national one. Even as the stereotype of Europe as the old and tired continent showed no signs of abating in the United States, the mid-century American infatuation with youth received a decisive impulse from the other side of the Atlantic. In opposition to post-Napoleonic efforts to restore as much of the prerevolutionary order as possible, a chain of "Young" movements formed across Western and Central Europe in the 1820s and 1830s. Most of them conjoined condemnations of the ancien régime with mystic calls for national reawakening.[34]

The Italian Risorgimento, which literally means "on the rise again," captured the imagination of antebellum reformers like few other foreign upheavals. Giuseppe Mazzini, Young Italy's charismatic leader, set the tone in 1834 when he spoke of the "same war" that "feeds the efforts of the young generations against the old" everywhere. Mazzini authored these lines from his Swiss exile, where he helped to bind Polish, Austrian, Swiss, and German revolutionaries into the first transnational fraternity of its kind: Young Europe. While Young Europe's pledge to rid the continent of old kings and aristocrats did not apply to US conditions, Mazzini's decision to limit membership in Young Italy to men under forty struck a chord with his American sympathizers. Curiously, Mazzini was one of the few liberal celebrities from the Old World who found admirers on opposing ends of the political spectrum, which speaks to the malleability of youth-themed reform. When Garrison's *Liberator* hailed Mazzini in July 1849 as an idealist who had been dreaming of "the regeneration of his country" since his youth, little seemed to separate the Boston abolitionist from O'Sullivan, who years earlier had gushed over the "high and holy cause" of Young Italy.[35]

But as the cumulative events of 1848 revealed, any rapprochement between the abolitionists' rejuvenation-through-repair and the New Democrat's rejuvenation-through-growth designs remained piecemeal. US antislavery societies passed resolutions that applauded Europe's revolutionaries for mounting the barricades on behalf of human rights and national self-determination, but they made their ultimate approval contingent on Young Europe's stance on slavery. Praising the new republican government in France for abolishing slavery in all its dominions, abolitionists found novel arguments for emancipating America's slaves. In a string of public declarations, they seized on examples of foreign antislavery legislation to turn the tables on their domestic rivals. Did Young America's dithering on slavery not expose them as distant relatives of Europe's doddering aristocracies?[36]

The accused scoffed at such intimations. Young Americans read 1848 as a milestone event in the global advance of liberty, seeing their vision of manifest destiny vindicated on both continents (see figure 2.2). In North America, the US soldiers returning victorious from Mexico had secured another huge chunk of land for their country's expanding settler empire. Turning eastward, Young Americans thought (naively) that they were witnessing multiple reenactments of 1776, this time on a transnational stage. Bordering on hubris, George Sanders continued to play godfather to continental revolutionaries long after their uprisings had ended in disaster. In early 1854, Sanders, who had accepted the position of US consul to London, hosted a dinner party in honor of George Washington's birthday that included some of Europe's most wanted radicals: the Italians Mazzini, Giuseppe Garibaldi, and Felice Orsini (who was guillotined four years later after trying to assassinate Napoleon III); the German socialist Arnold Ruge; the French republican Alexandre Ledru-Rollin; the Hungarian leader Lajos Kossuth (who had earned the abolitionists' ire for equivocating on slavery); and the Russian writer and activist Alexander Herzen.[37]

People back home either shrugged off Sanders's gathering or chided him for risking a diplomatic row with Europe's resurgent monarchies. Had the euphoria of the Young Americans been premature? In 1848, US voters sent two aging Whigs to the White House; the rise of the Free Soil Party started to tear apart the Second Party System; and liberal nationalism produced refugees, not stable governments. The tide of public opinion was turning, and suddenly it seemed as if the very idea of youth, cocksure and overconfident, was put on trial. Beginning in the mid-1840s, a series of caricatures appeared in British and US periodicals that made a laughingstock out of the chest-thumping Young American. English cartoonists working for the internationally renowned *Punch* magazine invented the image of the "young Yankee-Noodle," the uncouth man-child who kept picking fights with opponents more massive and mature than he was.[38]

US journals with Whiggish leanings followed suit. A caricature that appeared on March 26, 1853, in the New York–based magazine *The Lantern* compares Young Americans to a spoiled milksop who lacks the toughness of youths from other countries. "Boo-Hoo! 'Tain't that I mind the 'lickin, but to be knocked around by a blamed Foreigner, isn't my notion of Liberty and

FIGURE 2.2 Sheet music cover featuring an allegory of Young America, 1855. The young man proudly holding the Stars and Stripes epitomizes the boastful expansionism associated with the period's Young America movement. Courtesy of the Library of Congress Prints and Photographs Division.

Equality, no how!" wails the boy in front of his parents after he returns from an altercation with an immigrant his age. Other publications filled their pages with satirical drawings that portrayed Young Americans as precocious boys shaving their smooth faces and looking ridiculous in their gentlemanly attire and oversized top hats. In view of the turmoil that engulfed the Atlantic world after 1848, the subtext was clear: putting inexperienced, hot-tempered boy-men at the helm of state at a time that called for the wisdom of advanced age was a recipe for disaster.[39]

To a columnist writing for the *New York Daily Times*, Young America was more than a possible menace to national security. Its dangerous doctrines, he fretted, had already started poisoning the minds of the young generation. Strolling down Broadway on a sunny afternoon in June 1853, the author (whose background was most likely white and middle-class) came across a group of boys in their teens imitating the mannerisms of grown men in ways that made them look both "strange" and "repellent." More alarming, this "effeminate race of creatures" would crowd the saloons in upper Manhattan at night, "quaffing doctored brandy, spending money that is not their own, and boasting of vicious exploits, which . . . are generally inventions of their own prurient imaginations." Permitting this "strange hybrid between youth and age—depraved in morals, vulgar in sentiment, narrow in intellect, and stunted in growth"—to run wild on the streets of New York was a failure of fatherhood, a perversion of manhood, and, perhaps worse, a national embarrassment. Mischievous adolescents, in the author's eyes, were the harvest of a society that had reversed the authority that youth traditionally owed to old age. For its critics, Young America's insistence on a radical futurity that showed no allegiance to the past was neither rejuvenation nor youth. And if it was, they wanted no part of it.[40]

WAYWARD YOUTH MUST HAVE BEEN the last thing on Abraham Lincoln's mind when he rose to deliver his famous Gettysburg Address on November 19, 1863. The president had come to dedicate a cemetery that would become the final resting place for more than 3,500 Union soldiers. Many of the fallen had perished at an age just slightly older than the teenage New Yorkers that had made the *New York Daily Times* columnist indignant. With its staggering death toll, the US Civil War "marked a sharp and alarming departure" in American society "from existing preconceptions about who should die," as Drew Gilpin Faust noted. Young men, healthy and thirsting for action, were the first to die fighting in one of the earliest industrial wars that cost the lives of an estimated 640,000 soldiers. Looking at the freshly dug graves, Lincoln and his contemporaries were only beginning to grasp a dramatic shift: people who had become accustomed to thinking of themselves as young to the point of invincibility were now learning the painful lesson that death and loss were all-pervading and perhaps the true companions of obsessive youthfulness. Or were they?[41]

Lincoln was no friend of Young America; nor did he make common cause with the millennial reformers singing the praises of the water cure. In many ways, he went into politics as the antithesis of both. One of Lincoln's earliest public speeches, which he gave in January 1838 as a twenty-eight-year-old state legislator at the Young Men's Lyceum in Springfield, Illinois, ran over with admiration for the statecraft of the founders. Lincoln continued to venerate the revolutionary generation as he climbed up the ladders of the Whig and later of the Republican Party. In his debates with Stephen Douglas, he called the Declaration of Independence "that immortal emblem of humanity" and implored his fellow citizens to "return to the fountain whose waters spring close by the blood of the Revolution." Up until the second year of the war, when he moved forcefully against slavery by issuing the Emancipation Proclamation, Lincoln's politics of rejuvenation blended nostalgia for the founders with conservative reform. Lincoln distrusted gestures of radical newness, but he also profited from the youthful enthusiasm that swept the nascent Republican Party to power.[42]

Few grassroots organizations embodied this enthusiasm more vividly than the Wide Awakes. Army-like columns of Lincoln supporters who had adopted that name stormed onto the national stage during the election campaign of 1860. While rekindling some the generational fervor displayed by the Young Americans in their heyday, the Wide Awakes fused martial manhood and partisan youth involvement in a much more combative manner. First of all, they were younger demographically. Judging by the rosters of individual companies, its members were rarely older than twenty-five and could be as young as fifteen. Estimates about the organization's size differ. The half a million marchers mentioned by commentators at the time is an exaggeration (roughly 100,000 to 150,000 recruits is a more accurate figure), but it underlines the mass excitement that these uniformed Republicans stumping for Lincoln were able to spark in just a few months. Declaring themselves the voice of first-time voters, Wide Awake troops sprouting up in cities from Hartford and New York to St. Louis and San Francisco serenaded party favorites, held torchlight rallies, and formed bodyguards at Republican campaign events.[43]

The historian Jon Grinspan identified several factors that explain the Wide Awakes' exploding popularity in the North with young males from rural and urban, affluent and struggling backgrounds. Chief among them were the military-style demonstrations and intense fraternalism that gave these political novices a sense of civic importance rarely granted to American men around the age of majority. An effective media operation ensured rapid recruitment. Pamphlets and newspapers carrying images of earnest young men dressed in dark uniforms, holding banners with sketches of large eyeballs, and marching in unison to drumbeats, Grinspan elaborated, must have appealed to "northerners who felt emasculated by years of submitting to the Slave Power." The Wide Awakes' commitment to "waking up" a slumbering nation cast the Republicans as the true party of youth. In addition, the movement's projection of organizational prowess and sober discipline suggested that their rank and file possessed maturity beyond their age.[44]

This is not to say that the Wide Awakes' relationship with senior Republicans was entirely amicable. Carl Schurz was one of several Lincoln confidants who felt that the Wide Awakes sucked up too much oxygen and occasionally crossed the line between protecting and stalking party elders. Yet, like other top Republicans, Schurz never doubted the advantages of developing intergenerational ties within a party that claimed the purifying force of youth for all its members, regardless of age. A German refugee of 1848 who had escaped imprisonment and possible execution as a twenty-year-old student, Schurz appreciated that Wide Awake detachments were forming in immigrant communities in the North as well. To him, the sight of revolutionary refugees and native-born men rallying under the banner of antislavery vindicated the idea that immigration refreshed the lifeblood of every civilized nation rather than drained it, as nativist elements in the Republican Party had been saying. Laying out his vision of "True Americanism" in 1859, Schurz postulated that "nations which have long subsisted exclusively on their own resources will gradually lose their original vigor, and die the death of decrepitude. But mankind becomes young again by its different elements being shaken together, by race crossing race and mind penetrating mind."[45]

Schurz's rejuvenationist utopia did not extend equally to all groups of people. The same liberal nationalists who denounced slavery and aristocracy as outdated systems of hereditary rule had no qualms about inscribing gender and racial differences in their blueprints for democracy. The "free colony of humanity" that Schurz envisioned lay in the West. Native Americans living on that land were told to either assimilate or face annihilation. But even in moderate doses, this utopia was explosive enough to tear the United States in two. When the Civil War started in April 1861, many of the Union's earliest and most zealous volunteers were Wide Awakes. In St. Louis, pro-Lincoln militias composed of members of the local German gymnastic society, the *Turnverein,* and former Wide Awakes drew first blood as they were trying to capture a small secessionist force nearby (a number of those who escaped would join the Bushwhackers, a Confederate guerilla force made up mostly of youngsters in their teens and early twenties). The confrontation on May 10 left twenty-eight dead and sparked the extremely brutal fighting that agonized Missouri, and much of the nation, for the next four years.[46]

In the midst of all the carnage, rejuvenation assumed its most transcendent and most devastating meaning. Lincoln's Gettysburg Address is best known for crafting a vision of political immortality on the graves of the fallen. Brave men died so that this "nation might live" and experience a "new birth of freedom." Radical abolitionists wielded similar metaphors to defend the war. For Frederick Douglass, "national regeneration" through bloodshed was the only way to repair a "broken constitution," to "unify and reorganize" institutions putrefied by slavery and secession. Douglass's vision for a political refounding came with a stronger dedication to racial egalitarianism than Lincoln's, but the argument was the same. Douglass and Lincoln, middle-aged men both, constructed a causal relationship between the sacrificial value of young deaths and the potential for a redemptive national reset.[47]

For the soldiers who bore the brunt of the battle, reconstructing the body politic was mired in pain and grief. Staggering piles of amputated arms and legs generated an army of empty sleeves, and many disabled soldiers turned to a burgeoning prosthetics industry for help. According to conservative estimates, approximately 70,000 amputations resulting from battle-inflicted injuries took place between 1861 and 1865. Far from regaining the wholesomeness of their former selves, veterans wearing artificial limbs survived as symbols of lost youth and shattered manhood.[48]

The wounds of war continued to fester beyond 1865. Emancipated Black Americans saw in Reconstruction a path to the maturity of equal citizenship. "We stand in relations to all others, as youth to age. Other nations have had their day of greatness and glory; we are yet to have our day, and that day is coming," Douglass predicted in 1869. But that dream proved abortive, mainly because defeated Confederates converted their longing to restore a vanished world into racist violence. For the South to "rise again," newly enfranchised African Americans, in the eyes of Southern "Redeemers," had to be forced back into the status of subordinate wards, which the overwhelming portion of white Southerners and their abettors up North considered the appropriate age for people of color. In the mid-nineteenth century, some Americans aspired to give the past a new future to grow into; others wanted to reinstate a past devoured by the flames of war through intimidation and terror. In the lives of more than just a few people, the ecstasy of expectations resounding from water cure facilities, expansionist fantasies, and Wide Awake rallies had given way to the agony of despair. Still, the race for rejuvenation roared on, gaining fresh steam from new engines.[49]

CHAPTER THREE

Far Away, Back in Time

The Rise of Imperial Recreation

Infinite mighty young-old free,
Tawny and rough, profound
Full of silence of mystery,
Cradled in finite joy,
Young you are, as you e'er have been
Man-like and strong, you boy!
—Charles Wakefield Cadman, *The West* (1916)

The South had few defenders after the Civil War, and Harriet Beecher Stowe hardly appeared destined for that role. Her best-selling novel *Uncle Tom's Cabin*, which had catapulted her to international fame in the 1850s, made Stowe a persona non grata in the states of the former Confederacy. The loathing was mutual. Stowe's portrayal of slaveholder cruelty heightened sectional tensions and fueled the debate about how and when to end slavery. Astoundingly, the relationship changed from acrimony to amity within only a couple of years. During that time Stowe discovered a different kind of South, one in which calm seas, gentle airs, and mild winters made the fifty-six-year-old writer feel "quite young & frisky."[1]

When Stowe left Connecticut for Florida in early 1867 to visit her son Frederick, she traveled as a concerned mother, not as an abolitionist firebrand. Frederick had started over, running a cotton plantation outside of Jacksonville that the Stowes had rented for him. His business was in the red, yet Stowe was happy to see her troubled son look healthy and tanned. Reuniting with Frederick under sun-drenched orange trees made Stowe forget the heavy drinker that her son, a veteran of the Civil War, had become. Stowe's hopes for her son's recovery seemed boundless. The pace of reform mattered little in these lush surroundings. She was now living like a mistress on a piece of land farmed by hundreds of freedpeople who, according to Stowe, were learning to think and work for themselves and enjoy the fruits of their own labor. Stowe found a peculiar charm in the "quiet and repose" that hovered over this "perpetual flower-garden," where the sleep-stealing chills of cold New England nights had "given way . . . to the most childlike habit of slumber."

After deciding to make Mandarin County her winter habitat, Stowe became increasingly enchanted with Florida's vegetation. No month passed "without flowers blooming in the open air." Stowe marveled at the way in which "this wild, wonderful, bright and vivid growth" defied seasonal conventions. "When I get here, I enter another life," Stowe told the English novelist George Eliot in February 1872. "The world recedes; I am out of it; it ceases to influence; its bustle and noise die away in the far distance."[2]

Gilded Age speculators who began marketing Florida as a place of unique regenerative possibilities could not have wished for a better mouthpiece. *Palmetto Leaves*, an uplifting travel guide that the New England writer completed around that time, is often credited with spurring northern migration to the state. At the heart of Stowe's boosterism lay a profound paradox: How was it possible to escape the "bustle and noise" of industrial modernity and simultaneously lay the groundwork for its expansion? Would joining the drumbeat for the rapid development of the southernmost parts of the United States not corrupt the island of tranquility that had rejuvenated Stowe physically and spiritually? Precisely how Americans of the late nineteenth and early twentieth centuries confronted this paradox, in large parts by reassessing the relationship of aging, place, and modernization, is the subject of this chapter. Imperial recreation—animated by a revaluation of the outdoors as well as the near simultaneous invention of what David Wrobel called the "global West" and what Catherine Cocks termed the "tropical South"—lent renewed urgency to a basic question: Does age have a geography?[3]

Ailing white women pursuing rejuvenation away from the corrosive influences of civilization were not the first to ponder whether aging was as much a spatial as a temporal phenomenon. As chapter 1 demonstrated, eighteenth-century notions that white bodies would grow old faster in foreign climes had spawned the degeneration thesis, which regarded all living organisms in the New World as inferior. Fears of premature aging in the tropics also encumbered the British imperial project. Scrambling to explain the high mortality rates among colonial troops and administrators stationed in India, medical experts in the early 1800s held that exposing Europeans to excessive heat over a long period subjected them to fatigue and lethal diseases. Deterministic views about tropical climates spread across imperial communities, as did schemes to remedy the allegedly devastating effect of heat on white bodies. Strategies of racial revitalization ranged from building hill stations in British India, which grew out of the belief that higher altitudes could halt the accelerated aging of transplanted Europeans, to promoting therapeutic spas in French Africa and the West Indies. Designed to reduce colonialism's health hazards, all these places made youth, in the words of David Pomfret, "an essential co-requisite of empire."[4]

Zones with climates unfamiliar to white Europeans and North Americans did not turn into places of desire overnight. When Stowe began rhapsodizing about Florida's exotic fruits and chirping birds, most people still viewed the tropics as a cesspool of disease—an invisible menace that white men tasked with conquering inhospitable lands had to endure. Illness and death were rampant on the Oregon Trail as well. Countless settlers moving west in wagon trains perished before the journey was over. How, then, did the notion that going south (or west for that matter) would rejuvenate, not ruin, white bodies trickle into public consciousness? The answer lies in the intersecting politics of recreation and empire. Recent histories have emphasized that from the late 1800s to the mid-twentieth century, travel and tourism not only mimicked imperial thought and practice but also recast them as healthy, pleasurable, and innocuous. Materially, this rearticulation manifested itself in railroads, steamships, and later cars and airplanes that brought throngs of adventurers and leisure-seekers to faraway destinations once penetrated by explorers, missionaries, and soldiers. Culturally, it built on the conviction that Euro-Americans could impose their will on nature while containing all kinds of eco-biological risks.[5]

For the traveler to rewrite risk into opportunity and senescence into youth, overcoming the tyranny of distance was not the only precondition. Aging backward, some believed, hinged on managing another inescapable trait of modernizing societies: the acceleration of the pace of life. At once a product and catalyst of industrialization, nineteenth-century advancements in transportation and communication upended traditional biorhythms. Although acceleration was experienced differently in different places, an expanding capitalist economy powered by ever-faster systems of production and distribution affected larger segments of the world's population. A cultural preference for speed—reinforced by scientists, journalists, and politicians celebrating technological progress at every turn—mirrored ambitions of growth and greatness, toppling familiar life cycles and perceptions regarding the flow of time. Acceleration's Janus-faced character contributed to several modern maladies diagnosed by medical experts during the late 1800s. Neurasthenia topped the list. Developing the first clinical profile of nervous exhaustion in 1881, the American physician George Miller Beard portrayed neurasthenia as an illness of the white middle and upper classes. City dwellers groaning under the stress and strain of their hurried lives succumbed to headaches, depression, and "phases of insanity," turning them into depleted and senile wrecks irrespective of age. The only remedy, Beard trumpeted, was temporary withdrawal from the burdens of an urban existence and a simpler, nature-oriented lifestyle.[6]

Beard's suggestion that sufferers slow down and take time out from their chores before succumbing to an ever-more dynamic onslaught of aggressive stimuli exemplified a new kind of rejuvenation discourse that blossomed as the nineteenth century closed and the twentieth century began. Deceleration became the watchword of a transnational cohort of self-designated stress experts who saw in the dizzying tempo of work a major cause of accelerated aging. Though differing in their prescriptions, most of these fatigue scientists agreed that territorial niches untouched by escalating speed regimes would help exhausted subjects regain the freshness of their younger selves. Endorsements from physicians and patients visiting the first health resorts on the nation's southern frontier echoed this presumption. "The overworked and over worried class, will find here a most soothing climate to regain their lost energy or restore the nervous system to its normal equilibrium," reported a couple from Philadelphia who spent the spring and summer of 1896 in Southern California.[7]

Since empire was the soil on which many such "oases of deceleration" sprouted, this chapter addresses the sharp divides produced by various practices of imperial recreation. White sojourners seeking enclaves of rejuvenation in faraway lands proved harmful to Indigenous populations, creating lasting legacies of dispossession and neglect. The neurasthenic premise was as simplistic as it was racist: as long as exhaustion was conceived as the result of mental rather than physical labor, then those races stamped with possessing limited intellectual faculties were considered less prone to overuse them. But even among the privileged classes, the desire to make aging bodies resistant to the ailments induced by acceleration bred profoundly gendered practices. At one end of the spectrum were women confined to rest cures. The assumption was that nervous "invalids" of the "weaker sex" could only recover in states of total repose and inactivity. At the opposite end were men who sought to repair their battered masculinities by hiking in pristine nature, roping cattle, and going on expeditions or hunting trips that took them as far as South America and Africa. The frontier became their adventure playground or, to quote the historian Frederick Jackson Turner, their "magical fountain of youth in which America continually bathed and was rejuvenated."[8]

It is important to note that in most of these endeavors, deceleration rarely sparked revolutionary critiques of Western modernity. Taking a break from civilization was more strategy than ideology, a pathway toward reenergizing fatigued bodies and, ideally, immunizing them against future bouts of exhaustion. Silas Weir Mitchell, the physician who came up with the rest cure, was certain that white-collar workers who engaged in a "sturdy contest with nature" and "store[d] up a capital of vitality" kept up the nation's "pristine force and energy." Imperial recreation served as a crucial auxiliary to social Darwinism. Adherents believed that preserving the youthful efficiency of a particular people, specifically its best and brightest, would give them an edge in the race for global dominance. The link between the domestic and foreign surfaced in attempts to regenerate American manhood in thrilling and dangerous frontier exploits, but it also figured in turn-of-the-century campaigns to rebrand places like Florida and Southern California as tourist sites where youthfulness could be plucked like oranges from a tree. After examining these twin contexts, the chapter closes with an excursion into the world of camping, which developed into one of America's favorite pastimes in the early twentieth century. Wilderness enthusiasts, too, found it necessary to take time away from office desks and conveyor belts, contending that outdoor experiences in temperate climate zones offered just as much—if not more—revitalization.[9]

TO GROW YOUNG while accruing greater wisdom—this was "the true myth of America," wrote D. H. Lawrence. "Wrinkled and writhing in an old skin" at its birth, the country, with each step, experienced "a gradual sloughing of the old skin, toward a new youth." The British author's exceptionalist image of the United States replicated Turner's frontier thesis. Three decades earlier, Turner had famously located the wellspring of America's national character in the continuous cycle of birth and rebirth caused by three centuries of westward expansion. Perhaps Lawrence's inner eye also conjured up the silhouettes of the men who had entered the Euro-American imagination as true embodiments of that spirit. There was William "Buffalo Bill" Cody, whose Wild West Shows around 1900 sold epic performances of rugged individualism and frontier democracy to audiences in North America and Europe. There was Frederick Russell Burnham, the mercenary adventurer who dug for gold in Alaska and dined with Queen Victoria after fighting for the British in the Second Boer War. Towering over them all was Theodore Roosevelt. The rough-riding twenty-sixth president of the United States became the most potent envoy of an increasingly global American West.[10]

Neither of these frontier celebrities invented the script of the West as a place of physical and spiritual renewal on their own. That label is often pinned on one of Roosevelt's college chums, the writer Owen Wister. In his fictional exploits, Wister developed an appealing formula for how to remake decrepit weaklings into red-blooded men. Of all the popular cowboy novels penned during the Gilded Age, Wister's *The Virginian* (1902) stood out for creating an enduring model of the ideal western man: tough, fearless, chivalric. Critics discern in the novel's main character—a transplanted easterner who starts over on a cattle ranch in Wyoming and brings his enemies to justice in a final shootout—Wister's alter ego, the end result of a personal journey that began at a doctor's office in Philadelphia in 1885.[11]

Shortly after Silas Mitchell had diagnosed Wister with neurasthenia, the sickly financier took a leave from his banking job and boarded a train that took him out west. Spending the summer in Wyoming riding horses, hunting big game, and working under blue skies on the ranch of a family friend forever changed him. Wister's diary contains lengthy entries about majestic landscapes, stately animals, and the cleanest air a human being could possibly breathe. The local herdsmen intrigued him most. His feelings were ambivalent at first, reflecting the class conceit of an East Coast patrician who cringed at the coarse manners of common country folk. The longer Wister stayed, the more he felt drawn to the "barbaric virtues," the "reckless generosity &—a certain kind of tenderness bred of a wild life." More than forty years later, and after numerous holidays in Wyoming packed with cattle roundups, moose hunts, and camping trips in the mountains, Wister still harkened back to that first summer as his second birth, the starting shot of a dual act of recreation and creation. As he was reassembling his broken masculinity, Wister began the work of assembling the cowboy into a recuperative figure. The heroes striding through his stories are just that, walking reconciliations between primitivism and civilization, youth and age—lodestars for a nation fearful of losing its drive as it was ambitiously reaching outward.[12]

Wister's epiphany came at the cusp of a growing influx of middle-aged, affluent white urbanites who roamed the prairies for fun and fellowship. No doubt stoked by tales of recovery and regeneration, the fondness of genteel easterners for roughing it in the wide outdoors engendered a spate of networks and institutions. High up on the list—aside from hunting and conservation clubs—were the dude ranches, former cattle farms whose owners saw a business opportunity in offering paying customers authentic slices of western life. Although dude ranching did not peak until the 1920s, these rustic spas found an early cheerleader in Theodore Roosevelt. Like Wister, Roosevelt promoted his own errand into the Dakotas, where he had first gone in 1883 to overcome his infirmities, as a blueprint for fostering male camaraderie and national rejuvenation (see figure 3.1). Both themes helped launch Roosevelt's political career, which started with him lecturing the public on why

FIGURE 3.1 Theodore Roosevelt with his horse in the Dakota Badlands, 1883. Roosevelt championed the "West Cure" to reawaken the masculine instincts of white middle-class men suffering from "civilization fatigue." Courtesy of the Harvard College Library, Theodore Roosevelt Collection.

the United States needed to retain its fierce frontier spirit. In an avalanche of books and articles, the future president broadcast the "West cure" as the perfect blend of democracy and meritocracy. In Roosevelt's judgment, the out-of-doors rekindled "the best and manliest qualities" in the progenies of an aging elite. More importantly, he likened the fraternal order of the prairie to a melting pot in which the animosities of class and region dissolved into the unifying mold of the vigorous American.[13]

The vision of the West as a repository of white masculine values combined several temporalities. On one level, it came to grips with the nation's recent history. Less an expression of private nostalgia than a political act of coping with the past, the type of cowboy brotherhood romanticized by Wister and Roosevelt was inextricably tied to the goal of restoring fraternal bonds between North and South. For Wister, there was no better way to clasp hands over the bloody chasm than to exchange hearty handshakes at the prairie campfire. Only then did the men who "came riding from various parts of the compass" rediscover what the Civil War had tragically obscured—that they were bound together by a shared racial destiny. A Pennsylvanian, Wister modeled his fictional cowboys after idealized southern cavaliers. He hailed the "adventurous sons of Tennessee and Kentucky" who had migrated to Texas in the 1850s as the first real cowboys. Later, Wister presented his "Virginian" as the epitome of the gallant southern gentleman, prepared to rededicate his rebellious energy to a glorious national future.[14]

Curtailing the role of non-white Americans, Wister's literary reconciliation scheme was cut from the same cloth as other mainstream nation-building attempts of the time. Turn-of-the-century proponents of reunion believed that erasing memories of African American emancipation was necessary to overcome lingering hostilities between white Northerners and Southerners. Sovereign Black actors were in short supply in contemporary accounts of US expansionism. Almost without exception, these narratives, most of which were authored by white males, concealed just how substantial the African American presence in the West was in the late 1800s. Thousands of formerly enslaved men headed west in the decades after the Civil War, trying to elude the grip of their old masters and make a living as waiters, servants, ranch hands, even soldiers.[15]

The urge to push people of color out of the frame united white frontier afficionados across the sectional gulf who did not tolerate any racial disruption of their rugged brotherhood. Some Black settlers, however, made their voices heard. When they did, their stories suggested how far the African American rationale for heading west diverged from the rejuvenationist fantasies spread by Wister, Roosevelt, and other white mythologizers of the West. A case in point is the 1907 autobiography of Nat Love, a Black man born into slavery who claimed for himself all the prerogatives of a proud and independent cowboy. Love had learned to read and write early in his life, which was rare for African Americans of his generation. That gave him the literary ability to brag about his exploits as a cattle driver and rodeo performer. But while the famous author photo included in Love's memoir effortlessly appropriates the elements of white cowboyhood (hat, bandanna, saddle, lasso, and rifle), the memoir makes clear that men like Love went to the American West to escape, not reboot, a racial past mired in pain and suffering. If anything, they hoped to find a radically different future in a place that seemed to offer a greater degree of geographical and social mobility.[16]

The national future envisioned by the Roosevelts and Wisters, meanwhile, was that of a youthful Anglo-Saxon eager to break out of the confines of domesticity and domestic politics. "Is America a weakling, to shrink of the world work of other great powers?" asked Roosevelt two years after the Spanish–American War of 1898 had established the United States as an overseas empire. His answer was "No. The young giant of the West stands on a continent and clasps the crest of an ocean in either hand. Our nation, glorious in youth and strength, looks into the future with eager and fearless eyes, and rejoices as a strong man to run the race."[17] Roosevelt's diction betrays an intriguing conflation typical for men of his caste: they liked to juxtapose American youthfulness with the aging empires of Europe and East Asia. Appropriating the familiar imperial rhetoric of a forward-looking civilizing mission, Roosevelt yearned for a primal masculinity that would allow rejuvenated Anglo-Saxons to leap at their prey with predatory force.

Gender historians are no strangers to this balancing act. Michael Kimmel, Gail Bederman, and others have called attention to how white middle- and upper-class American men around 1900 sought to acquire "savage" traits to dispel fears of racial degeneration and shore up their sense of superiority. But whereas these scholars tend to dismiss rejuvenation as a by-product of remasculinization, I contend that making men manlier *and* younger was central to advocating a virile, youthful vision of empire. More than once, frontier trekkers spoke of their expeditions to the outer rims of civilization, where they hoped to rediscover their primal instincts, in time-traveling terms. After a clean kill in the wild made him feel one with the hunting prowess of his ancient forebears, the Californian politician and conservationist William Kent cheered, "You're a barbarian, and you're glad of it. It's good to be a barbarian . . . and you know that if you're a barbarian, you are at any rate a man." Chasing gold and glory in imperial borderlands, Minnesota native Frederick Russell Burnham considered the global frontier his fountain of youth. From that well, Burnham believed, "the gift from my ancestors of superabundant physical energy and strength" would gush eternal. His cheerleaders in the press played along. "Major Burnham is about 50 years old, but strong and hearty as a youth," the *New York Herald* raved in 1911. Few followed Burnham in making a career out of colonial warriordom, but his popularity in imperialist circles in Britain and the United States encapsulated the belief that being "a splendid savage" would mitigate the maladies caused by overcivilization.[18]

Though white women barely figured as actors in Anglo-Saxon frontier exploits, they were not entirely absent, either. Years before Burnham made a name for himself as America's premier scout, Fanny Bullock Workman broke with the conventions of Victorian womanhood by cycling thousands of miles in the imperial borderlands of India and North Africa. Born into an affluent Massachusetts family, Workman pioneered a new form of female travel writing that combined strenuous activity and adventure journalism. Together with her husband William, she wrote *Algerian Memories* in 1895, which documents the couple's experiences as they were biking across the Atlas

Mountains and commenting on local peoples and sceneries. Armed with a Kodak camera and a revolver, Workman took pride in her ability to explore exotic hinterlands that few tourists got to see. The trip itself was described as a journey into a distant past, dotted with thrilling encounters with natives whose supposedly pre-civilized ways stood in sharp contrast to the Workman's mastery of modern technology. Despite frequent punctures and flat tires, Workman extolled the regenerative virtues of cycling into the wild, embracing it as a form of emancipation from the monotonies of middle-class domesticity.[19]

Nowhere is the sequence of colonial travel, going back to the origins of the species, and self-rejuvenation spelled out more candidly than in Roosevelt's published account of his East African safari in 1909. One year after leaving the White House, Roosevelt realized his boyhood dream of dashing after lions, rhinos, and elephants in what today is Kenya, Uganda, and the Congo. The narrative voice detailing dramatic encounters with wild animals (the ex-president and his companions ended up trapping and killing more than 11,000 for "scientific" purposes) bore little resemblance to the customary bearing of a fifty-year-old elder statesman. Roosevelt's Africa was a prehistoric environment governed by interspecies violence, a society in infancy where white men could at once demonstrate superior skills and bask in the emotions of an intensely archaic masculinity. In casting big-game hunting as a battle for survival akin to the dangers once faced by his "earliest paleolithic ancestors," Roosevelt applied a key precept from one of the leading evolutionary theorists at the turn of the century. If the US psychologist Granville Stanley Hall was correct that individuals recapitulated the stages of human history as they evolved from childhood to adulthood, then inverting this "biological law" by going back in time might hold the key to turning back life's clock. Done right, it could inoculate men, races, and whole nations against the slackening of mind and muscles in an amenity-sated urban modernity.[20]

Readers might wonder how leading what Roosevelt called "the strenuous life" could be experienced as simultaneously invigorating and decelerating. In part, the answer lies in the high value white imperialists placed on primitivism in the decades before World War I. This is a tricky subject since this reappraisal was one-sided, Eurocentric, and rarely resulted in a greater appreciation of cultural difference. What it did result in was an intense longing for the unvarnished virility supposedly residing in "primitive" peoples living on the edges of the mapped world—a primal vigor that white men sought to tap into and harvest for their own benefit. Highly contradictory images of racial others proliferated as a consequence. In Buffalo Bill's Wild West spectacles, for instance, Native Americans morphed from being ferocious devils standing in the way of progress to honorable warriors deserving a just peace (a cynical move considering that the Native Americans had been slaughtered by the thousands). The dramatic coupling of bloody battles and peace ceremonies projected a natural equilibrium of the steady ebb and flow of historical time, which modern technology threatened to expedite beyond control. Roosevelt evoked a similar scenery toward the end of his African sojourn. Mingled with "the thrill of the fight with dangerous game" was "the strong attraction of the silent places . . . where the wanderer sees the awful glory of sunrise and sunset in the wide waste spaces of the earth, unworn of man, and changed only by the slow changes of the ages throughout time everlasting." Rather than ruling each other out, regenerative violence and a decelerated sense of time were presented as complementary desires.[21]

Nevertheless, rejuvenated imperial manhood remained a fragile construct, always fraying at the edges. Returning to the source meant walking a fine line between recapturing the right amount of youth and losing attributes associated with mature citizenship. By trying to make the old young again, some were ridiculed as infants in adult clothing. Roosevelt himself faced repeated criticism for disregarding diplomatic etiquette. It made him look like an excitable boy, not like a leader of men. Caricatures that made a mockery of the president show him sitting on a rocking horse, commanding toy armies, and using the Caribbean as the playground for his fleet. A variety of boy organizations that sprang up in the United States after 1900, including the Sons of Daniel Boone, the Woodcraft Indians, and the most influential of them all, the Boy Scouts of America (BSA), further shrank the distance separating boyhood from manhood. However, many of the middle-aged men infatuated with the boyish qualities of impulsiveness, exuberance, and playfulness never stopped worrying whether crossing that line all too zealously would make them appear unmanly in the eyes of their peers. Wister leveled that charge at his friend, the painter Frederic Remington, whom he had asked to illustrate one of his cowboy characters. To Wister's chagrin, Remington drew a soft-featured adolescent with big ears and a long neck, not the kind of daredevil the writer wanted. Their squabble ended after Remington added a mustache and fuller cheeks to make the hero seem more mature.[22]

For all the quibbling over how young the ideal man should be, these Old Stock Americans had one thing working in their favor: the frontier they idealized was young demographically. People over fifty rarely moved west of the Mississippi until the early twentieth century. A cowboy was considered seasoned at thirty, and miners were old when they reached forty. Advocates of transcontinental settlement encouraged healthy young men with strong backs to be in the vanguard. Pioneering, they cautioned, was no assignment for the old and infirm. As understandable as these warnings may sound in hindsight, they anticipated pessimistic views about aging that became more pronounced after 1900. At a time when the authority of influential pathologists began to hinge on equating aging with illness, growing old appeared more dreadful and undesirable than ever before. Even scientists like the émigré physician Ignatz Leo Nascher, who established geriatrics as a medical subfield in the United States prior to World War I, found it hard to resist a capitalist logic that dismissed mentally and physically depleted workers as "economically worthless." In a period in which negative attitudes toward older people were hardening, contemporary invocations of a crisis of masculinity went hand in hand with expressing repugnance at the visible markers of old age.[23]

Considering this correlation, it should come as no surprise that the rejuvenationist lingo of the men championing a muscular American empire had an ageist bent. Aside from racism, scholars often point to anti-feminism as the chief ideological outgrowth of cultures trumpeting the naturalness of white male privilege. The masculinist rejuvenationists of the Gilded Age and Progressive Era fall under that rubric. Misogynistic slurs hurled at confident women were frequent, and men who rejected the imperatives of empire were derided as soft and feminine. Woven into these discriminatory patterns was a third line of demarcation: anxious agers defined white imperial manhood as inherently youthful. In Wister's novel *Lady Baltimore* (1906), leading America into the world of the twentieth century was not a task for the elderly. The novel is set in a fictionalized version of Charleston, South Carolina, called Kings Port. John Mayrant, the protagonist, vacillates between honoring his elders and revolting at the sight of their decrepit bodies. "The town's ultimate tragic note," the narrator muses, was to see a young man like Mayrant with "his energetic adolescence" linger amid "the old timber of the forest dying, and the too sparse new growth appear scantily amid the tall, fine venerable decaying trunks," unable to heed the call of a world "full of future and empty of past." Here was a somber warning that failing to shoulder the responsibilities of empire would doom an entire nation to senescence.[24]

Underneath this warning, however, lurked a danger that the guardians of the frontier myth were reluctant to concede: the quest for lasting youth in colonial borderlands could breed its own kind of destructive restlessness. Similar to a drug addict striving to maintain a permanent high, the men who sought to regenerate themselves never ceased to view youth as a transient state—a flame that, no matter how often rekindled, was always on the verge of extinction. One who cracked under the Sisyphus-like pressure of pushing that stone up the mountain was Jack London. Masculine bluster concealed the writer's gnawing morbidity. Best known for creating a cast of human-animal characters driven by a youthful lust for exploration, London developed a serious form of gerontophobia. London's life and work allow for a variety of interpretations. Despite the author's professed socialism, many discern in him the poster boy for white expansionism because he spent the better part of his adulthood writing stories of struggle and survival while sailing around the Pacific. The private London was an anxious, deeply troubled artist who aspired to stay young out of an excessive sense of self-preservation. London's ageism surfaces repeatedly in his writings. He depicted a group of elderly natives as too weak to resist the onslaught of white settlers and told the story of an aging boxer who takes a merciless beating from his younger opponent. "Youth unquenchable and irresistible—and ever they put the old uns [*sic*] away, themselves becoming old uns [*sic*] and travelling the same downward path, while behind them, ever pressing on them, was Youth eternal," London's boxer ruminates in "A Piece of Steak" (1909). Against this backdrop, London's admission that he "would rather be a superb meteor, every atom of me in magnificent glow, than a sleepy and permanent planet" sounds like a futile rearguard action.[25]

London's meteor burned out in its prime. Worn down by alcoholism and depression, the writer did not live to see his forty-first birthday. Death took him on November 22, 1916. London may have gained some sort of immortality because the image that he was "youth, adventure, romance" personified outlasted him.[26] To others, his early demise showed that chasing a seductive myth across oceans was ultimately destructive—for the chaser and immeasurably more so for those standing in the way. Two-and-a-half years later, Roosevelt drew his terminal breath at the age of sixty. He never recovered from the physical ailments that had plagued him after returning from a final expedition in 1913 that had taken him into unmapped parts of the Amazon rainforest. By then, imperial recreation had already begun to shed its rough-and-tumble origins, gradually adapting to the tunes of mass leisure and democratic consumption.

IN 1908, Luella Day McConnell pulled off the greatest bluff of her life. Eight years earlier, she and her husband, a wealthy hotelier and boat operator who had made a fortune in the Klondike Gold Rush, had bought a piece of land on the outskirts of St. Augustine, Florida. The marriage did not last, but that did

FIGURE 3.2 Luella Day McConnell's "Fountain of Youth," St. Augustine, Florida, 1909. McConnell was one of the many Floridian grifters who wanted to make money off the Ponce de León legend. Courtesy of the State Archives and Library of Florida.

not hamper Luella's entrepreneurial acumen. When asked by friends why she sailed for Spain, she replied that she was going to dig up evidence that the small well on her property bore the name "Ponce de León Spring" for a reason. The trip emboldened her. Back home, McConnell declared that a fallen tree on her land had revealed a large stone cross. The cross, she explained, had been placed there by the legendary conquistador to mark the spot where he had located the "Fountain of Youth." In addition, McConnell announced that she had excavated a piece of parchment written in Spanish by one of Ponce's companions that presumably backed her claim.[27]

McConnell immediately began the work of turning her plot of land into a major tourist attraction. Members of St. Augustine's flourishing business community openly doubted her sanity, but they did not object that her discovery brought in visitors who checked into the city's posh new beachside hotels. From there, many took a stroll to the fabled fountain, where McConnell supplied paying customers with postcards and bottles of rejuvenating water (see figure 3.2). A car accident in 1927 cut McConnell's life short. Her pet project, though, continued to thrive. Local developer Walter B. Fraser bought her property and cashed in on the myth. Fraser contacted state and federal officials to have them endorse the historical significance of his site, threatening legal action against anyone who called him a fraud. Local scholars continued to bristle at Fraser's claims. In 1929, the St. Augustine Historical Society came out opposing the "silly and quacky" story, protesting that the Ponce de León craze impugned the city's reputation. A few years later, the National Park Service rejected the proposal to erect a national monument on Fraser's property as "immature" and "based entirely on conjecture." Among the five sensations advertised in Fraser's Fountain of Youth Park, only the Native American burial ground was deemed authentic. What Fraser lacked in scientific accreditations he made up for in brochures, roadside signs, and neon lights. His investments paid off. The idea of dipping a toe into magic waters lured enough tourists to Fraser's park to help sustain his operation throughout the difficult years of depression and war.[28]

Reviving an old myth was good business, not just in St. Augustine. During the tourist boom of the early twentieth century, remarks about the rejuvenating influence of southern destinations became ubiquitous. "Bathe Here and Find Youth," "Add Ten More Years to Your Life," and "Ponce de León Had the Right Idea"—all slogans created by nifty advertisers across the Sunshine State—illustrate just how fundamental rejuvenation was to selling Florida to enervated northerners. Trying not to be bested, the city of Miami established a separate publicity department in 1920 to market itself as the "city of eternal youth." Under tropical skies, a Miami broadside boasted in 1926 that "bronzed, erect old men" and "women delighting in new cream-and-rose complexions" were adding years to their lives.[29]

Ponce's legendary search for the fountain of youth gave Floridians a head start, but promoters for other leisure locations soon caught up. Southern Californians who joined the business of courting tourists to speed regional development promised equally rich rewards to the weary traveler. "Try it, as I did, and then come back and tell your friends what you have found," boasted a New Yorker who in 1922 sought respite from everyday troubles on the beaches of Santa Barbara and Los Angeles. "Not Youth's Fountain, but as near to that long sought for panacea as anything you'll ever find. . . . In three weeks I was re-made—a new man." Travelers opting for a vacation in the Caribbean could draw inspiration from similar messages. "Life begins anew for the cruise passenger in search of health and pleasure," stated a 1937 advertisement of the Hamburg America Line. "With renewed vigor, one wants to play again, to feel young again, and every opportunity to satisfy this desire is available." This script was extended to Hawaii later in the century, where beach boys and surfers contributed to the island's youthful image. Touting recreational tourism as a way life, none of these announcements implied that to enjoy the antiaging effects of warmer climates, prospective customers would have to settle in these regions permanently. Absorbing a healthy dose of tropicality for a few weeks in the safe and sanitary conditions offered by modern resorts would do the trick.[30]

Claiming rejuvenation in order to gain a competitive edge over market rivals was not unique to the tourist industry. What the commercialization of old colonial frontiers for recreational purposes shows is the pace at which enterprising individuals put the desire for regeneration in the service of generating modern brands. For turn-of-the-century promoters of the tropical South, creating enticing packages around their products meant establishing a positive relationship between vacationers and specific destinations marketed as rejuvenating. Branding, in J. E. Peterson's succinct definition, "is the application of a story to a product." Tourism entrepreneurs rarely missed an opportunity to lend charm and authenticity to their assertions that patrons staying at their sites would leave them revitalized.[31]

As with most such stories, the ad campaigns launched by boosters depicting Florida, Southern California, and Hawaii as places where people lived happier and longer lives masked inconvenient truths. To attract northern capital and consumers, rejuvenationists threw a veil of silence over long-standing concerns that hot temperatures carried grave health risks, especially for white Euro-Americans accustomed to cooler environs. These fears persisted even as newer germ theories of disease challenged climate determinists who held that two of the worst scourges that had imperiled white colonization of the Americas, malaria and yellow fever, were primarily the result of geography, not of microbes. Despite advances in public health, malaria remained a serious health hazard well into the twentieth century. In Florida alone, medical experts estimated in 1910 that one percent of patients who had contracted the disease died of it. Ten years later, researchers found that in some areas of the state, the infection rate could be as high as 80 percent. Boosters downplayed the problem. If they mentioned the sickly tropics at all, they usually did so in the past tense, stressing that modern science and technology had made the hot zones safe for travelers. For the British writer Stephen Graham, who toured the US-administered Panama Canal Zone in the early 1920s, the country's tropical possessions had become home to "a real new generation of imperial Americans rising in health and pride from what was once jungle and pestilence—the 'white man's grave.'"[32]

Others shifted the blame, suggesting that getting sick betrayed a lack of caution and self-discipline. Physicians like Jacksonville's Charles J. Kenworthy attributed "the slight indispositions affecting visitors" not to malaria but to bad decision-making. In his view, the illness was exacerbated, if not caused, by excessive eating, drinking, and lingering in unsafe places with "air poisoned by human breath." Kenworthy's diagnosis was part of a racist tradition that singled out the poor hygiene of non-whites as the main reason for high transmission rates (the notion that non-Anglo-Saxon peoples were the carriers of contagious diseases also stoked anti-immigration propaganda in early twentieth-century North America and Europe). Rationalizations that linked the numerical decline of Indigenous populations to issues of heredity and immorality were used to mute anticolonial voices that regarded the violent encroachment of Westerners as the main reason for shrinking native life expectancies. "Thickly populated with white people," the Hawaiian Islands "will be healthy, happy, and prosperous," predicted one US editor in 1890. His laconic remark "that the white population is on the increase while the natives are decreasing" marked the gradual disappearance of Polynesians as natural and inevitable. In the same way, Euro-American colonizers had been absolving themselves of all culpability for the demise of the Native Americans, dismissing them as a "vanishing race."[33]

Travel writers, even the younger ones, routinely juxtaposed the cleanliness of white sojourners with Indigenous bodies described as filthy. Nineteen-year-old Paul Siple, an Eagle Scout from Pennsylvania who joined an expedition to Antarctica in 1928, relished his shore leave in Panama but cringed at the destitution of the locals who lived in crowded quarters. He wondered how anybody but the "lowliest [racial slur]" could survive in such "foul air." Insinuating that the boundaries separating health from disease were medical as well as racial, Siple's account carried an implicit warning: rather than recapture their youth, tourists oblivious to keeping their distance from natives might end up hastening their own demise.[34]

Such sentiments were grist to the mill of segregationists, who tightened Jim Crow laws in the United States at the same time that germ theories were making headway. Starting in the late nineteenth century, tourist establishments under the jurisdiction of segregationists not only invested in clean water and air-conditioned rooms but also erected a social *cordon sanitaire* that linked well-being to race. Whites-only policies did not merely become standard practice at seaside hotels, restaurants, and swimming pools across the Deep South. In Southern California's coastal communities, white citizen groups resorted to intimidation and political maneuvers to bar Black and Brown Americans from frequenting popular beaches. Minority residents were charged exorbitant fees. Bus routes bypassed non-white districts. Cuban hoteliers and vendors, too, heeded the color line in interactions with their affluent northern neighbors. The African American writer Langston Hughes, who visited Havana in 1930, was not allowed to purchase a ticket to enter the beach "although they were sold quite freely to whites." Fair-skinned Americans openly applauded or silently condoned these measures. Streaming southward by the thousands, northern whites became accomplices of a system that helped spread Jim Crow across state and national boundaries.[35]

African American leisure-seekers did not take no for an answer. The development of non-white recreational opportunities in modern America was steeped in contestation and struggle. Navigating the geographies of anti-Black harassment was a vital skill that Black travelers had to acquire before they could even think of aspiring to the liberties of a tourist. "Vacation and Recreation without Humiliation" became the motto of *Travelguide,* a guidebook for African Americans with the means to afford a vacation that began publication in 1947. Like its popular but unassuming predecessor, the *Green Book, Travelguide* carried valuable information for mid-century African American motorists looking for hotels and restaurants in all states that served customers of color. It also adorned its front cover with photographs of beautiful Black models playing golf and sprawling on yachts. Representations of stylish Black bodies under palms challenged the notion that people of color did not know how to enjoy the pleasures of paradise responsibly. To the extent that the freedom to travel was claimed as a civil right, physical and emotional rejuvenation became inseparable from pursuing "a renewed sense of racial pride, cultural self-expression, economic independence, and progressive politics." In celebrating Black tourism's youthfulness, African Americans joyfully defied those who had long questioned their collective survival in a nation that treated them as second-class citizens.[36]

While the paths of the white and Black tourist rarely crossed, boosters still had to work their way around other obstacles traditionally associated with hotter climates. In the middle of the nineteenth century, northern critics of the US South amplified a strand of antislavery thought that did not spring from the desire to alleviate Black suffering. Searching for a culprit to explain the region's backwardness, they discovered a shiftless white underclass, illiterate and landless squatters who barely scraped by on the margins of plantation society. The insult "poor white trash" found first usage in pre–Civil War literary circles that tied poverty to defects caused by biology and geography. Middle-class observers saw both these factors wreak havoc on destitute rural whites and their offspring from the mountains of West Virginia to the swamplands of Georgia. Descriptions of these people as a "disease breed," writes the historian Nancy Isenberg, denigrated them to "clinical subjects," with "children prematurely aged and deformed with distended bellies." Classified by some as a distinct race, poor whites in the South were relegated to the mudsill of humanity, epitomizing the evolutionary decline of a once proud people who had traded their whiteness for liquor, rot, and dirt.[37]

Had Buffon, the French naturalist, been right after all? Northern reformers poured old wine into new casks. A series of field studies undertaken in the early 1900s shored up long-held views of the Deep South as a hothouse of degeneration. Pathologizing poverty as a hereditary and possibly contagious ailment, the eugenicist Charles Davenport worried as much about the north-bound migration of ill-bred Mississippians as he did about the influx of undesirable foreigners. Starting in 1909, the Rockefeller Institute in New York funded a research project aimed at eradicating hookworm, one of the so-called lazy diseases. In the judgment of one physician, more than 40 percent of the South's population had come in contact with the parasite, which survived in fecal matter and was most likely to infect humans walking barefoot on excrement-infested soil. Those who fell ill suffered from chronic exhaustion. In children, hookworm was said to lead to stupidity and stunted growth. To underscore its devastating effects, the Rockefeller scientists sent to study the poor white folk of Arkansas and Alabama published photographs that compared boys of the same age placed next to one another. Usually one looked tall and healthy; the other pitifully deformed and dwarfed by the disease. The images reinforced the stereotype of the indolent southerner, but a growing number of Progressive Era reformers preferred to talk about how scientific methods could help shrink, if not weed out, pockets of degeneracy that had stunted the development of a resourceful, intelligent, and durable white citizenry in that part of the country.[38]

From the Rockefeller Institute's social engineering optimism, it was only a small step to the promises of age engineering that pervaded travel advertisements to sunny destinations. The early twentieth-century tourist industry reversed the idea that whites moving into the tropics faced racial degradation. Precisely because the South possessed climatic advantages over the frost-blighted North, where the winter months brought all kinds of respiratory diseases to congested urban centers, modern vacation resorts could offer guests in need of relaxation the reinvigorating pleasures of an "eternal spring." Boosters crowed that perpetual sunshine would de-age white immune systems. Suspending the natural cycle of seasons sounded more like magical thinking than science, but advertisers ran with it anyway. Why "wait six days for summer," the Florida East Coast Railway beckoned in 1927, when "Springtime and the golden days along the Gulf Stream, lie just over the southern horizon?" Striking a more fanciful tone, another testimonial spelled out the ultimate prize awaiting weary travelers who had managed to escape the dull routines of their workplace. Enter the Southland's "enchanted isles," and "the Frost King may not follow, or claim him as his own." The very act of going south, it seemed, was already enough to escape aging and cheat death.[39]

Equating travel across space with travel back in time was a plot employed profusely by the mythologizers of the frontier. The tourist boosters did not merely imitate this theme. They ensured its viability through commercial repetition. Comparing a journey to California or Florida to trips that commenced in February and ended in June, travel promoters made a point of likening them to imaginary forays into a carefree realm of childhood and youth detached from the sorrows of adulthood. In its most romantic association, the tropical South brought to mind a reopened Garden of Eden, a sanctuary of curative innocence untarnished by history and civilization. As he was approaching Havana, one traveler fantasized about returning to "the promised land—the land of the cocoa and the palm, of my childhood's dreams of tropic fruits and gorgeous flowers." Others predicted tangible results that would emerge from rotating in and out of paradise. In addition to finding their minds and bodies rejuvenated, visitors could expect to live longer. "The health of the inhabitants of Florida is proverbial; many can now be seen who are ninety years old and upwards," affirmed a guidebook published in 1879. Peter C. Remondino, an Italian American physician and citizen of San Diego, echoed this sentiment in 1892, proclaiming that people residing in Southern California gained "ten years more with the additional benefit of feeling ten years younger during the time, for there is a rejuvenating influence about the atmosphere that is remarked upon and felt by all newcomers after a residence of several months."[40]

Those who raved about the prospect of rejuvenation through sunshine tourism put their faith in a mighty stellar ally: the sun itself. The rise of suntanning as an aesthetic practice cherished by white middle classes around the globe broke with preindustrial ideals of whiteness that treasured pale skin as a sign of nobility and superiority over the darker-skinned workers toiling in the fields. This revaluation was hastened by industrialization, during which sun-deprived children living in cramped dwellings and pallid-faced patients diagnosed with neurasthenia stoked fears of an impending civilizational decline. Introducing Americans to the glamour of sunbathing, twentieth-century tourist advertisers expedited this shift. Beach beauties sporting a glowing bronze demonstrated what it meant to incorporate youthful vigor and attractiveness into aging bodies. Absorbing this combination seemed especially meaningful to white women who sought liberation from Victorian norms of domesticity and propriety. Tanning, stated one fashion writer in

1921, permitted women to recapture freedoms long lost and to realize "that the sun and the wind are our friends again, as they were when the world was young." Modern girls with brown skins, thus, were cast as both progressive and natural, unlike older women stuck in the cage of prudery.[41]

All the while, sunbathing enthusiasts had to tread carefully so as not to alienate too many skeptics. Scantily dressed tourists signaling sexual permissiveness were a red rag to defenders of traditional gender roles. However, even health advisers who appreciated the revitalizing powers of sunlight (vitamin D was discovered in 1913) cautioned women against intentional tanning. According to some early twentieth-century physicians, relying on sunlight for beautification was a masquerade at best because it distracted sun worshippers from investing in the kind of nutrition and exercise needed to get in shape. In the worst case, beach lovers might find themselves covered with freckles and scars from hideous sunburns.[42]

Critics also called for moderation on racial grounds. In an age in which color lines were closely monitored, North American whites who chose to darken their skins had to make sure that in approximating the brownness of Central Americans, they would not be mistaken for one. For Jack London, such worries were unfounded. White men of his mold were keenly interested in salvaging from primitive nature the youthful potency that aging civilizations had lost. In London's stories, globe-trotting travelers who returned home with a healthy tan were hailed for doing just that. David Grief was the courageous and brawny English navigator of the South Pacific in London's *Son of the Sun* (1912). "Heavy muscled he was, but he was not lumped and hummocked by muscles. They were softly rounded, and, when they did move, slid softly and silkily under the smooth, tanned skin." Though appearing less than civilized, Grief, in London's portrayal, showcased his brownness as proof that Anglo-Saxons could dominate even the hottest regions of the globe. "Ardent suns had likewise tanned his face till it was swarthy as a Spaniard's. . . . Yet his blue eyes retained their blue, his mustache its yellow, and the lines of his face were those which had persisted through centuries in his English race." This was a far cry from contemporary calls to "go native," which romanticized non-white cultures as ethically preferable to Western imperialism. Abandoning the benefits of white supremacy was the last thing that the promoters of the tropical South had in mind. In its consumer-friendly, sun-drenched oases of deceleration, the governing logic of imperial recreation was to cash in on these benefits, not to dwell on their violent roots.[43]

We may feel tempted to laugh at Luella McConnell's charade of thrusting herself into the limelight of Florida's nascent tourist industry. We may also chuckle at the gullibility of the visitors who bought bottles of rejuvenating water at Walter Fraser's Fountain of Youth Park. There is no way of knowing whether wasting dollars on a dubious fairy tale had any measurable therapeutic effect, as unlikely as that might seem. The placebo that US sightseers might have gained on the nation's southern frontiers was probably less medical than cultural. The unprecedented visibility of youth-oriented leisure lifestyles, which first crested in the 1920s, raised the profile of recreational travel from which fatigued civilized subjects could arise resplendent. Tourists went south for a variety of reasons, but by purchasing a vacation in Florida, Southern California, or Hawaii, northerners paid considerable sums to acquire their own personal share of rejuvenation's mounting social stock. In a society that placed a high value on unaging bodies, gaining membership in this circle opened up alluring ways of reclaiming pasts and extending futures.

WHEN DEVELOPERS IN Southern California, Hawaii, Florida, and the Caribbean started touting their locales as "luxuriously hot," they were not merely talking about the climate. Until the expansion of the middle class after World War II, long-distance tourism remained a domain of the moneyed elites. Southward-bound vacationers had to be wealthy enough to travel for extended periods without having to make a living. The most affluent booked first-class cabins and stayed in opulent hotels on arrival. Hailed as liberating and rejuvenating, tropical tourism also invited charges of decadence. Were well-heeled northerners relaxing on the beaches of San Diego or St. Petersburg really repairing their stressed-out bodies? Or were they just carrying on with their fastidious routines? A 1928 brochure for a summer camp at Blue Mountain Lake, New York, gave a straightforward answer. Those who sought mental and physical reinvigoration should choose fresh country air, daily exercise, and group activities over "a vacation of idleness and trivial pleasures."[44]

Recreational camping originated in the late nineteenth century as the poor cousin of tropical tourism. For many Americans, it quickly grew into the more popular activity. The reasons that summer camping became one of America's most beloved pastimes were part economic, part cultural. Fun, rest, and health could be experienced for a relatively modest price, which made trekking off into the woods an affordable alternative for city slickers with thinner wallets. The lure of camping extended to the upper strata of white society, where the idea found some of its greatest champions. William H. H. Murray, a Protestant preacher in his late twenties from New England, set off the first outdoor craze in the 1870s. Thousands of northeastern urbanites followed in the minister's footsteps and spent their summers hiking, canoeing, and swimming in the Adirondack Mountains. Murray's best-selling *Adventures in the Wilderness*, which attained gospel-like status in the early camping movement, framed vacationing in nature as a uniquely transformative pilgrimage. Convinced that America's flora and fauna represented a national treasure more precious than anything Europe had to offer, Murray exhorted "all jaded minds" to "find that perfect relaxation" in the country's wilderness. "There, from a thousand sources of inspiration, flow into the exhausted mind and enfeebled body currents of strength and life." For muscular Christians like Murray who worried that Protestantism was becoming too sentimental and feminized, rustic recreation promised to reconcile spirituality with masculinity. A man of God, refreshed by nature, could once again preach "with elasticity in his step, fire in his eye, [and] depth and clearness in his reinvigorated voice."[45]

Unlike the transcendentalists of the pre–Civil War years, who idealized nature as a divine retreat for true living, camping advocates presented their errands into the wild in more utilitarian terms. The recesses of the woods were to be sought out for their practical benefits, not merely for their spiritual and aesthetic beauty. John Muir, the famous preservationist, rhapsodized that "mountain parks and reservations are useful not only as fountains of timber and irrigating rivers, but as fountains of life." *Harper's Monthly* carried the story of a journalist who looked death in the eye but recovered from severe tuberculosis after a trip to the Adirondacks. Recuperation ensued over an eighteen-month stay, during which nature had been "ridding the system of fever, checking the cough, putting flesh on the wasted body, and strengthening the flabby muscles." Readers were surely piqued by reports of worn-out businessmen who, after spending entire summers in the Rocky Mountains to reverse the damage done to their organisms by telephones, telegraphs, and locomotives, returned to their desks reenergized. Leisure, in this context, was neither escapist nor antimodern. Largely embraced as an antidote to the ills of civilization, camping upheld—rather than undercut—urban capitalism and its profiteers.[46]

Even a naturalist as contrarian as Ernest Thompson Seton moved within the bounds of that system. The Scottish-Canadian author and wildlife artist turned into one of the most sizzling critics of city life at the turn of the century. Yet, his harangues against civilization were never meant to foment a revolution. To Seton, a closet Darwinist, rejuvenation was larger than the individuals pursuing it. Unless white men stopped acting like a retired "house race" and began "living out-doors for at least a month every year, reviving and expanding a custom that as far back as Moses was deemed essential to the national well-being," the "physical regeneration so needful for continued national existence" remained out of reach. Seton's reference to Moses was not exactly a biblical gesture. It was his way of saying that camping unearthed pathways back in time that permitted modern Americans to reexperience the healthy communal living of ancient races—perhaps more so than the primitivist adventures of part-time cowboys and definitely to a greater extent than any sunshine vacation at a glitzy resort. Seton, who penned these lines in 1902, thought that Native Americans approximated this ideal best. To be sure, they were not flesh-and-blood people. They were romanticized projections that Seton sold as mirror images of the character traits—honor, ferocity, purity, fertility—he believed were crucial to rejuvenating Anglo-Saxons.[47]

If faux Native Americans were the first ingredient in Seton's recipe for national regeneration, children were the second one. Both coalesced in the Woodcraft Indians, which Seton founded in 1901 to save white youth, preferably boys, from the temptations of the city. The Woodcraft Indians were Seton's stamp on the budding transatlantic profession of youth workers who created a string of organizations that turned to the rugged outdoors in the hope of raising robust men and citizens. The fact that Seton's summer camps replaced tents with tepees and encouraged children and adolescents to imitate the ways of the "Red Man" and not those of the early pioneers triggered mixed reactions. Daniel Carter Beard, another influential US boy worker of the period, accused Seton of being naive at best or unpatriotic at worst. How was it possible for the next generation of Americans to sustain the vast settler republic their fathers had built if they identified with the same tribesmen their ancestors had vanquished in a struggle for land and manifest destiny? In an age rife with nativist resentment, it certainly did not help that Beard disparaged Seton as a foreigner.[48]

Despite their public row, both Beard and Seton aspired to a reformed manhood that was as concerned with masculinizing boys as it was with boyifying men. "Playing Indian" or "pioneer" was presented as an uplifting hobby for males of different age groups bound together by ties of gender, heredity, and camaraderie. In shouting cowboy yells and Native American war whoops with their young charges around the campfire, Seton and Beard imagined a conduit that transported overcivilized, middle-aged men back to the days of their own boyhood, where young manhood could be recaptured in a state of unfragmented purity. Dreaming of men who "still retained some of the urge of boyhood," Beard sought to rid the world of "gray-headed philosophers" and "money-getting baldheads," to him symbols of a society that had descended into fecklessness and cynicism. Seton's and Beard's tacit alliance came to a head when they joined forces with the most famous boy-man of their time. Together with Robert Baden-Powell, the British founder of the Boy Scouts, Beard and Seton formed a triumvirate that oversaw the inception of the BSA in 1910. No other youth organization devoted to the cross-generational socialization of boys and men in the twentieth-century United States attracted more members or attained a comparable public stature.[49]

Wrapped in the innocence of childhood, boyification nevertheless served decidedly unchildlike purposes. Except for a few self-styled radical alternatives, summer camps in the years before and after World War I (and up to the 1970s in parts of the South) heeded Jim Crow policies, denying equal access to youth of color. Mainstream campers were inclined to associate Black and Brown boyhood with immaturity and deviancy rather than with the potential for national renewal. Disparities of wealth and income punctuated the campers' rhetoric of inclusiveness. At the same time that affluent parents were thinking about how and where their children should spend their summer vacations, rural and working-class families continued to rely on the labor of their younger members. The growth of girl organizations, most prominently the Camp Fire Girls and the Girl Scouts of America (GSA), led to more camping opportunities for females. But the women campers who wanted their sex to benefit from nature's restorative powers were less inclined to seek rites of passage in reverse. Most women likely looked back at their girlhood as a time of domestic regulation and surveillance. Boyification, on the other hand, transformed colonial violence into exhilarating play, erasing the fact that imperial white manhood was forged in the cauldron of exploitation and oppression (see figure 3.3). The conquest of an entire continent vanished behind the veil of companionship that united boy workers with their young wards.[50]

The thin line separating homosocial from homoerotic desire further complicated relationships in male outdoor organizations, especially in such tightly regulated institutions as summer camps where adult staffers controlled almost every move of the younger lodgers. Beard's and Baden-Powell's fixation on young bodies bristled with pedophiliac connotations, and only recently did court orders tear down the wall of secrecy that the BSA had built since at least the early 1920s to conceal the dark twin of boyification: child abuse. Records long hidden from the public eye prove that boy-man homosociality has made the organization attractive to sexual predators. More jarringly, they reveal that its leaders systematically shielded scoutmasters accused of molesting boys for the sake of protecting the Boy Scout brand. Although the current leadership has vowed to do better, the problem of older

FIGURE 3.3 Boy Scouts at a summer camp near Gettysburg, 1913. Youth organizations such as the BSA permitted aging men to act out boyish fantasies and recast imperial practices as playful adventure. Courtesy of the Library of Congress Prints and Photographs Division.

men abusing their power over young bodies is bigger than the wrongdoing of any single organization.[51]

Entering the world of the twentieth century, Americans wondered more than ever how their relative age might affect their ability to compete with international rivals over markets, resources, and territories. In this race for global influence, youth became valorized on the individual as well as collective level: as the prerequisite for leading healthy and productive lives, and as a tool for strengthening the military, social, and economic security of states. New links between science and commerce, nature and nurture, stoked the public's desire to break the spell of aging. Rejuvenationist fads proliferated after 1900 at breathtaking speed. Antiagers promoting modern cosmetic, biomedical, and demographic interventions jostled for attention as did the sunshine worshippers and fresh-air enthusiasts who advocated the naturalness of their methods. All the while, the imperial foundations of recreation through deceleration sank into oblivion.

CHAPTER FOUR

Beauty from Trees

The Colonial Roots of American Cosmetics

Farewell to Age!
Grow young along with me,
the best is yet to be!
—Elizabeth Arden advertisement (1936)

How did Cleopatra wash her face? A soap advertisement from 1920 posed this question in bold letters. In case nobody knew, the ad revealed what archaeologists had supposedly gleaned from "hieroglyphic records": daily toilets with palm and olive oils brought about the "radiant cleanliness" that ensured the queen's unwaning beauty. Cleopatra's rebirth as a modern beauty icon grew out of a broader fascination with ancient Egypt that took hold of Europeans and North Americans during the early twentieth century. Archaeological excavations such as Howard Carter's discovery of Tutankhamen's tomb, neo-Egyptian symbols in art nouveau decorations, fashion design, and cosmetic ads all contributed to the early twentieth-century Westernization of Cleopatra. Few, however, claimed the legendary queen more doggedly than the men who ran the Milwaukee-based Palmolive Company. To sell their products, Palmolive presented images of Cleopatra that straddled the Oriental and the Western, the ancient and the modern. Women who wanted to stay attractive could trust Palmolive's "scientific formula" because it contained "no foreign substances" that would "poison the skin with blots and imperfections." Instead, it put "the greatest of modern luxuries . . . within the reach of all" by reviving old beauty secrets first discovered at a time "when ancient Egypt was young." With unblemished white skin, red lips, and subtle rouge, another fictional Cleopatra owed her good looks to the "beauty from trees." As she stands upright, wearing a bejeweled bra and radiating a mild eroticism with her arms folded behind her head, a Black slave is kneeling at Cleopatra's feet, ready to wash and rejuvenate her mistress.[1]

The visual metaphor of an enslaved African helping a whitened Cleopatra to preserve her youthful complexion conveys the disparities of gender, race, and empire in the creation of a modern mass market for personal care and cosmetic products. New soaps, creams, fragrances, and makeup touted as safe and affordable promised shiny skins and healthy hair to white women who were anxious about aging. Beauty, like rejuvenation, is an old ideal. Its commodification accelerated with astonishing rapidity after 1900, not least because of US commercial interests. New York City became home to two of the world's major beauty brands, the cosmetic powerhouses Helena Rubinstein and Elizabeth Arden. Both companies ushered in a century of near constant growth for an antiaging industry that has survived wars and depressions. In 2010, consumers across the globe paid more than $330 billion for all kinds of beauty services and products.[2]

Entrepreneurial initiative, globalization, and female empowerment are common themes in books that have investigated the swift rise of a business that probably tells us more about the democratization of rejuvenation practices in the twentieth-century United States than any comparable endeavor. But this democratization (for the lack of a better term) was inconsistent at best. Based on recent scholarship on the palm and coconut oil trades, this chapter foregrounds the extent to which commercialized desires to retain attractive appearances rested on extractive colonial economies. Without the oils harvested from palm and coconut trees in Africa and South Asia, the mass-market companies that transformed middle-class notions of charm, attractiveness, and taste would have never evolved the way they did. Accounts focusing on the strong women who stood at the helm of cosmetic multinationals cast an emancipatory veneer over the beauty business. Yet, the same industry profited from global supply chains that guaranteed access to raw materials and cheap labor. If the image of a Black servant holding Cleopatra's oil jug holds a deeper meaning, then the story cannot start with the crafty inventors who manufactured the creams and lipsticks sold to middle-aged women in Europe and North America. Rather, it has to begin with the sweat of Indigenous workers toiling on copra and palm oil plantations across the Global South.

The colonial labor regimes that sustained cosmetic rejuvenation practices in the northern hemisphere also furthered the racialization of beauty ideals. African workers who had to endure the dirt and stink that came with the taxing occupation of extracting oils from tropical plants stood on the lowest rung of an aesthetic ladder that associated cleanliness with whiteness. In the United States, race, gender, class, and age intersected in depictions of nonwhite peoples as unattractive. Equations of darker skin with ugliness were rooted in the visual cultures of slavery and segregation. Associations of that kind also found approving audiences after millions of poor immigrant arrivals from Southern and Eastern Europe had crowded together in urban slums.

White commentators were quick to see in such squalor proof of racial and social inferiority. Bodies thus dismissed might have been recognized as biologically young, yet nativists never ascribed much value to them. They were busy fantasizing about a future that belonged to a racially rejuvenated Anglo-Saxon nation.[3]

The great irony is that two of the three main characters in the making of America's modern beauty industry were women who did not quite fit that mold. One was the African American businesswoman Madam C. J. Walker; the other was the Polish-Jewish immigrant Helena Rubinstein, who entertained a bitter rivalry with the Canadian-born beauty magnate Elizabeth Arden. Their lives have been the subject of several inspirational rags-to-riches stories in which these women build their cosmetic empires in defiance of traditional stereotypes of race and gender. Feminist scholars have been hesitant to embrace them as heroines, in part because some blame the cosmetic industry for advancing a misogynistic preoccupation with outward appearance. Yet, even the fiercest critic would have to admit that Walker, Arden, and Rubinstein decisively reshaped definitions of what it meant to be beautiful. They advanced the view that preserving youthful attractiveness was the key to female success in an appearance-oriented culture that valued visible, measurable, and improvable markers of desirability.[4]

As fascinating as the careers of these three women are, this chapter is not a collective biography. It shows how their lives interfaced with a nascent culture of cosmetic rejuvenation that hinged as much on colonial labor as it did on transatlantic networks of trade and print, visual culture, marketing campaigns, and everyday consumption patterns for getting rid of wrinkles and age spots. This commodity chain, held together by the inequalities of race, class, gender, and empire, forms the narrative arc of this chapter. Moving from West African palm oil groves to North American beauty parlors and bathrooms allows us to track with greater precision how the imperative of attractiveness had real consequences for those whose labor fastened that chain but who were never meant to be attractive.

American protagonists of cosmetic rejuvenation did not present beauty and youth as temporary gifts. They framed them as conscious consumer choices that required money, discipline, and willpower. Even as the politics of gender and race generated different beauty standards for different groups, cosmetics was never simply about renewing biological skins. Social skins, too, needed to be kept young and tight in a capitalist society to meet the demand made on people that they appear healthy, dynamic, and youthful—irrespective of their actual age. Whether cosmetics aided or subverted women's rights is perhaps the wrong kind of question to ask. After all, the pioneers of the industry had to overcome long-standing associations of cosmetics with prostitution. Liberating to some, advocating skin-care products was upsetting to others. Twentieth-century Americans resorting to soaps, cremes, and makeup found themselves in a cultural crossfire in which they could experiment with forms of self-fashioning while being kept aware of their obligations to the body politic.[5]

FOR EUROPEAN BOTANISTS of the early modern period, figuring out the geographical roots of the oil palm proved a hard nut to crack. Drawing on anecdotes and plant extracts brought back by sailors in the 1570s, the Flemish physician Matthaeus Lobelius speculated that Portuguese explorers who had sailed to India deserved all the praise, dubbing the oil palm "the little Indian nut." South Asia and the Arabian Peninsula remained hot contenders until circulating travel accounts and testimonies shifted the focus to West Africa. In 1763, the Dutch botanist Nikolas Jacquin put his stamp of approval on the West African thesis. *Elaeis guineensis*, the Latin name he gave to the oil palm, entered the European scientific lexicon. Curiously, Jacquin's interest in the plant was first piqued in the Caribbean, where he sketched and described the tree as part of an expedition funded by the Habsburg Empire.[6]

Explanations about the tree's origins varied because it grew in different places. By the 1700s, palm oil had already crossed oceans and spurred trade outside Africa all the way to Indonesia and the Americas. Its presence in coastal economies across the early modern world had a lot to do with the crop's versatility. Precolonial African cultures bear traces of how palm oil was put to use in religious ceremonies, healing rituals, beverages, food, illuminants, personal hygiene, even in construction. Europeans visiting West Africa learned about the tree's high material and spiritual value. The Sherbro people of Sierra Leone turned the dangerous task of clambering up tall palms and cutting fruits into a masculine rite of passage; other communities forced enslaved workers to do the climbing and chopping. In the Congo region, the harvest commonly ended with festivities where locals pruned and sapped the trees to extract fluids that fermented into wine. An eighteenth-century European explorer found the wine "agreeable," noting that "it makes people merry and strong, and does not bring any headache like other wines."[7]

Colonization and capitalism transformed palm oil into a transatlantic cash crop. The slave trade catapulted palm oil overseas as it became part of the captives' diet during the Middle Passage and sustained enslaved fieldworkers in the Americas. Slave traders smeared grease from palm kernel on enslaved

Africans to make their skin shiny and increase their value at slave auctions. Palm oil experienced a second boom in the first half of the nineteenth century when Europeans began to appreciate its efficacy as an industrial lubricant, expediting the transition from animal-based oils and fats to herbal fluids that came to "grease the wheels of the industrial revolution." Large quantities of palm oil were imported to western metropoles, where they provided the fatty slush for candlemakers and fueled the development of urban street lighting.[8]

Another global market that emerged around 1800 centered on the oil's health benefits. Early botanical descriptions of the plant had already hinted at its recuperative powers. Excited by what he had learned from local users, an Englishman who surveyed the Gold Coast in the 1710s related that palm oil was "good for both the Back and Belly," claiming that a daily ration "mightily invigorates their nerves." Reports likening palm oil to a beauty elixir that protected the skin and hair caught the colonizers' attention. Worried about the lack of hygiene among industrial workers, middle-class reformers took a second look at Indigenous traditions of making soap from the tree's offerings. Criticism voiced by Enlightenment scientists that importing African washing rituals would amount to adopting primitive customs had curbed demand for the plant. But a new method developed in 1836 for bleaching red palm oil, which made it smell more agreeable to European noses, heightened its appeal to British and North American soap manufactures. In an era of unparalleled growth for soap producers, Liverpool became the main recipient of imported palm oil and, as a consequence, the world's leading center for soap production.[9]

Western brokers cast the palm oil business as a benign alternative to chattel slavery, yet the network and premium system established for palm oil resembled those used by slave traders in Africa. This was evident in how transactions were conducted at trading stations along the Niger Delta. After sailing into the area, palm oil brokers would set up shop on the hulks of abandoned ships to avoid diseases and limit contacts with locals. Weeks and sometimes even a month or two passed until Indigenous workers had retrieved the crop from inland sites and transported it to the ships. There was little the merchants and their hirelings from the northern hemisphere could do in the meantime except wait. Gambling, drinking, and sex with local women punctuated the boredom. At times, frustration with unfamiliar trading practices boiled over, leading to spouts of violence in which the better-armed whites usually had the upper hand.[10]

The power gap in the global palm oil trade continued to widen in the second half of the nineteenth century. As white imperialists were leveraging their technological superiority, soldiers and bureaucrats started wresting control of the trade away from West Africans. The clearing of tropical forests reduced the number of semiwild groves and prepared the ground for industrial-scale plantations. Cash-crop agriculture put an enormous strain on local cultivators who could not keep up with an international oligarchy of rubber and palm oil barons and the methods they employed to maximize yields. Huge fortunes were made. The Belgian agronomist Adrien Hallet alone held more than 71,000 acres of rubber and oil palm real estate in Africa and Southeast Asia. Hallet had secured his wealth with the blessing of the Belgian royal family. Given his connections to King Leopold's government, Hallet must have known about the atrocities that took place in the Congo Free State between 1885 and 1908. There is reason to assume that Hallet approved of coercive measures to increase production. Lashings and mutilations were widespread forms of punishment on plantations where African workers struggled to meet their quotas. As late as 1915, five years after slavery had been officially abolished in the Congo, a Belgian official conceded that the majority of the workforce consisted of people living in slavelike conditions. In British West Africa, colonial administrators and firms forcibly recruited Indigenous laborers to replace men, women, and children lost to sickness and death.[11]

Imperial regimes of labor and cash-crop extraction loomed large in the Philippines and US-occupied Samoa as well. After 1900, both places became major exporters of copra, the dried flesh of coconuts that came to provide a more refined kind of oil for mass-produced cosmetic products. By 1927, the Philippines shouldered about one-fifth of the world's copra supply, and America's nascent beauty industry benefited from the constant inflow of fine oils from US possessions in Southeast Asia and the South Pacific. There, too, traditional modes of harvesting collided with the new plantation system imposed from the outside. Although Samoans managed to retain a greater degree of independence in dealing with Euro-American planters compared to other colonized peoples, travel restrictions, taxes, and cash money introduced by German and US administrators (the islands had been partitioned between the two powers in 1899) pressured locals into selling their labor. Broken contracts, rigid schedules, and reports of abuse soured relations between planters and workers. "The foreigners only want to gain money through the lives of others," the Samoan leader Mata'afa Iosefo complained in 1903, emphasizing how much the Euro-American copra rush had unraveled native agricultural practices.[12]

Class disparities were another result of the increasing demand for copra. The development of local industries took a back seat in the Philippines.

FIGURE 4.1 A Filipino worker opening coconuts for copra, c. 1918. Cheap labor and raw materials imported from the colonies spurred the rise of the beauty industry in Europe and North America. Courtesy of the Library of Congress Prints and Photographs Division.

US business interests on the islands were largely limited to securing unrestricted access to their natural resources. A small group of prosperous Filipino landholders benefited from trading with the empire while plantation workers struggled to make ends meet (see figure 4.1). Many found themselves at the mercy of these wealthy "caciques," whom locals feared for wielding near unchecked power over their workforce. Resistance against this quasi-feudal system, which turned out to be quite compatible with the export-oriented economy established under US rule, boiled over in a series of rural uprisings in the early 1930s. People toiling on copra plantations joined forces with other agricultural workers to protest their degradation in the Colorum and Sakdalista revolts. Colonial authorities responded with mass arrests and punitive killings. Some survivors continued to push for reform. Many others took the same route as the crops they had collected: they migrated to the United States (until the US government severely limited the number of Filipinos allowed to enter the country in 1934).[13]

Few American consumers of hygiene and beauty products had a clear understanding of how fundamentally cash-crop capitalism had been upending the lives of the colonized. Companies like Palmolive wanted to make sure it stayed that way. In a promotional booklet published in 1925, Palmolive executives offered a behind-the-scenes tour of the main factory in Milwaukee. Carefully selected photographs guide the reader through the production process, showing massive soap kettles, modern machines, happy workers, and tidy offices adorned with exotic plants. Making soap was the province of professional experts, the booklet stated, "men who have devoted their lives" to manufacturing a product that could be "used on the most delicate skin or scalp without discomfort." But soapmaking was also "romance," taking its students "into the utmost corners of the world." There are probably few accounts of cosmetic colonialism more sanitized than this one. Erasing the industry's implication in imperial oppression, Palmolive executives assured the public that their business practices were as clean as the product they were selling. Judging by the growing popularity of soaps, cremes, and other antiaging substances sold at beauty parlors and department stores, buyers were taking the bait.[14]

CONTRARY TO PALMOLIVE'S assertion that white male professionals were the driving force behind mass-produced cosmetics, women were crucial for the market—and not just as paying customers. According to the historians Michelle Smith and Jane Nicholas, women's prominence in the ascent of manufactured beauty in the decades after 1900 indicate the extent to which "the logic of rejuvenation was feminized." In making this argument, Smith and Nicholas referred to the cosmetic routines taken up by an increasing number of middle-class women. These routines, in turn, were shaped significantly by female entrepreneurs and their substances, which promised rejuvenation to those who could afford them. By no means uncontested, this promise nonetheless helped normalize new ways of thinking about aging women. Wrinkles and spots became signs of personal neglect and their removal a moral duty.[15]

Helena Rubinstein and Elizabeth Arden built their careers on this prescription. Their feud is legendary; it even inspired a Broadway musical that depicted the two entrepreneurs as vengeful workaholics. Culturally and commercially, the women were pulling in the same direction. Arden and Rubinstein opened their stores in New York City just five years and a few blocks apart from each other. Arden made her debut in 1910 and achieved a major commercial breakthrough four years later when chemists helped her to come up with a fluffy pore cream that became an instant bestseller. At the end of the decade, Arden was setting her eyes on overseas markets where Rubinstein had already made first inroads. Before she set up shop in Manhattan in 1915, Rubinstein had run beauty salons in Melbourne, London, and Paris, experimenting with herbal preparations and developing her own makeup line. Department stores selling their products as well as a chain of parlors across the United States and Europe formed the pillars of Arden's and Rubinstein's rivaling empires. Private misfortunes punctuated the women's business success. Both women had to deal with unfaithful husbands. Arden's marriage to the American banker Thomas Jenkins Lewis could not have ended on a more humiliating note. After the divorce in 1935, Lewis switched sides and offered his services to Rubinstein.[16]

Although fierce competition drove the two women apart, it honed their skills when it came to recasting cosmetics as desirable and respectable. Prior to the twentieth century, "painted women" signaled decadence and vice, and the guardians of Victorian morality dismissed glitter as surface illusion for a deficient character. Men would encounter crimson lips and powdered cheeks in the underworlds of prostitution or in the frivolous court culture of the old aristocracies, not in the domestic sphere of respectable womanhood. Middle-class print culture routinely admonished women to pursue beautiful complexions without using rouge or lip coloring. If anything, temperance in food and drink would keep women young and attractive. People with makeup, on the contrary, had something to hide.[17]

It was this linkage of cosmetics with fakeness and promiscuity against which Rubinstein and Arden revolted—a rebellion that at once furthered and profited from changing age and gender norms. Writers who once had considered makeup disgraceful were nodding in appreciation of how the younger generation were starting to assert control over their own bodies. Public chatter about the "new woman" began in the late nineteenth century and grew louder as progressive voices celebrated educated, intelligent, and self-sufficient women who announced themselves to the world as socially and sexually independent beings. More than just an aesthetic corollary to the suffrage movement, new womanhood reflected the widening economic footprint of women in urban-industrial societies. Women attending all-female colleges and finding employment as nurses, clerks, and teachers had more money to spend and less need to rely on a male breadwinner. As always, the capitalist vision of buying the good life depended on the size of one's wallet. Without the disposable income required to shop for scents and substances from all over the world, women found themselves unable to participate in the cosmetic boom. Selling your labor for decent wages became a precondition for taking up the labor of beautifying your own body.[18]

If new womanhood sparked a revolution at all, it was a visual one. Around the turn of the century, a broad array of female types, from athletic girls sunbathing at the beach to Broadway actresses wearing mascara and lipstick, conquered the pages of magazines, newspaper ads, and department store displays. Whether developed for elite enjoyment or popular consumption, these images all shared the common currency of youthfulness. Down went ideas of female worth centering on invisible virtues such as piety and modesty. For the American woman to grow "braver, stronger, more healthful and skillful and able and free, more human in all ways," as the novelist Charlotte Perkins Gilman demanded in 1898, a different language was needed, one that valued dazzling appearance over a corseted morality. Her rejection of Victorian domesticity made the new woman renounce traditional ladyhood in favor of a girlishness that did not signify weakness or immaturity. Instead, the "modern girl" came to embody a practical feminism that aimed at enhancing women's mobility and fostered greater pleasure, individuality, and sexual freedom. Aging carried a twofold risk for women in the age of Gibson girls and glitzy flappers. Unless they kept up their looks, their aesthetic decline would be compounded by the loss of social relevance.[19]

In a flurry of advertisements and booklets, Arden and Rubinstein put the imperative of female rejuvenation front and center. Beauty, Rubinstein explained, was "more often developed than inherited," and every patron could attain "permanent youthfulness that is woman's greatest and rarest charm" through "care and caution." As early as the 1910s, female beauty entrepreneurs adopted the masculine language of science to persuade those who had been accustomed to viewing cosmetics as a frivolous pastime. Arden highlighted that her successful treatments were "the result of scientific knowledge gained by study, experience, and consultation with the foremost specialists and chemists." Likewise, Rubinstein sought to project expertise by labeling herself "the most famous scientist of beauty" who through "constant research" had learned how to give "the pearly skin of childhood" back to women. Their goal was to build trust in a rapidly growing portfolio of skin-care products. Convincing potential buyers that evading the "oppressive specter of old age" required little more than commitment and common sense was crucial in that regard.[20]

Most advertisements of the 1910s and 1920s chose a conversational tone to strike a balance between invoking scientific authority and presenting cosmetics as stylish antiaging for the masses. Female consumers were addressed as equal partners in the quest for ageless youth (see figure 4.2). Producers stressed the importance of customer initiative for making skins younger and

FIGURE 4.2 Advertisement for Helena Rubinstein beauty products, 1925. To sell antiaging
to the masses, Arden's and Rubenstein's cosmetic ads balanced gestures to science
with the promise of consumer empowerment. *Vanity Fair*, November 1925.

lovelier, tapping into a do-it-yourself spirit that fit neatly with the emancipatory optimism expressed by early twentieth-century feminists. "Keep your schoolgirl complexion and you can forget your passing years" was the reward awaiting the woman who chose Palmolive. Ideally, a visit to the beauty parlor and consultations with trained specialists resulted in individualized treatment plans that women could carry out at home. Rubinstein's "9 basic rules for beauty," which became the masthead of an ad offensive in 1927, emphasized that knowing one's own skin type, daily cleansing, and persevering in the "regularity of home treatment" were key to maintaining a youthful appearance. Arden, who had told women to "Be Your Own Complexionist" as early as 1914, promised similar outcomes with her three-step process of cleansing, toning, and nourishing. Women supplied with the proper creams and tonics, Arden asserted, could follow their daily beauty routines in virtually any bathroom as long as they mustered sufficient discipline and endurance. Perhaps more than any other consumerist mode of self-improvement, cosmetics made rejuvenation contingent on the right products and the right work ethic.[21]

Cosmetic ads can be read as perfect expressions of a modern consumer culture trying to "cash in on the women's sphere," as Kathy Peiss succinctly put it. The beauty industry's fusion of democratic capitalism with women's emancipation deserves to be taken seriously, especially since its leaders insisted that they had remedies for every aging face. Such declarations, however, conflicted with hierarchies of color and desirability that elevated some skins over others. Middle-aged white women were the primary market for white-owned companies, so vying for their attention with models who had lily-white skin and elegant facial features seemed like sound business practice. Linking beauty to immaculate whiteness had a disturbing history. While the exquisiteness attributed to white skin predates colonialism (European nobility famously desired paleness to distance themselves from the sun-weathered peasantry), Enlightenment scholars defined aesthetic perfection on the basis of race. Johann Friedrich Blumenbach, for example, believed that "Caucasian" white skin was the original color of humankind and that all other skin colors were just deviations. Theories positing a correlation between beauty and intelligence spread across societies remade by the transatlantic slave trade and by racist characterizations of Black people as ugly and primitive. Western nomenclatures of skin color branched out to include other races as Euro-American colonization engulfed more parts of the world. Red, the color that came to designate Native Americans, connoted "wild" and "aggressive." "Sickly" or "toxic" were traits ascribed to yellow, the color widely used to refer to people from East Asia. Profit and power converged in the cosmetic industry's preference for lighter skins. Selling products that reinforced Anglo-American notions of beauty meant colluding with white supremacy.[22]

At the same time, the gradually more heterogeneous lines and marketing strategies point to a growing awareness in the industry that obsessing too much about whiteness in a multiethnic population might backfire. Immigrant entrepreneurs both, Rubinstein and Arden could certainly relate to the observation made by the journalist Helen Macfadden that it "was quite possible here in the United States to join a Nordic skin to Italian hair and eyes, to color an English skin with a warmth of Spanish, Jewish, and Russian blood." The face of the country was changing while Americans were debating the pros and cons of being a nation of immigrants. In addition, the rise of sunshine tourism made many white women reconsider their natural indoor hue. Would a healthy tan not bring them closer to possessing the youthfully attractive bodies they craved? Tre-Jur, another New York-based cosmetic powerhouse known for enticing women to play with exotic looks, agreed when it stated in 1929 that "lily white complexion is 'passé.'"[23]

Major brands responded to the color craze of the 1920s by adding new items to their collections. Rubinstein's "Egyptian Mask," which she promoted as "treatment for rejuvenating aging, relaxed faces," was an attempt to exploit the same Egyptomania that had led to Cleopatra's resurrection in Palmolive ads. The popularity of darker shades, now that suntanning was all the rage, hastened innovations such as Rubinstein's "Gypsy Tan Powder" or, in Arden's case, face powders by the name of "Ardena Bronze" or "Spanish Rachel." Still, the melting pot aesthetics marketed by white stylists stayed within certain boundaries. Ethnicity, suspicious as identity, was admired for its ability to pronounce individuality in white women. Commodified in the form of rouge or powders, ethnic looks could be put on and rinsed off without leaving permanent marks. In case women went too far and returned from their summer vacations too dark and freckled, Rubinstein recommended skin bleachers so that Nordic types might again "lighten up the entire tone of their complexions."[24]

Readers may sense a paradox in the belief that the revitalization of white womanhood hinged on flawless white skin absorbing tinges of color. Advocates of color play did not. The new woman's determination to create her own style by consuming all the shades she wanted set her visibly apart from the stereotypical victim of neurasthenia, the pale homebound bachelor girl. In cosmetic's imperial marketplace, buying products with foreign names or supposedly exotic ingredients catered to white women's desire for confident selfhood. Inadvertently, Anglo-American females who felt that they had the entire globe at their disposal as they were browsing the skin-care collections of beauty salons and department stores upheld the colonial project. Cosmetic products wrapped in images of oriental splendor and colonial discovery offered conduits to distant sources of vitality and beauty, all waiting to be tapped in the service of keeping white women supremely enchanting. *Exercises for Health and Beauty*, a booklet published by the Arden Company in 1923, demonstrates how the cosmetic imperative and the colonial gaze worked in tandem. The booklet starts by juxtaposing "a women of the Orient—slothful, dull, heavy" with "a women of classical Greece—lithe, graceful, poised, beautiful." The Greek woman, the author explained, aged more slowly on account of her superior knowledge of how to live well. Thanks to the "undreamed of progress in the sciences," white women in the modern era, aided by substances from faraway regions, could do the same. To view skin-care regimens as the female equivalent of white men finding rejuvenation on African safaris is not a stretch of the imagination. The main point is to recognize that both practices relied on the labor of dark-skinned bodies to ensure the regeneration of racial identities.[25]

For all their cosmopolitan pretensions, Rubinstein's and Arden's fascination with ethnic variety did not include an appreciation for Blackness. African imagery in white beauty advertisements of the period was confined to few ornaments and fewer people in servant's garb. The fact that the powder boxes of white-owned companies solidified the color line seemingly left Black consumers with no choice other than emulation. In the hope of approximating an ideal that had been impossible to reach, many African Americans turned to skin lighteners. Bleaching, its advocates vowed, would make good looks available to Black women in a segregated society where even slight color modifications could better one's social status. African American periodicals of the Jazz Age amplified the trend to go brown by advertising creams that promised to brighten and lighten, much to the delight of an aspiring Black urban middle class whose members sought to shed old stereotypes.[26]

More than a few literati in the community begged to differ. Some worried that the rush to cover up Blackness would foster racial self-loathing. One columnist, in a February 1920 piece for the *Half Century Magazine*, slammed beauty companies "whose owners grow rich and retire to large dwellings all the while laughing at the gullibility of [African Americans]." Marcus Garvey, the Jamaican-born champion of Pan-Africanism, turned to poetry to celebrate Black women as authentically beautiful. Convinced that cosmetics were inimical to true beauty, Garvey lashed out at the colonial structures sustaining white-owned businesses and envisioned the day when Africans regained control in Africa, "restoring the pearly crown that proud Queen Sheba did wear." The Black social commentator George Schuyler scolded Black women who resorted to dangerous chemicals to appear less dark. Schuyler's opposition culminated in his novel *Black No More* (1931), a biting satire about a con artist whose scheme to whiten the entire Black race ends in violence and chaos.[27]

The outcry of a few Black commentators was insufficient to stem the tide of bleaching advertisements and their version of a "new negro" finding redemption in a rejuvenated whiter self. Erasing the harrowing legacy of slavery by shedding the stain of Blackness, bleaching vendors reasoned, should appeal to women and men alike; hence, several dealers addressed both sexes. An ad for Black and white ointment from 1919 contained a particularly dramatic appeal. "Race men and women protect your future," the advertisement urged. "Be Attractive! Throw off the chains that have held you back from the prosperity and happiness that belongs to you!" Judging by the observations of people who sauntered down the streets of Harlem during the interwar years, African Americans of property and standing were disproportionately light-skinned. Harlem Renaissance intellectuals who strove for racial renewal through art found themselves caught between two aristocracies, one of culture and one of color. While the former tied Blackness to artistic vibrancy, the latter fed aspirations for social distinction within the African American community.[28]

Madam C. J. Walker Manufacturing Company rose above the fray. Founded in 1910 by Sarah Breedlove, a Black haircare specialist who made a fortune with her method for repairing and refining Black hair, the Walker brand gained prominence as a symbol of African American race pride and business acumen. Breedlove, who changed her name to Madam Walker when she was still peddling her own hair growers and scalping conditioners door to door, was clear-eyed about the political significance of her work. "I want the greater masses of my people to take greater pride in their personal appearance and to give their hair proper attention," Walker declared. Charting a path to Black beauty, she knew, would have to involve dismantling the racist image of Black domestic workers as unappealing drudges who forfeited their youth the day they turned into the stereotypical "mammy." Walker's products expressed a vision of Black modernity in which making Black hair healthier and shinier would provide upward mobility to the granddaughters of enslaved cotton pickers. Only after Walker's death in 1919 did the company invest in skin lighteners. Walker herself had shunned products that extolled lighter complexions. As if to lend credibility to her feminist vision of racial progress, Walker built her business with the help of thousands of African American women whom she hired and trained as sales agents.[29]

Walker's combination of entrepreneurial ambition with political activism left a lasting impact on African American communities. She donated generously to the National Association for the Advancement of Colored People (NAACP) and called on President Woodrow Wilson to support anti-lynching legislation. The beauty schools she founded and hair salons she inspired became part of an evolving civil rights infrastructure (see figure 4.3). Profits made in Black beauty parlors enabled donations to Black colleges and paid for advertisements that sustained African American newspapers. The women frequenting these Black-controlled spaces, according to the historian Tiffany Gill, experienced degrees of freedom rarely obtainable in an otherwise oppressive environment. Uplifting Black women and making them feel confident, modern, youthful, and attractive was often framed in the language of collective responsibility. The slogan "Look your best—You owe it to your race" was used in an advertisement by Madam C. J. Walker that circulated in the late 1920s, suggesting that more was at stake than self-improvement.[30]

Although African American intellectuals of the Progressive Era generally dismissed talk of "race suicide" by their white supremacist counterparts, few

FIGURE 4.3 Students of the Madam C. J. Walker College of Beauty Culture in Chicago, c. 1920. Walker's business ventures made the point that African American women trained in self-care could obtain desirability, youth, and success. Courtesy of the Madam C. J. Walker Supplemental Collection, Indiana Historical Society.

denied that the horrors of Jim Crow threatened the survival of their race. Falling birth rates had different implications for a community that saw more of its children die from illness and more of its adult population succumb to state-sanctioned violence. Fears regarding the future of Black-to-Black romance—particularly the question of whether young Black men who had come under the spell of colorism would remain sexually attracted to dark-skinned women—exacerbated the problem. Where would all the healthy babies come from if not from women who, with the right hair and skin treatments, had upped their value on the marriage market? With demographics entering the equation, the road to female rejuvenation could easily swerve in the direction of a gender regime fixated on women's reproductive capacities.

Helping women make consumer decisions that would not only improve their looks but also strengthen the body politic was a concern voiced by cosmetic advocates across racial lines. Convinced that white women, too, "owed it to their race," Rubinstein acquired a reputation for telling women to powder up during hard times. During World War I, she called out women who were weighed down by the troubles of war, calling them detrimental to the nation's fighting morale. "Your patriotism demands that you keep your face bright and attractive so that you radiate optimism," claimed one of her ads, instructing women to get rid of the "war face." The same contention that makeup would boost confidence in victory reemerged after the United States had gone to war against Nazi Germany and Japan in 1941. Beautiful women, Rubinstein maintained, were in a better position to support the war effort and cheer up the soldiers in the field. To gauge whether such narratives stuck, the consumer's role in redrawing the social boundaries of cosmetics needs to be part of the analysis.[31]

"THE ERA OF ROUGE is upon us," the English essayist Max Beerbohm proclaimed with prophetic certainty in 1896. Considering the sharp rise of beauty advertisements in women's print journals over the next decades, Beerbohm's cultural instincts appeared to be ahead of the curve. Yet, the messaging of an industry tells us little about actual changes in consumer behavior. Cosmetics, Kathy Peiss reminded us, "came only gradually to Main Street" and slower still to the countryside. Its outward spread from the big cities was hampered by class and culture. Until the Great Depression and beyond, women working in factories or toiling on farms had other things to worry about than following Rubinstein's beauty rules. Even if they felt like covering up a spot here or removing a wrinkle there, chances that the local small-town drugstores carried a wider selection of metropolitan brands were usually slim.[32]

In the interwar years, the divide over the use of makeup reflected a larger cultural rift separating rural Americans with a strong attachment to traditional values from the more progressive outlook of the urban middle classes. Listening to religious conservatives of the 1920s, one might think that women masking their biological age with modern skin-care products were committing a sin against God's creation nearly as grave as schoolteachers who exposed children to the heresies of evolution. Evangeline Booth, the leader of the US wing of the Salvation Army, went on the record in February 1922 calling the woman who applied cosmetics "a cheat." Doubling down, Booth claimed that "many divorces are caused by the fact that wily ladies have deceived their husbands into thinking them better looking than they are." True beauty, she added, resided in the homely appearance nature had bestowed on women. Sharing Booth's alarm, the Harvard-trained Reverend Percy Stickney Grant declared Christianity "the greatest beauty parlor in the world" and implored his female parishioners to find happiness in faith, not fragrances.[33]

Pushback also came from less devout quarters. Voices from the medical community exhorted consumers to be more skeptical toward cosmetic products and not to discount possible negative side effects. Morris Fishbein, a physician with a reputation for hunting down quacks, took aim at the beauty merchants for luring women into a false sense of expectation with shiny brand names. Lurid slogans, according to Fishbein, were a poor excuse for being "poorly informed concerning the actual anatomy, physiology and pathology of the skin." Conservative guardians of taste and propriety organizing under the banner of "make women's faces clean" saw in the flapperization of college-age girls a massive problem. They applauded university presidents who banned the use of cosmetics on campus. All that anti-makeup advocates were doing, one skin disease specialist told a group of homeopathic doctors, was trying to keep harmful substances out of the hands of modern girls, who might otherwise turn "frightful, fat, and forty." One of the most widely read US advice writers of the 1920s, the columnist Dorothy Dix, sought the middle ground, recommending cosmetics for middle-aged women but faulting "very young girls" and "old women" for craving a youthful complexion that the former did not need and the latter had irrevocably lost. Rather than undermine the dignity of old age, elderly women should look to Grace Coolidge, the wife of the president. "First Lady Uses No Cosmetics and Arranges Her Hair Conservatively," the *Boston Daily Globe* wrote approvingly in its August 5, 1923, issue.[34]

A rare forum in which younger proponents of beautification could lay out their case came in the shape of a public debate organized by the Boston Girl's City Club in January 1924. The young debaters in favor of cosmetics convinced the judges, who unanimously declared them winners. They also managed to sway the crowd, who responded with applause and laughter. The girls arguing the other side showed up prepared as well. If the flapper generation believed that rouge and lipstick enhanced their individuality, one opponent of makeup contented, they were sorely mistaken. The pro-cosmetics faction shrugged off the intervention. For them, wearing makeup, even as young women, was a matter of modernity, not morals. "Why is it that wealthy women look so well—it is because they know how to use the best modern science has produced. Today it is the foolish woman who wrinkles and fades." Molly Walsh, the lead supporter of cosmetics, admitted that she would not press her case so hard if personal taste were the issue. But if the "first question a man asks about a girl is this: Is she good-looking . . . a girl owes it to herself to put her best foot forward." In these days of "social competition," Walsh bluntly stated, there were things a young woman had to do to get ahead.[35]

Whether Walsh and her companions were simply parroting what they had heard from adults or read in magazines is impossible to know. However, Walsh was on to something with her assertion that "social competition" was the primary stimulus that made women of different age segments invest in cosmetic rejuvenation. "Women, whether in business, on the stage, or in other occupations in which they are in contact with the public, consider a youthful appearance to be an economic necessity," was the plain verdict of the mathematician Adelaide Smith. Market research surveys, a new genre of capitalist writing born after World War I, indicate that urban professional women—many unmarried—became the most loyal customers of the nation's top beauty brands, Arden and Rubinstein included. Rouge, lipstick, and almost daily powder applications were popular among the twenty-year-olds, whereas thirty- and forty-year-olds were inclined to spend their money on creams and less on powder. Throngs of young stenographers and clerks spent their lunch breaks at Sears and Macy's, checking out new merchandise in the stores' makeup sections. It was this class of wage-earning women who turned the painted face into a business uniform.[36]

Consumers did not simply fall for the industry's glitzy promises; nor did they mindlessly apply the newest tonics. Women who wanted to master the art of staying attractive learned to be critical shoppers. Many became ardent students of compositions and treatment methods recommended by beauticians. Trying out different products was often preceded by conversations with a close friend or colleague whose advice on which soaps or cremes to trust counted more than advice found in brochures or magazines. If a friend felt that lipstick was too garish, better discard it before drawing attention to yourself and looking silly or, worse, vulgar. Ultimately, refashioning biological and social skins expressed some sort of personal dissatisfaction with one's age. Teenage girls like Margaret Parton, who in the 1930s shocked her mother "with charcoal on [her] lids, a spit curl, and a cigarette," saw in the application of makeup a fast track to adulthood. Older women, in contrast, could turn nostalgic on entering a beauty parlor, lamenting the loss of their youth and what once had made them lovely in the eyes of their partners. Although the scramble for lasting beauty did not devolve into intergenerational warfare, the middle-aged sensed they would not come out on top in a cosmetics arms race. As one forty-nine-year-old woman, who was struggling to survive in a "man's business," pleaded in 1937, "it is terribly important to me to retain as much youth as possible as long as I can, both mentally and physically." Losing their sex appeal in times of depression could mean economic disaster for aging women, especially when they had to compete for jobs and attention against twenty-five-year-olds.[37]

But the modern girl had a lot to lose, too, despite her relative advantage on the attractiveness scale. Retaining youthful appearances required money, diligence, and knowledge of how to exercise bodily self-care on a daily basis, regardless of mood or weather. A health study commissioned by the government of Ontario, Canada in 1923 dove deeper. Officials conducted up to 300 interviews with "business women" about their personal hygiene. Though limited to one region, the study provides a glimpse into the intimate worlds of wage-earning women's bathroom routines, the daily pressure to keep hair, nails, eyelids, teeth, and skins intact and shining. One female correspondent described the hassle best, noting "our physical condition deserves first attention, because upon this everything hinges. Better to be methodical and start at the head, gradually working our way to the feet. Make out a list. . . . Example: Brush hair, cold cream and massage face and neck, bathe eyes in boracic solution, extra special brushing of the teeth, using waxed floss drawn carefully between, manicuring finger-nails, bath and foot attention." Another letter writer warned that failure in efficiency, or trading body care for leisure, might lead to premature aging. Such ominous words cast a different light over the "Vienna Youth Mask," a facial treatment introduced by Elizabeth Arden in 1927. Would it rejuvenate the client, or would it rather make her disappear behind a regime of constant optimization?[38]

Marketed as female, makeup was nevertheless not exclusively lodged in the women's sphere. Men, too, gradually became a consumer force to be reckoned with, although those who worried about their appearance had obstacles to overcome, none bigger than the association of cosmetics with effeminacy. Men who started using toiletries for reasons of hygiene and style tiptoed into skin care rather than embrace the industry wholeheartedly. Anxieties about masculinity remained a strong impediment. As late as 1937, market analysts from New York doubted that "he-men" would "ever be a good market." The majority of office workers they interviewed consented to mild aftershave but found that "no regular guy" should want cremes and scents for himself. The emphasis on straightness was related to the early twentieth-century rise of queer culture in metropolitan areas, especially in New York and Los Angeles. Although the history of gay men's cosmetic practices has yet to be written, fashion and style have long been staples of queer identity. In the thriving gay nightlife of Greenwich Village and the Bowery, wearing flamboyant makeup signaled same-sex desire, and cross-dressing performances were a common sight at homosexual bars. Acting more discreetly during the day, white-collar homosexuals would resort to less conspicuous means of skin enhancement. The question of how many men, straight and gay, polished their appearance by secretly using their mothers' creams or claiming to shop for beauty items for their wives is difficult to determine.[39]

Plastic surgery was the one area of cosmetic rejuvenation where men figured prominently. Reconstructing limbs and faces reached unprecedented levels with the veterans of World War I, many of whom returned to their families scarred physically and emotionally. Disfigurements ranged from amputated arms and legs to noses blown off and faces horribly distorted. For the soldiers suffering from such drastic wounds, returning to the lives they had led before the war was near impossible. Increasing the number of disabled persons in society, wounded war veterans came to represent a defective manhood and served as constant reminders of the carnage of industrialized trench warfare. Pioneering plastic surgeons such as New Zealand's Harold Gillies and the Armenian-born US oral specialist Varaztad Kazanjian rose to the challenge of restoring male bodies mutilated in war by refining techniques of skin grafting and prosthetic dentistry. Hopes for rejuvenation, not just rehabilitation, drove these innovations. Public policy placed the disabled soldier in close proximity to the frail and feeble senior. Welfare agencies on both sides of the Atlantic framed the issues of veteran pauperism and old age poverty in strikingly similar ways. While not all returning soldiers needed assistance, charities like the American Red Cross Institute for Crippled and Disabled Men, founded in New York in 1917, received federal tax dollars to help wounded doughboys reenter the workforce and remove from them the twin stigmas of dependency and unsightliness.[40]

Again, racism constricted access to these services since white soldiers were deemed more worthy of repair than Black veterans. African American survivors of the slaughter were not just trying to salvage from the battlefields of Europe what was left of their youth. Just as disheartening was that they were returning to a country that was still to grant them the rights of adult citizens. The task of reintegrating into a Black community humming with controversy over white emulation and race renewal, skin bleaching, and hair straightening proved daunting on its own. The belief voiced by some reformers that the "New Negro" might eventually mature into a new race, more Brown than Black, prompted bitter disputes. In 1923, the historian and civil rights activist W. E. B. Du Bois hurled some of his choicest invectives at Marcus Garvey, one of the harshest critics of whitening. Why, Du Bois wondered, should Black women take their beauty advice from "a little, fat black man, ugly . . . dressed in a military uniform of the gayest mid-Victorian type, heavy with gold lace, epaulets, plume and sword"? Garvey shot back, claiming that Du Bois's blend of Blackness and white civilization was a thinly veiled disguise for hating his own skin. How African Americans of this period chose to identify was arguably more complex. But the politics behind arguments over which appearance projected the right kind of racial solidarity was hard to evade.[41]

Since white-run market research companies showed scant interest in non-white consumption habits, little is known about average African American buying patterns at the time. Yet, despite the clamor in the African American press that mimicking white fads undermined the ideal of authentic Black beauty, skin bleachers continued to sell well. The same was true of lightening creams such as Madam Walker's "Tan-Off," which the company recommended "for brightening sallow or dark skin" and promoted at Black beauty contests across the nation. Would such products light the path toward an African American future in which modern youthfulness and equal maturity stood in perfect equilibrium? Doubts remained. Perhaps no twentieth-century Black writer articulated them more forcefully than James Baldwin, who captured the Sisyphean folly of trying to erase Blackness when recalling his Harlem childhood in the 1920s: "One was always being mercilessly scrubbed and polished, as though in the hope that a stain could thus be washed away. . . . And yet it was clear that none of this effort would release one from the stigma and danger of being a [n-word]; this effort merely increased the shame and rage."[42]

Cosmetics entrepreneurs learned to juggle the ambiguities of their industry's adolescence. That is one reason why the trade thrived way beyond what its Progressive Era pioneers had imagined. Much of its expansion inside and outside the United States continued to be driven by imperial circuits of labor and resource extraction that outlasted the period of decolonization. Issues of child labor, the exploitation of migrant workers, and deforestation are stains on the palm oil business to this day. Only in 2022 did cosmetic brands join forces in an industrywide coalition to pressure palm oil suppliers into implementing more sustainable practices. This leaves the question of why the public has been so slow to wake up to the inequalities shored up by the beauty industry. A big part of the answer lies in its advocates, who have been quite successful in spreading the myth of cosmetics as soft rejuvenation. Because of the economic costs and health risks associated with genital surgeries and other hard forms of rejuvenation, cosmetics could prevail as the more innocuous variant. In covering up age spots with paint and powder, Americans have been doing their part to cover up that youthful appearances are often regained at the expense of others.[43]

CHAPTER FIVE

Renewing the Race

Sex, Demography, and Democracy between the Wars

Let me take you by the hand
Over to the jungle band
If you're too old for dancing
Get yourself a monkey gland.
—Irving Berlin, "The Monkey Doodle Doo" (1925)

As Joseph Wozniak awoke from troubled dreams one October morning in 1922, he did not find himself transformed into a giant insect. But there are definitely more pleasant experiences than waking up on a sidewalk in Chicago's Near South Side. Stretching off the slumber, Wozniak sorted his memories. What had happened? He and a good friend had been drinking at a nearby speakeasy. Howling saxophones, strangers, broken glass, a tussle, a running car at the curb. Suddenly, piercing through the brain fog caused by what must have been a serious hangover, a stabbing pain in his crotch made Wozniak wince. He opened his pants and froze—his genitals were wrapped in a blood-soaked bandage! After limping back home, Wozniak immediately contacted his doctor. Dr. Sampelinski confirmed Wozniak's worst fear—the war veteran from Wisconsin had lost one of his testicles. The culprits had vanished without a trace, except for the amputation that would leave a monstrous scar.[1]

Chicago's press had a field day with Wozniak's ordeal. Reporters assumed that he had become the latest victim of organ traffickers who had been targeting healthy males in the Windy City. Chicago in the Prohibition era was teeming with all kinds of crime, but the brutal precision exhibited by these gland snatchers made the most hardened law enforcement official shudder. One medical report surmised that the violent orchiectomy was conducted by an "expert surgeon" who acted on behalf of a "wealthy ancient" eager to have his shriveled sex organs replaced with younger ones. If there was a rich mastermind behind all this, he was certainly willing to pay an extraordinary sum for his libido. Wild rumors spread until the investigation centered on the St. Louis candy tycoon Henry Baurichter. Although the charges against Baurichter were dropped because of flimsy evidence, the media feasted on the story. The sixty-eight-year-old millionaire had just announced his engagement to a woman more than forty years his minor. He was also seen visiting surgeons who had begun conducting potency-enhancing operations on wealthy patients. Was this the reason why Wozniak's testicles, and those of several other unsuspecting young men, had disappeared?[2]

The dread caused by Chicago's gland pirates was short-lived. After a while, with no new thefts reported, men stopped worrying about waking up in dark alleys with an empty scrotum. Still, testicles no longer seemed off limits in the gray area where organized crime and modern medicine met. The postwar rise of surgical procedures intended to buoy the potency of aging males ran up against established norms of decency. But the transgressive character of these operations also made for spectacular headlines at a time when interest in rejuvenation was soaring across cultures and continents. Like other transatlantic media hypes of the period, sexual rejuvenation created its own language and celebrities. The two stars of the scene were the gland-engineering physicians Eugen Steinach and Serge Voronoff. Their names tower in almost every book on the subject. To "get Steinached" became a catchphrase in the English language, coined after the Austrian physiologist whose antiaging vasectomies put Vienna on the map as a mecca for men seeking to regain their virility. Steinach's fame was more than matched by the Russian-born French surgeon Serge Voronoff, who captivated audiences with his claim that grafting monkey testicle tissue on the gonads of men amounted to an elixir of youth. Before-and-after photographs showing visible changes in patients were meant to convince a wary public. At the height of his popularity in the mid-1920s, Voronoff boasted that he had operated successfully on more than a thousand men.[3]

From the start, the idea of crossing men and monkeys elicited as much incredulity and outrage as excitement. Rejuvenation doctors incensed religious authorities who blasted their experiments as an affront to God and nature. Cartoons made fun of old philanderers undergoing all kinds of therapies to recover their sex drive (see figure 5.1). Animal rights activists scored a major victory when Voronoff was denied a license to operate in Great Britain. Cutting out a healthy chimpanzee's testicles for the sake of making men younger, they protested, was "an offence against morality, hygiene, and decency." But what gradually pushed Steinach, Voronoff, and their disciples out of the limelight were charges coming out of the medical profession. Scientists had demanded proof that antiaging surgery worked. What they got instead was promotional literature and reports about prominent patients, including William Butler Yeats, Sigmund Freud, and Turkey's president Mustafa Atatürk, getting a rejuvenation operation. In 1928, the American Medical Association

FIGURE 5.1 Cartoon mocking the popularity of novel rejuvenation therapies, 1921. The boasts of rejuvenation surgeons such as Serge Voronoff, who claimed to have found the key to curing impotence, provoked much satirical commentary. *Chicago Tribune*, October 13, 1921.

questioned the viability of Voronoff's grafting methods, effectively labeling him a quack. The accusation that the advocates of surgical revitalization were all engaged in a colossal Ponzi scheme was overblown, but there is no doubt that the field attracted its share of charlatans. The greatest swindler of all was America's answer to Voronoff, the "Kansas Goat Doctor" John R. Brinkley. After gaining his medical diploma from a dubious source, Brinkley got rich emptying the pockets of affluent white businessmen who believed the prairie surgeon's claim that inserting goat gland material into their scrota would restore their sexual prowess. A carnival barker in both medicine and politics, Brinkley became a conservative talk radio host and ran for governor in Kansas in 1930 after losing his license to practice medicine. Barred from participating in the election because of a missed deadline, Brinkley nonetheless drew huge crowds with his populist attacks on the government, the medical profession, and the powers allegedly bent on destroying him and the American people.[4]

The stories of Brinkley, Voronoff, and Steinach have been told elsewhere to great effect, and I have no intention of squabbling with their biographers. It is understandable, maybe necessary, to place their public careers in the overlapping contexts of transnational medical research, the mass media and celebrity cultures of the Roaring Twenties, and the often-invoked modern crisis of masculinity. There is also much value in analyses that situate the commodification of body parts, human and animal, within evolving market economies that declared ability, endurance, and workplace performance the major yardsticks for measuring human worth. The new "glandular self" propagated by the period's rejuvenation doctors, the historian Michael Pettit explained, was at once an expression of late nineteenth-century conceptions of the human body as a machine "subject to wear and tear" and of the modernist hope in "humanity's ability to finally control" time.[5]

All these interpretations leave no doubt about rejuvenation's tendency to deepen class divisions and pathologize aging bodies, and rightly so. Where they falter is that they tempt readers to group the clinical interventions of the likes of Steinach and Voronoff together with other consumerist promises of optimization—"technologies of the self," as the French philosopher Michel Foucault termed them, which "permit individuals to effect . . . a certain number of operations on their own bodies . . . so as to transform themselves in order to attain a certain state of happiness, purity, wisdom, perfection, or immortality."[6] This chapter dissents from any suggestions that sexual rejuvenation was politically at home in a forward-looking progressive modernity or that it merely offered utopian futures to people moneyed enough to pay for them. Instead, the glandular craze of the 1920s opens a window onto a host of reactionary body projects. These were held together by the urge of privileged antiagers to revitalize not just themselves but more broadly the national and international orders built on hierarchies of race, gender, class, and colonialism to which they clung. Despite their eccentric personas, the resonance that monkey and goat gland doctors enjoyed can only be explained in full when we see them as tacit allies of other early twentieth-century biopolitical movements. Few of these movements were keen on upending the power structures that benefited them.

Eugenics fits that description best. Though the movement did not look the same everywhere, its adherents learned to wield rejuvenation as a tool for racist demography. And though eugenicists rarely shared the platform with glandular scientists, their policies were by no means at odds with each other. Before World War II, the United States was a world leader in eugenics, which proposed that the key to improving human populations lay in studying patterns of procreation. "Race betterment," a doctrine preached at the nation's two major centers for eugenics research, the Battle Creek Sanatorium in Michigan and the Eugenics Record Office in Cold Spring Harbor, New York, mirrored ambitions for creating a superior people—stronger, healthier, smarter, and more youthful. The prospect of failure sounded bleak: a sickly, senescent society weakened by disease, crime, and miscegenation, to many in the movement's vanguard the greatest boogeyman of all. For the American zoologist Madison Grant, whose book *Passing of the Great Race* became a white supremacist must-read, giving birth to mixed-race children was "a social and racial crime of the first magnitude." Eugenicists from both sides of the Atlantic nodded their approval. Far from being hailed as potential rejuvenators, young men and women of color were vilified as civilization's worst nemesis. Again, people obsessed about testicles. Stirred into action by eugenic teachings, several US states passed forced sterilization laws between the 1910s and the 1930s. An estimated 60,000 persons, many with a minority background, were cut open as a consequence of these laws. Here we find another troubling connection: the flip coin side of resexualizing aging whites was asexualizing non-whites stamped as "feeble-minded."[7]

"Make it new"—Ezra Pound's dictum for mending the fractures of tradition in modern society—chimed well with eugenic rejuvenation. But as this chapter reveals, the poet's words spoke equally to those fighting for more inclusive alternatives. Fears that Anglo-American civilization might collapse under the weight of political radicalism and economic depression intensified during the interwar years and, with them, appeals that democracy itself needed a rejuvenation bath. In the case of the United States, two distinct projects committed to that task deserve special attention: one artistic and bottom-up, the other legislative and top-down. Renewal was central to the Harlem Renaissance. Next to raising popular interest in African American music, arts, and literature, members of this movement presented their works as the gift of Black culture for the repurposing of American democracy. When the Great Depression brought the Harlem Renaissance to a halt, the New

Deal's vision of a more equitable society offered a rallying point for those repelled by the new men and women that dominated the iconographies of communism and fascism. The politics of age pervaded the interwar worlds of sexual revitalization, reactionary eugenics, and democratic reform. Which path toward a youthfully renovated United States was going to attract more followers at the dawn of the American Century was an open question.[8]

A YALE PROFESSOR holding views on population control that were more drastic than those held by Benito Mussolini is hard to imagine. Irving Fisher, an internationally renowned economist and social reformer, accomplished that feat. Traveling to Rome in September 1927 after hearing that Mussolini was interested to learn about his monetary theory, Fisher spent about thirty minutes in his presence. The meeting went well, and having "the probably most important political figure in Europe" listen to his ideas about how to stimulate the Italian economy flattered Fisher. What the American academic was hesitant to share were his ideas about how to invigorate the country's aging population, even though Fisher had plenty. He knew that Mussolini had embraced pronatalism just a few months earlier. "The more children for the nation, the better." The slogan that spelled disaster to the American was Italy's national creed now. So Fisher kept his mouth shut.[9]

Fisher was not the only American to approach Il Duce with high hopes. Like many of his colleagues who had been rapt by Mussolini's carefully choreographed image as the youthfully dynamic savior of an ancient culture, Fisher was disappointed that the fascist leader believed in large families, not in breeding people with inferior traits out of existence. Charles Davenport, the founder of the Eugenics Record Office, took another stab at convincing Mussolini two years later at a gathering of the International Federation of Eugenic Organizations in Rome. Together with the German racial hygienist Eugen Fischer, whose studies would inform National Socialist race laws, Davenport called on Il Duce to impose stricter eugenic measures. They told Mussolini that it was "not only masses that make up a people" and that the only way to avert "a veritable catastrophic plunge" in the vitality of Europe's time-honored cultures was "the preservation of human quality." Davenport admitted that the necessary measures "may sound an anti-social and anti-democratic note." But "setting a model to the world by showing that energetic administration can make good the damage that has already been done to our culture" allowed no delay. To Davenport's chagrin, Mussolini refused to change course. Maybe another dictator in the making would prove more inclined to set that model.[10]

US eugenicists' infatuation with Mussolini and later Adolf Hitler has been the subject of several books that shed light on an emerging right-wing international composed of Jim Crow segregationists, radical anticommunists, and violent anti-Semites. Their shared extremism on matters of race, gender, and heredity shatters the notion of a political firewall separating American democracy from tyranny abroad. However, belaboring the "Nazi connection" comes at a risk: it can obscure that the origins of eugenic rejuvenation in the United States were quite liberal. One way to begin the story is with a personal awakening. In 1898, freshly promoted to full professor at age thirty-one, Irving Fisher contracted tuberculosis, a disease that had killed his father and tormented him over the next three years. Surviving his brush with death gave Fisher a calling that lasted for the rest of his life: spreading the gospel of health in a society inhaling the toxic vapors of modernization. With the zeal of a fire-and-brimstone preacher, Fisher renounced alcohol, opposed smoking, turned vegetarian, and exercised twice a day. He also believed that with sound science and the right partners his own regeneration might be mapped onto the nation as a whole.[11]

Fisher's ideas about how to widen lifespans and stretch mortality curves gained the attention of other Progressive Era elites. Business executives took great interest in his models showing that more health and less death in the population meant increased productivity from the laboring classes and higher revenues for life insurance companies. Political leaders appreciated Fisher's comparison of national vitality to the protection of the country's natural resources. The analogy resurfaced in Theodore Roosevelt's "new nationalism" speech in Osawatomie, Kansas, on August 31, 1910, where the former president called "the health and vitality of our people . . . as well worth conserving as their forests, waters, lands, and minerals." Three years later, Fisher had secured enough funding and institutional backing to launch his boldest initiative yet: the founding of the Life Extension Institute (LEI). Part business venture, part health organization, the LEI entered the national conversation to "teach hygiene" and the "prevention of disease." But the organization's goals did not stop there.[12]

The portrait gallery inserted in the front pages of the 1915 edition of the LEI's best-selling manual *How to Live* reads like a photo album of the early eugenics movement in the United States. Davenport was in there; so was the German American physician Adolphus Knopf, the mentor of birth control activist Margaret Sanger; muscular Christians like the physical educator Dudley Sargent and the award-winning American football coach Amos Alonzo Stagg; the Scottish-born inventor Alexander Graham Bell, who patented the telephone; and the nutritionist John Harvey Kellogg, whose sanatorium in Battle Creek hosted a series of conferences to study and halt "race degeneracy." The book itself repackaged eugenics as popular self-help. Declaring "vital surplus" the biological currency of every human being, the authors urged readers to accumulate more of that surplus through a balanced diet, fresh air, daily exercise, more time spent outdoors, and regular medical checkups. Periodic examinations, rare at the time, were at the heart of what the LEI was promoting. The goal was to funnel more clients into the life insurance industry by convincing them that health was manageable. The authors wanted to reassure Americans that they were perfectly capable of enhancing their lives and recharging the life force of the nation. Acts of biological citizenship, if rigorously performed, could "bring about the hereditary improvement of the race, generation by generation."[13]

As *How to Live* demonstrates, the name "Life Extension Institute" was a misnomer of sorts. Paramount to prolonging life was the LEI's mission to lengthen middle age. Midlife, once associated with a point of no return after which bodies started to wither, was redefined as the life stage at which men (and less so women) reached the pinnacle of their mental and productive powers. Extending middle age became synonymous with keeping bodies fit, efficient, and capable of driving economic growth. "When such ideals are attained, work instead of turning into drudgery tends to turn into play, and the hue of life seems to turn from dull gray to the bright tints of well-remembered childhood," the authors wrote. Sentences like these cloaked the capitalist need for a vibrant workforce in the romance of rejuvenation. Sure enough, the identification of age with productive function transcended social class. The well-heeled, too, had to be "a well-spring of energy" for as long as they could. Bosses who tired quickly risked losing the respect of the workers under their supervision. "We shall then . . . have a class of men old in years but young in vigor," Fisher rhapsodized in 1916, "men who will be able to apply their accumulated experience to our most complicated problems of social and political life!" Youth and age, it seemed, no longer depended on what someone's birth certificate said.[14]

Few broadcast the idea that Americans should be their own age engineers more vehemently than the LEI's medical director. Eugene Lyman Fisk was a crucial figure in the recasting of old age as personal failure. Uncertainties regarding his own birthday might have nurtured in him a dislike of calendar dates. Fisk regarded the traditional notion that old age was the inevitable result of time as a cheap excuse. People got old not because they had to but because they were lazy and ignorant. Aging was reversible or at least preventable, in much the same way that machines ran longer with proper maintenance. Labeling old age "a disease," Fisk suggested that it could be studied and treated like one. Although Fisk did not participate in number games, he was confident that the right combination of science and willpower could propel average life expectancies beyond the one hundred mark. Had the previous decades not already witnessed the grand workings of progress? Longevity enthusiasts envisioned seniors who were happy, healthy, and active members of society. Like good social Darwinists, they insinuated that those worn down by decrepitude had themselves to blame. Worse, the old put a burden on the healthy, draining precious resources required to maintain the nation's forward trajectory.[15]

In the eugenic imagination, national security hinged on managing the relative age of a population. World War I was a wake-up call for many in the movement. Even though the conflict cost fewer American lives relative to the enormous casualties suffered by European countries, it confronted US citizens with the destructiveness of large-scale modern war. Fitness tests administered to US army recruits in 1917 and 1918 showed worrying results. Among those drafted, about one-third of the young men between ages twenty-one and thirty-one were found too weak and sickly for active service. For Fisk and other physicians, the lack of robustness diagnosed in American youth was unbefitting a great power—a generation young in years but with old bodies.[16]

Unlike Progressive Era reformers who were simply lamenting that masculinity was in decline, LEI scientists generated massive amounts of data to back up that sentiment. Their publications included tables comparing the "degenerative tendencies among nations." The United States looked bad in many of these comparisons. Countries like Sweden, Great Britain, the Netherlands, and Germany beat the United States in vital statistics, including average height, weight, infant mortality, and lifespans. Conservative reformers blamed activists on the left. R. Austin Freeman, the popular British author of detective fiction, got a rave review in the *New York Times* for arguing that the path to rejuvenation would be wide open once nations disavowed collectivist philosophies that enabled "the unfit to become completely parasitic upon the fit." All that welfare advocates were trying to achieve, Fisher grumbled at a 1914 conference on "race betterment," was "prolong the lives of . . . the defective classes." Echoing Fisher's complaint, Fisk crunched numbers to prove that banning alcoholic beverages was warranted on the same grounds. Prohibition, he argued, prevented demographic decay. Back in 1890, the temperance reformer Frances Willard had already warned that failing to keep white people sober would empower "the colored race" who "multiplie[d] like the locusts of Egypt." The subtext was clear: fast-aging youths and degenerate drunkards could not be entrusted with defending the nation against adversaries foreign and domestic.[17]

But who, really, was the enemy? Lothrop Stoddard claimed he knew. This is the journalist who was famously laughed off the stage in 1929 after challenging W. E. B. Du Bois to a debate over Black demands for equality. His ideas about race, eugenics, and the rejuvenation of whiteness, however, were no laughing matter. Stoddard's career received a major boost in 1920 with the publication of *The Rising Tide of Color*, a 320-page harangue about the demographic threat posed to white civilization by the world's non-white population groups. Cited favorably by luminaries in politics and big business, the book rehashed common eugenic arguments: that white nations experiencing declining birth rates were risking "race suicide"; that the US government needed to prevent the immigration of undesirables, in particular Asians and Africans, but also Jews and Hispanics; and that segregation was the safest barrier against a "mongrel America." When talking about the world war, Stoddard went from racist alarm to reproductive panic. "All European belligerents are dangerously impoverished in their stock of youth," shorn of "maximum driving power and maximum plasticity of mind." Portraying the war as a fratricide between white nations that left behind masses of old and crippled people, Madison Grant, Stoddard's mentor, resented that "from the breeding point of view the little dark man is the final winner." For Stoddard and Grant, senescence imperiled the restoration of "white world supremacy" as much as miscegenation and homosexuality.[18]

Such sentiments were not confined to the printed page. Men like Stoddard and Arthur Estabrook, Davenport's protégé, started traveling the country armed with lantern slide presentations and the simple message that America would perish if regular folks would not do their part to turn the demographic tide. Eugenic popularizers had already joined forces with child welfare advocates in the 1910s at so-called baby shows. Prize committees made up of pediatricians and laypeople evaluated infants on the basis of height, weight, and the circumference of chest, head, and abdomen. After World War I, these better baby competitions grew into larger events that involved entire families. Movement leaders generously sponsored the first Fitter Family contests, which usually took place at agricultural fairs in Midwestern and Southern states (see figure 5.2). Committees linked livestock breeding to breeding humans. From father and mother down to the youngest child, families were graded with the help of scorecards that listed physical and mental traits. Winners would receive silver trophies and firm handshakes from US senators,

FIGURE 5.2 Fitter Family contest at the Kansas Free Fair, c. 1925. Agricultural shows served as important hubs for recruiting rural Americans to the eugenicist cause, which aimed for demographic rejuvenation through superior breeding. Courtesy of the American Philosophical Society.

who thanked the contestants for helping to secure white America's biological future. That humans were judged like cattle did not seem to bother the organizers. Their main concern was that rank-and-file Americans do their reproductive duties.[19]

As more eugenicists won a favorable hearing in the court of public opinion, leading advocates of sexual rejuvenation took note. Their problem was that they could spend all day marketing surgical procedures for repairing male potency as effective; it was not enough to burst the bubble of immorality surrounding them. After the first patients with animal testicles in their bodies began to realize that they continued to age as if nothing had happened, the complaints started mounting. Not a few pundits cackled that rejuvenated elders might wake up one morning behaving like primates. Others feared that the rush to youth would make society not younger but only more perverse. When *Black Oxen,* Gertrude Atherton's novel about a woman rediscovering her libido after having her ovaries irradiated, was published in 1923, it was banned in some towns in the United States. The topic was considered too bawdy. Atherton herself added to the controversy by disclosing that she had gone to Vienna to become one of the first women to get treated by Steinach. Here, rejuvenation did not represent the freedom of new beginnings. Instead, it evoked the specter of moral decline.[20]

Eugenics offered the glandular faction a lifeline. Grabbing it allayed fears that transplanting goat or monkey glands would open the floodgates of hedonism and create an army of oversexed seniors. "Does any scientific discovery of the ages exceed this in its importance to the individual and the race?" Voronoff asked readers from war-ravaged societies in 1920. Not one, seconded the German American sexologist Harry Benjamin, who became Steinach's biggest promoter in the United States. How much more could humankind achieve, Benjamin wondered, if all the world's "aging intellectual, political, and industrial leaders would be 'Steinached.'" They would stay young as they grew older, postpone generational change, and compensate for lackluster birth rates. However radical the science, the politics of rejuvenation in these circles had a strong conservative timbre.[21]

This discrepancy becomes clearer when considering which bodies were deemed worthy of overhaul and which ones were being cannibalized so that others could become young again. An early pioneer of glandular medicine, Chicago surgeon Frank Lydston performed a number of testicular transplantations in the 1910s. If successful, Lydston boasted, the novel procedure might prevent older men from losing their wits. The doctor did not seem very picky as to where the organs came from. Experimenting on himself in January 1914, Lydston extracted the gonads of an eighteen-year-old who had died in a car crash and had one of them stitched into his scrotum. Color, however, was the one line he dared not to cross. A rabid racist who stamped African American men as beastly sexual predators, Lydston wanted to see Black males found guilty of a crime sterilized so their genes would stay out of white bloodstreams. Leo Stanley, the chief surgeon of Saint Quentin Prison north of San Francisco, begged to differ. He believed that white masculinity could actually benefit from implanting Black body parts. During his bloody reign that lasted almost four decades, Stanley operated on more than 600 inmates, asserting that his work would help "cure" violent crime, homosexuality, and the frailties of old age. Three of the first four "donors," all men who were executed around 1918, were non-white; one of them was Fred Miller, a young African American whose glands Stanley grafted onto a seventy-two-year-old convict. The senior, Stanley gloated, woke up with more "jazz and pep," radiating the "energy of a man many years younger than he" was. Those who think sexual rejuvenation was all talk and no action should ponder the depths of inhumanity to which some white antiagers stooped.[22]

All the while, the professors put a genteel face on the grisly business of racial regeneration, justifying their prescriptions as a matter of self-defense. A war was raging for the body of the nation, and patriotic citizens had to keep themselves young and fresh to score "a major racial victory." These words, spoken by Charles Darwin's son Leonard, ignited a roar of recognition at a New York gathering of eugenicists in September 1921. Three months earlier, Fisher had warned in a speech at the laboratory in Cold Spring Harbor that the "Nordic race" would "vanish" unless something was done to "breed out the unfit." Across the United States, people were tapping their feet to the music of eugenic rejuvenation. They were tapping them in the halls of Congress, which passed the Johnson–Reed Act in 1924 to curtail immigration from Southern and Eastern European countries and shut out people from Asia. They were tapping them in universities, 376 of which offered courses in eugenics by the end of the decade. They were tapping them at barns in central Iowa, where whole families were smiling into the camera of a Fitter Family contest, hoping that they would be the lucky ones to take home the silver trophy awarded for best human pedigree. No one was to say when the music was going to stop.[23]

IN THE COLONY OF JOY, white merrymakers were dancing to an entirely different tune. Eugene Lesche, a shrewd businessman and the founder of a spa for rich elders, stood on the stage of a dance hall somewhere in upstate New York, egging on the colony's geriatric patrons. "Move to the music . . . to the gaily primitive rhythms of the first man. Be Adam again, be Eve. Be not afraid of life." He signaled to the jazz band to take it up a notch. Ecstatic tunes filled the room "with life and soul," and as the Black musicians picked up the pace, the dancers became more confident and less inhibited in their movements. Lesche's followers grew, and they began referring to him as the "New Leader" and to themselves as "New Men" and "New Women." Most appeared satisfied with the results of their "African exercises." Losing themselves to the music worked wonders on their tired bodies. Until disaster struck. A group of jealous Wall Street widows bickered for Lesche's attention; a love triangle broke up the band. One day shots rang out in the dance hall, causing the old to faint and the less old to run for their lives. That was how the Colony of Joy ended, leaving behind only mockery in the press and a stunning claim: Lesche, the great leader, was actually a Black man—"passing as white!"[24]

Neither Lesche nor the jazz retreat that made wealthy white New Yorkers believe they could pass as young existed in real life. Both were works of fiction conjured up by Langston Hughes, one of the most stirring voices of the

Harlem Renaissance. When "Rejuvenation through Joy" went into print in 1933 as part of a collection of short stories, Hughes had already seen a lot of the world. After finishing high school in Cleveland, he spent one year in Mexico, where he lived with his divorced father, and sailed to Europe and Africa working on a steamship. His rise to literary fame in 1920s Harlem was interspersed with temporary stays in Paris and London. In 1932, Hughes embarked on a seven-month tour of the Soviet Union together with twenty-two other African American artists, actors, and filmmakers. Appreciating the freedom of movement in a country unencumbered by Jim Crow restrictions, Hughes traveled from Leningrad to Turkmenistan to see what communism looked like on the cotton fields of Soviet Central Asia. As the train was rattling south, the Black poet enjoyed sitting in an unsegregated passenger car. Whenever the mood felt right, he took out his jazz albums and record player, playing Louis Armstrong and Duke Ellington to fellow travelers used to the sounds of a balalaika.[25]

To call Hughes the most influential jazz ambassador of the twentieth century who never mastered an instrument is not an exaggeration. The poet's task, he noted, was to put "jazz into words," to mimic the music's riffs, improvisations, and fiery exchanges. Hughes's early poems did just that, elevating the vibes and vernacular of Harlem's pulsating nightlife to a form of art. More than music, jazz sprang from the core of the African American experience. It was "one of the inherent expressions of Negro life in America: the eternal tom-tom beating in the Negro soul—the tom-tom of revolt against weariness in a white world, a world of subway trains, and work, work, work; the tom-tom of joy and laughter, and pain swallowed in a smile." Hughes wrote these lines, which became a cornerstone statement of the Harlem Renaissance, in response to an essay penned by George Schuyler in 1926. Schuyler had mocked the idea that an independent African American literary tradition could thrive in a white republic. Hughes (see figure 5.3) rejected that premise. Imitating an exhausted civilization was the worst thing a young Black artist could do. No middle ground seemed to exist between what one of Hughes's readers called "the fragile, sterile iciness and conventionality" of the whites and the "beating fire and laughter and virility" of Black culture. Instead, young Black artists should connect with the aboriginal vigor of their ancestors retained in jazz and blues and harness it for the cultural emancipation of the race.[26]

Primitivism was a fine line to walk if you were Black in the United States. Nostalgia for an imagined state of nature pervaded the modernist landscape. The seeds laid by painters like Paul Gauguin or Pablo Picasso, who felt invigo-

FIGURE 5.3 Portrait of Langston Hughes, 1943. A defining voice of the Harlem Renaissance, Hughes saw jazz music as advancing African American renewal but also as subject to white misappropriation. Courtesy of the Library of Congress Prints and Photographs Division.

rated by their encounters with the Global South, sprouted into opportunities for artists eager to discard staid bourgeoise conventions. Africa was suddenly en vogue in Western art, celebrated as a place unburdened by the cultural sclerosis brought about by industrialization and total war. Once signs of debauchery, nudity and savagery were being reframed as a tonic against modernity's diseases: congested cities, sexual repression, soulless technology. Josephine Baker, who danced to transatlantic stardom on stages in New York, Paris, and Berlin, spent much of her career catering to this urge, whipping theatergoers into a frenzy with her lascivious moves.[27]

Yet, it was one thing to feel rejuvenated by the primitivist surge and quite another to be caught in its gaze. For as much as white peddlers of the "primitive" craved the undiluted energy associated with it, they still viewed it as inferior and less evolved. The infantilization of colonized peoples can be traced back to the days of Columbus, but one is struck by how much Western artists and educators in the early twentieth century relied on children to convey the values of savagery. Gauguin's Tahitian paintings, replete with seminude underage girls posing in wild nature, represented the antithesis to European decadence. Youth organizations such as the Woodcraft Indians and the Boy Scouts encouraged white middle-class children to "play Indian." The fundamental difference between these two settings was that in one, the young were supposed to mature into responsible adults whereas their development appears arrested in the other. White primitivism, in its most extreme form, could not bear the thought of people of color growing up. The conduit to an Eden-like paradise, where cynical souls might be refreshed and fatigued bodies restored, would be irrevocably lost. Euro-Americans practicing colonialism, thus, were more than inclined to treat the "primitive" as another resource to plunder and possess.[28]

Alain Locke, one of the leading theorists of the Harlem Renaissance, was well aware of this predicament when he collaborated with thirty-three African American intellectuals for an anthology that hit the shelves in 1925. Boldly titled *The New Negro*, the book announced a seismic shift along the lines of age and agency. Critics have labeled the anthology disjointed, but imposing uniformity on a new generation of African American artists was never the intention. The point was to emphasize the diversity of this creative class, forged in the crucibles of migration and urbanization, and to use new representations of Blackness to debunk the old ones—monolithic "stock figure[s] perpetuated as a historical fiction." Actual youth was crucial to shedding this fiction and, with it, the inferiority complex it had bred in the descendants of the enslaved. Many Black artists were still trying to find their voice, molding words, playing with style, and experimenting with substance, but that did not matter as long as they ended up providing "a healthy antidote to Puritanism." A "lusty vigorous realism" propelled them forward, past Jim Crow's degrading minstrel shows and racial slurs. "Thoroughly modern" of their own volition, they cared little about meeting white expectations. "If America were deaf, they would still sing," Locke remarked.[29]

But America was listening. Jazz swept the country from coast to coast, influencing those enthralled by it in dress, language, and attitudes toward racial mixing. Already nightclubs in New York, San Francisco, and Chicago were opening their doors to jazz lovers regardless of skin color. Though still small at a time when segregation was the norm, this burgeoning interracial clientele, largely urban and middle class, raised urgent questions on both sides of the color line. A strikingly optimistic assessment flew from the pen of the Jamaican-born critic Joel Augustus Rogers, who viewed jazz as a potential game changer in US race relations. In his contribution to Locke's anthology, he described the music as both authentically Black and decidedly transnational. Its hybrid mix of influences contrasted vividly with the "sordidness" and "sorrow" of "convention-bound society." However, Rogers was not interested in passing aesthetic judgment. He wanted jazz to carry out a "popular mission," to put its "mocking disregard of formalities" in the service of tearing down artificial barriers in human relations. For Rogers, jazz was "rejuvenation," plain and simple: it "recharged the batteries of civilization with primitive new vigor" and permitted Americans to start over after the horrors of war. Rogers's concept of rejuvenation was transactional. He presented jazz as "a balm for modern ennui" in a depleted white culture. In return, Rogers hoped that African Americans would gain recognition and rights for the restorative work they performed.[30]

Rogers's faith in jazz as a leveler and maker of interracial democracy sounds overly upbeat in hindsight. To Hughes, it also sounded premature. He believed that the paramount task of modern Black art was to create safe spaces in which African Americans could be sincere, smart, beautiful, and alive *as* African Americans. Hughes kept insisting that jazz was empowering. Grinning "jungle joys" in the heat of the music allowed Blacks to cast off the shackles of racist oppression and reconnect to their primitive—in a sense their younger precolonial—selves. The "eternal tom-tom" was theirs to treasure, not for whites to steal or scorn. Even if jazz had this revivifying effect on a dying aristocracy, there was little evidence that the ruling class, once refreshed, would be willing to give up their privileges. Reading white appraisals of the Harlem Renaissance must have confirmed Hughes's suspicion that whites frequenting Black neighborhoods in search of release did not have African Americans' best interest in mind. The renowned journalist H. L. Mencken showered *The New Negro* with toxic praise, lauding the book as a "phenomenon of immense significance" before maligning the great mass of Black people as "two or three inches removed from gorillas." Hughes distrust of white patronage also shone through in more cordial interactions. Winold Reiss's famous 1926 portrait of Hughes positions the Black poet in front of a blue art deco background, with Hughes looking longingly away, as if he wanted to evade the painter's judging eye. Compared to Rogers, Hughes understood art in essentialist terms, but his essentialism was a form of self-defense. In a country where some African American men were cheered for their exuberant art while others were being lynched, interracial partnerships could only be brittle.[31]

The same can be said of the Black musicians who, barred from performing at upper-crust clubs, found themselves playing at bars and bordellos run by notorious mobsters. Prohibition-era gangsters hired jazz bands to mark urban territory and lure white customers into their establishments. Black band members, in turn, sought a stable income and protection from police violence. But in the underworlds of Chicago, New York, and New Orleans, mafia bosses wrote the rules. Few were concerned with the safety of the people working for them. Black performers could be fired at a moment's notice, and most were treated little better than porters or busboys. In the eyes of the state, the symbiotic yet uneven relationships that evolved between leading African American jazz musicians and powerful mobsters, including Al Capone and Mickey Cohen, hardened associations of Blackness with crime. Once the party stopped, Black lives were still demeaned and endangered by racist terror.[32]

Hughes's anger at these exploitative mechanisms was palpable, even when clothed in satire. Hilarious at times, "Rejuvenation through Joy" stands as a sober warning against the kind of utopian interracialism outlined by Rogers. To be frank, Hughes does not invalidate the idea at the core of the story. The primitive jazz, along with the swaying exercises, actually reinvigorates the wealthy seniors residing at the Colony of Joy, much more so than the other youth cults of the day. Lesche's motives, however, are monetary all along. His shady business practices are only overshadowed by the gullibility of his customers who purchase a product they can neither grasp nor control. The pact between Lesche and New York's moneyed elites is symbolically etched into the instruments of the musicians, who sell their rejuvenationist labor to the highest bidder. "It's unbelievable how they need what we got," Lesche's companion Sol says at one point. But this inversion of power relations does not last. The same therapeutic force that renews the aging representatives of the old order also props up its racist and capitalist foundations. Greed and envy lead to Joy's downfall, washing away the egalitarian promise found in jazz.[33]

Hughes arrived in the Soviet Union a tired man, fatigued by the life-sapping realities of segregation but also exhausted by members of his own community. Exposing mainstream rejuvenation as a siren song that lured people of color into a white supremacist trap was a message not every Black person was willing to hear. Instead, African American newspapers celebrating Black excellence in the arts also featured advertisements for rather dubious products. Beginning in 1923, major Black dailies opened their columns to a revitalizing compound named "Korex." Black men who had taken these pills, the ads bragged, no longer suffered from "lost manhood" and felt young, like they were thirty again. Korex turned out to be a massive scam. In 1927, the man operating it out of Kansas City was sentenced to two years in prison and payments totaling $10,000. Other African Americans did not reject eugenics wholesale. Their contention was that its teachings could be tweaked to enhance the biological fitness and hence the respectability of the Black race. Even an organization as reputable as the NAACP was prepared to dance on that tightrope, lending its support to Black beauty pageants and better baby contests. That African Americans were a people uniquely gifted with talent and youth was a proposition that few Black leaders disagreed with at the time. Where they differed was whether that gift needed to be confidently shared or cautiously guarded.[34]

IF THERE EVER WAS a mass spectacle devoted to promoting the new man in the liberal democratic mold, the national jamboree held in Washington, D.C., over ten hot July days in 1937 came pretty close. More than 27,000 Boy Scouts from all corners of the United States, plus a couple hundred youths from other countries, built a tent city on the National Mall, where they entertained several high-ranking celebrities, including President Franklin Delano Roosevelt (FDR), with their camping and woodcraft skills. The organizers emphasized that American scoutcraft was not the only thing they had come to celebrate. "Over the world we hear the tramp of the feet of youth . . . in so many places youth exploited, youth regimented, youth mobilized for selfish aims," BSA executive George J. Fisher noted. But not in Washington, where the boys were listening not to "shouting dictators" but to "the spirits of Washington and Lincoln that were among them." This was not an assembly of doddering old men and flabby youths, as foreign propagandists had sneered. "Democracy is young," another BSA official exclaimed, and there was no reason its defenders should bow to "the goose-stepping black shirts or brown shirts of Italy and Germany."[35]

It is hard to tell whether American youth workers who made these statements meant what they said, or whether they were whistling in the dark. Questions about democracy's true age sparked passionate disagreements in a world roiled by economic woes and ideological extremes. Radical alternatives articulated on the left drew inspiration from the October Revolution of 1917, which ousted Russia's teetering liberals and projected a bright future for the working classes. Bolshevism was steeped in the rhetoric of generational warfare. Party leaders whitewashed mass death and suffering with metahistorical narratives of aristocratic grandfathers and bourgeois fathers being dethroned by revolutionary youth—according to Lenin, the only force capable of waging "a self-sacrificing struggle against the old rottenness." Political gerontocide was to pave the way for the creation of the new Soviet person, a youthful citizen-comrade uncompromisingly committed to freeing humanity from the twin evils of capitalism and imperialism.[36]

To those watching from afar, the Soviet revolt against hereditary systems of privilege signaled a perilous inversion of traditional age relations. Youth and rejuvenation sat in opposite corners, staring each other down. The same revolution that victimized millions of children also proved empowering to young people identifying with the cause. Young adults and teenagers flocked en masse to the Red Guards, the Komsomol, and other revolutionary institutions, ready to tear down the remnants of the old order. Stories of thirteen-year-olds denouncing their fathers to the political police threatened to further erode adult authority in societies where, like in Russia, the war had left a demographic void. The need for acquitting "the old" was particularly pressing in light of postwar disputes about who was to blame for the immense loss of young lives—disputes that carried the tonality of ageism rather than party politics. More often than not, the red scares gripping Western nations after the Bolshevik coup evolved into full-fledged youth scares. In conservative readings of the communist script, young people dancing at jazz clubs, drinking alcohol, and dating without their parents' permission figured as vanguards of a dangerous alien ideology. Once these deviants started wearing their political colors openly, these fearmongers warned, they would not hesitate to make short shrift of their elders' values, perhaps even of the elders themselves.[37]

Mortal enemies on the battlefield, fascists and communists glorified youth-driven action in similar ways. Both actively recruited young foot soldiers to guarantee the durability of their regimes. But unlike their adversaries on the left, far-right ideologues enlisted youth for the rejuvenation of mythic national pasts. From Mussolini's March on Rome in 1922 to Hitler's rise to the chancellorship in 1933, interwar fascists staged their "seizures of power" as virile acts carried out by revolutionaries who were young in body and spirit. Claiming to be one with youth, they turned age into a moral-political category—a remarkable move for radical nationalists who held the biological foundations of race and citizenship sacrosanct. Shouting "Make Way, You Old Men!" as their boots thundered on cobblestones, Nazi militias expressed their determination to crush the feeble custodians of Weimar Germany's democratic constitution. Young/old binaries marked the distinction between a muscular fascism and a liberal order depicted as weak and sclerotic. For the Nazi publicist Alfred Rosenberg, the supporters of democracy were automatically old, regardless of whether they were sixteen or sixty-six. Senile liberals, Rosenberg added, were easy prey for "parasites" bent on exploiting the *Volk*. Ageism and antisemitism worked in tandem in caricatures that portrayed Jewish bankers as portly old men with top hats and exaggerated facial features lusting for young blonde virgins. For the nation to awake to new life, fascists declared an all-out war against senescence, which they located less in actual seniors than in groups they excluded from their vision of a rejuvenated national community.[38]

Americans following the violent rise of these alternative modernities during the Depression years could not find solace in the fact that an ocean separated them from distant regime changes. Interwar communism and fascism were global movements, and their allure extended to US households. Youth activist Viola Ilma, the founder of the left-leaning American Youth Congress, wanted her country's rising generation to work for a better society with the same kind of idealism that she had experienced when she visited Berlin in 1933. Meanwhile, conservative Americans traveling to Europe often returned with a sense of dread, wondering whether the clouds of conflict that hovered over the new dictatorships forecast bad political weather for the United States. Young people growing up materially deprived and morally disoriented appeared particularly prone to be led astray. On his trip to Hungary in 1935, the clergyman Daniel A. Poling was taken aback by the masses of militarized adolescents who were "marching for war, and not for peace." These were not the rebellious young revelers of the twenties. These were uniformed fanatics ready to lash out at everyone who stepped out of line. "What of our own young people?" the journalist Maxine Davis asked her American readers in 1936. "They have been living through the same dark days that caused their foreign brothers to see Hitler and Mussolini and Lenin appear as leaders bathed in light. Can we depend on them now to live and work and carry on in our own beliefs in democracy, individual liberty, and freedom? Or will they, cynical, dissatisfied, revolt against the established order and lead us into strange and dangerous ways?"[39]

Preventing the young from revolting was one of the New Deal's objectives. But first, FDR and his team of reformers had to keep the old from collapsing. FDR's famous 1932 campaign pledge to put the nation on the road to recovery happened at a time of crushing want. Roughly 20 million Americans were out of a job. Stocks and average wages had been plummeting, and homes and farms were lost to foreclosure. Countless people, including children, went to bed hungry. The platform that got Roosevelt elected was a balancing act. It lauded the resiliency of the liberal creed while blaming a feckless Republican elite for grossly violating it. A sacred tradition had been damaged and needed to be repaired through "direct, vigorous action," Roosevelt promised at his inauguration on March 4, 1933.[40]

The Democrat in the White House could not afford to be modest. His job was to bring relief to millions of Americans, but also to prove to the world that liberal democracy had enough muscle to bounce back from an existential crisis. This was a tall order, especially for a politician who had been sitting in a wheelchair ever since a polio infection had paralyzed him from the waist down. Presenting to the public an image of himself as able-bodied—Roosevelt forbade any pictures that showed him immobilized or reliant on physical assistance—became a crucial corollary to underscoring the fitness of the nation over which he presided. To project the masculine strength the office of the presidency required, FDR had learned to walk short distances with leg braces and stand upright clutching the speaker's podium. With his muscular upper frame and disarming smile, Roosevelt exuded a boyish optimism, a cheerful can-do spirit that made him seem qualified for the difficult task of reconstruction that lay ahead.[41]

Having reclaimed some of the vestiges of his younger self, Roosevelt set out to win the trust of the nation's youngest men. The Civilian Conservation Corps (CCC), established four weeks after FDR had taken the oath of office, became a centerpiece of that effort (see figure 5.4). In terms of numbers and duration, the CCC was among the most impactful agencies growing out of the New Deal. From its inception in 1933 to its war-related demise in 1942, the CCC gave employment to more than 3 million young men between the ages of eighteen and twenty-five. Living together in army-like camps and working under the open skies, the enrollees built roads, modernized national parks,

FIGURE 5.4 Poster promoting the Civilian Conservation Corps (CCC), 1939. More than a relief program for young men, the CCC symbolized the US government's effort to "rejuvenate" liberal democracy against the twin threat of economic depression and foreign dictatorships. Courtesy of the Wisconsin Historical Society.

and planted billions of trees. Sending young men into the "great outdoors" to learn discipline and companionship clearly echoed the Progressive Era roots of organizations like the Boy Scouts, which Roosevelt admired.[42]

On an international scale, the CCC was the New Deal's answer to the masculinist vision of rejuvenating civic pride through the taming of nature. Not only was the United States able to pull off what Germany was trying to achieve with the Nazi Labor Service. More importantly, the country, under the Roosevelt administration, sought to prove that mass schemes used to mobilize and strengthen bodies in dictatorships worked even better when adjusted to the goal of fertilizing democracy's aging soil. Letters written by young enrollees show that faith in the CCC's regenerative qualities trickled down into the consciousness of the rank-and-file. John E. Hussey from Johnstown, Pennsylvania, discovered "a new born fighting spirit" within him and declared that joining the CCC had made him a better American. Karl Kidd, another young volunteer, agreed. Working with others to improve the nation's parks and roads had built in him "a strong and more enduring faith . . .

that restores belief in one's physical, mental and spiritual self, in his associates, and in the future."[43]

Such testimonials were hardly representative, and the optimism of some volunteers faded quickly once they left camp and struggled to find a job. Still, they were music to the ears of policymakers who contended that the dozens of federal programs and agencies created to combat the Depression were bold but far from extreme. In seeking to reconcile the nation's youth with a reformed capitalism, New Dealers wanted the United States to appear young again. They were, in the words of the media tycoon Henry Luce, aiming for the "rejuvenation of the now decayed and outmoded idea of democracy itself." Although Luce disliked FDR and criticized much of the New Deal, he appreciated the rehabilitation effort. Roosevelt's antiradicalism also surfaced in his "Quarantine Speech" in Chicago on October 5, 1937. Rather than prescribe dangerous therapies, he wanted to boost the nation's immune system against a spreading "epidemic of world lawlessness." Rejuvenation meant keeping the historical core of US democracy intact, its established hierarchies of race and gender included.[44]

All this was accompanied by a state-sponsored explosion of visual culture that centered on the regenerative value of shared physical labor. The Works Progress Administration (WPA), installed in May 1935, hired more than 50,000 artists who made crafts, sculptures, and paintings for government buildings. About 1,400 murals alone would embellish the walls of post offices across the country, many of which showed muscle-packed workers standing at assembly lines or bringing home a bountiful harvest. Such depictions had been a preferred tool of artists affiliated with labor unions and socialist groups who used murals to spread revolutionary ideas. This was less the case with the public artwork paid by the WPA, which replaced an emphasis on class struggle with representations of masculine camaraderie that extended across all sectors of the economy. The message emanating from these murals was that the country's ailing institutions could be strong-armed back to the confidence and health of a young man. America's manly workers with their big shoulders and patriotic hearts would get the job done.[45]

The CCC encapsulated this element of conservative reform. The New Deal's version of affirmative action, as historian Ira Katznelson contended, was largely white and male, focused on recuperating the male breadwinner who had been forced to stand in long lines outside soup kitchens. Some New Deal programs catered to both sexes. The CCC, however, excluded women (despite the efforts of First Lady Eleanor Roosevelt to launch a smaller corps for females). Its leaders hated the idea of women competing with men for jobs and leadership positions in mass organizations. African and Native Americans were admitted but placed in segregated camps. Indigenous men took jobs under the auspices of a separate corps that recognized tribal institutions. At the same time, government officials discouraged native peoples from leaving the reservations. African American volunteers, on whom the Depression had taken a harsh toll, were given work in Black-only camps where conditions were meager. The CCC's director, Robert Fechner, was relentless about enforcing racial discrimination. A white Southerner who sought to avoid any substantial breach of the color line, Fechner oversaw a nationwide classification system that marked areas where Black workers were housed with a "C" (for "colored), in part to keep them distant from white communities that harbored suspicions about unmarried African American men.[46]

As the decade went on, blatant displays of racism proved harder to square with the New Deal's lofty vision of a fraternity of citizens serving a common cause. In the age of mass politics, national vitality was increasingly measured by how many young and fit bodies the state was able to muster. Whether these bodies had the same worth and status was a secondary issue. US elites understood that they were facing a worrying trend. Democracies were perishing. In Europe alone, thirteen out of twenty-six states that had been republics in 1920 had turned into dictatorships by 1938. And the United States was not just any democracy, even less so by its own standards. The world was watching whether Americans were capable of outmobilizing and outperforming their youth-obsessed fascist and communist rivals. In this global-ideological standoff, calls to take full advantage of the nation's subaltern manpower gradually drowned out eugenic voices clamoring for racial purity.

Still, lukewarm tolerance was often the best that non-white Americans could hope for. When Fred Ames, a Black Boy Scout from Rhode Island, was told by local Scout executives that he better skip the 1937 national jamboree in Washington, D.C., because the color of his skin would make him a target for bigots from the South, the NAACP rose up in protest. Talking a young Black patriot out of making the trip to the nation's capital, Assistant Secretary Roy Wilkins declared, was wholly inconsistent with the "tolerance and fair play" that characterized "real American citizenship." The jamboree organizers scrambled to repair the damage. Ames eventually traveled to Washington at the personal invitation of Chief Scout Executive James E. West of the BSA. After a cordial handshake and a brief exchange of niceties, Ames was shown his quarters: an all-Black section of the campground, furnished with its own segregated dining facility. The liberal new man, it seemed, gladly accepted the sword of democratic pluralism reforged in a time of crisis. But when it came to striking a blow for racial equality, the blade turned out to be disappointingly blunt.[47]

The New Deal's record on race has been hotly debated. The devil is in the details, and for every objectionable decision that reinforced segregation, one can find evidence that many of the social policies of the 1930s ended a long period of governmental neglect toward the suffering of minorities. Conservatives denounced FDR's government as a socialist cabal precisely because of programs such as the "Indian New Deal." The threat of a far-right power grab also split the eugenic community, with some turning their backs on the belief that the "unfit" should be weeded out instead of being granted the right to a happy life. Others continued to openly express their admiration for Hitler's Germany. Lothrop Stoddard received red-carpet treatment when he visited Berlin in 1939. Harry H. Laughlin, the superintendent of the Eugenics Record Office and a staunch supporter of forced sterilization, greeted the eugenic policies of the Nazi regime as a milestone on the road to creating a master race. Heidelberg University returned the favor in 1936. Its medical faculty awarded Laughlin an honorary doctorate for his research, which had given Nazi legislators a template for their own compulsory sterilization laws. US eugenicists' cordial ties with German race scientists persisted throughout the decade. Preventing the dystopia of a "people without youth"—code for the looming extinction of the white race—overrode any attempt at democratic reform.[48]

Langston Hughes felt nothing but contempt for people like Laughlin. Yet his opinion of Roosevelt was not much better. Hughes had returned from the Soviet Union convinced that white Americans had a long way to go until they were prepared to cast off their blinders and realize that the thing they called democracy was not worth preserving. Seeing how the Depression had turned his beloved Harlem from a center of cultural vibrancy into an almshouse hardened that stance. "I'm tired / O' waitin' on Roosevelt, / Roosevelt, Roosevelt. / Damn tired o' waitin' on Roosevelt," Hughes wrote in 1934. For the disenchanted poet, a national effort that promised to make the country whole again while leaving its poorest citizens exhausted was a sham. As the United States was edging closer to another world war, its landscapes of rejuvenation were as fractured as ever. With an ominous geopolitical threat nearing, few cared to take a deep hard look at these fault lines.[49]

CHAPTER SIX

Boy Nations

Rejuvenating Defeated Germany and Japan

When I was 11 my parents
had raised me the wrong way
Kilroy made the effort
taught me human rights
& the UN Charter
reinstructed me.

—Yaak Karsunke, "Kilroy Was Here" (1967)

The fate of America's Caesar hung in the balance when he arrived on Capitol Hill on May 3, 1951. General Douglas MacArthur had been summoned before the Senate to defend his record in East Asia, where the United States and its allies were bogged down in a vicious war against communist North Korea and China. In his opening testimony, which went over six hours, MacArthur did not pull any punches. He railed against his recent dismissal, called for the complete annihilation of the enemy, and slammed President Harry Truman's foreign policy as spineless. When asked about his time as the Allied commander of occupied Japan, MacArthur's frown suddenly disappeared. Gone was the irascible general whose inclination to ignore Truman's orders had led to his firing. Underscoring the tremendous progress the Japanese had made since the end of World War II, MacArthur now talked like a loving father about his children. He explained that despite its ancient origins, Japan was by no means an old culture. "Measured by the standards of modern civilization, they would be like a boy of twelve as compared with our development." Raised the right way, a preadolescent Japan could mature into a reliable ally. His tutelage had laid the groundwork, MacArthur insisted, and Americans better think twice before replacing him with a second-rate commander.[1]

This kind of language was not unique to how MacArthur vindicated his postwar assignment. In 1943, while the campaign to subdue the Axis powers was in full swing, the Swiss author Emil Ludwig held that Germany had forfeited any right to be treated like a responsible adult. Here was a nation that had strayed from the path of civilization and decided to follow the pied pipers of militarism and conquest instead. The only hope for correction lay in demoting the country back to a childlike state and placing it under rigorous supervision. Germany, Ludwig wrote, had "to be handled as a gifted but dangerous boy who must be watched and controlled by strict though well-meaning masters." Ludwig joined a group of Western intellectuals who were deploying metaphors of immaturity and dependency to convince US citizens that lengthy foreign occupations were necessary to fundamentally alter the national character of America's enemies. Viewed in that light, Nazi Germany came to resemble a boyish rogue state, a juvenile delinquent who had misbehaved so severely that the full force of US parental authority was needed to put him in his place.[2]

Mid-century Americans could well afford to feel like they were the adults in the room. The Japanese attack on Pearl Harbor on December 7, 1941, effectively submerged the insecurities of the Depression Era. Old doubts were washed away by a steely determination to defeat the Axis menace. World War II revealed to many the awesome reach of US power as the nation's soldiers stormed foreign beaches and its factories churned out guns, tanks, and airplanes at unrivaled speed. Declaring the twentieth century an American one, Henry Luce once again gauged the country's relative age. A big maturity test was underway that would show whether "the most powerful and the most vital nation in the world" would be able to leave behind childish things and assume the mantle of leadership. For Luce, isolationism had been akin to an adolescent caught up in selfish pursuits. The true badge of political adulthood came with accepting the duties and opportunities of US international influence. Men like Luce described the era of the world wars not only in terms of collective sacrifice but also as a period of national ripening. They found in age an appropriate yardstick for gauging their country's ascendancy and the responsibilities that entailed.[3]

This chapter deviates from the others in that it approaches rejuvenation as something Americans did not merely practice on themselves. Lowering the age of foreign dependents became a meaningful component of US imperial policy in an era of fierce global-ideological conflict. My use of the word *imperial* is deliberate because putting a rejuvenationist glaze on US postwar occupation drew on earlier forms of colonial tutelage. The history of Western colonialism is stacked with examples of expanding empires rationalizing unequal power relations between the conquerors and conquered on the basis of age. Claims of intrinsic differences that gave imperialists cover for annexing the lands of others were never just expressed in overtly racist ways. Discourses of infantilization offered a softer yet equally cunning case for empire, especially since they were capable of accommodating more progressive models of modernization and development. Infantilism often operated in tandem with racism and sexism, applying the same arguments used to consign women to second-class citizenship to colonial subjects. Comparisons of women and people of color with children cast both as too irrational and immature to thrive without benign masculine protectors. The result was degrading epithets such as "little brown brothers," which was how advocates of a strong US presence in the Philippines liked to call the locals.[4]

Readers may chafe at putting the Allied crusade against Nazism alongside the subjugation of non-white peoples. Let me assure you that I would be the last person to endorse such cheap analogies. There is a world of difference between the young GIs who liberated the oldest Nazi concentration camp in Dachau and the US soldiers who, forty years earlier, had tortured Filipino insurgents by pouring water down their throat. Yet, it bears remembering that identifying overlapping dynamics in two seemingly unrelated historical contexts does not make them morally equivalent. Advocates of US colonial rule after 1898 and pro-occupation policymakers after 1945 both needed to mobilize public support for costly overseas interventions with no clear end dates. In both cases, Americans put out narratives of manly civilizers exporting liberty and progress to benighted parts of the globe. And in both cases, local populations experienced forced rejuvenation, during which occupiers stripped them of their adult privileges and hence of their claims to sovereign citizenship.

Forced rejuvenation was not the only principle that governed relationships between victors and vanquished in the aftermath of World War II. The kind of retributive justice practiced at the international war crime trials of Nuremberg and Tokyo required treating imperial Japanese leaders and their Nazi counterparts as fully accountable adults. Nor did forced rejuvenation look the same in occupied Germany and defeated Japan, as US citizens viewed both countries through different lenses. Overall, however, ageist tropes deployed to justify the exercise of disciplinary power over these boy nations undergirded US reeducation policies in the 1940s and 1950s. The boyhood metaphor gained plausibility from the fact that the war had left the Axis nations in demographic shambles. Fatherless children, war widows, and the relative absence of men in their prime contributed to the image of dysfunctional societies incapable of renewing themselves without intervention from the outside. In portraying the loss of national sovereignty as a loss of maturity, the victors inverted a common stereotype: a supposedly young United States took on the role of ersatz parent of older nations thrown back into a state of quasi-colonial infancy.[5]

When reeducators talked about boys instead of girls or children more broadly, they did so for a reason. Enemy nations had to be reconstructed in alignment with US interests. This included making sure that nonconforming gender identities would not gain any traction in the process. In fact, many of the programs implemented to teach Japanese and German survivors the values of American-style democracy mirrored the wish to return to prewar assumptions about the proper relationship of men and women. At a time when national clocks were reset to the very beginning—the Germans called it *Stunde Null* ("zero hour")—women were often the first to clear the rubble and rebuild. Female civic participation increasingly clashed with the expectation that women play their part in restoring a natural order of separate spheres and leave the task of learning the hard lessons of democratic statecraft to boys and men. Embracing a conservative approach to nation-building helped reeducators deflect from the sexual permissiveness among US servicemen and local women. Part of a larger project of collective purification, compliance with traditional gender roles would transform former enemies into fledgling, well-ordered democracies and facilitate their reentry into the family of free nations.[6]

Apprentices were everywhere in the postwar laboratories of reeducation. Labor leaders were taught to see in capitalism a partner rather than a predicament. Journalists were expected to unlearn the propaganda methods of the past and refamiliarize themselves with liberal conventions of objective reporting. Housewives were encouraged to find self-fulfillment in adopting a modern consumer lifestyle. Young people got the most attention. The historian Petra Goedde gave a compelling explanation for why US officials put youth front and center. First, young people were regarded as less encumbered by the past and more malleable than their elders. Second, youth represented a form of "infantile citizenship" that could only prosper with fatherlike guidance—according to Goedde, the perfect formula for imposing "democracy on another people through essentially undemocratic means." Friendly exchanges between local children and US soldiers, whether these involved chocolate bars and candies, boxcar races or joint summer camps, evolved into symbolically charged events, with the occupiers standing in as benign schoolmasters and the children as representatives of a forcibly rejuvenated but grateful population.[7]

The argument proceeds in three steps. The first part sketches colonial precursors to post-1945 US reeducation schemes, particularly the tendency to infantilize subjugated peoples. Five decades of US colonial rule in the Philippines, Hawaii, and Puerto Rico offered a treasure trove of experience for scientists, philanthropists, and military and state officials trying to turn hostile populations into junior partners of America's free-world empire. The second section takes a close look at the West German case, where reeducation veered between suggesting to locals that political adulthood could be regained through good conduct and inviting them to distance themselves from the crimes committed in wartime. The focus then shifts to Japan to discuss the extent to which racist perceptions of East Asia accounted for differences in how infantilization and democracy promotion played out in both countries. Whenever feasible, those rejuvenated against their volition will get a say as well. Counteracting the occupiers' intentions, some rejected the infant citizen label outright while others shrewdly sought to use it to their advantage.

"GOSH! I wish they wouldn't come quite so many in a bunch, but, if I've got to take them, I guess I can do as well by them as I've done by the others!" Political cartoons featuring a fatherly Uncle Sam taking dark-skinned children under his wing were hard to miss in the summer of 1898. Taking stock of the recent victory over Spain, *Puck Magazine* printed one such cartoon by Joseph Keppler Jr. that showed Uncle Sam running a foundling asylum together with Lady Columbia. In the background, four children are holding hands, dancing merrily inside the asylum walls. Each one signifies a territory or people already under US jurisdiction or influence (Texas, California, Mexico, Native Americans). Standing at the front gate are Uncle Sam and Lady Columbia, both staring in amazement at a basket of four crying babies handed to them by two strong arms tattooed with the words "Manifest Destiny." The babies, two Hispanic, one Polynesian and the other one South Asian, bear the names Cuba, Puerto Rico, Hawaii, and the Philippines. Viewers at the time would have instantly recognized them as Spain's former colonies, which had come into the United States' expanding imperial orbit.[8]

There is a lot to unpack in that image. The maternal and the masculine traits of the nation are clearly anchored in the adult couple, with Uncle Sam dominating the picture as the asylum's chief proprietor and protector. His development into a figure of imperial authority was gradual rather than sudden. Many turn-of-the-century cartoonists liked to align Uncle Sam, the personification of assertive Yankeedom, with jingoistic themes of national pride and condescension, but critics of empire made him an object of rhetorical struggle by presenting him as an advocate for restraint. Reworking Uncle Sam into America's educator-in-chief was an attempt to reconcile both positions and consolidate his meaning as the embodiment of a powerful, stern, yet also kindhearted force for good. Louis Dalrymple's *School Begins,* published

FIGURE 6.1 Louis Dalrymple, "School Begins," 1899. Published in the aftermath of the Spanish–American War, this cartoon justifies US imperialism by depicting the new colonies as unruly children in need of Uncle Sam's guidance. *Puck Magazine*, January 1899.

in January 1899, was another famous caricature that disseminated this motif (see figure 6.1). It depicts Uncle Sam in a classroom setting trying to teach discipline to four new students. Cuba, Puerto Rico, Hawaii, and the Philippines, all portrayed as disgruntled children of color with adult faces, are unhappy with their situation. They have a hard time following their instructor. His rod, meanwhile, points to the blackboard behind the young colonials, which reads: "The U.S. must govern its new territories with or without their consent until they can govern themselves."[9]

Rewriting colonial annexations into an empire of care relied heavily on such iconographic arrangements. A skeptical public, it seems, had to be swayed into believing that expanding the nation's influence abroad was not driven by selfish greed but by an intrinsically righteous Americanism. Those who were not easily convinced were exposed to ridicule. In May 1899, Dalrymple depicted the opponents of overseas expansion as old "aunties," suggesting that they lacked proper manhood and patriotism. Empire was presented as a higher duty, much like the moral obligations of fatherhood. Keppler's Uncle Sam does not actively seek new children but accepts the ones placed in his custody. Imperialists across the globe held that they were bringing an advanced culture to backward tribes. Seen from this vantage point, images of foster fathers or teacher-student relationships reflected the same assumptions that resonated from the French civilizing mission or informed the poet Rudyard Kipling's famous plea that Anglo-Saxon Americans assist their British cousins in taking up the "white man's burden." What made trans-imperial narratives about raising "new-caught sullen peoples, half devil and half child" so effective was the way in which they trivialized colonial violence. Instead of shining a light on the deadly volleys fired from Euro-American rifles, they feigned parental concern over unruly children who had to be chastised once in a while.[10]

US cartoonists did not pick blonde girls with blue eyes to infantilize distant populations. The children they drew were dark and petulant, often poorly clothed or half-naked to evoke associations of racial inferiority. Contrary to white children, the caricatured colonials lacked not only proper manners but, more significantly, proper families. Colonial wars of subjugation, including the Philippine–American War and the Moro Rebellion that broke out after the United States had taken control of the archipelago, left countless children orphaned. Drawings that depicted natives as fatherless and mother-less youths made light of the deliberate destruction of Indigenous families. To the general public and policymakers who consumed these generalizations, they suggested that aboriginal peoples did not have any traditions that white societies were bound to respect. Mainstream Americans thought of Filipinos and Puerto Ricans more as cultural than literal orphans. Without a capable white male pedagogue willing to engage in the selfless work of racial uplift, they would face extinction.

Portraying island children in the company of domestic minorities tells a story of imperial continuation rather than a tale of an inexperienced young nation entering the world stage. The older students in Uncle Sam's class, African and Native Americans in particular, figured as allegorical warnings about the dangers of regression. In a drawing printed in the *Minneapolis Journal* in October 1898, well-behaved colonial youths sit on a school bench and watch a vigilant Uncle Sam rebuke a native boy for failing to pay attention. Dalrymple's cartoon contains a similar dynamic, sketching two possible futures: the new colonies can either follow in the footsteps of former territories like Texas and California that have matured into states, or they can fail to keep up like the Native American student in the back who is holding his primer upside down. A Black boy cleaning the windows, shown in the print's upper left corner, occupies the lowest rung of the racial ladder. Trying to educate him seemed like a waste of time. Savagery was never far removed from the colonials. The implication was that ignoring Uncle Sam's instructions would throw them back to the primitivism from which domestic peoples of color appeared incapable of emerging. Only time would tell whether the islanders would move up the ladder of civilization, or whether they would have to stay indefinitely in America's imperial orphanage as uncivilized wards.[11]

Sentiments similar to the infantilism propagated in imperial print culture can also be found in reports and letters from US soldiers dispatched to the colonial frontier. Much of what individual servicemen wrote echoed the pronouncements of political and military leaders who characterized the peoples they were determined to rule as grossly underdeveloped. Speaking in Manila in December 1903, William Howard Taft explained that it was the declared policy of the United States to preserve "the 'Philippines for the Filipinos' for their benefit, for their elevation, for their civilization." Were the United States to withdraw its "guiding hand" too early, "chaos, conscription, and corruption would follow inevitably." General Nelson A. Miles, who commanded the invasion of Puerto Rico, addressed its inhabitants in likeminded spirit in July 1898. His men had come to protect the islanders and secure for them "the advantages and blessings of enlightened civilization." Rank-and-file colonizers were no less condescending than their superiors. Emmanuel Rossiter, who served under Miles in Puerto Rico, referred to the natives as "grown up children, with all a child's natural affection and trust." Mary Denison Thomas, wife of the contract surgeon Jerome Beers Thomas, made similar observations on her trips to the Philippine countryside in the early 1900s. Equipped with a portable camera, Thomas took snapshots of local people, often children, in front of bamboo fences and mud huts. Comparing the Filipino struggle for independence with the American Revolution struck her as utterly absurd. The America people, Thomas wrote to a friend, came "from a stock accustomed for years to education and thought," while the Filipinos "are like bright children who are capable of learning but have as yet not the rudiments of knowledge." Facing an uncertain colonial future, the conquerors tasked with exercising US power in unfamiliar lands found in such tutelary language a familiar hierarchical framework.[12]

That framework, to be sure, was not applied evenly; nor did feelings of kinship spring naturally from first encounters. Soldiers ordered to crush the Filipino resistance mocked the idea that the locals were "little brown brothers." One song they sang sharply distinguished between Taft's familial rhetoric and the bloody work in which they were engaged. The soldiers had a point: to quell the uprising, they resorted to scorched-earth tactics, torture, and mass killings. The failed insurgency resulted in the death of more than three-quarter of a million Filipinos, more than all of the casualties of the US Civil War combined. How can one uphold the facade of fraternalism in the face of such unspeakable violence? This is where children came into play, literally as well as figuratively. Sherman Kiser, a US officer stationed on the southern peninsula of Zamboanga, tugged at American heartstrings with his work among Moro youth. In September 1914, Kiser founded a local Boy Scout troop, teaching the sons of his former enemies the American scout law and scout oath. Learning first aid, treating wounded animals, and saluting the Stars and Stripes constituted two rites in one—one of passage, in which local youths were initiated into the youth movement's masculine Americanism, and one of reconciliation, in which a US colonizer could shed his warrior identity and evolve into an older brother, redeemed by the friendship he experienced in the company of the boys. Kiser's Moro scouts became darlings of the mainland press. Their story helped rehabilitate the nation's self-image battered by war and rejuvenate faith in the goodness of the US imperial project.[13]

At the same time, the idea that shared play might regenerate the colonizer and masculinize the colonized stood in critical tension with the racist notion that the natives might never be able to mature beyond a certain stage. This ambiguity, however, was not entirely frustrating. Just as the fraternal variant of colonialism did not require the older brother to treat the younger sibling as his equal, US soldier-educators could argue that molding defiant populations into loyal subjects of the empire was the ultimate goal of development. Uncertainties about how to grade the collective age of non-white peoples had a major advantage. It allowed imperialists to keep on infantilizing their subordinates and continue to move the goalpost that marked their entry into political adulthood. Why relinquish custody when nobody could be exactly sure whether Filipinos, Puerto Ricans, or Hawaiians would prosper without a committed guardian? Theodore Roosevelt's son, Theodore Jr., turned into a fierce critic of Philippine independence after his governorship of the islands had ended in 1933: "With such militancy and incompetence at the helm, I wouldn't be surprised to see the movement there go to waste in but a few years." He was wrong, but as late as 1937, men like Roosevelt felt comfortable claiming that the premature transfer of sovereignty spelled political disaster for both sides.[14]

Formal independence came in 1946, in no small part because of the tenacity of Filipino activists who refused to wait for an imaginary rubber stamp that would certify their fitness for self-rule. The process was messy. Delayed by partisan strife and interrupted by World War II, Filipino futures bounced back and forth between the US government granting the islands commonwealth status and securing prerogatives for American businesses and the military. Colonial subjects striving to break the shackles of imperial tutelage had to work against perceptions of non-white inferiority grounded in race as well as age. At a time when unabashed biological racism had begun to raise more eyebrows, denouncing decolonization as a form of child abandonment became an effective cloaking device for imperial exploitation. Liberal elites who laid the groundwork for modern human rights after learning about the monstrosities that had occurred in the Nazi death camps could no longer dodge questions about colonialism's racist foundations so easily. Childhood, on the contrary, remained "deceptively universal," to quote the historian Tara Zahra, and parental authority was considered a timeless fact—the most natural and innocuous of all unequal relations. A perfect symbol of humanitarian concern and postwar renewal, childhood became the bridge linking the official end of US colonial rule in the Philippines to the establishment of occupation regimes in Japan and Germany, which happened just one year apart. Had Keppler been alive in 1946, he might have decided to update his cartoon. Uncle Sam, having dismissed one of his wards into an uncertain future, is asked to receive a new batch of charges: two nations, stamped with the mark of infancy, in dire need of reeducation.[15]

THE SOLDIERS ESCORTING Catherine Filene Shouse must have envied her endurance. The fifty-four-year-old wealthy philanthropist showed no signs of tiring as she was hurrying through the narrow alleys of Heidelberg, the second stop on her multi-leg journey across West Germany. Shouse was keen to learn how much progress the US military had made since army personnel had joined the effort to democratize Germany's postwar youth. Judging by how she responded to the warm welcome she received, she was visibly enthused. Shouse first visited the boys' center of the Heidelberg branch of the German Youth Activities (GYA) program, replete with pastimes and classes in which local teenage boys discussed similarities between the US Constitution and the Basic Law of the newly founded Federal Republic of Germany. Her next appointment was with a group of girls in an adjacent building. "What I observed, I liked," Shouse noted in her diary. Seated at a table decorated with West German and US flags, the girls displayed their handicraft and serenaded their benefactress with a selection of German and English songs.[16]

Two years earlier, in August 1948, Shouse had toured Germany for the first time since the 1930s. The country stood high in her affections. Shouse, the granddaughter of German-born entrepreneurs who had migrated to Boston, was a lover of classical music and believed in the power of the performing arts to transcend nationalism. Hitler had strained the emotional bond that connected Shouse to Germany, but the dictator had not broken it. Traveling the war-devastated country with her husband Jouett Shouse, a former Kansas congressman, and watching hungry children play on heaps of rubble awakened her to a clear sense of what had gone wrong. The Germans had a split identity—old and civilized in matters of culture, yet shockingly immature when it came to politics. Shouse hoped that reeducation might achieve a healthy equilibrium. Back on the East Coast, she lent her fundraising skills to setting up the General Clay Fund, which collected donations from women's clubs and distributed them to GYA centers across Germany. Helping ailing children was the work of reconstructing a disoriented nation. "For many years I inclined to the opinion that the German people are incapable of self-government. The Weimar Republic was a failure. Successively, they had Bismarck, the Kaiser, and Hitler." Witnessing the fruits of that work on her 1950 trip convinced Shouse "that the American occupation had at least partially opened their eyes to a form of government and a way of life of which they formerly were entirely ignorant and the merits of which they are now seriously weighing."[17]

When the Axis nations had surrendered, Shouse was not alone in doubting whether that kind of ignorance could ever be remedied. The desire for vengeance was strong. In an opinion poll conducted in 1944, only 8 percent checked "reeducate, rehabilitate" for Japan, while almost half of the participants favored harsher methods of subjugation. Wartime Americans were almost as livid with the Germans. Ideas about how to punish them ranged from Treasury Secretary Henry Morgenthau's plan to hurl the country back to the preindustrial age to extreme talk about mass castration. All too radical designs were soon discarded, but not because victory had made hating the enemy obsolete. Rather, the task of ruling over an estimated 150 million people proved so daunting that the US military had to pick their battles. Denazification was largely limited to a few high-profile trials, Nuremberg among them. Few Germans were confronted with damning footage documenting the horrific crimes committed in concentration camps, and fewer Nazi officials were converted with questionnaires. Enlisted soldiers ignored the army's fraternization ban from the get-go. Sexual relationships with Fräuleins were quite common. Many GIs also quickly warmed up to local children, putting a smile on their faces with a bar of chocolate.[18]

The difficulties accompanying the first months of the occupation were compounded by uncertainties about precisely how the United States should wield its dominance in a postwar world. Should victory hasten the demise of colonial empires? Was self-government even desirable on a planetary scale?

The grandiose rhetoric of the Atlantic Charter, with its universal appeals to freedom and self-determination, was as unspecific as Woodrow Wilson's World War I slogan "to make the world safe for democracy" had been vague. But if occupation lacked a clear strategy, let alone a grand vision, it at least needed some sort of rationale to persuade servicemen who longed to return to their families that it was not yet time to get out of their uniforms. Geopolitics came in handy, especially since the rapidly deteriorating relationship with the Soviet Union gave the United States a menacing villain to contain. Liberal internationalism no longer seemed viable without the supremacy of US arms. The larger the communist threat loomed, the more Americans were inclined to regard their former enemies as the lesser evil. When Walter Lippmann popularized the term Cold War in 1947, the United States had already come to accept the role of provider and protector of defeated peoples.[19]

Reeducation's roots go back further. The term gained currency during the early 1940s in academic circles with ties to the US government and military intelligence. An interdisciplinary group of scholars, including the anthropologist Margaret Mead, the developmental psychologist Erik H. Erikson, and the neurologist Richard Brickner, sought to disprove the notion that Germany was incurable. The terms they injected into the public debate, including "collective therapy," "de-hypnosis," "re-birth," "mental reconstruction," and "mental hygiene," reflected the group's growing confidence that they could provide theoretically informed solutions to complex political problems. "Our hope of success lies not simply in an aroused public opinion," noted Margaret Mead in 1943, "but in the development of social science." Childhood figured prominently in their scientific formulas, both as object and analogy. Drawing on Mead's field work in Papua New Guinea, Brickner speculated whether the German obsession with race purity was an advanced version of the primal fears of island populations used to living in relative isolation. Erikson was fond of drawing parallels between New Deal policies that had promoted the education of Native Americans—peoples whom white settlers had long considered childlike—and current plans to reeducate German society based on anthropological and psychoanalytic expertise. He argued that since the Nazi mentality was the result of childhood experiences prone to produce authoritarian characters, that mentality could be studied and possibly undone with therapeutic rigor. Once they disowned their "monster father," the Germans would "once more emerge as good customers" and develop a democratic character of their own.[20]

Hollywood movies in which Germany featured as a troubled boy amplified the scientific community's hopeful narratives of rehabilitation and enlightenment. A case in point is the 1943 motion picture *Tomorrow, the World!* A coming-of-age drama about a Hitler Youth member who had moved in with his American uncle, the movie details the family's struggle to make the boy shed his Nazi beliefs. Emil Bruckner, the boy, grows increasingly violent. Hurling antisemitic slurs and lashing out at Americans of diverse ethnic backgrounds gets him into trouble. All the while, his family does not lose faith in him. Emil finds redemption in the end when, impressed by the perseverance of those around him, he opens up about his traumatic past and begins a new life in democratic America. *Tomorrow, the World!* is easy to dismiss as sentimental wartime propaganda, but the story of the regeneration of an adolescent led astray by National Socialism anticipated the reeducators' ambition to purge all the ancient pathologies from what they understood to be the German national character.[21]

If Emil Bruckner reinforced the myth of childhood innocence, the millions of real-life Emiles roaming the streets of postwar Germany proved instrumental in transforming cold-blooded villains into infantilized victims. Not long after General Dwight Eisenhower had exempted children from the fraternization ban, the Army began assembling the personnel and infrastructure that would form the backbone of the GYA. Launched in September 1946 for youths aged ten to eighteen, the GYA pursued a two-pronged strategy. To gain the locals' trust, its representatives signaled that they would provide food, leisure, and education to aimless, possibly delinquent youngsters under the condition that Germans gave democracy a chance. To win over the men under his command, Lucius D. Clay, the US military governor for Germany, presented young people as most likely to overcome the fanaticism of the past. Posters attached in military installations told soldiers that "not everything German is bad. Let German youth show you some of the good." The disciplinary subtext should have been obvious to any US servicemen: rather than have sex with local women and risk venereal disease, spend your free time with wholesome activities such as helping kids. In an interview with the military newspaper *Stars and Stripes*, Clay explained why he believed youth to be the key demographic. Properly guided, they would inject "some fresh blood" into the old and worn-out Weimar elites and constitute "the greatest hope for restoring Germany as a peaceful nation along democratic lines."[22]

Activities sponsored by GYA centers opening up across Bavaria, Hesse, and West Berlin ran the gamut from team sports, civics courses, and Soap Box Derby competitions for boys (see figure 6.2) to handicraft, cooking, and singing lessons for girls. Army clubhouses had playrooms with toys for smaller children and reading rooms whose shelves were stacked with books

FIGURE 6.2 German teenager Alfred Hänle receiving a warm welcome in Akron, Ohio, 1950. US government officials sponsored such trips to the United States to showcase the ripening of a younger, more democratic West Germany. Courtesy of the Schlesinger Library, Harvard Radcliffe Institute.

donated by US schools and private households. Careful planning went into the GYA's annual summer camps. Children of different ages hoping for a taste of US-style prosperity applied for one of the much-coveted spots in these camps. Young Germans who made a strong impression on the organizers were given a chance to meet with Americans their age. One such moment came on December 20, 1948, when 200 handpicked US and German teenagers gathered in the same courtroom in which leaders of the Nazi regime had been tried and sentenced two years earlier. "With amazing maturity and alertness," as an army reporter phrased it, the students gathered in Nuremberg discussed issues related to securing world peace, symbolically turning the page on past atrocities. Occasions like this one announced to the world the ripening of a new, younger Germany, bound to their American benefactors in gratitude and friendship.[23]

Overall participation was impressive. What started as a trickle of a few thousand children expanded in just three years into a tide of more than 1.4 million registered children and teenagers who took advantage of the program's recreational offers. By 1949, internal statistics estimated that roughly 600,000 youths were visiting GYA facilities each month. Whether the young Germans left them more democratized was harder to measure. Officials who had poured significant resources into the program had a vested interest in claiming that they did. Reframing the occupation as an apprenticeship in democracy, an article published by the State Department in 1951 basically declared "mission accomplished." Every dollar invested in youth work was a dollar well spent, for what the world was witnessing was the emergence of a rejuvenated Germany where a "healthy nationalism" had become "the most effective antidote to the influences of Neo-Nazi and Communist." Or as another article pithily stated, "GYA is our dam against the red tide."[24]

However, indifference to reeducation was not uncommon among the occupied. Postwar Germany was a land of scarcity. Hunger stoked misgivings toward the new masters, and daily struggles for food and clothing left little room for weighing the pros and cons of democracy. Quite a few GYA volunteers complained that adolescents joined with outsized notions of American material abundance and left frustrated when they did not get what they wanted. Others regretted that some youths refused to mingle with people their age on sectarian grounds. Interviews conducted by Army officials in GYA centers revealed a mixed picture. Fears of juvenile delinquency were rampant in the postwar years, and parents turned to the occupiers in the hope that a hierarchical organization like the US military would help them discipline their young. For one mother from Bayreuth, sending her children to

American youth activities had little to do with democratic pedagogy and everything to do with teaching them "obedience toward their elders." Young people who participated in the interviews stressed the material benefits of reeducation. Assuming that they did not want to bite the hand that fed them, many said what their benefactors wanted to hear—namely, that their understanding of democracy had improved thanks to the GYA. What that meant in practice was impossible to determine, also because the interviewers did not define the content of the values included in their questions.[25]

When Americans spoke of democracy, the historian David Potter noted in 1956, they often meant abundance as well. In certain situations, the stereotypical notion that the United States was home to a "people of plenty" was more curse than blessing. For Europe's educated elites, American power was manifesting itself primarily in the form of a military-consumerist complex. They viewed the United States as a nation rich in goods but poor in culture, and the crass materialism ascribed to the sole Western superpower continued to nurture anti-American sentiments. Not all European intellectuals saw it that way. Some younger Europeans became ardent readers of Henry David Thoreau, Herman Melville, Mark Twain, and Ernest Hemingway. In 1953, the twenty-four-year-old West German poet Hans Magnus Enzensberger praised the evolving literary canon of a still young democracy as a source of postwar regeneration. A Belgian author who attended an American Studies seminar in Salzburg, Austria, in 1951 defended American literature on the grounds that it was exempt from "snobbishness" and "free from the burden of senility" weighing on a tired, old continent. Culture could preclude cooperation, but it just as much inspired visions of a rejuvenated Europe joining the work of proselytizing a democracy of the mind, not just of things.[26]

All this made the occupiers feel good about how they were schooling the Germans. With countless German men killed in the war and many more Wehrmacht soldiers imprisoned in prisoner of war camps, GIs must have thought they had been stationed in a land of women and children. Images of a feminized Germany made it easy to envision its inhabitants as infantile citizens, but embracing that notion too tightly would have created an entirely different set of problems. It would have meant postponing the transfer of sovereignty to a point at which teenagers democratized in the late 1940s would have reached their forties or fifties, an age considered appropriate for statesmanship. In addition, overemphasizing German immaturity would have made it seem reckless for Americans to grant the new West German leadership a supporting role in defending the "free world" against communism. Curiously, MacArthur, who considered Japan an infant nation, could not fathom how that same metric might apply to the Germans—for him a nation "as mature" as the United States and therefore much harder to correct. A balance had to be struck in the nation-building process between rejuvenating former enemies in the spirit of liberal democracy and drawing on the experience of elders free from the taint of fascism. Konrad Adenauer, the leader of the Christian Democrats, was seventy-three years old when the Bundestag elected him chancellor of the Federal Republic of Germany on September 15, 1949.[27]

Since the Western Allies could ill afford to alienate the middle-aged, adult reeducation took on the tonality of partnership rather than tutelage. Behind closed doors, military staff pondering how to best instill pro-American sentiments in German teachers or union leaders made no bones about their supposed illiteracy in all things democratic. A memorandum written in May 1947 by an official in the Office of Military Government for Bavaria bluntly stated that "by tradition or training, Germans are unduly submissive to authority." At the same time, reeducators were concerned that their policies would backfire if such verdicts went public. Germans might favor paternalism, yet US officials conceded that working with conditions as they were ultimately meant helping locals acquire new civic identities within institutional frameworks that the Germans knew and cherished. "What is democracy worth if school reform can be imposed against the will of the people?" asked Waldemar von Knöringen, the leader of Bavaria's Social Democrats who had returned from exile and emerged as a fierce critic of plans to replace the traditional German three-tiered school system with US-style high schools. More than merely resisting reeducation, Knöringen's objection shows that the occupied did not hesitate to turn the language of democratic citizenship against their guardians.[28]

To placate adult professionals who wanted to be treated as such, US government officials stopped speaking of reeducation or reorientation and began using less degrading terms, like "democratic orientation." As one report noted about the Germans' dislike of occupation terminology, "They say they are a nation of grown-ups and should not be retrained, reeducated and reoriented. They say they have had for many centuries their own valuable experience and tradition." What they would like instead was that "Americans should rather be friends with whom to discuss mutual problems than teachers who talk down to them." A range of exchange programs implemented in the latter half of the 1940s facilitated this shift. From 1946 to 1956, more than 12,000 German politicians, professors, bureaucrats, teachers, youth workers, labor leaders, judges, and journalists visited the United States on guided tours administered by the State Department. Reeducation remained important, and the organizers clearly aspired to rearing a liberal-minded German elite. Publicly, these trips during which German professionals—overwhelmingly male and middle-aged—got to intern with US colleagues or catch up on the newest research were advertised as enabling cultural dialogue and knowledge transfer between two peoples. Meeting on an international platform of shared expertise promised benefits to both sides. The Americans could clothe their strategic interests in altruism. German visitors, on the other hand, seized the opportunity to escape the realities of defeat and place themselves in the vanguard of their nation's reconstruction efforts.[29]

We know that much because the participants were debriefed by State Department officials on their return. Most appreciated leaving behind dark memories of the war, if only for a short time, as well as the feeling of having been thrown into a state of dependency. Music correspondent Hans Stückenschmidt praised the atmosphere of cordiality and mutual respect that made his time in the United States "the most wonderful experience" of his life. Kurt Pfister, a teacher from West Berlin, echoed this sentiment when he confirmed in glowing terms that his American hosts had treated him like a peer, not like an ignorant student. Again, most Germans tried not to upset their sponsors, while the organizers tried to impress the visitors from overseas with picture-perfect versions of the American way. Candidates and hosts were carefully screened, and travelers were kept on tight schedules. Officials boasting that the tours gave Germans an appreciation of the rich variety of life in a model democracy had regional differences in mind. Seeing more than just New York, Philadelphia, or Chicago meant spending time with white middle-class families in other parts of the country. Exposing erstwhile citizens of Nazi Germany to the stark inequalities of Jim Crow, for example, was not part of the agenda.[30]

But the few who insisted on seeing how the other half lived could not be held back. Josef Schilling, a trained mason and Bavarian trade union executive who spent the summer of 1949 meeting labor representatives in different parts of the United States, told his counterparts that the picture would be incomplete without addressing the situation of Black workers. Schilling cared little for diplomatic niceties. He called the states in the South "reactionary" on the question of race relations. More shocking to his hosts, he added that America could not be called a free country as long as it allowed discrimination to fester in its midst. Schilling warned his American colleagues that "communism [would have] a good ground among" African Americans if the white majority continued to ignore their grievances. In a stunning move, the Bavarian labor leader turned the tables on the nation that had set out to reeducate him. Perhaps it was the United States, Schilling suggested, that should take an extra class in how to make democracy true for all its citizens.[31]

Scaling back to political adulthood from a place of forced rejuvenation came with an obligation. In exchange for being readmitted to the family of free of nations, the occupied had to consent to their status as junior partners in a liberal imperial order with the United States on top. The boundaries between rejuvenation and infantilization were kept deliberately hazy. While representations of German children in the context of reeducation signaled that the country had abdicated its power as creators of culture, the same representations also pointed to the brighter narrative of a rejuvenated Germany that could be redeemed from a horrific past and become one with its saviors. Some parents worried that the GYA was intent on converting their young ones into "Little Americans"—or "*kleine Amis*," as Germans called them. Others resented that reeducation smacked of the "elementary schooling given to children, colonial people, and illiterates." However, most West Germans apparently believed—if only for pragmatic reasons—that encouraging their young ones to showcase the rehabilitation expected from them would speed up the (re)maturation of the nation as a whole.[32]

Sovereignty in America's free-world empire was granted as well as graded. Like a master who reminded his apprentices that their ripening depended on his willingness to support their growth, US representatives considered themselves the final umpires of German development. Despite supporting official statehood, John Foster Dulles, who was secretary of state under President Dwight D. Eisenhower, expressed "grave doubts" about West Germany's reliability as late as 1953. If unleashed prematurely, the reeducated living on the frontiers of the Cold War, Dulles feared, might be tempted to "again turn to the methods of yesteryear." Big brother had come to stay, watching the young democracy's every move.[33]

GROWTH IS THE natural law of nationhood. However, if a nation grew in unhealthy ways, a reset was warranted. On September 2, 1945, a few hours after representatives of the Japanese government had signed the surrender of their country on board the USS *Missouri*, MacArthur broadcast his thoughts over the radio. Although the arms of a mighty democracy in its prime had defeated a wicked enemy, this was not the time for revenge. Rather, a rescue mission begun ninety-two years earlier was waiting to be completed. It had all started with Commodore Matthew Perry, who, according to MacArthur, had "brought enlightenment and progress" to a barbaric people. But instead of developing peacefully, Japan had proved incapable of wielding the gifts of science and technology responsibly. World peace depended on acknowledging Japanese ineptitude and recognizing America's duty to exorcise old patterns of "superstition" and "force." MacArthur was confident that "the energy of the Japanese race," if correctly channeled, would "enable expansion vertically rather than horizontally." Liberating a once hostile oriental people from ancient "fanaticism" had worked wonders in the Philippines, now a "model for this free new world of Asia." Why should taking a rejuvenated Japan by the hand not yield the same result?[34]

MacArthur's victory speech hints at some of the major themes and contexts specific to the US approach to reeducating Japan. Though many of the policies carried out in the two former Axis nations sprang from the same impulses—dismantling inherited authorities, pacifying warrior societies, rearing pro-American states—neither served as an overarching model for the other. Of all the factors that cut through the notion that reeducation rested on a shared foundation, geography and race were the sharpest. When Americans looked across the Atlantic Ocean in the early 1940s, most were ready to accept the argument that the Nazi menace represented the failure of a cultured European society that had degenerated into adolescent madness. Not so in the case of Imperial Japan. Long before President Franklin Delano Roosevelt vowed to avenge Pearl Harbor, his compatriots had viewed the Japanese as upstart children, undeserving of the respect granted to civilized nations. The ageism Japan experienced in transpacific relations corresponded with the regular nativist flare-ups against Japanese migrant communities on the West Coast. Many were caught in the whirlwinds of the "Yellow Peril," a racist discourse that paradoxically cast Asians as a threat to Anglo-Saxon dominance while at the same time ridiculing them as unmanly, feminine, and even childlike. Japan's victory over Russia in 1905 punctuated the white supremacist myth but did not demolish it. On the contrary, the more people of color called out the inconsistency of the myth, the harder some white commentators pushed back against idea that the Japanese would someday outpace the United States. To borrow a phrase from the missionary and scholar Sidney Lewis Gulick, Japan's rapid rise to a regional power more resembled the "the crudity of a boy in his teens."[35]

Orientalism provided the loosest of frameworks for mid-century Americans projecting a seamless transition from colonialism in the Philippines to the military occupation of Japan. The Japanese themselves were not innocent of othering Asians, cultivating a sense of superiority vis-à-vis their neighbors that accompanied their conquests in the 1930s and 1940s. In the estimate of the historian Gerald Horne, Japan's brutal expansionism thrived on ruthless reinterpretations of European and North American colonialism. Japanese propagandists were trying to find allies among the Asians they had subdued by portraying the war as payback for decades of white rule. US policymakers developed their own reading of the Pacific theater as a full-fledged race war. "If Oriental peoples," with the Japanese taking the lead, were to "have independent and civilized peoples," the New Jersey congressman Charles Eaton warned in 1943, the "United States . . . might be pushed off the map." Wartime characterizations of the Japanese as devious barbarians who deserved no mercy stretched from the battlefield to the home front, where Americans of Japanese descent were stripped of their rights and forced to live behind barbed wire. Intense hate gripped both sides in the war, which took on more savage forms than the fighting on the Western front in Europe. In terms of disregard for human life, banzai charges and kamikaze attacks were not that different from the terror bombings of Japanese cities, conventional or nuclear.[36]

Having obtained Japan's unconditional surrender, the United States quickly readjusted its racist lens on the defeated. Victory meant that hierarchical relationships of civilization and order were to be restored, with the exception that the Japanese were now subject to an imperial pedagogy that blended reeducation with forms of colonial tutelage the United States had practiced in the Philippines. To illustrate, consider the overhaul of the Japanese school system, which began just a few weeks into the occupation. The Civil Information and Education Division (CIE), founded in the fall of 1945, was tasked with severing the schools' ties to Shintoism, which the occupiers believed was a religion that had fostered a totalitarian cult of personality around the emperor. The CIE's suggestions for reform ended up in a report that recommended the following changes: demilitarizing education, replacing schools segregated by class with comprehensive coeducational ones, adopting a romanized alphabet called *Romaji*, and introducing child-centered learning models from the Progressive Era. As in the German case, the occupiers wanted the Japanese to unlearn "habit[s] of obedience to authority" and incorporate into their curricula US-style courses in civics, politics, and democratic ethics.[37]

When it came to liberalizing Japanese education, the occupiers found willing partners among social segments traditionally shut out from the country's higher institutions of learning (see figure 6.3). Japan's old elites were the primary target of forced rejuvenation, while disadvantaged groups had some reason to rejoice. Opportunities for women increased when the US military

FIGURE 6.3 Japanese girls in a newly rebuilt Catholic school in Tokyo, 1946. Liberalizing the education system was a centerpiece of the postwar occupation of Japan, which paired orientalist tropes of immaturity with US-style modernization. Courtesy of the Library of Congress Prints and Photographs Division.

began to remove gendered restrictions from secondary schools and promote all-female colleges. Equal adulthood, to be sure, remained a far cry, also because the realities of sex work fostered images of Japan as a geisha nation. This contradictory trope invited Americans to portray their former enemies as weak and helpless while highlighting that contacts between GIs and local women often occurred within the framework of prostitution. The gendered dimensions of the US occupation caused ripples of opposition in the Japanese public. In an effort to distance themselves from the reformers, the country's top universities resisted CIE policies by adding new graduate-level studies. Some Japanese newspapers juxtaposed the immoral conditions of female sex work with nostalgic images of lost imperial purity and glory.[38]

Debates over the proper place of women in postwar Japanese society point to the tenuous middle ground that the nation occupied in US reeducation schemes. A former colonial power itself, Japan could hardly be considered a civilizational toddler. If its clocks had to be set back, it was not because the country had lacked exposure to modernity. Rather, the Japanese, through proper schooling, had to be weaned away from a distorted understanding of the modern. Seen as superior to other Asians, they still figured as wayward children who needed to be disabused of any illusions of supremacy. A cartoon published in a Pittsburgh newspaper six days after the Japanese surrender illustrates this stance perfectly. Titled "The First Lesson," the cartoon depicts a classroom under US control. The children, racialized as ugly Asians with oversized buckteeth, watch indignantly as their new teacher, General MacArthur, bursts into the room. He has come not to uplift the defeated but to reeducate them. Their excessive lust for power rested on a horrific delusion, a deranged mass hysteria to which no real adult would succumb. The spell had to be broken; the Japanese had to grow anew. Before getting permission to return to the world of mature nation-states, the politically illiterate boy-men had to be taught how to speak, think, and act properly. Understanding that "Japan *lost* the war," the message written on the blackboard, was a necessary first step.[39]

Homi Bhabha's concepts of "hybridity" and "mimicry" can help to unravel this semicolonial relationship. Exchanges between the occupiers and occupied were hybrid in the sense that the ruling party, while cognizant of existing disparities, increasingly pursued reeducation on the basis of reciprocity. The joint sense of mission that emerged from daily interactions between US personnel and Japanese civil society groups interested in national renewal paved the wave for reforms that were neither American nor Japanese, but blended both systems. Admittedly, the idea of partnership at first held little romance for those who had survived a murderous war. Both sides worked together out of naked self-interest. Order ensured sustenance, and vice versa. Strategically, US officials had more to gain from nurturing interpersonal relationships, professional and conjugal. Adopting children orphaned by the war, welcoming thousands of Japanese "war brides" to North American shores, and bringing young women scarred by the atomic bomb dropped over Hiroshima to the United States for plastic surgery were presented as important steps toward reconciliation.[40]

For the Japanese, entering the postwar Western family as its youngest member was a promise and a price it needed to pay. There is little indication that the formally reeducated who regained their sovereignty in 1952 relished their infant status in national and international relations. Mimicry, which Bhabha theorized as imitating the dominant imperial culture to the point of subversion, remained one of the few remaining outlets for defiance. The contested terrain of filmmaking in postwar Japan bears this out. Hollywood companies had made inroads into the Japanese movie market as early as the 1920s. Given these prior entanglements, using film to promote pro-American ideology seemed a rational choice for the occupation regime. Japanese moviemakers who wanted a piece of the pie had to consent to US censors screening their products and demanding changes to scenes that struck them as disagreeable. According to the historian Hiroshi Kitamura, contests over the relationship of artistic freedom and political appropriateness reflected "the uneven power dynamic of the occupation." Local filmmakers quickly learned to speak the language of civil rights to push back against the occupiers' patronizing and—as the Japanese asserted—undemocratic conduct. *The Bells of Nagasaki*, which recounted the story of a scientist who died from leukemia following the atomic explosion at Nagasaki, was one such movie that made it onto the big screen, mainly due to the tenacity of its directors. Censors told Shochiku, the Japanese film company that produced *Bells of Nagasaki*, to delete all references to the nuclear blast, which would make the Americans look like the bad guys. The filmmakers delayed and deflected. All they were doing, they replied, was exercise their right as artists to inquire into "the truth" and tell a story about "the beauty of human love." Released in 1950, the movie received favorable reviews and started a conversation in Japan about the unresolved physical and psychological consequences of the atomic bombings.[41]

Postwar reconstruction consisted of many roads to recovery—some congested, some aborted, others long and winding, and others not taken. In holding up to boyified nations the maturity of statehood as compensation for having to endure the primacy of America's liberal empire, reeducators glossed over persisting contradictions in how they went about (re)building democracies at home and abroad. To heal the wounds of war, US elites privileged repairing families and nations over addressing the lingering inequities of race and class. Forced rejuvenation mirrored the broad antiradical consensus forged by Western elites after 1945. After youth-obsessed autocrats had pushed the world to the brink of destruction, rejuvenation itself had to be purged of its worst excesses. Combative disruption of the old, trampling over the accumulated wisdom of the ages, the fascist cult of violent regeneration, communist class warfare—all were branded as dangerous aberrations from a healthy balance between youth and experience.

Widely portrayed as the decade of family values and anticommunism, the conservative 1950s reflected a newfound appreciation for moderation and restraint that many rejuvenationists of the interwar period had lacked. Seasoned leaders—Eisenhower in the United States, Konrad Adenauer in West

Germany, Shigeru Yoshida in Japan—enjoyed majority support. Tested and proven ways that were extolled, for example, in Adenauer's 1957 campaign slogan "No Experiments" were advertised as preferable to the iconoclastic furor of prior decades. Already, however, the seeds of the next youth revolts were beginning to sprout. Growing up with television, rock and roll, and more money to spend, the children of the Greatest Generation found ways to burst out of the frame of sanitized middle-class conformity that emanated from almost every Normal Rockwell painting of the period. Teenagers rebelling against the "square" culture of their parents inspired transnational imitation and exchange. Models of intergenerational cooperation that US reeducators had relied on in occupied Japan and West Germany were no longer "swell" (if they ever were).[42]

Disillusionment ran deep once cultural upheaval merged with political protest. The German poet Yaak Karsunke, who had first tasted US freedom at a GYA center when he was eleven years old, expressed his anger about the Vietnam War in verse. His 1967 poem "Kilroy Was Here" testifies to the profound sense of betrayal felt by an entire generation of West Germans who had been raised to admire the self-styled leaders of the free world. Instead of cheering up children with chewing gum and Coca-Cola and teaching youths "such words . . . as fairness and democracy," Kilroy was now dropping napalm bombs on villages in Southeast Asia. On the smoldering remains of what once was a budding friendship, Karsunke left a pithy phrase: *Wir sind geschiedene Leute*—"We're going our separate ways."[43]

CHAPTER SEVEN

Wipe the Slate Clean

The Countercultural Rebellion

Your old road is rapidly agin'
Please get out of the new one
If you can't lend your hand
For the times they are a-changin.
—Bob Dylan, "The Times, They Are a-Changin'" (1964)

A veritable children's crusade was heading east in the 1960s and 1970s—children not in body but in spirit. The thousands of travelers leaving their homes in North America and Europe to encounter unfamiliar cultures in far-flung Asia were tourists of a different kind. They did not take the plane or stay at lush beach resorts. Most considered themselves hippies, young men and women who were making a virtue out of escaping the conformities of consumer capitalism and defying the Cold War military-industrial complex. Some spent weeks, if not several months, on dusty roads, covering up to 11,000 miles in battered cars and hand-painted buses until they reached the end of their pilgrimage, places they associated with recovery from modernity's mindless routines. Cities like Kabul in Afghanistan, Varanasi in India, and Kathmandu in Nepal became destinations where backpackers would mend their sores and meditate on how to rejuvenate the world.[1]

Regular folks shook their heads at the long hair, tie-dyed clothes, and granny glasses that had become the hallmarks of a new movement. Its adherents, in turn, felt nothing but contempt for the nine-to-five jobs and pledges of allegiance of their elders. Parents fretted about young people congregating in city parks and on sidewalks, talking, preaching, kissing, dancing, and inhaling strange substances. How kids who had enjoyed the comforts of postwar prosperity were throwing it all away exceeded their elders' comprehension. Courthouses, churches, office buildings, and army barracks—all symbols of a rotten establishment—were the last locations the hippies wanted to frequent. "What is happening to our young people?" was a question posed with increasing alarm in middle-class households in the United States, Canada, and Europe. But rather than return home to get lectured about their conduct (or maybe receive a good spanking), the young dropouts liked to snap back: "No, what has happened to YOU?" To Rory MacLean and his fellow trekkers en route to India, the straitjacketed adulthood created by late-stage capitalism was a form of cultural death more depressing than a proper burial. "We divided society into 'them' and 'us,' our optimistic innocence lost as we exiled ourselves from Eden at home and abroad. . . . But I hungered for the perfect destination," MacLean confessed. "I still wandered along the trail of wonders, believing in a family of man, yearning to complete the greatest journey bopping to the best songs of all time."[2]

Few hippie travelers explained why they had chosen to become flower children in such poignant prose. The themes MacLean touched on—loss of innocence, exile, hunger for redemption—resonated with countless self-professed young idealists who became the face of the period's counterculture. The term is fraught with difficulty. Though widely used as a catchall category for the antiestablishment revolts of the 1960s, countercultural movements were hardly unique to that decade. Theodore Roszak, the Princeton-trained historian who coined the term in 1969, did not care much about historical precedents when looking for a name to describe the antiauthoritarian revolts happening around him. "Counterculture" was his way of giving coherence to campus rebellions, civil rights struggles, antiwar protests, demands for women's liberation, and young people's frustration with an increasingly sterile and morbid Western civilization. Roszak's critics have faulted him for imposing uniformity on different movements with distinct agendas, as well as for lumping together diverse communities who did not always get along. Others have questioned the all too rigid separation of mainstream and counterculture, given that the constant cross-pollination of styles and ideas connected both spheres. Still, the term stuck, also because the youthful dissenters, eager to extricate themselves from a repressive society, wanted it to stick.[3]

Former activists reminiscing about the sixties as an era of political awakening rarely forget to mention the perceived generation gap that united different countercultural movements. Age awareness played a crucial role in the making of a radical young avant-garde ready to take on the powers that were. "Don't trust anyone over thirty," words spoken by the free speech activist Jack Weinberg in November 1964, captured the sense of a gaping divide between youth against adult society. Demonstrating youth's power to shape the national conversation, students and teenagers demanding greater inclusion for women and minorities gave new momentum to suffrage reform. Legislators complied in 1971 with the ratification of the Twenty-Sixth Amendment, which lowered the minimum voting age from twenty-one to eighteen. For people younger than that, feminists advocated trauma theory as a means to psychoanalyze and treat all kinds of negative childhood experiences. On the other side of the age spectrum, the psychiatrist Robert N. Butler coined the term "ageism" in 1969 to protest the declining respect for older people and institutions. Finally, metaphors of puberty have appeared in the works of historians trying to weave the baby boomers, adolescent rage, and the sixties into a coherent narrative.[4]

This was a profoundly age-conscious society, in short, for which young and old were far more than biographical markers. Having the right age was tantamount to standing on the right side of history. In contexts where people felt the need to manufacture identities in opposition to the staid and geriatric, rejuvenation was imbued with immense cultural power. How should the story of a decade be told in which the young led the charge for national rejuvenation like never before (with the exception of maybe the Wide Awakes introduced in chapter 2)? One crucial aspect involved the effort to deny youth to the nation's elites, the leaders in government and big business whom the activists accused of turning society into a numb mass of comatose shoppers and flag-waving automatons. Maturity, in this reading, was no longer synonymous with responsible citizenship. It meant accepting racism, militarism, patriarchy, greed, and indifference toward distant suffering as unfortunate yet probably unreformable facets of human history. Empathy and critical thought degenerated at the same pace that growing up resulted in developing the life-sapping habits of consumer capitalism. Preventing these "one-dimensional men," as the philosopher Herbert Marcuse called them, from prolonging their grip on power was integral to the project of renewal pursued by the New Left.[5]

As much as this countercultural critique was anchored in reality, the story goes further. Instead of simply recording the ageist sensibilities of student protesters, hippie travelers, and psychedelic explorers, this chapter depicts their assumed monopoly over questions of who was really young and authorized to bring about change as part of a larger transgenerational tug-of-war over the meaning of rejuvenation. Should rejuvenation be snatched from the privileged and thrown into the dustbin of history? Could it be reprogrammed to revive the dream of a more inclusive America? Or was Peter Braunstein correct in observing that the period's infatuation with youth spawned a pervasive "culture of rejuvenation" that was pretty much up for grabs for anyone determined to seize it?[6]

I will answer as best I can, yet not without some additional caveats. Protest in the 1960s was youthful but barely unified. The question "How old are you?" rang different in different settings. There was the roar of community at music festivals like Woodstock, where hundreds of thousands of attendees, most of them in their early twenties, chose music over a war led by men in their fifties and sixties. There was the sound of challenge in conversations involving middle-aged civil rights leaders and young freedom riders who decried the pace of racial progress as too sluggish and criticized the old guard as too moderate. But there were also echoes of estrangement in the disappointment of young feminists who grew frustrated with a male-dominated student movement. In their opinion, too few backed the assertion that birth control was key to delaying motherhood and preserving women's youth. Disagreements about where the politics of age began and where it ended cut across partisan lines. Inflected by race, class, and gender, rejuvenation's role as an engine of change remained contested between social groups as well as within them.

In some corners of the counterculture, ripping youth from the claws of the establishment was not enough. Hippie intellectuals ascribed an almost mystical quality to persons cutting the cord that bound them to adult society and its many surrogate parents (presidents, governors, police, and college bureaucrats, to name a few). Dropping out, they propagated, involved going back and reuniting with one's inner child, an unpolluted version of the self buried underneath the wreckage of modernity. Beat poet Tuli Kupferberg spoke for many when he idealized the child as the truest revolutionary of all. The power of childhood, Kupferberg implied, "would make the ugly beautiful—the sick healthy—the poor rich—the soldiers peaceful." Conservatives called the followers of the politics of love "stupid, insane, naïve children." Kupferberg took the insult as a compliment. Only those who remained children at heart could "save" humankind. In the hippie universe, embracing a second childhood was celebrated as redemptive and democratic. It leveled differences and restored a purity of thought and soul that had wilted under the gruesome constraints of the grown-up world.[7]

Youth activists in the transnational 1960s, while special in terms of their social diversity and geographical reach, were not the first to venerate children as a source of moral regeneration. Accounts in which the hippies feature as descendants of the early nineteenth-century romantics, who crafted mournful elegies about man's corruption in civilization and the loss of innocence, are legion. Even drugs seemed a like distant conduit. Samuel Taylor Coleridge, a regular opium user, yearned through his poetry to hold on to "the sweet scenes of childhood." LSD-guru Timothy Leary promoted psychedelic trips as pathways to a childlike state of natural wonder. Not everyone on the left understood the appeal of this Peter Pan–like refusal to grow up. Dissenters championing racial equality and class solidarity through radical political action largely rejected Leary's flower children antics as escapist middle-class fantasy. Children should be emancipated, not imitated. What they needed was liberation from an education rooted in authority and coercion. Even before the conservative crackdown on the counterculture got underway, New Left and Black Power protesters criticized hippie rejuvenation as misguided. If youth were to build a more humane world, retreating into a privileged fortress of childhood into which anger and pain could not intrude might only invite condescending laughter from the very elites whose old ways had to go and never return.[8]

These divisions were already surfacing in the early 1960s, when the counterculture was still in its infancy. At the end of the decade, the fault lines had cracked wide open. Perhaps these ruptures were the inevitable by-product of a "youthquake" that shook continents and prompted millions of young people everywhere to rise up against the status quo. Admittedly, students and teenagers were not alone in sticking their heads out, and many were happy for every adult who joined them on the barricades. With nonconformist youth in the vanguard, rejuvenation lost its conservative veneer and turned into an instrument of sweeping reform—what the historian Arthur Marwick described as the "*permanent* transformation of relations between men and women, adults and children, Blacks and whites, provinces and metropoles, in lifestyles, and in the abolition of the furtiveness and guilt that surrounded sex in the late 1940s and 1950s." What this transformation entailed other than burying stuffy conventions remained a matter of debate. So did the question of whether chasing an imagined childhood, be it through narcotics or other hedonistic pursuits, would be enough to rouse society out of a deep stupor. But the establishment was far from asleep and had no intention of going away. The system and those sustaining it turned out to be quick learners, sounding the drumbeat of rejuvenation for their own purposes.[9]

SIXTIES REJUVENATION BEGAN with an uprising against mass death. The insurgency took place in the fall of 1957 and spanned about 9,000 words. The Philadelphia-based magazine *Dissent* had decided to publish a controversial essay by the author Norman Mailer. "The White Negro" received mixed reactions and a rather harsh one from James Baldwin. His friendship with Mailer cooled considerably over the essay's portrayal of Black men as hypervirile lovers. Shot through with racism, Mailer's tone was also thick with existential angst. All around him, he saw people going about their daily lives, clinging to illusions of safety and security in order to forget that they were teetering on the brink of extinction. The two gravest threats of the early Cold War, "instant death by atomic war" and "slow death by conformity," required a different response. Mailer found one in the hipster, a radical nonconformist who was singularly devoted to unshackling himself from civilizational restraints. Mailer declared the hipster, a thoroughly male character, the natural ally of Black people. His immoderate embrace of present thrills made him an outcast, not unlike African Americans, who had known what it meant to stare death in the eye for more than three centuries. The defiant joy of a people surviving in the twilight zone of totalitarianism and democracy had much to teach a complacent white culture. The hipster understood this, which is why he was most alive when "exploring all those moral wildernesses of civilized life which the Square automatically condemns."[10]

Mailer's view of Black culture vacillated between admiration and objectification. Similar to the white primitivists who had pioneered the first slumming vogue during the 1920s, Mailer fetishized the most expressive and salacious aspects of African American life. This was unabashed cultural appropriation, yet one that Mailer deemed justified given the stakes involved. The bigger problem for him was how to escape the gravitational pull of the Cold War logic of mutually assured destruction, which made Americans prefer a sedative suburban existence. Against the nightmare of a nation resembling a giant retirement home, Mailer pitted a vision of radical self-rejuvenation. Less devoted revolutionary than individualist rebel, the hipster resisted the postponement of gratification stipulated by middle-class morality. A "philosophical psychopath" by circumstance, he would rather act out his "infantile fantasies" than surrender to "old crippling habit[s]" that alienated him from his innermost desires. Going back "to the source of their creation" was a perilous journey of self-discovery that could easily descend into violence. But it was ultimately necessary to "lessen the tensions of those infantile desires and so free [oneself] to remake a bit of [one's] nervous system." For Mailer, the true enemies of youth were lethargy and apathy. Defeat them, and you might get a shot at living life to its fullest.[11]

"The White Negro," which some regarded as the opening salvo of the counterculture's war against the national security state, left others dumbfounded. How could there be any value in the pseudo-allyship of the hipster if he bent toward the same infantilism that whites had invoked to relegate people of color to second-class citizenship? Black writer Ralph Ellison blasted Mailer's essay a few months after publication "as the same old primitivism crap in a new package," and he had a point. At the time of Ellison's intervention, the civil rights movement was picking up momentum. African Americans were demonstrating for equal citizenship, not for selfish hedonism. Young people were putting their lives on the line. Determined to topple segregation, Black college students organized sit-ins and launched voter registration campaigns across the South. Many endured beatings and arrests. In the summer of 1963, school-age African American children marched for civil rights in Birmingham, Alabama, showing maturity beyond their years. Youth politics in the Black freedom struggle bore little resemblance to the white hipster's rebellious youthfulness. In fact, both appeared to move in opposite directions.[12]

Rejuvenation's two sides—one empowering young people, the other encouraging adults to "grow down" in pursuit of their true selves—persisted throughout the protest-filled 1960s. Finding a middle ground proved difficult, as the authors of the Port Huron Statement realized. The student activists who met at the southern tip of Lake Huron in Michigan in June 1962 wanted a fresh start, both for themselves and for US democracy. Students for a Democratic Society (SDS) was the name they gave their collective body. The New Left they envisioned was part rebirth, part patricide. The labor leaders of old, the students found, had been co-opted by the country's power elites and had forfeited their role as agents of social justice. SDS members were equally concerned about the state of the American working class, whom they saw as rudderless and sedated by middle-class values. Tom Hayden, the main author of the Port Huron Statement, delivered his coup de grâce to socialist orthodoxy by declaring the university the locomotive of progress: "Many of us began maturing in complacency. As we grew, however, our comfort was penetrated by events too troubling to dismiss." What promised to be a golden age turned out to be an age of stagnation—sclerotic, without fantasy, wary of creativity and idealism. The only ones still "imbued with urgency" and longing to be "the spark and engine" in the "search for truly democratic alternatives" were students, according to Hayden. They first needed to remove from old gowns what the West German student movement referred to as "one-thousand years of rot." Once the university ceased to be a conformity-producing assembly line, it could serve as a hub for social change.[13]

The SDS's call for a youth-led participatory democracy rested on a daunting calculation. Amplifying student voices on campus appeared doable; whether university reform would function as a dress rehearsal for starting over on a national scale was a different matter altogether. The first test came with the free speech fights at Berkeley and Ann Arbor in 1964 and 1965. Student protest erupted after the administration of the University of California, Berkely imposed new restrictions on political activity on campus. The First

Amendment became a rallying point for a diverse coalition of liberal and socialist student groups who wanted to bury the anticommunist frenzy of the fifties. The campaign to free higher education from McCarthyism also nurtured a broader critique of patriarchal supervision. Students across the nation started speaking out against university boards treating them like children—a contradiction that seemed especially glaring in light of the fact that many had been playing major roles in demonstrations off campus. Lana Taylor, a student at Spelman College who went to jail for participating in a sit-in at an Atlanta diner in 1961, was one of them. Taylor was dismayed that "the institution was just working against the thing that they were supposed to be fostering—growing up and maturity."[14]

This was a common sentiment: colleges operated as the extended arm of a paternalistic system, and instead of treating students like young citizens, they were prolonging the same unruly adolescence that delinquency experts had been decrying as the source of numerous social ills. For Berkeley's free speech activists, seeing the administrators adopt a hard line only heightened the contradiction. The conflict came to a head on December 2, 1964, when 5,000 students engaged in a campus-wide strike. After police broke up a nonviolent sit-in demonstration inside the administration building, the Board of Regents held out an olive branch. They hired a new chancellor who was more supportive of the free speech movement's demands, even as they insisted that they would not surrender their right to regulate campus activities. Regardless of the outcome, one thing had become abundantly clear. The children of the duck-and-cover generation were no longer crouching under their desks. They were standing on them, looking their elders straight in the eye and telling them to listen.[15]

If the "crust of apathy" lying over the nation was to be broken, building new universities on the ruins of the old would not suffice. The mandate SDS activists gave themselves went further, culminating in calls for a strong student-worker alliance. Students' criticism of labor unions' ebbing vigor certainly did not help. Organized labor had little interest in joining the New Left as junior partners, and watching young activists reach out to factory workers and educate them on how to confront the system left a bad taste in their mouth. Michael Harrington, whose book *The Other America* inspired Lyndon B. Johnson's "War on Poverty," felt the sting of exclusion in his interactions with the Port Huron delegates. "Here I was: I was thirty-four. I'd been a youth leader for so long that people were joking that I was 'the oldest young socialist in America.' . . . Up comes this younger generation. I think that they are ignoring my honest, sincere and absolutely profound advice. And this struck at my self-image." In their crusade to rejuvenate the promise of US democracy, student activists also targeted men like Harrington. The Old Left, in their estimate, had become obsolete and thus unfit for rejuvenation. That did not sit well with middle-aged radicals, who took offense at being labeled outdated.[16]

Cooperation was more likely to happen when ageism was less pronounced. Among the methods the American SDS developed in concert with their European counterparts were the "work-ins," during which students took jobs at warehouses and factories to bond with regular working people. The rationale, according to a SDS leaflet, was to "get a deeper understanding of the problems workers face" as well as to make them partners in protest. Students who participated in these work-ins filed glowing reports about how the discussion groups and movie nights they organized prompted white workers to utter their disgust of the Vietnam War and to stand in solidarity with people of color. Building permanent bridges remained onerous, however. Even the most enthusiastic young activists found it "difficult to strike a balance between being too timid and being too gung-ho." Lecturing workers on Southeast Asia instead of understanding the things they needed to do to make a decent living was the surest way to cut a conversation short. Attempting to learn from past mistakes, the youths constantly reminded themselves that work-ins had to be spaces of mutual learning in which nobody saw their age and rank as liabilities.[17]

For the most part, middle-aged workers, even the more conservative ones, tolerated the presence of students on the shop floor. Any kind of "wise-guy attitude," however, made them lash out. At a large trucking company in New York City, two hippies felt the heat when they preached the gospel of scarcity to employees who had been working night shifts for years. They were asked to leave and never come back. Student radicals who believed that the country had to rejuvenate on their terms were walking on a tightrope with no end in sight. Play down your convictions to fit in, and you become a researcher rather than a revolutionary. Speak out too confidently in a blue-collar environment, and workers will feel insulted. Both sides expected the other to undergo a rite of passage; neither fully acquiesced. On May 8, 1970, the uneasy truce between workers and students broke down in New York's infamous Hardhat Riot. Hundreds of fuming construction workers armed with huge American flags ripped into an antiwar demonstration on Wall Street, injuring more than seventy students with their helmets and fists. The relationship was never the same again. Students denounced conservative white workers who supported Richard M. Nixon as "labor fascists." The hardhats, who had come to break some noses, had seen enough. Pampered college students, they fumed, were out of line and needed to be put back in their place.[18]

In resenting the erosion of white patriarchy, the hardhat rioters had much in common with Southern segregationists. Dismissing adult Black men as "boys" had long been a staple of the Jim Crow South. There was a reason that African American workers held up signs saying "I Am a Man" at the 1968 Memphis sanitation strike, which drew Martin Luther King Jr. to Tennessee. Toward the end of his life, King was facing mounting criticism from a younger, more militant wing of the movement. Although the boundaries separating racial moderates and Black Power advocates were more porous than frequently reported, the civil rights movement experienced its share of intergenerational strife. Newer studies of the movement contend that nonviolence was more tactical than normative and that appeals to pacifism impeded attempts to recruit more young Black men for the cause. Many felt emasculated seeing peaceful protesters, old women and children included, firehosed to the ground and brutally beaten by the police, with no means to defend themselves. White supremacy was the enemy, yet the respectability politics of senior civil rights organizations like the NAACP was seen as the problem.[19]

One influential proposition for rejuvenating the Black freedom struggle came from Stokely Carmichael, who took over the chairmanship of the Student Nonviolent Coordinating Committee (SNCC) in 1966. Carmichael's frustration with King's leadership had grown over the course of the sixties. Talking to Black youth across the South made him understand the futility of simply repeating the party line and calling for patience. "Of course, I was uneasy with it," Carmichael remembered, "to have to counsel restraint. Say what? Telling folks not to confront racism? . . . One faction—a loud faction of the youth—was restless. But discipline was holding." Tired with the pace of progress and the lack of white support, Carmichael began to share the restlessness he initially sought to contain. His call for "Black Power," which he uttered in June 1966 at a rally in Greenwood, Mississippi, marked Carmichael's divorce from gradualism. Culturally, the movement's young foot soldiers coveted a new look, sporting Afros and dashikis to convey race pride. Politically, Carmichael and other Black Power advocates suggested that the African American freedom struggle was at an impasse, fenced in between a fatigued Black leadership and a white majority unwilling to change. "Frederick Douglass said that the youth should fight to be leaders today. God knows we need to be leaders today, because the men who run this country are sick," Carmichael declared in front of a group of students at Berkeley. Young Black activists faced a choice: either follow their elders' fallacious dream of

FIGURE 7.1 Alfredo Roostgard, "Black Power," 1968. Revitalizing African American masculinity by aggressively countering the racist stereotype of Black men as weak and submissive was a core concern of the Black Power movement. Courtesy of the National Museum of African American History and Culture.

integration, or follow the example of students in other parts of the world, who were in the vanguard of their countries' anticolonial struggles.[20]

Several self-defense groups that emerged in the final two years of the 1960s opted for taking up arms. Gender and age were critical elements in the formation of the Black Panther Party, which fashioned a militant Black masculinity projecting aggressiveness and coolness (see figure 7.1). Unapologetic about brandishing weapons in public spaces, the Panthers, clad in black leather coats and berets, developed a revolutionary style that found imitators across the globe. Making a conscious effort to win over Black youths, members denigrated their opponents as "Uncle Toms" and bootlicking old fools. Condemning the old to obsolescence probably got in the way of developing the kind of larger movement the Panthers hoped to build. At the same time, their ageism was consistent with their belief that the moderate civil rights policies of the past had made African American genocide more likely. The Young Lords, a group of Puerto Rican nationalists modeled after the Black Panthers, thrived on the same distinction. Founded in 1968, the Young Lords carried out a series of urban guerrilla actions in Chicago and New York City to forge Latinx-Black coalitions and renew interest in Puerto Rican independence. Here, too, rejuvenation meant empowering young people against an older generation of Hispanic-American leaders perceived as too timid to fight back against the counterrevolution.[21]

Although women flocked to these movements in significant numbers, Black Power focused on the rejuvenation of African American manhood. In the eyes of Panther ideologue Eldridge Cleaver, centuries of white oppression had left Black males psychologically and literally castrated, unable to perform their patriarchal duties to protect and provide for their families. Other party frontmen echoed Cleaver's masculinist convictions, with some branding feminism as a sinister white plot to weaken the Black nationalist project. To be fair, the misogyny experienced by politicized young women in the sixties was not unique to the Black Panthers. Sexism hampered meaningful partnerships between male and female activists in the student movement as well. Most young women who joined the SDS refused to see women's rights issues as marginal matters. Those who took the stage arguing that fighting patriarchy at home and imperialism abroad were two sides of the same coin, as the feminist Ellen Willis recounted, "were laughed at, patronized, called frigid, emotionally disturbed man-haters" and, worst of all in left-wing circles, "apolitical." Despite resolutions to the contrary, the male-dominated New Left struggled to make gender equality (even more so gay and lesbian rights) a core component of their revolutionary agenda.[22]

Democratizing the American body politic, thus, rarely extended to a broader commitment to assisting women in taking control of their own bodies. As access to contraception increased, feminists became more adamant about locating the prime of female youth in women's ability to have children later in life or, if they so desired, to have none at all. In the women's rights literature of the 1960s and 1970s, the stay-at-home moms venerated in the postwar ideal of the nuclear family were almost indistinguishable from the children these mothers were supposed to raise. Maternal care furthered women's dependency, making them adults in name only. Motherhood was not incompatible with activism. That was borne out by the roughly 400 middle-aged women who staged a "mothers' protest" in front of the White House in June 1965 to demonstrate against the Vietnam War. Still, young feminists chafed at the public perception of mothers calling for their sons to come home as emotionally and politically naive. Modern women, they held, needed to carve out identities for themselves distinct from the superficial college girl or the exhausted, trapped housewife.[23]

Female rejuvenation during the sixties did not stop with demands for political inclusion and greater career opportunities. As one might expect from the so-called sexual revolution, it involved an extensive reconsideration of women's sexuality. A new candor about bodily pleasures articulated in countercultural spaces prompted a series of advice books that encouraged Americans to talk more openly about their sexual preferences. *The Joy of Sex*, Alex Comfort's charts-topping 1972 manual, told women fifty and older that a healthy sex life could be as invigorating as a balanced diet and regular exercise. Feminists defending the right of every woman to have an orgasm sneered at the beauty culture of their mothers and grandmothers. Staging a protest outside a Miss America pageant in Atlantic City in September 1968, a group of women liberationists slammed "the gospel of our society," which dictated "according to Saint Male: women must be young, juicy, malleable—hence age discrimination and the cult of youth. And we women are brain-washed into believing this ourselves!" Rather than hoping to regain their youth, most middle-aged women seeking to improve their sex life were pursuing self-fulfillment. Redefining female sexuality as "a life-long journey," as the historian Leslie Paris put it, connected aging women to their younger selves, but not in a nostalgic way. More importantly, it helped them release some of the anxiety associated with entering their thirties and forties, a stage in the female life course rarely associated with personal growth.[24]

In challenging common conceptions of aging women, second-wave feminists could build on the example set by queer authors who created counter-hegemonic stories around their older protagonists. *Sister Gin*, a 1975 novel written by June Arnold, takes a defiant approach to the subject of menopause. Contrary to portraying the last period as a negative turning point in women's lives, the novel presents the end of female reproductive capability as a liberating experience. The main character Su, an aging lesbian from North Carolina, finds unexpected vigor and a new partner. The absence of biological children is reframed as an empowering moment of rebirth. Instead of nurturing her own, Su campaigns for the Democrats during the 1972 presidential election and adopts "anger" as her true inner child. Political defeat notwithstanding,

Su keeps "spouting off," eager to seek retribution for the wrongs she had to suffer in her earlier life.[25]

Scholars of the counterculture have been grappling for decades with the question of when the period started and when, exactly, it ended. This is a futile debate to have because the ferment of rebellion took off in so many directions, with varied outcomes for the people involved. Speaking of a single culture of rejuvenation makes little sense considering the sheer multitude of youth-themed protest movements vying for the spotlight. In this increasingly discordant choir, few voices sang together in total harmony. However, there was one melody that resonated with leftist students, Black youths, feminists, and queer activists alike: a shared disdain for an ecumenical ideal of youth that permitted senior men to act as if they were its natural guardians. Preventing the regeneration of an older culture of national complacency was the one thing young leftists could agree on, and Cold War elites were the last group they wanted to see reenergized. Meanwhile, one group continued to look for another tune entirely, one that would propel them back to the days of their childhood.

TIMOTHY LEARY WAS so convinced that he had discovered the Fountain of Youth that he did not mind walking into the lion's den. On April 10, 1967, Leary, wearing a white gown and beaded necklaces, found himself sitting in a TV studio in Queens, New York, ready to parry the arguments of his opponents. His antagonist onstage was a formidable debater. William F. Buckley, the conservative intellectual and host of the popular talk show *Firing Line*, began the exchange by ripping into Leary's movement and calling the man opposite to him "the pope of what he chooses to call a new religion." Buckley, who felt emboldened in front of an audience of students in traditional suits and with neatly combed hair, made no secret of his disdain for mood-altering substances. Excessive drug use was the problem of "poorly adjusted people," of young men and women drowning their own incapacity to deal with the world as it was and resorting to narcotics. Throughout the debate, Buckley pointed out that taking LSD could cause serious health damage. His biggest indictment, though, was reserved for the claim that mind-enhancing drugs would unlock a higher reality. That, scoffed the conservative celebrity, was "utter, total gobbledygook."[26]

Buckley was right about one thing: Leary, the trained psychologist and hippie intellectual, did not yield a single inch. He defended the creativity unleashed by psychedelic drugs with the confidence of an evangelist. His opponent's accusations, Leary replied, reflected a poor understanding of the issue.

FIGURE 7.2 Timothy Leary at the Human Be-In in San Francisco, 1967. Psychedelic activists advocated the use of LSD to return to an imaginary childhood free from the constraints of modern adulthood. Photograph by Lisa Law, courtesy of the Division of Work and Industry, National Museum of American History, Smithsonian Institution.

The overwhelmingly young psychedelic revolutionaries took drugs precisely out of a heightened sense of responsibility. They were displaying "a level of awareness" that Leary could "only dimly grasp" and say Godspeed to as it passed him by. Age, Leary argued, was "the only important political division of the United States today." On one side, there were the many Americans, "particularly over the age fifty," who "when the word drug is mentioned, think of some opiate, of something that is an escape . . . something that you take if you are a failure." Younger, more enlightened minds had debunked that false perception, proving that "psychedelic drugs intensify consciousness." Learning how to use them wisely and correctly was the only path to a "philosophical and religious experience" through which people could detach themselves from "fake prop society and go back." Leary opposed outlawing drugs. But when asked which warning label he would prefer to see on LSD packages, he quipped that the label should read "LSD can cause death and rebirth."[27]

Leary and his disciples liked a good joke. But jesters they were not. Three months earlier, at a "human be-in" of 30,000 people in San Francisco's Golden Gate Park, Leary had gained notoriety for uttering the words that became the mantra of his movement (see figure 7.2). "Turn on, tune in, drop out" amounted to a psychedelic declaration of independence. Of all the addictions that beset humanity, tradition was decried as the greatest. Mainstream culture, the worst drug of all, rewarded compliance with false highs such as larger homes, bigger cars, and higher salaries. Psychedelic intellectuals sought liberation from the materialist cravings generated by consumerism, using clinical language to describe modern society and its institutions as one big insane asylum. The inversion of madness and sanity became a recurring theme in hippie literature. Nowhere did that theme figure more prominently than in Ken Kesey's 1962 novel *One Flew over the Cuckoo's Nest,* which relates the power struggles between medical staff and inmates in a mental hospital. The book ends tragically with the mercy killing of the protagonist Randle McMurphy, who led a futile rebellion against an institution dedicated to smothering in its patients all desire for joy.[28]

Where McMurphy failed, the Beatniks tried to succeed with poetry. In convention-defying, obscenity-sprinkled verse, Beat writers like Allen Ginsberg and William Burroughs urged the younger generation to "break out of the plastic mass into human flesh and blood, vulnerability and tenderness." Taking readers on a tour across America's darkest alleys and highest planes became a signature move in Beat literature. Jack Kerouac's best-selling novel *On the Road* (1957) inspired young people to embrace travel as a physical and philosophical act of sovereignty. Ideally, the hippie backpackers who walked away from the trappings of consumerism experienced their trips as a rite of passage more satisfying than those offered to a first-time voter at the ballot box. In celebrating geographical and ecstatic voyage as self-discovery, the Beatniks of the 1950s exerted a major influence on the psychedelic experimenters of the 1960s. Out of Ginsberg's and Burroughs's friendship with Leary, a radical theory of rejuvenation began to crystallize. Combining art and drugs, they held, might be the key to rewiring middle-class adults to an earlier, freer state of existence—a process that LSD advocates referred to as "deconditioning."[29]

The kind of time travel espoused in psychedelic circles stood in sharp contrast to the hypermasculine regeneration touted by Theodore Roosevelt sixty years earlier. Whereas their imperialist fathers and great-grandfathers had cherished raw, unbridled adolescence, LSD promoters homed their sights on early childhood, which to them was the optimal locus of rejuvenation. In the years after World War II, different groups developed a fascination for the drug. The US government authorized clandestine experiments to determine whether LSD's hallucinogenic effects could be turned into a psychological weapon. Psychiatrists who started using LSD in therapy were the first to note that patients were comparing their trips to temporary forays back into the world of carefree play. "I plummeted down, I felt myself growing smaller and smaller. . . . I was becoming a child . . . a very small child" was how one female recollected the impact the pill had on her. The chemical reactions LSD induced in human brains were not well understood, except that they caused childlike sensations and extreme mood swings. Trips sent users on emotional roller coasters; they would giggle and fool around one minute, then suddenly bawl like toddlers. The British writer Aldous Huxley, himself a proponent of throwing open the doors of perception through mind-altering substances, called these experiences a "second childhood." Without them, men and women would remain trapped in civilization's iron cage, unable to wrest their deepest, immaculate selves from conformity's grip.[30]

Psychedelic missionaries vowed that their exaltation of the adult-child sprang from social impulses, not selfish ones. Residing in Millbrook, New York, from 1963 to 1968, Leary and his followers conducted a series of consciousness-expanding workshops. Most followed a two-step process. The first step was to throw out all the mental garbage—to "take LSD to wipe the slate clean of all that Madison Avenue-Big Business-Behaviorist crap." The second step aimed at the reforging of social relations. In an essay published as early as 1931, Huxley described this reforging as follows: "If we could sniff or swallow something that would, for five or six hours each day, abolish our solitude as individuals, atone us with our fellows in a glowing exaltation of affection and make life in all its aspects seem not only worth living, but divinely beautiful and significant . . . then, it seems to me, all our problems . . . would be wholly solved and earth would become paradise." The religious overtones are hard to miss. Leary's politics of ecstasy elevated children to the position of God-like teacher and Jesus-like savior. Hippies embodying younger versions of themselves by adopting colorful nicknames and wearing playful costumes recognized each other as part of a spiritually rejuvenated human family, at one with nature and its creatures.[31]

The New Left, for the most part, begged to differ. The ties holding together the student and psychedelic movements were dangerously frayed. During the height of the hippie demonstrations in 1967 that became known as the "Summer of Love," they snapped in two. Tom Hayden did not hold back his contempt, stating that the hippies were peddling "absurdity masquerading as politics." Their idealization of childhood innocence smacked of pointless nostalgia, or worse, a form of anti-politics that left the youth's revolutionary potential rotting by the roadside. Relationships between Black Power and the mostly white flower children could also turn quite adversarial.

In February 1968, the Oakland chapter of the Black Panthers called on its members to stop harassing the hippies: their pacifism might be badly misplaced, but they were not the enemy. Eldridge Cleaver had less patience for Leary's messiah complex. Their paths crossed in 1970 in Algeria, where Cleaver had established an outpost of the Panthers. He soon regretted playing host to Leary, who had barely made it to Algeria after breaking out of a California prison. The two fugitives from the US government did not get along. Cleaver called Leary "apolitical" and an "opportunist" who had his "mind blown out by acid." His followers, Cleaver continued, were just as deluded for thinking they were changing society by dropping out: "You're doing nothing except destroying your own brains and strengthening the ends of our enemy." Leary and his wife literally got away with a black eye. The Panthers seized their drugs and held them captive until they managed to slip away under the cover of darkness.[32]

Of all the accusations leveled against the psychedelic movement, the charge that its adherents were living in a shallow politics-free zone was the easiest to fend off. Why, then, would Nixon call Leary the most dangerous man in America? The hippies' deep suspicion of elites who confused masculinity and advanced age with authority transcended the spiritual realm. Rather than protest individual policies, hippie dissidents identified maturity as the actual problem, hopelessly entangled with militarism, racism, sexism, and imperialism. Leary was quite explicit about why he believed love and play to be far more potent tools of subversion than communist manifestos or civil rights marches. "The result of the psychedelic revolution is going to bring down the American Empire," Leary confidently stated in his debate with Buckley—not by disgruntled citizens resorting to "violence and force" but in the "only effective way: a familial turning on together, a protest of flowers and beauty." The surest manner to defeat the terror associated with modern American adulthood was to dismantle it with the weapons of childhood.[33]

For all the frenetic reclaiming of a purer past in the interest of building a better future, the hippies were treading on a well-trodden path. In attempting to regenerate society, they rebooted the age-old Euro-American dream (which was older still than its close cousin, the rags-to-riches Dream) of starting history afresh. That same return mentality had been the subject of a book written by a literary scholar on the eve of the countercultural rebellion. R. W. B. Lewis's *American Adam*, which came out in 1955, contended that since the nation's violent birth, each generation of Americans had set out to improve their country by dreaming it all up again. Likening the United States to the biblical Adam, writers and reformers of various stripes had donned the mantle of blissful innocence to stake out futures for humankind unburdened by history. At first glance, Lewis's thesis, mired in Cold War exceptionalism and biased toward canonical white male authors, seemed a bad fit for the youth movements of the 1960s. However, parts of Lewis's analysis could be read as offering a template for heroic rejuvenation in the Age of Containment. A distant kinship also existed with the Protestant revivals of the nineteenth century. The rites of rebirth vaunted by the hippies bore a striking similarity to antebellum preachers at camp meetings, who had been whipping worshippers into ecstasy with the promise that paradise was just one conversion away. LSD simply punched the ticket all the way back to the beginnings of creation, the original moment of wondrous innocence, nothing more.[34]

Hippie rejuvenation was not without its dark undercurrents. Psychedelic explorers failed to draw a clear boundary between idolizing childhood and treating actual children with questionable intent. Together with his partner Richard Alpert, Leary invited parents to stay at Millbrook with their small children, hoping to study the latter and learn from their spontaneity. The experiment was short-lived because the men became tired of childcare. Meanwhile, most hippie communes in the United States and elsewhere were teeming with children. Collective modes of childrearing, in which extended families took on the role of biological parents, were writ large in these settings. Individual experiences varied, of course, and many adults with a communal upbringing cherish memories of spending their days surrounded with plenty of playmates, animals, and grown-ups acting like older brothers and sisters.[35]

Anecdotal evidence suggests a bleaker picture. In some cases, the rejection of nuclear family norms resulted in carelessness and neglect. For Sean Gaston, growing up in an anarchist collective that went by the name of Strange Farm resembled a "Lord of the Flies" situation. The feeling of empowerment that came from interacting with adults without boundaries evaporated once basic needs went unaddressed. "French toast was the only thing I knew how to cook, and that was how I kept myself alive," Gaston remembered. He stank terribly and was full of lice. His nightly resting place was under a staircase (he had no bed). Sometimes, when the weather was nice, he slept outside beneath an old bus. Gaston's mother did not seem to mind. She was busy exploring her sexuality in a commune that disavowed private property and monogamy.[36]

Child abuse is a difficult subject to broach. To this day, it rarely figures among the sinister moments of the sixties' counterculture, such as the Manson family murders or the deadly Altamont Speedway Free Festival. Even if one assumes that hippie communes attracted fewer child molesters than closed institutions like juvenile detention centers or the Catholic Church, witnessing older housemates indulging in sex orgies night after night could leave deep psychological scars. Forced to shuttle between the revolutionary ethics of free love and a terrifying lack of privacy, the writer Elizabeth Shé had damning words for her countercultural childhood. "The free love movement," she noted, "set me up for a lifetime of sexual, emotional, and physical abuse." Drugs were a constant source of potential harm. Given that most communes prided themselves on their radical egalitarianism, children often enjoyed unrestricted access to marijuana and LSD. Some adult communards actively encouraged minors to join their psychedelic sessions, regardless of the negative impact hallucinogens might have had on younger bodies. Though horrific reports about sexual violence, pedophilia, and cultish behavior have not cropped up in more than a few instances, flower childhood seemed to revolve less around children's well-being.[37]

Contrary to popular perception, hippie permissiveness in childrearing did not simply grow out of the movement's antiestablishment attitudes. Age itself was seen as an oppressive construct that needed to be torn apart in order to advance the emancipation of all human beings. Renouncing the age restrictions of bourgeoise society became necessary for specific countercultural performances of rejuvenation to work. The presence of real children helped to authenticate these performances and possibly also to gloss over the absurdity of Leary's ultimate drop-out nirvana, which he shared on a ferry boat in San Francisco harbor in February 1967: "I am going to go away to a beach and live on the beach. I am going to take LSD once a week and I am going to take hashish once a day at sunset and I am going to have babies and I am going to learn from our babies." Leary's words spelled trouble for the counterculture. In the following years, conservatives would jump on such statements to paint the hippies as unpatriotic potheads and dangerous subversives bent on stealing America's most precious resource: its children.[38]

NOT QUITE TWO YEARS after the Vietnam War had ended, the singer and former beauty queen Anita Bryant opened a new front in the ongoing war over America's youth. The days of the flower children had passed, but not the forces of immorality who, according to Bryant, had reappeared in the gown of homosexual rights to wage a vicious assault on the traditional family. Together with fellow conservative Christians, Bryant took a stand at a public hearing in Miami on January 18, 1977. The protesters railed against an ordinance that would outlaw discrimination against gay men and lesbian women in Dade County, Florida. Calling gay rights a "peril to the nation," Bryant protested that the ordinance interfered with the "divine right" of mothers "to protect our children in our homes, our businesses, and especially our schools." Likening gays to kidnappers, she declared that "homosexuals cannot reproduce—so they must recruit. And to freshen their ranks, they must recruit the youth of America." Stopping the enemy from breaching the gates required extraordinary measures. This included escalating differences in sexual orientation into a struggle over which Americans got to speak for and own youth and thus survive.[39]

The raucous birth of Bryant's antigay coalition, which she shrewdly labeled "Save Our Children," mirrored the rightward shift of large numbers of white middle-class Americans during the crisis-ridden 1970s. But it also marked a pivotal moment in the consolidation of what I like to call the conservative child. Both political idea and breathing subject, the conservative child emerged as a reactionary bulwark against the surges of left-wing rejuvenation preceding it. Ideologically, it served as a linchpin connecting the suburban white middle-class values of the 1950s to the New Right's "morning again in America" nostalgia of the 1980s. Racist youth played an important role in the forging of the New Right. White children and teenagers who felt threatened by Black youth's aspirations to equal citizenship wrote angry letters to governors and presidents, demanding that their right to a happy childhood be protected. Taking these conservative minors seriously disrupts the assumption that children are somehow naturally progressive. Anti–civil rights youth involved in building a new Republican coalition turned their supposed vulnerability into a political asset while putting an innocuous face on old racist prejudices.[40]

Still, the conservative child gained its greatest efficacy (and later its greatest value for the Reaganite project of national rebirth) as an anti-rejuvenationist figure. An increasingly frantic emphasis on child protection, coupled with parents' adoption of civil rights rhetoric, enabled a white constituency that thought of itself as the last line of defense against racial and sexual minorities luring American youths away from the safe spaces of home and church. The "silent majority" had no interest in young and old people trading places. Young idealists striving to broaden US democracy were a thorn in the flesh of conservatives. Vice President Spiro Agnew and clergyman Norman Vincent Peale winced accordingly. They blamed their countercultural opponents for raising "demanding little tyrants" who trampled on everything that had made the United States the last, best hope on earth.[41]

Agnew's boss in the White House understood that juxtaposing insurgent youth with imperiled childhood accrued significant political capital for his side. In the eyes of left-wing protesters, Richard Nixon was the perfect villain. Shifty and awkward, he lacked the youthful charisma of John F. Kennedy, who defeated Nixon in 1960 and inspired countless young admirers to enter public service. Eight years later, Republicans found their winning strategy in a harsh law-and-order message. Television ads showed burning houses and ranting students. Nixon curried favor with voters by pledging to restore safety on the streets. Given the baby boomers' entry into political life, Nixon could not afford to ignore the youth vote entirely. The Republican nominee reached out to the Young Americans for Freedom, a devoted cadre of conservative student activists, and dallied with young female delegates waving "Nixon Is Groovy" signs at the 1968 Republican National Convention. The closing theme of Nixon's acceptance address, however, was childhood. His image of the nation in 1968 was that of children of all races born into a dystopian hellscape. Robbed of their future by the "peddlers" of "filth" and narcotics," they were condemned to "a living nightmare of poverty, neglect, and despair." What was needed were decent citizens marshaling the forces of faith and patriotism to repair these broken childhoods and end "the long dark night for America." Sidestepping the question of whether young people had just grievances, Nixon declared child saving a mainstay of the modern conservative movement and one of the touchstones of American exceptionalism.[42]

In order to turn child protection and colorblindness into conservative shields against the era's civil rights gains, the Republican Party could count on a growing army of women activists. The role of the white middle-class "homemaker" in organizing bottom-up resistance against liberalism, feminism, and antiracism has been amply documented by historians such as Lisa McGirr, Michelle Nickerson, and Rebecca Brückmann. Their works detail how a culture of conservative countermobilization, stretching from the court-ordered desegregation of public schools in the late 1950s to the antibusing demonstrations of the early 1970s, succeeded in painting government intervention on behalf of discriminated minorities as infringements on the right of mothers to decide how their children should be brought up. The notion that a powerful left-wing conspiracy was preying on the nation's children fueled the campaigns of Phyllis Schlafly, one of the most capable grassroots organizers of the 1970s. With a string of newsletters, distributed by her organization to stoke opposition against the Equal Rights Amendment (ERA), Schlafly infused a combustible stew of anti-feminism, homophobia, and constitutional theory into households across the nation. Were the ERA to become the law of the land, Schlafly cautioned in August 1973, it would "invalidate all the state laws" that gave "the wife her legal right to be a fulltime wife and mother, in her own home, taking care of her own babies."[43]

These examples make clear that the affective potential of vulnerable childhood offered far greater boons to conservative anti-rejuvenationists than restless youth. Claiming to act on behalf of one's children gave license to venting raw emotions: the fear that universities were popping out hordes of un-American teachers keen on indoctrinating the nation's boys and girls, or the anger directed at government bureaucrats for launching affirmative action programs that critics rejected as dangerous social experiments at the expense of the smallest Americans. Liberals hoped that their policies would produce young citizens less stuck in old ways and more committed to widening the circle of we beyond the pale of whiteness. For conservatives, this was exactly the pickle. Again, childhood provided a convenient backdoor, allowing reactionary whites to cloak their opposition to racial integration in the ostensibly colorblind mantle of child protection. As one father confronted New York City's Board of Education tasked with desegregating the city's public schools, "Do you honestly believe that you can . . . ship our children to some slum school . . . to spend their lunch hours in streets that are civic cesspools . . . without a fight on your hands?" Enraged parents siding with the letter writer could claim that these were not the words of a malicious racist, merely those of a concerned parent. Civil rights supporters saw through the charade, lambasting it as a dishonest attempt to deny children of color the right to a good education.[44]

The West has a long history of aligning childrearing with efforts to prolong white privilege. The conservatives of the 1960s and 1970s belong in that lineage. Countercultural activists wanted to rejuvenate US democracy by expanding it. Their adversaries on the right sought to prevent this from happening. They shot back with a conservative vision of childhood that was oddly resistant to development and that prized continuity over the change that comes with growth. For those looking for sprinkles of rejuvenationist thought in the early New Right, the pronatalism of the antiabortion movement is a good place to start. But even there, the religiously motivated concern for the rights of the unborn overrode calls to enforce maternity among white women as a means of demographic control (not until the early 2000s did pro-lifers become more susceptible to the racist panic that the United States was changing into a minority-white country). It took Ronald Reagan to spread an upbeat narrative of national rebirth in lieu of the darker anti-rejuvenationist message of his predecessors. Reagan's 1980 campaign slogan "Let's Make

America Great Again" tapped into a nostalgic mood. It expressed the belief that the script for a better future lay in reclaiming the optimism of past generations, and that a timeless suburban picket-fence idyll was waiting to be recovered. Reagan's acceptance speech at the Republican National Convention contained the word "renew" or "renewed" seven times, "restore" four times, "rebirth" once, and used verbs like "reestablish," "reaffirm," "redeem," and "recapture." The semantics of rejuvenation had entered the modern conservative dictionary. That book, however, has rarely spoken to more than half the country.[45]

There is endless speculation over what would have transpired had the young people who challenged the status quo in the transnational sixties gotten their way. Some dreams descended into delusions; others were crushed beyond recognition. But even as age alone proved insufficient to bring about the change the protesters desired, a larger story about youth's place in American society persisted: that of young people uniquely capable of identifying injustice and of acting forcefully on behalf of the greater good. Within that frame, parents no longer had the right to call their children "prone to shallow commitments," as Holly V. Scott stated. With young people taking up the reins of rejuvenation, the tables were beginning to turn. All of a sudden, adulthood stood in the court of public opinion, accused of being the real delinquent. Conversations about why and how youth mattered continued to produce different and highly contingent answers. For conservatives, though, clawing their way back to the switchboards of rejuvenation meant moving farther to the right and further into the past—to an imaginary time when those standing outside the halls of power had not yet tasted the forbidden fruit of defiance.[46]

CHAPTER EIGHT

Exercising for the New Age
Building Neoliberal Bodies

Just Do It.
—Nike (1988)

On a slightly overcast day in June 1984, US servicemen stationed in West Berlin took off their boots and put on their running shoes. With the Summer Olympics in Los Angeles just a few weeks away, Army Command ordered the soldiers serving on the front lines of the Cold War to demonstrate that they were good athletes. The Berlin "Brigade Run" took members of the Sixth Infantry Regiment on a ten-mile run around McNair Barracks in Lichterfelde. Photographs show the soldiers sweating and pumping toward the finish line but also grateful for the diversion. Local Berliners contributed to the festive mood by cheering the runners on and handing out fruits and beverages. These were exactly the scenes the organizers had hoped to generate—images of a fighting force that, a decade earlier, had been troubled by drugs, racial conflict, and war fatigue. The "Be All You Can Be" Army of the early 1980s wanted that chapter closed, promising young men adventure, camaraderie, and fraternity in fitness.[1]

An ocean away from the soldiers jogging up and down the streets of West Berlin, women were converting their own living rooms into private exercise studios. Their icon was Jane Fonda, the movie star and activist whose workout videos sparked a movement. Fonda's conversion to aerobics dated back to a foot fracture she suffered in 1978, which made it impossible for her to return to ballet, the sport she loved. She tried staying in shape with aerobics, and what started out as an alternative soon became a personal revelation. Growing up at a time when females were not supposed to exert themselves, the forty-year-old (born December 21, 1937) Fonda found herself "stronger and more limber, and I look and feel better than when I was twenty." The younger, more physical womanhood embodied by Fonda rapidly conquered a mass market. Her 1981 book, in which she described her daily workout routines, sold millions of copies. More successful still were Fonda's string of aerobics videotapes, some of which stayed in the top ten of Billboard's videocassette sales chart for over forty weeks. "America Shapes Up," *Time* magazine pronounced in November of that year. On the cover were five well-toned white men and women, four of them middle-aged and one a senior, holding up photos of themselves burning calories at their favorite sports.[2]

Fonda, a fervent critic of the Vietnam War, and the US Army probably would have never pulled in the same direction had it not been for the fitness craze that has swept the United States since the late 1970s. Journalists researching the subject estimated that in 1961, less than a quarter of all Americans were exercising on a regular basis. That percentage, according to a Gallup Poll conducted in 1987, had jumped up to 69 percent in the same year. As with most statistics, the statements made were probably more reflective of changing social norms than an accurate representation of everyday practices. Countless US citizens remained indifferent to the rising tide of images celebrating muscle-packed athletes. Others stayed away from fitness centers because they could not afford membership or because they suffered from a physical disability. Sooner or later, however, the unfit had to pay a social price. "Nerd" and "couch potato" did not become insults out of nowhere.[3]

Indeed, the breadth of the fitness craze continues to amaze, even more so since scholars have long refused to treat it as a serious phenomenon. That neglect is partly rooted in the dismissive attitude of some of the period's leading intellectuals. The decline in public trust in government following the Watergate scandal led to intense soul-searching about where the nation was headed. Diagnoses of the seventies as a time of self-indulgence were amplified by warnings about the perilous effects of retreating into privacy. For the novelist Tom Wolfe, who famously labeled the seventies "The Me Decade," finding oneself had become the obsession of an entire generation. Chiming in from the vistas of sociology, Richard Sennett predicted nothing less than "the end of public culture" if Americans surrendered to "the tyrannies of intimacy." Two years later in 1979, the historian Christopher Lasch elaborated on Wolfe's and Sennett's observations in a book titled *The Culture of Narcissism*. Instead of responding to the fractures of the present by repairing the sinews of community, Americans, Lasch bemoaned, had become enamored with spectacular self-realization. In Lasch's analysis, the throngs of adults who were spending their evenings in neon-lighted gyms and their weekends in funky discotheques were not merely a symptom of national malaise. Worse, they were feeding it.[4]

My purpose here is not to quarrel with Lasch or prove him wrong. His arguments will be dealt with at proper places in this chapter. I want to build on the work of other historians to try to understand why ideas of youthfully slender and sculpted bodies rose to dominance in the last quarter of the twentieth century and how these ideas shaped popular perceptions of antiaging as a sign of personal achievement in an age defined by the consolidation of neoliberalism. The term "neoliberal" has become such a hot potato that it better be defined precisely. I take it to mean more than a theory developed in opposition to New Deal liberalism that seeks to curtail the government's role in economic affairs and blurs the distinction between citizens and consumers. Applied to individuals, the neoliberal creed could mutate into a biopolitical straitjacket that, to quote Jürgen Martschukat, compelled its wearers to "work on themsel[ves], have life under control, get fit, ensure their own productive capacity, and embody these things in the truest sense of the word." The tension between liberty and compulsion, self and society, is a fundamental one. So is the question of whether rejuvenation through fitness, based on the assumption that regular exercise yields physical, civic, mental, and moral rewards, created opportunities for more meaningful lives or whether the confluence of work and workout ethic undercut that promise.[5]

Previous generations of Americans had been subject to similar exhortations. Some of the earliest proponents of a muscular citizenship included German-speaking immigrants who transplanted the Turner movement to the United States in the wake of the European Revolutions of 1848. Another cornerstone of modern physical education was laid by Progressive Era reformers who viewed athletics as vital to building character—white male character, to be exact. This was also the mold in which the first two real fitness celebrities were cast. One was the German-born strongman Eugen Sandow, who bulged his muscles in front of cheering crowds across the United States and the British Empire in the 1890s and early 1900s. While Sandow's vaudeville shows put bodybuilding on the map, the self-styled exercise guru Bernarr Macfadden built an entire business empire on it. *Physical Culture*, the journal Macfadden started in 1899, became an immediate success. Several readers were without a doubt drawn to Macfadden's publications because they carried pictures of scantily clad men and women (which got Macfadden in trouble with the law). Most of all, they hammered into the minds of millions of Americans that "weakness is a crime," and that the infirmities caused by aging could be reversed through healthy eating and sports.[6]

Acknowledging these forerunners is important for making sense of the marriage of neoliberalism and fitness in the latter part of the twentieth century. But they cannot fully explain it. The wellness hype that began in the 1970s, as well as the twin crisis it addressed of an economy gone bad and of a national body in disarray, differed from its precursors in size and substance. One difference concerned changing gender roles. The women who hoisted the banner of fitness as the second wave of feminism was cresting did so against the backdrop of increasing divorce rates and bitter fights over abortion rights and workplace equality. For many, breaking a sweat in the gym became crucial to shedding the stigma of women as the weaker sex, and not a few men felt threatened by women touting their physicality outside the realms of sexual intercourse and childbirth. Nasty remarks were a common nuisance. Kenneth Cooper, the medical doctor who coined the word *aerobics* in 1968, had a reputation for dropping some casual sexism when addressing women athletes. "If running is not your cup of tea," Cooper commented in his first book, "swimming is second best and definitely ladylike. You can wear your pretty bathing suit and socialize around the pool." In Cooper's opinion, women should exercise just so much that they could keep their tummies tucked in.[7]

Growing anxieties about expanding waistlines were another characteristic of the neoliberal body project. Although overweight people had been the target of ridicule long before 1970s, associations of corpulence with economic success, especially in older men, had kept the pathologization of fatness within certain limits. That changed with the gradual spread of a low-fat ideology that extended to the highest levels of government. In 1977, Democratic Senator George McGovern told Americans that "too much fat, too much sugar or salt, can be and are directly linked to heart disease, cancer, obesity, and stroke, among other killer diseases." McGovern's statement reflected a growing consensus in the medical community that called on Americans to avert a national health crisis (on top of the economic one) by cutting back on high-fat foods. More than ever, a proper diet consisting of fruits, vegetables, poultry, and fish promised longer, happier, and more productive lives. Losing weight became a choice—much like the cosmeticians of the early twentieth century had talked about removing wrinkles from a woman's aging face. Tolerating excessive body fat, on the other hand, was cast as a mark of irresponsibility or inability. Disadvantages of class and race rarely figured as possible causes.[8]

A third trait that gave structure to the ideal of self-governing individuals turning flabby bodies into toned ones was a profound reevaluation of midlife. Middle age offers a useful lens for scrutinizing the fitness boom of the 1970s and 1980s. Few Americans who found purpose in physical exercise during that period appeared driven by a yearning for lost youth. This classic theme was certainly present, yet it often vanished behind a collective effort to transform middle age, which most imagined to begin in one's thirties and end with retirement, into a time when reinvention was possible and a fuller vitality achievable.

If *becoming young* was not a primary concern for middle-aged gym-goers, *keeping up with the young* was. Not all fitness and anti-fatness programs aimed at rejuvenation. What they held out was the prospect of a midlife in which the biological clock would tick more slowly and less menacingly.

This sounded like a tall order given that "midlife" first gained the public's attention in conjunction with the word "crisis." Invented by psychologists in the 1960s and claimed by feminists in the 1970s, the term came to be used for adults living in abundance yet gripped by a stifling fear of their own mortality. Left untreated, midlife crises might lead to depression and suicide, but even milder cases raised the specter of an epidemic of outwardly successful adults weakened by a dip in energy and creativity. If people went through a midlife crisis, what was supposed to be the prime of life deteriorated into a string of hollow routines and dissatisfying obligations. Midlifers, it seemed, were beginning to despair over getting old rather than do something to improve their here and now.[9]

That "something" could be different things to different people. Reaching forty made some men tremble and battle the unease of walking on wobblier knees by buying a new leather jacket or, if their wallet was big enough, an expensive car. Others ventured into spiritual experiments, again others into sexual escapades to fill a gaping hole in their lives. Yet, the hole persisted. Keeping one's body slim and fit while juggling all the responsibilities of middle-class adulthood, from raising children to securing a decent income, was increasingly advertised as a way to rekindle the fire. To be sure, even as people from different segments of society jumped aboard the fitness train in pursuit of a flashy new lifestyle, the disparities of wealth and social status decided which seats were assigned to whom. Few managed to exercise themselves to the top, and experiences of exhilarating joy when working out alone or with others were hard to come by without the necessary money and spare time. The overwhelmingly white, suburban, and materially privileged middle-agers who got into the act could not care less. What they cared about was pushing back the walls of youth and old age that were closing in on them and repurposing their bodies into sites of personal fulfillment. Conservatives like Lasch begrudged that "the prevailing passion" of the day was to "live for the moment." But in lashing out against society's plunge into hedonism, they were missing a larger point about the neoliberal body project. Unwittingly or not, the sweat produced in muscle gyms and aerobic studios continued to grease the wheels of American capitalism.[10]

THE ASTRODOME IN HOUSTON was packed to the last seat when Billie Jean King took Bobby Riggs to school. An additional 90 million Americans sat in front of their television sets and watched the top-ranked female player in the world humiliate the former number one in men's tennis. King won in three straight sets 6–4, 6–3, 6–3, dealing a blow to all those who had doubted that a woman athlete could ever trounce a male opponent, even one who was past his prime. No regular tennis match, the contest between the twenty-nine-year-old King and the fifty-five-year-old Riggs on September 20, 1973, made for great entertainment. Riggs played his part as the male chauvinist pig to perfection. In the run-up to the match, he sat on Johnny Carson's "Tonight Show" couch and told the host that a woman's natural place was "in the bedroom and in the kitchen." Riggs rarely passed a microphone without calling the women's movement a joke. To the delight of his fans, Riggs strutted on the court wearing a bright yellow sports jacket with "Sugar Daddy" stitched on the back.[11]

The "Battle of the Sexes," as the media dubbed the King-Riggs showdown, was soaked in politics. That same year, the struggle over the ERA entered a fierce new phase as conservatives were launching a nationwide campaign to prevent its ratification. Antifeminist rage also centered on the Supreme Court, which nine months earlier, in its Roe v. Wade decision, had decreed abortion legal throughout the first trimester of pregnancy. What women should and could do with their bodies was a question that hovered over the Houston Astrodome like no other. A committed feminist, King knew that much when she walked out into the arena to face Riggs. "The women's movement is important to me," she said to a reporter from ABC minutes before the match, and she had to come to show the world what a woman with the right kind of attitude and discipline was capable of. No, Riggs had not "psyched her out." To prepare for the match, King had quietly lifted weights and talked to several coaches to find the weaknesses in Riggs's game. It paid off.[12]

Get in gear, and you can accomplish anything—that was the heartening lesson the women of America took away from that night. Symbols can be overrated, but scoring a win for women's rights meant something in a world used to linking achievement with masculinity and femininity with reproduction. Traditionally, women's bodies were supposed to be healthy, not necessarily fit or strong. "Wo-He-Lo," an anagram for Work, Health, Love, was the name of the first camp opened by the Camp Fire Girls, the earliest all-female outdoor organization in the United States, established in 1911. Luther Gulick, one of Camp Fire's founders, made it clear that the girls under his supervision were not to engage in strenuous activities like boys their age. "The bearing and rearing of children," he declared, "has always been the first duty of most women, and that must always continue to be." Around the campfire, white middle-class girls and young women learned to cook, keep the forest clean, and make their own dresses in order to prepare for the duties of motherhood. Teaching gendered skills in girls' organizations suggested that youth was not something that women had to pursue as long as they were able to dispense it—in the shape of healthy offspring for the nation.[13]

Gulick's belief that athletics should be used to build bodies concordant with their innate gender was shared by most early twentieth-century physical educators. In the case of women, this meant prescribing exercises that would increase their attractiveness and their ability to withstand disease but bar them from competing with men. To scare females into compliance, doctors cautioned women that vigorous movement could impair their fertility. There was ample commentary about women suffering pelvic damage from riding bikes, and the myth that running too fast or too long might make their uterus fall out remained largely intact until the 1960s. If that was not enough to deter women from wanting to gain a muscle or two, the self-proclaimed guardians of the "fairer sex" would play the aesthetics card. No sensible man, they asserted, wanted to marry a muscular jock or have children with a manly woman. Dancing was one of the few physical activities deemed proper for women, one even the devoted masculinist Granville Stanley Hall endorsed, who called it "one of the best expressions of pure play and of the motor needs of youth." Done right, dance education would teach women how to control their emotions and submit to a male partner.[14]

The roadblocks to female sports were slowly and cautiously removed. Much of the trailblazing work was done by individual athletes. Deciding to be their own roles models, pioneers like the weightlifter Abbye Eville-Stockton, who became one of the first recognized female bodybuilders in the 1930s, saw no reason why women should not have muscle-packed shoulders. Before that, swimming had generated an uptick in women's sports in the interwar years. Gertrude Ederle, who won gold and bronze medals at the 1924 Olympic Games in Paris, swam across the English Channel in 1926, a feat that earned her a ticker-tape parade on her return to New York City. Swimming developed into a popular pastime for both sexes because it accommodated competing urgencies. The press lauded female swim stars as envoys of modern womanhood, proud of their body and confident in their newly won rights. At the same time, photographs of toned women in swimsuits emphasized their beauty and desirability. Whatever gestures toward female emancipation these images contained, the outlets publishing them were as much interested in their sex appeal. "Business Girls Should Swim for Better Posture," Macfadden's flagship magazine *Physical Culture* recommended in

July 1937. As long as grace trumped gender equality, white fitness entrepreneurs were happy to serenade the modern female athlete for their own benefit. This, in a nutshell, was the problem. Hearing someone say that women should improve their bodies to stay young as long as possible gave little indication about their motives. Was it a clarion call to social progress, a eugenicist directive, a coping mechanism, a shrewd business scheme, or something else entirely?[15]

The ambiguities of fitness returned with a vengeance as the women's liberation movement was struggling to maintain momentum. Feminists like King, who insisted that advancing a physically rejuvenated womanhood was key to breaking glass ceilings, used all the media at their disposal to spread that message. A sports avoider in her youth, the editor of *Ms.* magazine, Gloria Steinem, nevertheless became an ardent cheerleader of the "politics of muscle" after observing the joy some of her close friends had found in "joining gyms, becoming joggers, or discovering the pleasure of learning how to yell and kick in self-defense class." In Steinem's estimate, the social acceptance of strong women was inextricable from the fight against patriarchy. "Yes, we need progress everywhere, but an increase in our physical strength could have more impact on the everyday lives of most women than the occasional role model in the boardroom or in the White House." "Fighting back" became common parlance in 1980s aerobics, be it against saggy breasts or abusive men who, as Fonda said, deserved to be punched in the face. For the militant faction out in the streets, having muscles was not enough, either. Radical groups such the Black Panther women and the Weatherwomen demanded for themselves the same right to revolutionary violence asserted by their male comrades. At an antiwar demonstration in Chicago on October 9, 1969, about sixty women wearing helmets and armed with wooden sticks and pipes confronted the police. Here, fitness was not just seen as a prerequisite for equal rights but for armed struggle as well.[16]

Other leading feminists of the 1970s and 1980s were reluctant to champion women's rejuvenation through fitness. Betty Friedan never really warmed to the sight of housewives in sweatbands. Following the 1963 publication of her massively influential *The Feminine Mystique*, which blew up the notion that women's contentment depended on domestic bliss, Friedan did not consider sports a major battlefield for the movement that she helped to spark. This deserves mentioning because her activism has been credited with pressuring President Richard Nixon into signing Title IX into law in 1972, which boosted female sports by ending sex-based discrimination in educational institutions that received federal funds. Friedan thought that women who worked out so they could look a certain way were captive to the beauty industry, which, Friedan believed, had stifled women's true potential. There was a slippery slope in fitness culture, especially when it led to commercials of young fashion models in formfitting clothes. Susan Sontag concurred. She assailed the chauvinist cliché of "physically weak, frail" women who men constantly had to "defend" and saw little use in redefining physical exercise as a female domain if the purpose was to conserve youth for as long as possible. In a society that penalized women more harshly than men for showing the signs of aging, this was a race that women were bound to lose. Fitness thus conceived, these feminists cautioned, risked becoming just another tool for sustaining men's rule over women.[17]

Many practitioners saw it differently. If the women's movement was stalling, perhaps the ladies had not done enough to find liberation within themselves. Iowa native Judi Sheppard Missett did not identify as a feminist when her fitness venture lighted a fire among the housewives of San Diego County. Three years earlier, in 1969, Missett had devised "Jazzercise," a curious mix of high-energy dance, yoga, and kickboxing while giving dance classes in Chicago. But it was in the white suburbs of Southern California, the neighborhoods that helped to spawn the modern Republican Party, where Jazzercise burst onto the scene. Having moved to the West Coast, Missett was cautiously optimistic that her business idea might take root in a soil sprinkled with sixties ideas about the importance of attaining a healthy body-soul equilibrium. The crowds that turned up to get a spot in her classes surpassed her wildest expectations. The military wives moving to Missett's heart-pumping choreographies gave Jazzercise a conservative flavor from the get-go, but the workout's any-woman-can-do-this appeal soon secured Missett a nationwide following. By the end of the 1970s, with the help of television ads, certification plans, and ultimately a franchise system, Jazzercise had grown into a mass sensation.[18]

Jazzercisers defied clear labels. Although they had grown tired of the postwar cult of domesticity, overthrowing patriarchy was not their main concern. "We were different from those women marching in the streets" was Missett's candid confession. In her opinion, women would gain much more from focusing on the small personal victories they could attain as part of her community—that confidence boost resulting from mastering the newest high-energy exercise program or that feeling of economic independence that came with taking over a franchise. Dropping a few pounds in the process could mean all the world at a time when middle-aged women started worrying about their figures. The fashion industry did its part, displaying slender bikini models and launching new trends like actress Gloria Swanson's signature clothing line that bore the telling name "Forever Young." Jazzercise classes were hardly an extension of the youth culture of the 1960s. The promise they held out to suburban housewives was that they did not have to age as fast as their mothers had.[19]

The most innovative thing one could say about Jazzercise and later aerobics was that they were hastening a revolution that they had not started. Ironically, conservative straight women who refused to look their age were usurping a trend rooted in gay and lesbian culture. Even before the 1970s, homosexuals had sought out sex-segregated fitness facilities precisely because they offered opportunities for bonding and intimacy found in few other locations. That regular housewives were now streaming into the studios, adopting a body-conscious aesthetic familiar to gays as they were working out, might have helped to normalize same-sex attraction in parts of the country. That acceptance was brittle, though. Once the AIDS epidemic arrived, the mood swung back, and homophobic Americans pilloried gay gyms as cesspits of disease and sin.[20]

Taking female recreation inside, first into school gyms and church basements and then into glitzy studios, gave women a safe space that females exercising outdoors lacked. Scary media reports of joggers being sexually harassed and raped spotlighted women's vulnerability, prompting many to do their routines behind the walls of state-of-the-art establishments or simply at home in front of the television. Commercial ambitions merged with a sincere interest in winning women over to a new form of exercise advertised as chic, effective, and secure. The white middle-class gym of the post–civil rights era promised women a "wild and woolly workout" at a safe distance from the allegedly wild and dangerous world of the inner cities.[21]

In that sense, the fitness and dance studios mushrooming from coast to coast expressed a new colorblind outlook that began to take hold of mainstream society. Suggesting a creative blend of Black and white America, Jazzercise was the brainchild of a blonde Midwesterner with a disarming smile and poor intercultural skills. Missett's brand was by and large a white-bodies-matter movement. African American musicians must have scratched their heads in disbelief, trying to find the jazz in Jazzercise. Representations of Black women in the movement smacked of tokenism, and their actual participation remained marginal. Many had to work in blue-collar jobs that left them too exhausted to go to a gym after work, even when they had the money. Class differences were compounded by the racist aesthetics of the period's fitness industry. Advertisers preferred women who were lean and white. The novelist Toni Morrison would not have called physical beauty "the most destructive idea in the history of human thought" had she not protested the denigration of Black bodies inherent in this ideal. And had Langston Hughes been alive to witness the spread of Jazzercise, he might as well have seen in Missett a white 1970s version of Eugene Lesche.[22]

African American distrust of white exercise initiatives ran deep, but so did Black women's attempts to acquire fit bodies despite the constraints placed on them. Ever since the demise of Reconstruction, the appeals made by members of the African American community that Black women needed to stay in shape had taken on a survivalist tone. Organizations from the Tuskegee Institute to the underfunded Black branches of the Young Men's Christian Association (YMCA) and the Young Women's Christian Association (YWCA) touted physical exercise for girls and young women in regions with rampant disease and high infant mortality rates. In the second half of the twentieth century, the African American press continued to portray healthy and physically mobile Black women as integral to the struggle for civil rights. Health indicators, however, showed troubling trends, caused in part by the growing presence of fast-food restaurants in Black neighborhoods that suffered from a shortage of upscale groceries and recreational options. The image of the Black body in the white media of the 1970s and 1980s veered between untenable extremes. There was the racist caricature of the lazy and overweight "welfare queen," invoked by Ronald Reagan during his 1976 presidential campaign to discredit the welfare state. Then there were Black superathletes like basketball hall of famers Earvin "Magic" Johnson and Michael Jordan and the track and fielders Carl Lewis and Florence Griffith Joyner, who reached stardom after their gold-winning performances at the 1984 and 1988 Summer Olympics. Disentangling fitness from politics was a luxury that minority groups in the United States, particularly women of color, could hardly afford.[23]

But even if the white mainstream rejected the notion that contemporary dance-exercise programs could be a vessel for social change, paying customers generally wanted to feel empowered by the fast-paced choreographies they were taught. There was a lot of pseudo-spiritual talk of cleansing and renewal in these classes and increasingly frank gestures toward sexual liberation. Lotte Berk, a German-Jewish professional dancer who acquired some notoriety in 1960s London, was probably as explicit as one could get when telling her students that "if you can't tuck, you can't fuck." Berk's US admirers had to be a little more subtle about marketing the erotic elements of their fitness plans to Protestant housewives. They did not have to say much because the "get-fit" girls posing in commercials in their tight body suits spoke a clear language. As the competition was heating up, the titans of the industry grew bolder, realizing that sex sold. "They want to be seduced, can you believe it?" a thirty-five-year-old Missett purred into the camera as she was tilting her pelvis with two mustached male dancers in one of her 1982 workout videos. Singer and actor Olivia Newton-John had already jumped on the aerobics bandwagon with the release of her raunchy single "Physical" in 1981. The iconic music video, which won the Grammy Award for best video, shows Newton-John wearing a low-cut white leotard over her blue leggings, teasing a group of overweight men who are desperately trying to drop a few pounds. Both the lyrics and the video invert conventional gender roles. Here, a sexually assertive woman gets to body-shame the chubby men, whose clumsy movements render them laughingstocks.[24]

Watching the "Physical" music video today, one is tempted to be cynical and say that the women who entered the 1970s protesting for political power got bedroom power instead. True, Billie Jean King beat Bobby Riggs fair and square, and just for one day, the alliance of fitness and a rejuvenated feminism seemed refreshingly uncomplicated. Outside the arena, rougher winds prevailed. Teetering between identity politics and market choices, self-improvement through physical culture could be claimed by emancipators seeking rights for women and minorities as well as by groups disinclined to support such endeavors. Hollywood's invention of the muscular superhero, which provided the visual backdrop for Ronald Reagan's presidency, lionized an ideal of strongmanship that no woman could possibly match. Once corporate America discovered the benefits of fitness, questions of workplace performance, motivation, and absenteeism appeared in a new light. "The physically fit employee" emerged as a white-collar paragon at about the same time that *Forbes* magazine "gently admonished" managers to stay in shape or risk being pushed aside by younger hotshots. Leftist sensibilities were definitely not the reason company gyms started proliferating in the mid-1970s (see figure 8.1).[25]

The millions of sports-enthused Americans who aspired to be inducted into a new physical avant-garde had little in common, except perhaps the desire to take charge of their personal lives in an age in which larger collective units seemed to be splintering into smaller, more intimate parcels of belonging. The sports medicine physician Robert Brown captured this mood best. "We have control over few things in our lives," Brown said in 1978, so "exercise is one of the only means we have to gain a sense of mastery and self-actualization." Fitness may have been "part of a youth kick," as Brown's colleague from the University of Pennsylvania, James E. Nixon, estimated in

FIGURE 8.1 Fitness center in an office building, c. 1985. Seeing an opportunity to boost productivity by keeping employees young and fit, Corporate America latched onto the workout boom of the 1970s and 1980s. Photograph by Carol M. Highsmith, courtesy of the Library of Congress Prints and Photographs Division.

1973—a culture in which nobody could afford "to appear not young anymore." But there was more, above all the fear of losing one's prime of life to an ever-bleaker world of dysfunctional institutions run by corrupt old men, as well as the realization that fit bodies and the fitness to rule were more tightly interwoven than ever.[26]

WHEN YOU WORK for McDonald's, the sky is the limit. At least this is what an ad for the fast-food giant published in the April 1978 edition of *Black Enterprise* suggests. Its main piece is a photograph of Harry Cromwell, a middle-aged African American man who is introduced as "Director of Operations" for New York, New Jersey, and Connecticut. For the purpose of this ad, Cromwell got up from behind his desk and put on his running shoes. The photograph shows him jogging down the street to highlight the "special ingredients" expected of an aspiring Black businessman, such as ambition, energy, and decisiveness. Printed in a magazine that stressed that "quick bucks" could be made selling Big Macs and Quarter Pounders, the ad conveyed that the relationship between McDonald's and Black America was fundamentally a healthy one.[27]

The advance of fast-food chains in Black communities across the United States easily lends itself to caricature. No book has made this point more persuasively than Marcia Chatelain's award-winning study *Franchise: The Golden Arches of Black America*. Where others see the main culprit for rising obesity rates, Chatelain provides a much more nuanced account of Black food entrepreneurs' efforts to harness free-market solutions to solve the problems of hunger and crime in struggling neighborhoods. But even a book as judicious as Chatelain's cannot overlook the disastrous health effects caused by the onslaught of high-fat, high-cholesterol foods. To this day, children of color growing up in poor districts where "fried carryout" reigns supreme are almost twice as likely as white children to contract type 2 diabetes, and 1.4 times at greater risk of becoming obese. This gap is exacerbated by a neoliberal discourse about race and health in which African Americans appear overly addicted to fast food and in which overweight people bear sole responsibility for their dietary choices.[28]

It is far from coincidental that the story documented by Chatelain, weight-based discrimination, and the stigmatization of fat-making foods by the nation's fitness impresarios took off at around the same time. In 1972, the physiologist Ancel Keys, who devoted his career to proving that dietary fat was the chief cause of heart disease, popularized the body mass index as the best scientific method for predicting obesity. "Why Do I Make Myself Fat?" asked America's major teen magazine *Seventeen* in March 1973 after alarming reports about overnutrition in children had gone public. Concerns over losing excess weight were frequently voiced in some of the most popular sitcoms of the early 1970s. In a telling episode of the *Bob Newhart Show*, Bob grudgingly acts on his doctor's advice to drop a few pounds. Armed with charts that tell him how to exercise, what to eat, and which foods to spurn, Bob goes on a strict diet. Wild mood swings ensue, yet Bob stays the course, always mindful of the doctor's warning that "every extra pound of fat takes a year off of life." After much strain and laughter, Bob ends up ten pounds lighter, much to the delight of his wife Carol, who finds her husband young and sexy again.[29]

Stories of diets unlocking the portal to a younger self echo back in time. Gluttony ranked as one of the seven deadly sins in medieval Christian theology, and Renaissance writers hailed successful fasting as a triumph over evil that would be rewarded with youth and beauty. Such fantasies, however, barely resonated outside the ivory tower. Scarcity was the norm in early modern societies, and hunger was a constant companion of the laboring classes.

When US nutritionists around 1900 began calculating the worth of food in calories, their main goal was to promote a dietary regime based on grain, meat, and dairy products. They thought that this would enhance the performance of workers and soldiers. Early twentieth-century food policy, the historian Nick Cullather concluded, revolved around the needs of capitalism and empire. Personal eating habits, let alone slimming down, remained a secondary concern.[30]

A group of food scientists with ties to the eugenics movement were among the first to question that assumption. The doctrine "eat right and live longer" gained a wider following as a result of the health campaigns conducted by Irving Fisher's Life Extension Institute and John Harvey Kellogg's Battle Creek Sanatorium. Adamant that "race betterment" involved what people put in their bellies, Kellogg blamed the meat industry for ruining the health of the best and brightest and advocated vegetarianism as the surest path to recuperation. The Philadelphia-born businessman Sanford Bennett seconded Kellogg. He declared that periodic fasting combined with regular exercise had freed him from the "conditions of age" and allowed him to "become, physically, a young man again." Similarly, Macfadden's dream of a hardened white manhood rested on fitness advice and dietary prescriptions. Adhering to both, Macfadden promised in 1915, would make middle-aged men "throb with vitality" and give them "the buoyancy, vivacity, energy, enthusiasm, and ambition ordinarily associated with youth." Healthy eaters, according to Macfadden, practiced moderation, avoided white bread, and limited themselves to two or three meals per day (see figure 8.2). To underscore the significance of nutrition to his rejuvenation plan, he related the story of a woman "who had lived over eighty years of age" and remained "as agile, as clearheaded and as capable as a young woman in the heyday of her youth." Her youth tonic was simple: eat but "one article of food at a meal." Books that connected aging and eating sold well in an era shaped by a mounting public fascination with science-based rejuvenation. Like the beauticians, they touted softer interventions to make people younger than the procedures peddled by the period's gland grafters.[31]

Not until the boom years of the 1950s, however, did US authorities declare their first all-out war on fatness. Like the more famous Red Scare, the obesity scare was rooted in Cold War anxieties about the lack of national vigor in the face of a frightening enemy. As waists were getting bigger in the prosperous parts of the country, the medical and pharmaceutical lobbies knocked at government doors to warn about the dark sides of affluence, personified by the overeating office worker and the gorging housewife. Negative portrayals of

FIGURE 8.2 Cover of *Physical Culture*, 1924. Bernarr Macfadden's popular magazine amplified the notion that healthy eating and regular exercise were key to attaining the highest form of citizenship.

the latter expressed a general disregard for female decision-making, and the gendered stereotype of the woman who ate too much because she could not handle stress shored up theories that cast obesity as a disease of the mind. As a result, doctors were told to treat overeating as they did alcoholism or depression, with drugs. Diet pills flourished, and the hope was that overweight mothers would respond positively to the appetite-reducing stimulants that were now aggressively hawked in women's magazines. Pharmaceutical companies who made a fortune off this obesity panic drew on all the scientific support they could get to contend that fat mothers not only aged faster but also set a bad precedent. They found their cheerleader in the German American psychiatrist Hilde Bruch, who faulted mothers for instilling in their children "oral fixations" that led to compulsive eating practices.[32]

Food control, fitness advocacy, and female self-help all converged in the Weight Watchers, one of the most recognizable upshots of a culture that proclaimed that exercise and eating were two sides of the same coin. The organization's founder, Jean Nidetch from Queens, New York, liked to present her invention as an all-American success story. What began in 1961 with a pledge in Nidetch's living room expanded into a sprawling business venture that sold diet products and opened meeting centers where clients received instruction on how to eat their way to a leaner body (see figure 8.3). Sisterhood and surveillance reinforced each other from the outset. Meetings could take on the character of emotional group confessions. Members who had not met their quotas would ask for forgiveness, hoping that encouragement from their fellow Watchers would harden their resolve to eat less and better food. This fusion of Protestant work ethic and revivalism was on full display in May 1973 when Weight Watchers celebrated its tenth birthday in a crammed Madison Square Garden. Standing out in a star-studded lineup featuring the comedian Bob Hope and the singer Roberta Peters were twenty so-called big losers, who received loud cheers for dropping 100 pounds or more thanks to the program. "I have self-confidence and self-liking like I never had before. My social life has blossomed beautifully," one female "big loser" told a reporter outside Madison Square Garden.[33]

The preoccupation with slimness could be compensatory as well as utilitarian. For those who found sweating disgusting but wanted to be svelte nonetheless, dieting might have looked like the more desirable path. In addition, the gospel of renunciation preached by Weight Watchers and kindred nutrition entrepreneurs offered weight reduction methods free from Big Pharma, which had come under public scrutiny after five women had reportedly died from diet pill abuse. But whether some fads praised eating

FIGURE 8.3 Jean Nidetch speaking at a Weight Watchers meeting, 1969. Few self-help organizations did more to link obesity to obsolescence by promoting weight loss in terms of a life-affirming makeover. Photograph by Philipp A. Harrington, courtesy of Evan Harrington.

pineapples only, recommended swallowing nothing but milk for seven days, or extolled the virtues of protein shakes, almost all promised their customers happier relationships and economic rewards. "Start Monday to look great on Saturday" was the slogan devised by the maker of the Slender Blend shake in 1971 to woo middle-aged women. Again, gender mattered. Diet ads for men tended to speak more about making minds sharper and bodies more energetic, traits that would give the male provider a competitive edge in the marketplace. For the same reason, one of the first issues of *Men's Health* in 1986 declared that "guys" needed to "eat right" not because they had to have thin waists, but because they "needed to stay on top of business." The ground was prepared for promoting grass-fed beef, high-protein salads, and other age-erasing superfoods purposely coded as masculine.[34]

Bad eaters, like non-exercisers, were increasingly caught in the crosshairs of a wellness movement that penetrated the nation's workplaces. In November 1979, CBS News anchor Dan Rather introduced the concept to a larger audience in a segment of *60 Minutes*. The physician John Travis, whom Rather interviewed for the segment, defined wellness as a form of self-care that reframed health as an "ongoing, dynamic state of growth." Though presented as less expensive than traditional medicine, wellness tended to benefit those who were already well-off. Giulio Esposito, an executive with a major West Coast firm, joined the program to get rid of his constant headaches. He told Rather that learning how to handle stressful situations with the help of a biometer had made him feel vivified and ready to soar. Its congruity with capitalism made wellness an ideal playground for corporate elites. Established in 1979, Johnson and Johnson's LIVE FOR LIFE program, which aimed to make the firm's employees "among the healthiest in the world," routinely assessed their fitness, weight, and eating habits. The objective was to cut health care costs and boost productivity. Neoliberalism disappeared behind the change-your-life spirituality emanating from the nation's leading wellness gurus. Few television personalities of the 1980s and 1990s built their brand more fervently around the New Age mantra of self-optimization than Oprah Winfrey. More than once, Winfrey turned her popular afternoon show into a wellness sermon. Her monologues were peppered with salesperson mottoes such as "The number one thing you have to do is to work on yourself," or "It does not matter where you come from . . . you are responsible for your life." Oprah likened midlife to an ongoing journey where the best still lay ahead. Dramatic makeovers were a crucial component in Oprah's wellness performances. In 1988, she carted sixty-seven pounds of animal fat onstage—the amount of weight she had allegedly dropped with a liquid protein diet.[35]

Wellness's before-and-after culture made a spectacle out of portraying a person's transformation on live television. Celebrating some visible changes, however, implied that others deserved to be censured. The pressure to conform broke hearts and damaged bodies. Some Weight Watchers left their neighborhood meetings more depressed than before because they could not carry the weight of expectations bearing down on them. The dangers of self-starvation crashed national headlines in February 1983 with the death of the singer Karen Carpenter, whose obsession with being skinny had cut her life short. By the mid-1980s, stories of young women and teenagers suffering from eating disorders were flooding mainstream media. Fitness stars who got rich off the thinness craze remained hesitant to speak out. A rare moment of candor came in December 1987 when aerobics tycoon Jane Fonda allowed a glimpse into her lifelong struggle with bulimia. Fonda's admission, though, did not dent her popularity. Even after the interview, she continued to profit from her multimedia empire, which told women all over the world to "go for the burn."[36]

Overweight people did not endure the onslaught of fat-shaming silently. Some translated the call to be the captains of their own destiny into organizing against what the queer theorist Robert McRuer has termed the modern fitness regime's "compulsory able-bodiedness." Accepting people the way they looked became a cause célèbre for fat activists beginning in the late 1960s. Taking his cue from contemporary radicalisms, Lew Louderback demanded "fat power" because, as he wrote somewhat parochially, "now that ethnic and racial prejudice are out of fashion, the public finds itself with nobody left to be bigoted about except the fat." A militant splinter group that went by the name of "Fat Underground" prided itself on being more inclusive. Their 1973 manifesto deployed Marxist rhetoric ("Fat People of the World, Unite!") to align their group with campaigns against other oppressive structures in society. More significantly, these fat liberationists marshaled medical evidence to push back against the claims of the "reduction industry," which labeled heavier folks categorically unfit. Ultimately, Fat Underground shared the fate of many sixties-inspired emancipatory cells. Their numbers were too small and their goals too radical for the vast majority of Americans to tip the scale in favor of an egalitarian, antiracist, and queer-friendly body politics.[37]

Curiously enough, the authors of the Fat Liberation Manifesto ended up inserting a sentence that heralded the new zeitgeist like no other: "We fully intend to reclaim power over our bodies and our lives." Few declarations had such broad appeal in a society that was so fractured and yet seemed bound together in fierce attachment to a democracy of self-ownership. Experiments in remaking identities with cookbooks and workouts did not fill the political voids left by a decade of protest. But neither did the baby boomers suddenly begin to "bowl alone," as the sociologist Robert Putnam famously asserted. Rather, post-1960s Americans relied on each other in underappreciated ways to redefine what made adulthood meaningful and to carve out for themselves spaces of development traditionally reserved for younger people. As the boundaries separating liberal from conservative America were hardening, the boundaries of middle age were silently redrawn.[38]

CARL JUNG HAD BEEN DEAD for more than twenty years by the late 1980s, so he had no say in his latest resurrection. Not long after his passing in 1961, the Swiss psychologist had become a household reference in countercultural communes eager to travel to the outer rims of the human soul. When Jung's name began popping up in US medical journals two decades later, his theories about childhood and death were barely cited. What fascinated psychologists of the Reagan era was a somewhat obscure article that Jung had written in 1930. *Die Lebenswende* ("Turning Point in Life") discarded the traditional image of the life course as a rising and falling staircase. Jung believed that middle and old age were rife with opportunity yet also different from the ones younger people should pursue. "The afternoon of life," Jung's metaphor for the second half of the staircase, needed to be understood as a developmental phase in its own right. Attempts to turn back the clock were not just futile but harmful because they meant chasing pasts that did not have a future. Some of Jung's American students were taken with the ideas that he had formulated during the Great Depression because, just maybe, they constituted an important puzzle piece for solving the depression epidemic plaguing the United States and other Western societies in the last quarter of the century.[39]

Thinking about midlife expanded noticeably in the decades after World War II. Erik Erikson's "eight ages of man," which started the trend, rejected pessimistic readings of middle age as a period of stagnation and decline. Erikson theorized that "generativity," his term for caring about and guiding the young, peaked between the years of forty and sixty. Failure to nurture and act on that sentiment, Erikson believed, made midlife rudderless, complicating the postwar search for order. Adults who had emerged relatively unscathed from the carnage were in high demand in a world thrown into political uncertainty and demographic disarray. Wary of mass spectacles of rejuvenation, the conservative educators of the 1950s found in the totalitarian assault on parental authority the culprit responsible for the wreckage of the last world war and the threat of a third one. Television shows like *Father Knows Best* or

Leave It to Beaver presented the nuclear family headed by loving mothers and affable fathers as a haven of stability. White middle-class fatherhood in particular underwent a remarkable metamorphosis. The sheer number of babies born during the boom years not only made married couples look for more spacious housing in the suburbs. It also raised questions about how men could support their wives and do their part in raising the children of a young superpower. For the historian Gary Cross, the 1950s marked the arrival of the "pal dad," the cheerful weekend "pops" who met his sons halfway as he was taking them to summer camp and Little League games.[40]

However, what some enjoyed as a temporary recess from adult routines turned into an unwinnable expectations game for others. Men who had grown up under the patriarch's rod felt torn between representing the authority of a male breadwinner and enacting the precepts of postwar childrearing experts who called for greater leniency in parent-child interactions. This profound contradiction at the heart of Cold War fatherhood is often overlooked in explanations of why the midlife crisis discourse started when it did. When New York State Senator Thomas Desmond deplored in 1956 that many of his countrymen "slump[ed] into middle age grudgingly, sadly, and with a tinge of fear," he was not talking about burnouts caused by working long hours—a term that had yet to be invented. An identity confusion stood at the heart of the problem, one that kept middle-class fathers from developing the tools they needed to square the conflicting demands of home and office. Building character while growing older did not become easier in the antiestablishment furor of the following decade. The counterculture was starting to slam the Norman Rockwell fathers of the 1950s, labeling them shallow and insincere. Adult development took a back seat, drowned out by graduate students attempting to dismantle many of the institutions their parents held dear.[41]

But in the quieter niches of academia, the seeds of the midlife market from which the fitness craze would sprout were already being planted. Researchers who placed middle age under the looking glass came from different disciplines. Developmental psychologists and psychiatrists left their marks on the object as did scholars affiliated with newer schools in market research and the behavioral sciences. As was to be expected, different findings emerged from these fields. Canadian psychoanalyst Elliot Jacques, to whom we owe the phrase "midlife crisis," detected a crossroads that could either lead to despair or set off surprising bursts of creativity. Fixated on aging men (women, Jacques held, simply went through menopause), his notion—namely, that patients who had passed thirty or forty could avoid existential pain with the right kind of psychological skills—was a paradigm shifter. The journalist Gail

Sheehy turned to the psyche to illuminate how to best transition to and out of midlife, even as she rejected Jacques's chauvinism in her 1976 book *Passages*. Several years later, Daniel Levinson argued that dealing with the "disparity between what he is and what he dreamed of becoming" could cause storm and stress in men comparable to a second adolescence. Finding the route to midlife happiness was possible, though. Not without selfish motives, psychoanalysts and their allies in the press advised therapy for those struggling to find new purpose as their hair was graying.[42]

Around the same time, social scientists started to put their own spin on the pliability of middle age. Orville Gilbert Brim had just become president of the Foundation for Child Development in 1974 when he began veering from his subject. Changes in personality and behavior, he asserted, could be as dramatic in midlife as in the first two decades of human life. Brim had gained that insight while observing youngsters, only to realize that their parents were evolving right beside them. Brim's early research earned him the scorn of his child-study peers, who kept insisting that growth was the domain of the young. Brim persevered, and his claim that adulthood possessed greater potential for reinvention than childhood or old age attracted followers and, more importantly, donor money. But even before his advocacy peaked with the founding of the Mac-Arthur Foundation, the multimillion-dollar research conglomerate dedicated to studying adult development, Brim struck a much more upbeat tone when talking about midlife. The business community appreciated the lack of gloom in Brim's approach. Market researchers Elizabeth Hirschman and Morris Holbrook joined the chorus in 1982. Commenting on a process well underway, the two scholars found adults around the age of forty particularly prone to "hedonic consumption." For midlifers, shopping had to be a "multisensory" experience, and the lifestyle products they bought had to be "emotion laden" because consumers were expressing themselves through ownership of things. The implications of Hirschman and Holbrook's study was sufficiently clear: midlife was little more than a commodity, and middle-agers who wanted to ditch their old identity in a capitalist society could always buy a new one.[43]

Leftists were not the only ones who frowned on the belief that consumption would alleviate the problems of aging. Christopher Lasch spurned the self-consciously fit and slim middle-agers for another reason. Closet rejuvenationists at best, they clung "desperately to their own youth," Lasch wrote, driven by an "irrational terror" that had clutched the "heart of a dying culture." For Lasch, the manic shopper, the diet queen, and the sporty yuppie were different manifestations of the same "narcissistic personality," the "typical form of character structure in a society that has lost interest in the future."

The future Lasch envisioned was tinged with nostalgia—a time in which parents discovered longevity in their offspring and "the cult of youth" had not yet "brought all forms of authority (including the authority of experience) into disrepute."[44]

Like many conservative critics, Lasch did not criticize the neoliberal "cult of the self" for the rampant inequalities it shored up. He worried most about its corrosive effects on traditional institutions—chief among them the family. The fear of growing old, Lasch maintained, had made the refusal to grow up less scandalous, with dire consequences for a nation whose social health depended on young adults having children and raising them properly. *The Culture of Narcissism* did not stoop to the level of the white extinction panic stirred up in Lothrop Stoddard's *The Rising Tide of Color* six decades earlier. Lasch, however, was not shy about identifying villains. A major one, in his view, was the sexual revolution, which allegedly had given women a false sense of freedom by shredding the ideal of motherhood and replacing it with images of middle-aged Lolitas hungering for "sexual excitement to satisfy all their emotional needs." Real feelings had gone out the window. Lasch concluded that women, unmoored from the ethos of procreation, had begun to acquire a toxic selfishness masquerading as self-fulfillment.[45]

While Lasch's texts dovetailed with the family-values conservatism of the antifeminist movement, they also exemplified the backlash women continued to face for acting their age as they saw fit. As Leslie Paris has emphasized, ageism weighed heavier on female shoulders in a society that, to quote Susan Sontag, considered women "old as soon as they are no longer very young." Lasch was on to something with his observation that middle-aged women were talking more assertively about maintaining an active sexual life. His accusations of frivolity, however, ignored the feeling of self-acceptance that aging women drew from unlearning the inhibitions placed on them by older codes of propriety and from asserting their right to be libidinous. A revitalized midlife and sexual citizenship, the right to enjoy one's body outside the confines of procreation, converged at workshops like the one sponsored by Lonnie Barbach, a sex therapist out of San Francisco, in December 1976. There "well-dressed, middle-class white woman of all ages," not your typical radical feminists, learned about their genitals and how to rub themselves to orgasm. This may sound like a poor substitute for the political setbacks the women's rights movement had to endure, most notably the ERA's slow and painful death. Yet in claiming such spaces for themselves, these women made a point about wanting to enjoy at least some of the freedom and impulsiveness granted to younger people and also to men their age.[46]

Women who made aerobics a central component of their leisure time took a similar line. Based on a collection of interviews that historian Melanie Woitas conducted with middle-aged aerobicizers, there is little evidence that the wish to turn back the biological clock had driven the women to exercise. If anything, the fun and fellowship they experienced while working out made them think less about their numerical age and more appreciative of having a great body in their forties and early fifties. This is not to suggest that stretching the frontiers of an active midlife was far from their mind. Most answers indicated a strong belief that growing old and staying young did not rule each other out, provided one was truly fit. Fonda herself returned to this theme time and again. "I feel better, I am stronger, I have more endurance, more energy than when I was in my twenties," a fifty-six-year-old Fonda told a reporter in 1990. "I always think age is more a function of how you feel about yourself than the actual chronological numbers." Fonda bragged that she did not mind working sixteen or seventeen hours on a movie set. At the end of the day, she was still fresher than the younger people around her. A return to youth no longer seemed necessary. Midlife was the place to be if you wanted to turn things around "and maximize the potential that you have as a human being."[47]

It is probably not a surprise that Fonda reigned as the queen of exercise as long as she did. She had mastered the language of fitness to perfection, a state so elastic in its meaning yet so universally desired. Arriving at the verge of a life stage that earlier generations had barely associated with growth, adult Americans who went through midlife in the period from Watergate to the fall of the Berlin Wall learned to embody the afternoons of their lives differently. Big business and televangelists hailed self-reliance, which meant taking care of all aspects of one's life—economic, spiritual, and physical—as the proper response of a people who had lost faith in government. But despite all the individualist noise, Americans did not go for the burn entirely of their own volition. Many started craving youthfully fit and attractive bodies because their opposites were increasingly maligned: the exhausted worker who faltered at the first breeze of competition; the binge eater who lacked the discipline required of a responsible consumer-citizen; the "welfare queen" who was making a fortune cashing Social Security checks that were not hers. In a society that embraced colorblindness but continued to associate Black bodies with laziness and crime, people of color had steeper hills to climb when it came to approximating white middle-class ideals of the perfect midlife. But even the less disadvantaged who reached their hilltops more quickly often found themselves sliding down again, only to try their luck at another one. Again,

The Great Gatsby comes to mind. "Tomorrow we will run faster, stretch out our arms farther . . . And one fine morning."[48]

I will give Betty Friedan the last word. Never a big exerciser, Friedan finally uttered her resounding no to the fitness mystique at age sixty-five. She no longer felt like she had to run away from the inevitable or endure the humiliation that so often befell a senior feminist. Friedan proudly proclaimed that she had discovered her "fountain of age." Drinking from that less-crowded well, she wrote, had brought unforeseen liberation and, with it, the knowledge that breaking old inhibitions worked best once the word *old* stopped being a disgrace. There was something strangely perverse about the graying of America, Friedan noted. The nation's leaders had been boasting life expectancy records every year yet kept flinching at the sight of wrinkles and wheelchairs. Amid deepening divisions, the illusion of staying young appeared to be the one bubble Americans remained loath to burst. Soon, that bubble would expand, absorbing technologies that promised to drastically alter the impact of time on human bodies.[49]

CHAPTER NINE

Transhuman

Rejuvenation's Final Frontier

Make my limb
Make my life long
Take my parts
Make me evolve.

—Zero Nine, *Grievances—Manufacture, Customize* (2017)

In the fall of 2020, people were anxiously waiting for good news to come out of the world's leading laboratories. Immunologists had been racing against time to develop a vaccine against COVID-19, which had already caused more than 10 million deaths across the globe. At the same time, speculation was heating up that the virus might not just be defeated in a lab but had possibly been generated in one. The group of scientists who drove up the hills of Palo Alto wanted to leave all the clamor behind. Their destination: the mega-mansion owned by the Russian-born physician and venture capitalist Yuri Milner. Participants got tested and wore masks. Apart from that, the pandemic faded into the background. A tech billionaire who had become insanely rich from investing in Facebook and Twitter, Milner hosted a two-day conference on his property where another question loomed large: how to set up a new biotech lab dedicated to reverting the aging process.[1]

Altos Labs, the antiaging company that emerged from the conference, almost slipped under the public radar. That changed when reports started surfacing that the freshly launched start-up possessed the financial firepower of a major corporation. With $3 billion in the bank, Altos Labs was able to staff its board of directors with luminaries from bioengineering, cell research, and artificial intelligence, Nobel laureates among them. The company's stated mission, which centers on scientific collaboration to unravel "the deep biology of cellular rejuvenation programming," is spanning three continents. In January 2022, Altos Labs announced that it would open two laboratories in California, one in the Bay Area and the other in San Diego. It would also start a third lab in Cambridge, England, and work with stem cell scientists based in Japan. Its outlook was markedly global. Although the company has not unveiled its wealthy backers, it was clear to everyone in the business that this was Silicon Valley's newest attempt to cheat death. One name in particular kept making the rounds: Amazon founder Jeff Bezos. If Bezos was serious about colonizing space, longevity would come in handy. The forecasts sound anything but discouraging. Very soon, wrote journalist Andrew Steele in January 2023, "we may see the first drug that targets the biology of aging itself," which would "kickstart the greatest revolution in medicine since the discovery of antibiotics."[2]

With all the excitement surrounding the latest push for rejuvenation, one can be coaxed into thinking that Ponce de León might have had better luck had he landed in California. Silicon Valley's start-up lifestyle, drenched in a sunny libertarianism and the fetishization of innovative thinking, is as close to resembling an early twenty-first-century version of the legendary Fountain of Youth as anything else. Parsing myth from reality can be challenging, especially when the object of inquiry is one of the world's largest tech hubs. A magazine for electronic products, acknowledging the region's growing importance for the silicon-based production of semiconductor chips, gave the southern San Francisco Bay Area its nickname in 1971. By then, Silicon Valley had already begun to garner a reputation for punishing stasis and rewarding risk takers. The first to enter its pantheon of whiz kids were eight young employees who had quit their jobs at Shockley Semiconductor and outcompeted their old boss with their own computer chip firm. Others followed: the two Steves, Jobs and Wozniak, who revolutionized personal computing in the late 1970s; University of Illinois graduate Marc Andreessen, who came to Stanford in 1994 to develop Netscape, the first commercially successful web browser; Mark Zuckerberg, who moved to Palo Alto in 2004 and oversaw Facebook's growth into a social media behemoth. Together, these tech iconoclasts tell a story too exuberant to be true. All you need is a research university, venture capital, and brilliant minds uninhibited by tradition and overregulation. Nothing should be impossible, not even rewriting the laws of aging.[3]

Of course, the story is far more complicated, and Big Tech had to learn the lesson that no brand is immune to falling from grace. Yet, the digital elite do not spend a lot of time licking their wounds. While Meta and X (formerly Twitter) are slashing jobs, the list of superinvestors hedging their bets on rejuvenation keeps getting longer. Even before Altos Labs was established, some of the Valley's most illustrious names had appeared on the roster of antiaging start-ups. Google's Larry Page, for instance, has been associated with Calico, a firm that wants to develop therapies for extending healthy life spans well into realm of 140 or 150 years. PayPal cofounder Peter Thiel gave $3.5 million to the Metuselah Foundation, a Virginia-based nonprofit that promises to "make 90 the new 50 by 2030." In 2016, Thiel's interest in adding years to his life gave rise to vampiric analogies. Already a political renegade for supporting Donald Trump, Thiel reportedly stood at the forefront of a rather eccentric prolongation method. Numerous media sites conjectured that he had signed up for a treatment during which younger people's blood coursed through his veins. The story sounded spectacular enough to become fodder for the film industry. HBO aired an episode of the satire *Silicon Valley* in 2017 in which the series' tech villain is shown in the company of his own "blood boy."[4]

For all the emancipatory vibes emanating from Silicon Valley, critics advise caution. All these endeavors, some say, amount to little more than narcissism on steroids. Look behind the curtain, and you see a plutocratic vanity project befitting the oversized egos of a few billionaires who do not want to die. As this book has shown, the notion that rejuvenation serves the rich and powerful is not without precedent. Presuming that we are witnessing a new chapter in America's century-old struggle against fading youth, how exactly does it differ from previous ones? The short answer is more money, faster computers, and better microscopes. Over the last several decades, scientists have pursued rejuvenation on increasingly smaller scales, zooming in on the level of individual cells. Starting with Ernest McCulloch and James Till, whose experiments on rodents made them pioneers in working with stem cells, research in that area gradually migrated to humans. In 1998, the biologist James Thomson isolated human embryonic stem cells. The medical community erupted with joy. Therapies for diseases long deemed uncurable, among them blindness, Parkinson's, and advanced cancer, seemed within reach. Stem cell technology's most recent feats, which included finding ways to regenerate muscles in mice with the help of proteins, have garnered much applause. Stanford scientist Vittorio Sebastiano, true to the Silicon Valley spirit, stoked expectations for saying that a blueprint now existed for promoting "rejuvenation in multiple human cell types." That kind of confidence was probably last expressed in the 1920s by the admirers of Eugen Steinach and Serge Voronoff.[5]

One hundred years later, the battle against aging is no longer being fought under the microscope alone. The digital revolution has electrified a movement that seeks better and younger bodies outside the confines of biology. Transhumanists see themselves as rebels against the natural world into which they were born. But they are also disciples of a secular faith, the belief that machines can deliver humanity from the miseries of an earthly existence. The union of technology and flesh, according to Mark O'Connell, is one of transhumanism's chief aims, and it is in many ways tailor-made for the internet age.

The movement has no agreed-on leaders, no leather-bound canon of texts, and no geographical center. What its adherents share is a general frustration with the limitations of the human body. They lament its vulnerability and detest its mortality. They chuckle at the uninitiated who dismiss them as a bunch of nerds sitting in their moms' basements and watching endless reruns of Ridley Scott's *Blade Runner*. The most vocal transhumanists are, by and large, accomplished adults, some with impressive scientific credentials. "We have reached our childhood's end," trumpeted the philosopher and futurist Max More as early as 1999. He brashly added, "We will no longer be slaves to our genes."[6]

There is a lot of testosterone dripping from More's statements. Descriptions of transhumanism as a movement encouraging macho behavior have surfaced more frequently after observers pointed to some of its troubling corollaries: grand gestures of space cowboyhood, the glorification of daring for daring's sake, demographics dominated by white Euro-American males, and the prevalence of technologically enhanced white cis-gendered bodies. Even if there is nothing inherently sexist or racist about the longing to live forever, the casual references to slavery and emancipation coming out of the mouth of wealthy white futurists are bound to make people of color cringe. Transhumanists resist such labels, claiming that the quest for biotechnological liberation would leave no one behind. Defeating illness and aging, they assert, is one of the last missions that can unite a divided planet. Imagine the good that can arise out of transcending a species known for its violent outbursts and provincial fear of others![7]

The verdict may still be out, but the ethical concerns raised on rejuvenation's final frontier are unlikely to go away. Nor should they. I approach the subject with the humility of a historian who understands that intentions, however noble, and actual change barely march in lockstep. I also believe that writing this book has earned me the right to voice my discomfort with a utopian philosophy that seems more interested in boarding escape pods to a not-so-distant future than in solving the problems of the present. Radical life extension has become a regular headline at tech conferences, yet life expectancies in the United States have been falling. How does ending the tyranny of death help us to stop global warming? Why should we care about uploading minds to high storage servers when human bodies continue to be devastated by guns, addiction, and warfare? True, transhumanism's optimism can be contagious. Its unshakable faith in the human capacity for progress is reminiscent of the Enlightenment's enchantment with the prospect of human perfectibility. Yet, more than two centuries after the likes of Jefferson and

Franklin walked the earth, we ought to know better. Atrocious crimes have been committed on behalf of scientific ideals, and invocations of reason have echoed from the most unequal of regimes, which denied basic rights, at times even the right to exist, to those they despised. If the millennialist dreamers are unaware of this history or, worse, openly dispute that the abuse of rationality is part of the Enlightenment tradition, then count me a skeptic.

I am not aiming for a hatchet job, and blanket condemnations are not helpful for understanding a heterogeneous cross-border movement. While this chapter will not give a detailed account of the contests between different biomedical and transhumanist schools and their varying politics, any treatment of the subject should at least acknowledge that these turf wars exist. In concluding this book, I plan to take at face value the predictions of today's tech elite that we are approaching the end of aging as we know it. With Silicon Valley driving many of these changes, this story is as much planetary as it is American. Those who expect a panoply of minutiae regarding the latest breakthroughs in nanotechnology or artificial intelligence (AI) will likely be disappointed. My interest remains with discursive patterns and social practices, if only to find out how much old rejuvenationist wine is still flowing from transhumanism's casks. A major part of the critic's task has to be, to riff off a quote by the immortal Jeffrey "The Dude" Lebowski, to "look for the person who will benefit."[8]

LIKE REJUVENATION, the transhuman desire to amend bodies beyond their corporeal confines is older than the term suggests. The robotic turn of the early twenty-first-century represents "the culmination of the 400-year philosophic project of modernity," as the philosopher Robert Frodeman put it. Because of this drawn-out process, a critique of that project needs to take the long view. Parallel to the rise of the machines that fired the Industrial Revolution, mechanistic descriptions of humanity spread throughout Western societies. The idea that human bodies operate like well-oiled machines that possess all the components necessary to nourish and sustain themselves is older still. For the seventeenth-century English naturalist Robert Boyle, God's genius had manifested itself in creating "living automatons," where "the body of man be indeed an engine, yet there is united to it an intelligent being." References to the Almighty pervaded early modern mechanistic literature. Both rational and wondrous, the body-machine was ultimately assembled by divine will.[9]

Deviations from this view became more common once the mechanization of bodies and body parts left the realm of metaphor. In the remote corners of the technological advances made during the nineteenth century, some engineers turned their talents to manufacturing artificial limbs. The fake hand crafted in 1845 by the Englishman George Cayley was a product of this era, as was the prosthetic leg invented by the disabled Confederate soldier James Edward Hanger, which replaced less comfortable wooden pegs. Further innovations followed in the contexts of medicine, mass production, and electronic communication. None of these developments, however, fundamentally upended the perceived separation of mind and matter, of machines and humans. A serious integration of these spheres did not take place prior to the twentieth century. Movies like Fritz Lang's Weimar classic *Metropolis* (1927) projected visions of human-machine symbiosis onto the big screen. A group of Soviet scientists who called themselves "biocosmists" or "immortalists" dreamed of inventing the ultimate revolutionary tool—the abolition of death. Norbert Wiener's 1948 book *Cybernetics* helped give birth to the cyborg, a living organism enhanced by technological devices. Not long after their literary inception, cyborgs and other computerized hybrids attained popularity through blockbuster films and television series such as *Star Trek, Star Wars, RoboCop,* and *Terminator.* Though often portrayed as menacing and hostile, cyborgs have mesmerized parts of their audience who believe that the benefits of a cybernetic future outweigh its risks.[10]

The list of Hollywood productions that have glamorized the theme of individuals getting a new lease on life or attaining quasi-magical powers with the help of technology is near endless. This also happens to be the formula that made Disney-owned Marvel, which specializes in superhero movies, one of the biggest media franchises in the world. The relationship between film and fandom is complex, but the grassroots growth of transhumanism cannot be explained without it. When the biologist Julian Huxley, Aldous Huxley's brother, added the word *transhumanism* to the lexicon of the modern natural sciences in 1957—the year in which the Soviets launched Sputnik and set off the space race—few took note. Thirty years later, the first small organizations and local groups were dotting the landscape. Many of the 1980s sci-fi clubs did not mind being situated at the fringes of society. Members met in garages and backyards, tinkering away at replicas of their favorite spaceships from *Star Trek* or *Star Wars.* Others tried their hands at programming their own biofeedback machines or speculated about cryonic techniques of low-temperature freezing, a method through which organisms might be resurrected after an extended period of time.[11]

The post–Cold War years witnessed attempts to weave different futurist scenes into something akin to a virtual transhumanist family. In 1992, Max

More and Tom Morrow founded the Extropy Institute. Its email lists and digital newsletters broke new ground at a time when the internet was still in its infancy. More was the perfect envoy of Extropy's higher-further-faster mentality. After moving from England to Southern California, he changed his last name to "More" because he wished "always to improve, to never be static." He wanted "to get better at everything, become smarter, fitter, and healthier." More's enthusiasm for extolling the virtues of self-optimization echoed the mindset of a Reagan-era executive, but it also caught fire with the tech avant-garde during the Bill Clinton and George W. Bush years, who wanted to clothe the transhumanist movement in official garbs. The establishment of the World Transhumanist Association (WTA) in 1998 the marked the first big step in that direction. Positioning itself as cosmopolitan and nonpartisan, the WTA mixed human rights rhetoric with SDS-style participatory democracy. Its two founding documents were the *Transhumanist Declaration* and, befitting an online movement, the Transhumanist FAQ. "We envision the possibility of broadening human potential," WTA declared, "by overcoming aging, cognitive shortcomings, involuntary suffering, and our confinement to planet Earth."[12]

Ever since its inception, the WTA has inspired a series of transhumanist platforms whose authors have attempted to summarize the movement's core values. Influenced by the famous charters of liberal internationalism, above all by the 1949 *Universal Declaration of Human Rights*, the transhumanist document nevertheless differs from its liberal precursors. Centering the question of rights around "sentience" rather than humanity marks the sharpest contrast between the two. Curiously, sentience, which in the broadest sense describes the capacity to have feelings, had evolved into a moral bedrock of the animal rights movement before transhumanist intellectuals usurped the concept. However, making humans recognize that animals are just as capable of experiencing joy and pain does not figure as a top priority. Animal rights activists tend to see a fig leaf where transhumanists proclaim an article of faith. When transhumanists call for a redirection toward "sentient entities," according to the philosopher Michael Hauskeller, a true "meeting of species" is not what they have in mind. Rather, they want to expand the scope of rights-bearing subjects beyond the confines of biological humans and grant legal protection to highly advanced, self-aware machines. Istvan's Transhumanist Bill of Rights, which he posted to the wall of the United States Capitol building, makes a similar point (see figure 9.1). Its latest version posits a seven-tiered hierarchy with inanimate objects at the bottom and "hybrid biological-digital awareness" at the top. Dogs are ranked at level-four capacity, one level below "sapient" forms of lucidity.[13]

FIGURE 9.1
Campaign poster of the Transhumanist Party, 2015. Dedicated to spreading a "pro-science culture," the party calls on all governments to develop tools that will give their citizens the means to "overcome involuntary aging."

Nick Bostrom, one of the WTA's main architects, stated in hindsight that removing the blemish of "cultishness" from transhumanism was a major reason for forming that body. Contrary to what the Swedish-born philosopher suggested, however, the brotherhood to which he had pledged himself cannot shed that stain so easily. Part of its reputation for promoting sectarianism stems from the loosely organized hacker groups who have subscribed to the movement's no-limits, open-boundaries doctrines. Few better represent the anarchic streak in transhumanism than the free-spirited computer geek. Proudly independent and exceedingly talented, the stereotypical geek is a young white male in his twenties. He snubs institutional loyalties and follows his inner compass. He likely attended university but just as likely lost interest and dropped out. Like Mark Zuckerberg, he claims that he "probably learned more coding from random side projects" than at the courses he took in college. At the peril of pushing the cliché too far, the geeks' relationship to the world of their parents is mostly transactional, if not cynical. Some secretly dream of following in the footsteps of the fictional character Thomas Anderson from the movie *The Matrix*, who one day awakens as Neo and saves humanity by learning how to bend the computer-generated simulation to his will.[14]

Another community that regularly pops up in discussions about transhumanism's antecedents is the Italian futurists. Notorious for their love of speed and disruption, the artists around the poet Filippo Tommaso Marinetti shared a distaste for tradition that critics see replicated in Silicon Valley's tech elite. "We stand on the last promontory of the centuries! Why should we look back, when what we want is to break down the mysterious doors of the Impossible?" Marinetti bellowed in 1909, almost a hundred years before similar sentiments spread through the hallways of Big Tech. The fast and furious Italians who rhapsodized over blazing furnaces and roaring cars could be laughed off as postadolescent adrenalin junkies were it not for their toxic politics. Theirs was a fanatical youth cult that wanted men older than forty to end up "in the wastebasket like useless manuscripts." They glorified war, "the world's only hygiene," and emphasized "the love of danger, the habit of energy and fearlessness" over "moralism, feminism" and "every opportunistic and or utilitarian cowardice." The futurists' ruthless embrace of technological progress foreshadowed the twentieth century's most extreme ideologies, most notably fascism. In their view, all that counted was rushing toward the world of tomorrow, one of "eternal, omnipresent speed." The faster that values like kindness and restraint got out of the way, the better.[15]

The futurist analogy can be a potent weapon in the hands of transhumanism's opponents. A megalomanic hater of past things and ideas? Look no further than Anthony Lewandowski, the cofounder of Google's self-driving car program Waymo, and you might be listening to Marinetti's American heir. At least this what *Wired* contributor Rose Eveleth implied. Lewandowski is on the record for saying that "the only thing that matters is the future. I don't even know why we study history. It's entertaining, I guess. . . . But what already happened doesn't really matter. You don't need to know that history to build on what they made. In technology, all that matters is tomorrow." As with most historical analogies, the futurism connection needs to be handled with care. At the most basic level, transhumanists believe in longevity, not in people dying young. Italian futurists would have balked at today's ideas about life extension and prolonging youthful vitality to the outer rims of old age and beyond. Transhumanists are also disinclined to romanticize war. Many treat the world wars and atrocities such as the Holocaust as evidence of humanity's vices that tradition has failed to eradicate. In 2019, Bostrom called civilization getting "devastated by default" the biggest threat facing our species. By that he meant a doomsday scenario in which one discovery could enable any person with basic computing skills to unleash annihilation on a scale surpassing the destructive force of nuclear weapons.[16]

Bostrom's "vulnerable world hypothesis" has bred few additional pacifists. In most transhumanist circles, the prospect of future wars elicits shoulder-shrugging fatalism. Few seek it, but many are also pragmatic about the fact that war and technological change have a nasty habit of converging. "If necessity is the mother of invention, then war is surely its father," declared Raymond Kurzweil, Google's director of engineering. Unlike Lewandowski, artificial intelligence pioneer Kurzweil is an avid reader of history. He talks a lot about World War II and about Alan Turing in particular, the English mathematician whose idea that computers were intelligent beings ripened while the Germans were bombing British cities. Kurzweil's admiration for Turing's work is enormous. Here was a scientist who helped defeat the Nazis with a stroke of genius, giving proof of humanity's capacity for giant leaps of knowledge in moments of existential crisis. Turing's prediction that machines would start to outperform humans around the turn of the millennium earned him the posthumous title of transhumanist prophet. In Kurzweil's self-serving narrative, Turing epitomizes the heroic inventor who parts the waters of history with sheer resolve.[17]

My semi-veiled allusions to the Old Testament are not accidental. In envisaging an arc that bends toward the separation of flesh and mind, transhumanists are navigating a fine line between rationality and religion. This seems counterintuitive, given that so many leading proponents identify as atheists. But their denial of God's existence has a soft underbelly. They pledge allegiance to the legacy of the Enlightenment yet feel comfortable invoking the Christian themes of redemption and resurrection. Kurzweil's lasting contribution to the transhumanist body of thought is his singularity thesis, which holds that humans would one day morph into "spiritual machines." Materialist readings focus on a technological point of no return after which humans would forever shed their biological frailties and evolve into beings with unprecedented creative powers. What these readings gloss over is the religious imagery that Kurzweil and others deploy to make that transition palatable. They describe the liberation of thought from the limitations of the biological form as an essentially spiritual undertaking. Bodies would stop to decay, organs would no longer rot, much like in Christian eschatological traditions where eternal life is bestowed as a reward on humans who have reached a certain state of righteousness. The only major differences, it appears, are that technology has taken on the role of the messiah. Scientists, not priests, now stand between mortals and the afterlife.[18]

"The data, the code, the communications. Forever Amen." This was how the software developer Anders Sandberg, clothed in black and standing in the middle of his room, concluded a pseudo-sermon that he had allowed the makers of a documentary to capture on film. After invoking his version of the holy trinity, Sandberg turned to the four corners of the room. With outstretched arms, he made the sign of the cross, hallowing the memory of four computer-age apostles: Charles Babbage, Alan Turing, Ada Lovelace, John von Neumann. Sandberg is perhaps not the best representative of the movement's clerical undertow. He may also enjoy a good parody. But the evangelical fervor displayed by Sandberg and his fellow futurists has yet to fade. According to their script, salvation lies in becoming one's own ultimate programmer, in intrepidly evolving to a stage of development where godlike powers beckon to the faithful: mind-to-mind communication, extraterrestrial travel, and a form of immortality detached from religious loyalties. Reconcilement with traditional faiths is possible but not mandatory. For the ethnobotanist Terence McKenna, the harbingers of this future had already arrived at the turn of the millennium. "We are now living in the age of the Holy Spirit," he remarked shortly before his death in 2000, "and the internet is its vessel."[19]

Searching for transhumanism's ancestors feels like entering a maze with no marked entrance and no known exits. Like other sprawling intellectual endeavors that preceded it, the movement's hunger for legitimacy is rapacious. In trying to persuade the rich and powerful, its advocates can be gleefully idiosyncratic, catering to different ideological tastes and spiritual sensibilities. This suppleness leaves observers with a dizzying mélange of ideas and influences that makes it difficult to pin a political label on transhumanism that will stick. Silicon Valley's tech avant-garde will continue to defy such attempts anyway as they are increasingly focused on creating their own segregated reality. What they do not and, frankly, should not have is exclusive control over who gets to write their history. Because if the radical life extensionists and their ensemble of ultrarich donors get what they want, their eulogies are not going to be written in this century or the next.

BUSINESSMAN JAMES STROLE has had few qualms about turning the fountain of youth into a money sprinkler. Customers strolling through his "marketplace of your future" can shop for the latest products from the nation's leading antiaging brands: supplements that enhance brain function, pills that activate cellular renewal, AI-supported tests that measure individual biomarkers, you name it. The marketplace has been conveniently nested in the grand ballrooms of hotels that have hosted the RAADfest, the annual "Revolution Against Aging and Death" conferences of the Coalition for Radical Life Extension (CRLE). Keynote speakers come from different parts of the antiaging stratosphere. InfoSpace founder Naveen Jain has been a regular contributor to the meetings, as has the transhumanist frontman Ray Kurzweil. Strole, who refers to himself as an anti-death activist, established CRLE in 2016. The septuagenarian with the wrinkleless face of a thirty-year-old takes great pride in his invention. He calls the RAADfests "the Woodstock of radical life extension," where everyone chips in to create "a huge bonfire of life to consume aging, sickness, and death." His mission, Strole declares, is to bring cutting-edge rejuvenation solutions to Main Street in ways that work for the average consumer, not just for the affluent tech manager. Fittingly, CRLE welcomes all who seek everlasting youth into their fold—as long as they can afford the whopping conference fee of $679.[20]

Judging by the brand names swirling around the exhibition halls, CRLE aficionados are all over the place. The services offered at the annual conferences run the entire gamut, from rejuvenating red-light panels and next-generation gene therapies to AI-assisted stem cell treatments and pet longevity programs. Wordy claims and glitzy labels obscure differences between attempting to lengthen life spans and trying to make bodies younger. For antiaging researchers, these differences very much exist, and when pressed, they will tell you why they matter. Rejuvenation scientist Aubrey de Grey, one of the scene's superstars until he lost his job as chief science officer of the SENS Research Foundation over sexual harassment allegations, objects to being grouped with the transhumanists, though he respects their work. De Grey, sensing misgivings in parts of the older generation, does not want "the general public [to] think we're all out to create a whole new species." Neither does he like the longevity tag. He thinks it distracts from his goal of repairing the damage that aging causes in otherwise healthy bodies.[21]

This kind of jockeying for the pole position is not unusual among public-facing scientists. Strole, however, would not have it at the RAADfests. The tone struck by the organizers is remarkably ecumenical, and the competing factions are happy to suspend their rivalries once the show starts. To kick off the 2018 festival in San Diego, Strole hopped out onstage together with his partner Bernadeane, a toned eighty-one-year-old in a leopard catsuit. Through blaring electronic dance music, the couple greeted the flock with the words, "If you ask me, no one here needs to die anymore!" The formula will ring familiar to any student of the self-help industry—motivation hucksters broadcasting stories of personal growth and cheering crowds getting hooked on the idea of achieving the best version of their selves. This congregation wanted more still: reaching that optimal state and keeping it. Kurzweil, who appeared on video call, reassured the faithful that this was not a castle in the sky. By 2045, thanks to further advances in bioengineering and the computer sciences, humanity could finally bid farewell to dying of natural causes. The immortalist creed preached at the RAADfests connects Californian beachboys, frequent-flyer executives, and Botoxed seniors. Under the auspices of some of the most vocal antiagers, Kurzweil's plea to "live long enough to live forever" is no cause for embarrassment. It has ushered in a new covenant.[22]

An us-versus-them mentality is a common feature of groups who feel misunderstood yet profoundly superior to others. The transhumanists and their allies at CRLE are getting their fair share of pushback. Credentialed gerontologists have declined speaking invitations, fearing it would damage their reputation. Instead, many joined the growing chorus of critics who have doubted the science behind spectacular longevity announcements. Cell biologist Leonard Hayflick, who taught medical microbiology at Stanford, gently mocked de Grey's work, calling its success as likely as the attempt to reverse gravity. Some of Hayflick's mainstream colleagues are more forthright in their denunciation. They regard RAADfest as an assembly of pompous half-frauds and self-righteous grifters. "Gerontology is science, and immortalism is religion," commented the pathologist Matt Kaeberlein in 2018. In his estimate, there was "no scientific basis" for the belief that human technology could ever outwit death. The federal government apparently agrees: the US Food and Drug Administration (FDA) has yet to approve any treatment designed specifically to stop people from aging.[23]

Rejuvenation has always been more of a trap than a fountain, and some react with schadenfreude to wealthy people getting scammed by wealthier ones. Not Francis Fukuyama. What concerns the conservative intellectual who acquired celebrity status with his post–Cold War thesis about the end of history is not so much the pretentiousness of life extension utopias. He seems more worried about their corrosive effect on communal relations. Fukuyama came out the gate swinging in September 2004 when he nominated transhumanism as "the world's most dangerous idea" in an article he wrote for *Foreign Policy*. Fukuyama arguably does not qualify as the best advocate for the sanctity of human life, considering that he initially supported the US invasion of Iraq. Yet, his intervention deserves to be taken seriously because it reflects a broader unease about the rapid advances of the digital age. Fukuyama's interest in the subject dates back to the late 1990s, when he first raised his voice against genetic cloning and DNA manipulation in humans. Suspicion gave way to alarm in his 2002 book *Our Posthuman Future*. It was a somber warning that liberal democracy might not survive the biotechnological revolution.[24]

Fukuyama maintains that in trying to trick nature, biogenetical developers are toppling the moral foundations of post-Enlightenment liberalism. The very essence of what it meant to be human was under attack. Fukuyama's animus toward transhumanist visions of progress impelled him to settle old scores with a somewhat cartoonish version of postmodernism, which he trashed at one point "as a kind of Nietzschean relativism that said there is no truth." Along these lines, he presents efforts to repair human bodies with biotechnological means as an outgrowth of the flawed notion that all reality is socially constructed. Fukuyama's indictment is most damning in passages that link the antiaging engineers of our time to the social engineers of some of the twentieth century's worst dictatorships. Both parties, according to Fukuyama, share an instrumentalist view of humanity, "pounding the square peg of human nature into the round hole of social planning." The ones who do not go through are either degraded or discarded. The result is a deeply anti-egalitarian, anti-human society that jettisons fundamentals such as love, hope, sorrow, and friendship in favor of some vague promise of significantly lengthened life spans that few roboticized humans would ever get to enjoy. We might one day wake up in a digital apartheid state, Fukuyama portends, without even caring.[25]

Predictably, the transhumanist camp was up in arms about Fukuyama's words. Had he really declared the machine man of the future the distant cousin of the new men of Soviet communism and National Socialism? One of the first to fight back was Bostrom, who belittled Fukuyama's anthropocentric ideas as antiquated. Bostrom refused to be lectured about the dangers of moral relativism by a man whose belief in a timeless human core flew in the face of evolutionary science. That concept, Bostrom countered, was inconsistent with scientific findings about fluctuating gene pools and the similarities between humans and primates. It also led Fukuyama, a reactionary bioconservative in Bostrom's eyes, to take a fallacious stance on equality. Saying that technologically augmented humans should not be equal under the law would be historically "akin to excluding people on [the] basis of their gender or the color of their skin." In just a few paragraphs, Bostrom had turned the tables on Fukuyama. Or so he thought.[26]

Once the genie of dystopian anti-transhumanism was out of the bottle, nobody could put him back in. Right-wing conspiracy peddlers seized on Fukuyama's pessimistic outlook and warped it beyond recognition. After the election of Barack Obama to the White House in 2008, segments that portrayed Silicon Valley's tech bubble as part of a money-rich, globalist cabal bent on subjugating traditional Americans featured heavily on the *InfoWars* channel, where Alex Jones ranted about a "terrible discovery," allegedly exposing how deeply liberal elites were invested in enslaving decent, god-fearing people and overriding them with machines. Such narratives are on par with the far-right Great Replacement theory, which evokes sinister images of dark-skinned immigrants overwhelming white Americans and Europeans. Anti-transhumanism melds effortlessly with anti-globalization, white nationalism, and antisemitism. In the netherworlds of QAnon and other right-wing conspiracy networks, the notion of optimizing human beings devolves into a regime of terror headed by tech billionaires who want to live forever while seeking to make huge swathes of the white population infertile.[27]

It is difficult to say what exactly makes these theories stick other than their vile careers on the internet. A big part of their appeal lies in their ability to cook up a toxic stew of cultural grievances and mounting economic inequalities, which Silicon Valley has come to symbolize to many who struggle to keep up. But even as online trolls subject tech leaders to the basest slander, there are few innocent victims here. Elon Musk does not appear to worry that much about the growing gap between the rich and poor, the climate crisis, or the persistence of racism. He is also surprisingly critical of his longevity-loving peers. People who refuse to die, Musk asserted, would only cause stasis and keep alive old ideas. In July 2021, Musk stunned the public, which was still reeling under the impact of the COVID-19 pandemic, by listing "population collapse" as the biggest threat facing the planet today. It was not the first time the owner of Tesla and X (formerly Twitter) had voiced his fears about declining birth rates, which he associates with overaged societies suffering from catastrophically low production rates. Demographers are unimpressed by Musk's projections. While numbers are declining or stalling in East and

Southeast Asia as well as most of Europe and North America, African and Middle Eastern populations continue to grow. What is driving the underpopulation thesis? The wish for more children or the desire for the right kind of children? Musk, who is a father of twelve, once tweeted, "Doing my best to help the underpopulation crisis." This sounds a lot like the cries of "no race suicide here" that filled the air at Theodore Roosevelt's campaign rallies more than 120 years ago.[28]

Those looking for hard evidence that rejuvenation continues to tilt between individual longings to stay young and the biopolitics of elite survival should turn to the Collins Institute for the Gifted, one of the latest Silicon Valley ventures. Founders Simone and Malcolm Collins, who have three children and plan to have ten, are not the kind of couple who would show up at a RAADfest. They are committed pronatalists with a strong preference for physical and mental excellence. Apart from devising meritocratic homeschool curricula, the Collinses are outspoken supporters of genomic prediction, which allows couples with deep pockets to select the "fittest" embryos from a plethora of in vitro fertilized eggs. The matchmaking service they created caters to "high-achieving" individuals, the kind of people Simone hopes will breed "the new dominant leading classes in the world." Though the Collinses, who say they are "secular Calvinists," are clever enough to tiptoe around blatantly racist remarks, their passion about finding permanence in their genetically flawless children implies they are striving to perpetuate a techified brand of white Protestant supremacy. When told by her interviewer that some folks called them "hipster eugenicists," Simone Collins could not help but put on a wry smile. She insisted that their project was future oriented. And yet, it exudes an unpleasant odor from the past.[29]

The stench of age segregation hovers over the pronouncements of another tech tycoon who has pledged himself to found a nation for anti-agers. Unlike the wonkish Collinses, the forty-six-year-old multimillionaire biohacker Bryan Johnson proudly parades his toned torso in front of the camera to show how far he has come on his mission to become a young man again. In March 2024, Johnson drew cheers from a crowd of longevity enthusiasts in West Palm Beach, Florida, after unveiling his plan to build something akin to a don't-die state. Finding the right kind of island or acreage would take time, the millionaire admitted, but the failure of today's governments to provide people the therapies they needed to de-age their bodies was reason enough to start acting. Membership requirements, not just the monetary ones, would be dauntingly high. Citizens in Johnson's antiaging nation would have to forego pizza and doughnuts, get up at five every morning, and sweat through hour-long daily workouts in order to gain access to state-of-the-art rejuvenation therapies. This would not be a place for the weak-willed. With health and youthfulness declared the prime yardsticks of human worth, there is little about Johnson's cultish dream of beating death that does not reek of fanaticism.[30]

A lot of Big Tech leaders who lean to the right politically attempt to rebut the charge of neo-eugenics by saying they are not Nazis. But neither were Irving Fisher and Charles Davenport. The narrow definitions of eugenics favored by today's transhumanists and pronatalists are politically motivated. All they do is brush under the carpet concerns that using technology to rear humans who are smarter, fitter, and younger would very likely magnify existing inequalities. True to their libertarian credentials, Peter Thiel, Elon Musk, and other superrich advocates of enhanced procreation slam state-run efforts at population control as immoral and ineffective. But on the question of who gets to live for how long in their techno-utopian future, their language is strikingly evasive—except for the assertion that intellectually less talented individuals outbreeding more gifted ones would ruin civilization in the long term. For the same reason, Musk promoted the movie *Idiocracy* in 2006, in which the ignorant populate the planet after the intelligent stopped having children. Pedigree still matters for a small elite obsessed with colonizing space and defeating age. For a change, Francis Fukuyama can claim vindication.[31]

LOUD GASPS FILL THE AIR at a train station in New Orleans. Monsieur Gateau, one of the city's finest clockmakers, has just unveiled his masterpiece. The giant clock he built is of a peculiar kind: it runs backward. Sensing the confusion, Gateau tells the audience that he made it that way. His vain hope was that the clock might indeed turn back time and thus bring back his son and all the other young men who died in the last war. Offering his apologies, the blind Gateau steps off the scaffold and exits the terminal, never to be seen again. This poignant scene marks the beginning of the 2008 movie *The Curious Case of Benjamin Button*, which is inspired by a short story of the same name written in 1922 by F. Scott Fitzgerald. In the movie, the clock's life span and that of its protagonist, Benjamin Button, are roughly the same. And both serve as allegories for a mighty desire: the wish to restore youth.

It is perhaps altogether proper to close this book with a tale about an American who grows only younger. The second most haunting character Fitzgerald birthed into literature after Jay Gatsby, Benjamin Button does not age like everyone else. He lives his biological life backward, from the cradle into which he is first placed as a septuagenarian infant to the grave that he enters as a baby whose memory of himself vanished, until "over him there were soft mumblings and murmurings that he scarcely heard, and faintly differentiated smells, and light and darkness." The movie's ending moved me to tears. Later, it made me think about what it means to deviate from a normal life course. In the original telling, Benjamin is at the peak of his powers around the age of forty. His company accumulates a fortune, and he returns a hero from the Spanish–American War. Yet the glory days do not last. Benjamin grows estranged from the woman he once adored, who envies her husband's youthful looks. He gets distracted easily, tumbles from one affair to the next, and eventually moves in with his son Roscoe, now outwardly older than his father. The clock keeps ticking backward, and Benjamin continues to rejuvenate.[32]

Pondering over Button's curious case after years of researching this topic, I wonder whether it offers a far more penetrating gaze on America's youth obsession than many acknowledge. When Benjamin stares into the mirror, he might be catching a glimpse of something larger than himself—the momentary delight of a culture that takes "a naive pleasure" in appearances and refuses to contemplate rejuvenation's devastating costs. Something might be terribly wrong, but why bother when there are so many exciting things left to do. The parties, the dancing, the opportunities for getting richer, for climbing up the political ladder, for expanding one's own frontier and that of the nation. Think of it! If your throat ever tightens with anxiety, do not despair. There will always be other people who will bring instant relief, who will pick up the tab and carry the burden.[33]

Surely, two-and-a-half centuries of US history cannot be squeezed into a single short story. Looking back at the characters highlighted over the last eight chapters, however, it will not be difficult to find many who, in some shape or form, embodied Buttonesque traits, each tailored to specific circumstances. From the moment of the nation's inception, youth has exercised an almost irresistible pull on Americans of various origins, and fantasies of salvaging it from the unrelenting march of time justified extraordinary, occasionally even violent action. In that regard, a sense of kinship extends far back into the past—to the Young Americans who espoused Manifest Destiny as their young nation was pushing westward, to the Progressive Era masculinist lust for reinvigorating imperial adventure, to the declaration of an "American Century," which legitimized US leadership over an aging West. Long before policymakers recognized the political importance of young people, they had discovered age as an instrument to build their own nation and gain an edge over its competitors.

Besides feeding the illusion of America's undying forward trajectory, of a nation absolved from the calamities of others, rejuvenation has kept filling people's pockets. The rise of consumerism across the industrialized world, a process in which the United States played first fiddle, rested on the willingness of the middle classes to pay enormous sums for things they did not need for basic sustenance. Lasting youth changed from myth to a machinery of attraction, with multiplying shops and department stores selling the latest cosmetic products to the modern woman who was told to brace herself against growing old. Beauty and fitness remain gendered concepts, and men, too, have not relinquished the concern for projecting an aura of long-lasting masculinity. Unmaking aging became the domain of those who "made it," a perfect symbol for a capitalist society where the face of capitalism itself is supposed to bear no wrinkle.

"Rage, rage against the dying of the light." The words of the Welsh poet Dylan Thomas speak to us still. Nobody should be ashamed of their feelings toward death, but our fear of dying should not serve as an excuse for casting as losers those who simply grow old. We now live in a world in which eighty-year-old presidents think they have to project energy by jogging across the stage. Such antics prompt a good laugh on social media. Reducing them to entertainment, however, only shows how little we care about their history and the many casualties that history has produced. Keeping America young has been hard work for a majority who never got to sip from its fountains. The immense economic muscle the United States acquired during its adolescence would never have been built up without the uncompensated toil of its enslaved Black population. Nor would its twentieth-century beauty industry have flourished the way it did without the backbreaking labor performed on African and South Asian plantations. That labor nurtured the belief that youth did not have to be a "vanishing act," that the iron chain of aging and time could indeed be broken. With one big caveat. Youth tended to elude those whose lives were repurposed to rejuvenate the bodies of others—bodies that were overwhelmingly classified as white. Factor in race and class, and aging has a quadruple standard.[34]

Is this just an American story? Definitely not. The two major geopolitical rivals of the United States, China and Russia, are openly relishing the prospect of American decline, and their autocratic alliance is built on a shared foundation of "development and rejuvenation." For Xi Jinping, this means more than getting a facelift. After decades of restraint in foreign policy, China is awash in jingoism, threatening the use of force as it seeks to seize Taiwan and dethrone the United States. Vladimir Putin, seething with resentment over the collapse of the Soviet Empire, has already chosen regeneration through bloodshed. Russia's brutal invasion of its neighbor Ukraine has caused unspeakable pain in that country while exposing the ugly grimace of an aging autocracy. To allay its demographic crisis, Russia has been kidnapping thousands of Ukrainian children from the occupied territories and forcing them to grow up as Russians. In atrocious fashion, one people are decimated so that another may feel rejuvenated.[35]

Let us return to familiar shores. The war on aging is a vital thread in the American narrative. It is also a troubling one. Like so many causes embraced for purportedly noble ends, the results that it begot benefited few, bewildered many, and left many more broken. Like the myth of the United States as the place where humankind would be renewed and its sins washed away in the wellspring of new beginnings, the language of age is misleadingly universal. It glosses over the fact that membership in America's communities of rejuvenation is limited today, just as it was in the late eighteenth century. Zoltan Istvan knows that. Asked about the biggest hurdles facing the Transhumanist Party ahead of the upcoming 2024 election, Istvan had a simple answer: food. "We need these technologies. . . . I don't want to die from aging. . . . But it's very hard to realize those things when you're hungry or super poor or can't get a job." There is little to disagree with here. Personally, I cannot think of anything more obscene than the top one percent pumping billions of dollars into extending their lives while average Americans have seen their loved ones die at younger ages. Maybe rejuvenation is not meant to stick, like Istvan's ambitious little bill of rights that kept falling off the sandstone wall.[36]

Notes

Prologue

1. O'Connell, "600-Hundred Miles in a Coffin-Shaped Bus"; Istvan, "Revolutionary Politics Are Necessary for Transhumanism to Succeed."

2. Freneau, "The Rising Glory of America," 82–83; "The Age of the Elderly Candidate: How Two Septuagenarians Came to Be Running for President," *The Guardian*, October 29, 2020.

3. Baumann, *Mortality, Immortality and Other Life Strategies*, 137–38; US Census Bureau, "America Is Getting Older," June 22, 2023; "Covid and Race," *New York Times*, June 9, 2022; "U.S. Life Expectancy Declines Again, a Dismal Trend Not Seen Since World War I," *Washington Post*, November 29, 2019. The most recent study of old age in modern America is Chappel, *Golden Years*.

4. For a broader perspective, see Honeck, Alexander, and Richter, "Mapping Modern Rejuvenation," a special issue of the *Journal of Social History*. On the myth of the United States as the "land of youth," see Woodward, "The Aging of America," 584.

5. Historical studies of modern rejuvenation are rare and few. See, for example, Trimmer, *Rejuvenation*; Stoff, *Ewige Jugend*; Pettit, "Becoming Glandular;" and most recently Stark, *Cult of Youth.*

6. Graff is quoted in Wegs, "Working-Class Adolescence in Austria, 1890–1930," 440.

7. Syrett and Pomfret, "Concepts of Youth," 39.

8. My conceptualization of age is drawn from Field and Syrett, *Age in America*, 1–5; and Mintz, "Reflections on Age as a Category of Historical Analysis." On embodied identities as social performance, see J. Butler, *Gender Trouble*, 34.

9. My usage of the term "body project" as a form of cultural and social labor involving individuals and entire societies is inspired by Brumberg, *The Body Project*. On demographic developments in US history, see Klein, *A Population History of the United States*; and Hoff, *The State and the Stork.*

10. Red Hot Chili Peppers, *Californication*. For the distinction between "soft" and "hard" rejuvenation, I rely on Stark, *Cult of Youth.*

11. J. Locke, *Two Treatises of Government*, 228–29. On Locke's involvement in the slave trade, see Glauser, "Three Approaches to Locke and the Slave Trade," 199–216. The survivor of the Roanoke colony is quoted in Kupperman, *Roanoke*, 72. Some ethnologists speculate that the Fountain of Youth myth has Native American origins; see, for instance, Hultkranz, "The Immortality of the Soul among North American Indians," 223.

12. Paine, *Common Sense*, 40.

13. On transcendence as a concept in body history, see Forth, "Corpulence, Modernity, and Transcendence in the Early Twentieth Century."

14. Sontag, "The Double Standard of Aging."

15. See Klein, *The Atlantic Slave Trade*, 72, 98, for the origins of the transatlantic palm oil trade.

16. On the infantilization of non-whites in the context of empire, see Paisley, "Childhood and Race."

17. Hobsbawm, *The Age of Extremes*. On the transideological career of the "New Man," see Chen, *Creating the New Man*. For a good overview, see also Bauernkämper, "Der Neue Mensch."

18. Fitzgerald, *The Great Gatsby*, 218.

Chapter One

1. "William Barton to George Washington, August 28, 1788," in Abbot, *Papers of George Washington*, 476–78.

2. US State Department, *The Seal of the United States*, 16–18; Nigg, *The Phoenix*, 318–19.

3. Barton, *Observations on the Progress of Population*, 1–2.

4. "A Lotion for Preserving and Whitening the Teeth," *Royal Magazine*, December 1, 1766, 305–6. On Washington's teeth, see Chernow, *Washington: A Life*, 438.

5. On early baldness cures, see Segrave, *Baldness*, 66. "Nature's Grand Restorative," *Companion & Weekly Miscellany*, June 22, 1805, 270–71.

6. Vitalism blossomed in France but also spilled over to North America. Fischer, "Vitalism in America," 501–30; Blumenbach, *Über den Bildungstrieb*. Cohausen, *Hermippus Redivivus*. Hufeland, *The Art of Prolonging Life*, 185–89.

7. Haber and Gratton, *Old Age and the Search for Security*, 4–19, provide a useful overview of the historiography of old age in the early United States. On juvenile involvement in revolutionary-era protests, see Bell, "From Saucy Boys to Sons of Liberty."

8. Harrison, *Juvenescence*, 100–101.

9. "Diary of John Adams, August 7, 1756," in *The Adams Papers, Diary and Autobiography*, vol. 1, 39–40; "John Adams to Nathan Webb, probably October 15, 1755," in *The Adams Papers, Diary and Autobiography*, vol. 1, 4.

10. See also O'Brien, *Narratives of Enlightenment*, 205.

11. On the prominence of *translatio imperii* in British American revolutionary discourse, see Kupperman, "International at the Creation," 104; Morse, *The American Geography*, 469.

12. Brückner, *The Geographic Revolution in Early America*; Jefferson to Benjamin Chambers, December 28, 1805.

13. See, among others, Onuf, *Jefferson's Empire*, 6–7.

14. Buffon is quoted in Dugatkin, *Mr. Jefferson and the Giant Moose*, 27. On the origins and spread of the degeneration thesis, see also Thomson, *Jefferson's Shadow*, 101–17.

15. Kalm, *Travels into North America*, 81; De Pauw, *A General History of the Americans*, 18. See also Dugatkin, *Mr. Jefferson and the Giant Moose*, 36–37.

16. Malthus, *An Essay on the Principle of Population*, 343–44; On Malthusianism in the early United States, see also Hoff, *The State and the Stork*, 28–30.

17. Hoff, *The State and the Stork*, 33.

18. See Thomson, *Jefferson's Shadow*, 107–8; Jefferson, *Notes on the State of Virginia*, 47–141, 161–72. On the moose, see Dugatkin, *Mr. Jefferson and the Giant Moose*.

19. The dinner scene is recounted in Jefferson, "Thomas Jefferson's Anecdotes of Benjamin Franklin, December 4, 1818," 462–65. See also Hamilton, "The Federalist No. 11, November 24, 1787," 345–46; Adams, "John Adams to Philip Mazzei, December 15, 1785," 45.

20. On conspiracy theories in the early United States, see Hünemörder, *The Society of the Cincinnati*; Rush, "On Old Age [1789]," 345. Newspaper articles from the early 1790s echo Rush's thesis; see, for instance, "Remarks on Longevity and Fruitfulness," *American Museum, or, Universal Magazine* (Philadelphia), April 1, 1790; St. John de Crèvecoeur, *Letters from an American Farmer*, 52–53.

21. For solid data, see Klein, *Population History*, 88–92; See also Appleby, *Inheriting the Revolution*, 63.

22. Savage, *Liberty in the Form of the Goddess of Youth*.

23. Wallach, *Obedient Sons*, 40–46, discusses the significance of youth in the First Great Awakening. See also Hart, *America's Remembrancer*, 8.

24. John Cleaveland is quoted in A. M. Baldwin, *The New England Clergy and the American Revolution*, 130; Warren, *History of the Rise, Progress, and Termination of the American Revolution*, vol. 3, 323, 335.

25. "Adams to Elbridge Gerry, April 17, 1813," *Founders Online*.

26. Field, *The Struggle for Equal Adulthood*.

27. Brooks, *Poor Richard*, 29. On the descriptive terms used for pregnant woman before the late eighteenth century, see Klepp, "Revolutionary Bodies," 917.

28. On population growth in colonial America, see Hoff, *The State and the Stork*, 19; Franklin, *Observations Concerning the Increase of Mankind*, 10; Jefferson, *Notes*, 167; Madison, "The Federalist No. 10," 263–70.

29. Klepp, *Revolutionary Conceptions*; Klepp, "Revolutionary Bodies," 928.

30. Adams, "Abigail Adams to John Adams, March 31, 1776," 370; Anonymous, *The Female Advocate*, 22; Kerber, "The Republican Mother."

31. Dunaway, *The African-American Family in Slavery and Emancipation*, 114–49; see also Appleby, *Inheriting the Revolution*, 63.

32. See W. Johnson, "Time and Revolution in African America," 152–54; Douglass, *Narrative of the Life of Frederick Douglass*, 1.

33. Windon, "Superannuated: Old Age on the Antebellum Plantation"; Berry, *The Price for Their Pound of Flesh*.

34. Jefferson, *Notes*, 271–72; Jefferson, "Jefferson to Edward Bancroft, January 26, 1789," 492.

35. Douglass, *My Bondage and My Freedom*, 362; See also Duane, *Suffering Childhood in Early America*, 125–64.

36. See, for example, the collection of essays in Jackson and Bacon, eds., *African Americans and the Haitian Revolutions*.

37. See Sinha, *The Slave's Cause*, on the significance of the Haitian Revolution for the African American freedom struggle (34–64) and Watkins's quote (63).

38. See Duane, *Suffering Childhood*, 136–37; "Jefferson to St. George Tucker, August 28, 1797," 519.

39. Kupperman, "International at the Creation," 106–7. The Iroquois influence thesis remains controversial; Canasatego is quoted in Olson, *Benjamin Franklin's Vision of Community*, 36.

40. Jefferson, *Notes*, 115–27. On Native American longevity, see, for example, "Remarkable Instances of American Longevity," *Pennsylvania Magazine* (July 1775): 314–15; "Old Age Respected by the Creek Indians," *Massachusetts Magazine, or, Monthly Magazine of*

Knowledge & Rational Entertainment, July 1, 1792; and "Indian Longevity," *Medical Intelligencer* (Boston), December 7, 1824.

41. Rochefoucauld-Liancourt is quoted in Brandenburg, "A French Aristocrat Looks at American Farming," 163.

42. Jefferson, *Notes*, 326. See also Conn, *Americans against the City*, 11–24.

43. "Jefferson to William Ludlow, September 6, 1824," in Peterson, *Thomas Jefferson: Writings*, 1496–97.

Chapter Two

1. Washington, *Sojourner Truth's America*, 175–76.

2. On Ruggles's hydropathic work, see Hodges, *David Ruggles*, 155–98.

3. There is no academic biography of Wesselhöft, only an unpublished typescript: Starr Willard Cutting, "Robert Wesselhöft: in Germany a leader of early nineteenth century student-life and a confessed revolutionary, in America the founder and director of the first Brattleboro water cure establishment, 20th century," c. 1930, Brooks Memorial Library.

4. For a good overview, with the journal's circulation figure, see Cayleff, *Wash and Be Healed*, 3.

5. On water cure centers as sites of female liberation, see Sklar, "All Hail to Pure Cold Water!" 64–70, and more recently Haynes, *Riotous Flesh*, 19.

6. On nineteenth-century heroic medicine, see Sullivan, "Sanguine Practices."

7. *Water-Cure Journal*, preface to the bound volume for 1852. On stagnant and shrinking life expectancies, see Klein, *Population History*, 112–14; Van Buren's eating habits are documented in Bumgarner, *The Health of the Presidents*, 57–58.

8. Shprintzen, *The Vegetarian Crusade*, describes the Grahamites (10–38) and the scholar's quote (33).

9. On the compatibility of hydropathy and temperance, see also Bradley, *Water*, 155–80; Cordell, "Alcohol and Temperance," 73.

10. See Mintz, *Huck's Raft*, 88; *Youth's Temperance Advocate* (New York), no. 1–39 (November 1839–February 1843), 71.

11. For the struggle surrounding early minimum drinking age laws in Europe and North America, see R. Phillips, *Alcohol*, 199–204; Cold Water Army, *New Jersey Juvenile Temperance Band: True Likeness*.

12. See Cole, *The Journey of Life*, 114–18; Currier, *The Drunkard's Progress*.

13. "Garrison to Edmund Quincy, August 10, 1848," in Merrill, *The Letters of William Lloyd Garrison*, 580. On Wendell Phillips, see Stewart, "Heroes, Villains, Liberty, and License," 179. Douglass is quoted in Hodges, *David Ruggles*, 181.

14. Wright, *Six Months at Graefenberg*, 229.

15. General histories of US abolitionism that touch on these aspects are Sinha, *The Slave's Cause*, and McDaniel, *The Problem of Democracy in the Age of Slavery*.

16. On Garrisonian respectability, see McDaniel, "The Fourth and the First," 129–51; Bartlett, *Wendell Phillips*, 280; W. Phillips, "Public Opinion," 43; Austin, *The Life and Times of Wendell Phillips*, 29.

17. Hodges, *David Ruggles*, 174. Garrison is quoted in Washington, *Sojourner Truth's America*, 177; Anonymous, *The Metropolis of the Water Cure*, 21; "Important Letter from Adam Shook," *The Daily Scioto Gazette* (Chillicothe, Ohio), September 12, 1850.

18. See Sklar, "All Hail to Pure Cold Water!"; Haynes, *Riotous Flesh*, 19.

19. Boyer Lewis, *Ladies and Gentlemen on Display*, 83. For an example of professional medical criticism of hydropathy, see King, *Quackery Unmasked*.

20. On Charles Follen Garrison's death, see Alonso, *Growing Up Abolitionist*, 57–61.

21. Hawthorne, "Rappacini's Daughter"; Hawthorne, *The Blithedale Romance*.

22. See, for example, Woodson, "Doctor Wesselhoeft and Doctor Rappacini"; Hawthorne, "Dr. Heidegger's Experiment."

23. "American Habits in Eating and Drug-Taking," *Water-Cure Journal* (June 1848): 91.

24. De Leon, *The Position and Duties of "Young America."*

25. On Young America and the Democratic Party, see Widmer, *Young America*; Eyal, *The Young America Movement*; Power Smith, *Young America*.

26. Widmer, *Young America*, includes the O'Sullivan quote (14) and discusses Young America as a slogan for US literary nationalism (93–124). The working-class angle is discussed in Lause, *Young America: Land, Labor, and the Republican Community*. For prints from the era in the Library of Congress, see Anonymous, "Young America denims" (c. 1858); Lilienthal, *Young America* [tobacco] (c. 1860) and *Young America* [ship] (c. 1860).

27. Field and Syrett, *Age in America*, 2; See also, in the same volume, Grinspan, "A Birthday Like None Other," 86–102.

28. "The Spirit of Young America," *Chicago Daily Tribune*, December 15, 1853; Train, *Spread-Eagleism*, viii, xii.

29. R. E. May, *Manifest Destiny's Underworld*, 112; For a contrarian account that paints Walker as a democratic nation-builder, see Michel Gobat, *Empire by Invitation*.

30. On Margaret Fuller and Young America, see Widmer, *Young America*, 109. The gender dimensions of manifest destiny are discussed in Greenberg, *Manifest Manhood*. On white women's political involvement, see also Varon, *We Mean to Be Counted*.

31. See Eyal, *The Young America Movement*, 8, 91. "Webster and Calhoun," *Raleigh Register*, September 12, 1849.

32. "The Duty of the Democratic Party," *United States Magazine and Democratic Review* (November 1839): 439–40.

33. The quote from the literary reviewer appeared in "Fogy Literature," *United States Magazine and Democratic Review* (May 1852): 398. On Young Carolina, see Wallach, *Obedient Sons*, 132–33. On the "Silver Gray Whigs," see Holt, *The Rise and Fall of the American Whig Party*, 588–97; Thoreau, *Walden*, 11.

34. Whitman, "Song of Myself," 78. For the European roots of Young America, see Eyal, *The Young America Movement*, 94–96; and Wallach, *Obedient Sons*, 118–24.

35. The reception of the Italian unification struggle in pre–Civil War America is the subject of Gemme, *Domesticating Foreign Struggles*. Mazzini is quoted in Gemme, *Domesticating Foreign Struggles*, 119; "Joseph Mazzini," *Liberator*, July 27, 1849; "The Revolutionary Secret Societies of Modern Italy," *United States Magazine and Democratic Review* (September 1841): 276.

36. Honeck, *We Are the Revolutionists*, 14–15, 26–28.

37. See Roberts, *Distant Revolutions* for US responses to 1848. On the Sanders dinner and the controversy surrounding it, see Eyal, *The Young America Movement*, 93.

38. See, for instance, "What? You Young Yankee-Noodle, Strike Your Own Father?" *Punch Magazine*, March 14, 1846.

39. "Young America," *The Lantern* (New York), March 26, 1853. Other examples are "Young America—Youthful Aspirations," *Yankee-Notions*, October 1, 1853; "Young America, 1776. Young America, 1856," *Yankee-Notions*, February 1, 1858.

40. "Young America," *New York Daily Times*, June 16, 1853.

41. Faust, *This Republic of Suffering*, xii.

42. Lincoln, "Address before the Young Men's Lyceum in Springfield, Illinois, January 27, 1838"; Lincoln, "Speech at Lewistown, Illinois, August 17, 185."

43. On the Wide Awakes, see Grinspan, *The Virgin Vote*, 117–19; Grinspan, "'Young Men for War.'"

44. Grinspan, *The Virgin Vote*, 117.

45. See, for instance, Schurz, "Carl Schurz to his wife Margarethe, August 16, 1860," 218; Schurz, "True Americanism," 54.

46. On liberal nationalism and the limits of democracy, see Hahn, *A Nation without Borders*, 270–317. On the early violence in Civil War Missouri, see Goodheart, *1861*, 233–39, 258–61.

47. Lincoln, "Address Delivered at the Dedication of the Cemetery at Gettysburg, November 19, 1863," 22–23; Frederick Douglass, "The Mission of the War," *New York Daily Tribune*, January 14, 1864.

48. B. C. Miller, *Empty Sleeves*.

49. Douglass, "Our Composite Nationality," in McKivigan, Husband, and Kaufman, *The Speeches of Frederick Douglass*, 281. A still foundational work is Foner, *Reconstruction*.

Chapter Three

1. Harriet Beecher Stowe to Calvin Stowe and children, March 10, 1867, Folder 85, Beecher-Stowe Family Papers, Schlesinger Library, Harvard Radcliffe Institute.

2. H. Stowe, *Palmetto Leaves*, 128–38; C. E. Stowe, *Life of Harriet Beecher Stowe*, 463, 469–70. See also Hedrick, *Harriet Beecher Stowe: A Life*, 329–52.

3. Wrobel, *Global West, American Frontier*; Cocks, *Tropical Whites*.

4. Pomfret, "Imperial Rejuvenations." See also Jennings, *Curing the Colonizers*.

5. See, for example, Cocks, *Tropical Whites*; Merrill, *Negotiating Paradise*; and Skwiot, *The Purpose of Paradise*.

6. G. M. Beard, *American Nervousness*, vii. On the nineteenth century as an age of acceleration, see Osterhammel, *The Transformation of the World*, 74–76.

7. Schaffner, *Exhaustion*, 111–49; Edwards and Harraden, *Two Health-Seekers in Southern California*, 99–100.

8. The phrase "oasis of deceleration" appears in Rosa, *Social Acceleration*, 115, 158. See also Frederick Jackson Turner, "Address at the Dedication of a New High School Building in Portage, Wisconsin," *Portage Weekly Democrat*, January 3, 1896.

9. Mitchell, *Wear and Tear, or Hints for the Overworked*, 6.

10. Lawrence, *Studies in Classic American Literature*, 57–58; F. J. Turner, "The Significance of the Frontier in American History."

11. On Wister, see Bold, *The Frontier Club*, 27–28, 55–64.

12. Wister is quoted in Scharnhorst, *Owen Wister and the West*, 10.

13. See Kimmel, *The History of Men*, 53–54; Roosevelt is quoted in Dalton, *Roosevelt*, 98.

14. Wister's affinity for white southern manhood is examined in Silber, *The Romance of Reunion*, 188–96.

15. Blight, *Race and Reunion*, remains the best synthesis of this subject. On African Americans in the postbellum West, see Bold, *The Frontier Club*, 131–33.

16. Love, *The Life and Adventures of Nat Love*, 96.

17. Roosevelt is quoted in Stratemeyer and Copeland, *American Boys' Life of Theodore Roosevelt*, 297–98.

18. Bederman, *Manliness and Civilization*; Kimmel, *Manhood in America*; "Out Doors (undated)," box 57, William Kent Family Papers, Yale University Library; Offenburger, *Frontiers in the Gilded Age*, 74; "Animals in Africa," *New York Herald*, March 1, 1911; Kemper, *A Splendid Savage*, 3.

19. Bullock and Workman, *Algerian Memories*, 89–95, 104–10. See also the unpublished paper by Cardon, "Fanny Bullock Workman."

20. On Roosevelt's African safari and Hall's recapitulation theory, see Bederman, *Manliness and Civilization*, 77–120, 207–13.

21. See Slotkin, *Gunfighter Nation*, 78–79; T. Roosevelt, *African Game Trails*, xi.

22. On the caricatures, see Banta, *Barbaric Intercourse*, 305–15. On boy scouting and the group's forerunners, see Honeck, *Our Frontier Is the World*, 20–31. See also Merchant, *My Dear Wister*, 181.

23. The age structure of nineteenth-century settler populations in the US West is addressed in Courtwright, *Violent Land*, 61–63; Nascher, *Geriatrics*, vi.

24. Wister, *Lady Baltimore*, 156–57.

25. London, "A Piece of Steak," 295. On London's personal credo, which he supposedly shared with close friends a couple months before his death, see London, *Jack London's Tales of Adventure*, vii.

26. Strunsky, "Memoirs of Jack London," 13.

27. Reynolds, *The Landing of Ponce de León*, 6–8; "Fountain of Myths," *Chicago Tribune*, January 6, 1992.

28. Gollner, *The Book of Immortality*, 139; US Department of the Interior, "Proposed Fountain of Youth Natl. Monument, Florida." This collection of correspondence includes "Herbert Kahler to Verne Chatelain, January 18, 1934."

29. For the slogans, see Kilby, *Finding the Fountain of Youth*, 28, 78; "City of Eternal Youth," *Miami Herald*, November 14, 1920; "Will You Take the Priceless Gift of—Life?" *Vanity Fair* (January 1926): 16.

30. "Decide Now, Spend Your Vacation in a Different Place," *New York Times*, June 8, 1922; Cocks, *Tropical Whites*, 85. On California, see also Culver, *The Frontier of Leisure*; on Hawaii, see Skwiot, *Purpose of Paradise*.

31. Peterson is quoted in Viktorin et al., *Nation Branding in Modern History*, 4.

32. "The Campaign against Malaria and Mosquitoes," *Florida Health Notes* 5, no. 9 (September 1910): 141; Patterson, "The Trials and Tribulations of Amos Quito," 164, 167; Graham, *In Quest of El Dorado*, 163.

33. Kenworthy, *Climatology of Florida*, 43–44. On the "disappearance" of the natives of Hawaii, see Lozano, "U.S. Settler Colonial Climates," 192.

34. Siple is quoted in Honeck, *Our Frontier Is the World*, 81.

35. See Culver, *Frontier of Leisure*, 71–72; Hughes, *I Wonder as I Wander*, 12.

36. Digitized versions of *Travelguide* are available through the New York Public Library Digital Collections; A. R. Jefferson, *Living the California Dream*, 13.

37. Isenberg, *White Trash*, 135.

38. Isenberg, *White Trash*, 194–200.

39. These promotions and testimonials are described in Cocks, *Tropical Whites*, 84.

40. Levis, *Diary of a Spring Holiday in Cuba*, 11; Atlantic and Gulf Railroad, *Guide to Southern Georgia and Florida*, 67; Remondino, *The Mediterranean Shores of America*, 118.

41. Dixon, "Saving Your Face from Sunburn"; see also Cocks, *Tropical Whites*, 110–23.

42. Cocks, *Tropical Whites*, 116–18.

43. London, *A Son of the Sun*, 12, 28.

44. Quoted in Paris, *Children's Nature*, 3.

45. Murray, *Adventures in the Wilderness*, 22, 24.

46. Muir, *Our National Parks*, 1; Cook, "Camp Lou"; Aron, *Working at Play*, 177.

47. Seton, *The Birch-Bark Roll of the Woodcraft Indians*, 1–2.

48. On the Seton-Beard feud, see Deloria, *Playing Indian*, 95–127.

49. Beard, *Hardly a Man Is Now Alive*, 205. See also Honeck, *Our Frontier Is the World*, 30–31.

50. This is the main argument of Honeck, *Our Frontier Is the World*. On gender and race segregation in early US summer camps, see Paris, *Children's Nature*, 49–51, 189–225.

51. See Honeck, *Our Frontier Is the World*, 281–82.

Chapter Four

1. Palmolive Advertisement, *Harper's Bazaar*, 55, no. 11 (November 1920): 112a; "When Ancient Egypt Was Young," Palmolive Advertisement, *Ladies' Home Journal* (July 1918): 70; "Beauty from Trees," Palmolive Advertisement, *Ladies' Home Journal* (July 1925): 45.

2. For good overviews, see Jones, *Beauty Imagined*; Berghoff and Kühne, *Globalizing Beauty*; Weinbaum et al., *The Modern Girl around the World*. The figure is taken from Jones, *Beauty Imagined*, 1.

3. On the racist underpinnings of modern beauty standards, see Painter, *The History of White People*, 59–71; and Jha, *The Global Beauty Industry*.

4. A best-selling account of the Arden-Rubinstein feud is Woodhead, *War Paint*. See also Fitoussi, *Helena Rubinstein*; L C. Johnson, *Behind the Red Door*; and Bundles, *On Her Own Ground*. Netflix turned Bundles's biography of Madam C. J. Walker into a miniseries in 2020 starring Octavia Spencer (Lemmons and Davis, *Self Made*).

5. The term "social skin" was introduced by the anthropologist Terrence Turner, "The Social Skin," 83–103.

6. On the origins of the global palm oil trade, see Robins, *Oil Palm*, 25–41.

7. Robins, *Oil Palm*, 16–22, 20.

8. Lynn, *Commerce and Economic Change in West Africa*, 3, 42–46.

9. Robins, *Oil Palm*, 32–41, 37.

10. Robins, *Oil Palm*.

11. The significance of palm oil in the era of high imperialism is explored in Haiven, *Palm Oil*. On Hallet, see Maat, "Agriculture and Food Production," 190–203; Robins, *Oil Palm*, 115.

12. Gothwaite, *Trade in Philippine Copra and Coconut Oil*, 12–21; Snodgrass, *Copra and Coconut Oil*, 27–29; Droessler, *Coconut Colonialism*, 22–57, 45.

13. Kerkvliet, *Peasant Rebellion in the Philippines*, 96; on Filipino migration to the United States, see Kramer, *The Blood of Government*, 397–407.

14. Palmolive Company, *A Day in the Palmolive Factory*, 4, 10.

15. Nicholas and Smith, "Soft Rejuvenation," 906.

16. On the parallel rise of Rubinstein and Arden, see Woodhead, *War Paint*, 36–102.

17. Peiss, *Hope in a Jar*, 37–60.

18. On the "new women," see Matthews, *The Rise of the New Woman*.

19. Perkins Gilman, *Women and Economics*, 149; Weinbaum, *The Modern Girl around the World*.

20. Rubinstein, *Beauty in the Making*, 2. See, for example, these various cosmetic ads for Rubinstein and Arden products, taken from the digital database *Cosmetics and Skin*, https://www.cosmeticsandskin.com, accessed January 3, 2023: Arden, "Know as I Do, the Art of Making Yourself Beautiful" (1919); Rubinstein, "Fresh Laurels for Valaze" (1919); Rubinstein, "Beauty and the Individual Idea" (1918); Rubinstein, "The Pearly Skin of Childhood (1913); Arden, "To Grow Old Is More Difficult than to Die" (1914).

21. Palmolive, "Why Fade at 30?" *Ladies' Home Journal* (December 1922): 57; Rubinstein, "9 Basic Rules for Beauty" (1927), *Cosmetics and Skin*; Arden, "Will You Do Three Things for Loveliness?" (1923), *Cosmetics and Skin*; Arden, "To Grow Old" (1914), *Cosmetics and Skin*.

22. Peiss, *Hope in a Jar*, 98; On the aestheticization of whiteness, see Painter, *The History of White People*, 59–90.

23. Macfadden, *Help Yourself to Beauty*, 129; Tre-Jur is quoted in Peiss, *Hope in a Jar*, 151.

24. Rubinstein, "Valaze Egyptian Mask Treatment" (1920), *Cosmetics and Skin*; Rubinstein, "Enhance Your Beauty with the Cosmetic Masterpieces of Helena Rubinstein" (1929), *Cosmetics and Skin*; Arden, "The Smartest Tan Is from Elizabeth Arden" (1929), *Cosmetics and Skin*; Rubinstein, "'Valaze' Home Treatment for Restoring Complexion after Summer Exposure" (1920), *Cosmetics and Skin*.

25. Arden, *The Elizabeth Arden Exercises for Health and Beauty*, 3. See also Hoganson, *Consumer's Imperium* on how empire expanded the consumer choices of US middle-class women.

26. On bleaching and race in an international context, see Thomas, *Beneath the Surface*.

27. *Half Century Magazine* is quoted in Rooks, *Hair Raising*, 41; Garvey, "The Black Woman"; Schuyler, "Unnecessary Negroes"; Schuyler, *Black No More*.

28. "Bleach Your Dark Skin," *New York Amsterdam News*, January 4, 1919. See also Dorman, "Skin Bleach and Civilization," 47–80.

29. Walker is quoted in Bundles, *On Her Own Ground*, 269. On Walker's recruitment policies, see Ayana Bird and Tharps, *Hair Story*, 77–79.

30. Gill, *Beauty Shop Politics*, 32–60; Advertisement for Madam C. J. Walker Products, "From a Slave Cabin to Riches and a Benefactress of Her Race" (c. 1928).

31. Rubinstein, "The War Face"; Woodhead, *War Paint*, 103–5, 253–96.

32. Beerbohm, *A Defense of Cosmetics*, 6; Preiss, *Hope in a Jar*, 168.

33. "Ethics of the Powder Puff," *Boston Daily Globe*, February 15, 1922; "Church as Beauty Parlor," *New York Times*, May 23, 1921.

34. Fishbein, *Fads and Quackery in Healing*, 225. See also "Women Must Ban Cosmetics," *Boston Daily Globe*, July 23, 1923; "Flapper's Cosmetics Alarming Physicians," *New York Times*, April 13, 1922; "Ethics of the Powder Puff;" "Mrs. Coolidge Begins by Getting a Shampoo," *Boston Daily Globe*, August 5, 1923.

35. "Defenders of Rouge Winners of Debate," *Boston Daily Globe*, January 15, 1924.

36. Smith and Rockwood, *Modern Beauty Culture*, 169; Peiss, *Hope in a Jar*, 171, 169–70.

37. Parton is quoted in Peiss, *Hope in a Jar*, 188; M. S. P. to Gertrude Atherton, September 26, 1937, box 7, Gertrude Franklin Horn Atherton Papers, Bancroft Library.

38. Ontario Division of Industrial Hygiene, *Health Confessions of Business Women*, 167, 225; Arden, "There Are Some Modern Miracles," *Cosmetics and Skin*.

39. Peiss, *Hope in a Jar*, 158–59. On the queer histories of New York and Los Angeles, see Chauncey, *Gay New York*; and Faderman and Timmons, *Gay L.A.*

40. Linker, *War's Waste*, 3. On plastic surgery as a form of masculine regeneration, see Ramsbrock, *The Science of Beauty*.

41. Du Bois, "Back to Africa," 539; Garvey, "W. E. Burghardt Du Bois as a Hater of Dark People." On the debate over brownness in the African American community, see Haidarali, *Brown Beauty*.

42. Walker, "Free Sample of Tan-Off," Digital Images, Item ID M1250_R0004_TAN _OFF.pdf, Madam C. J. Walker Papers, Indiana Historical Society; J. A. Baldwin, "East River, Downtown," 80.

43. "Cosmetic Brands Join Forces to Lift Leverage on Oil Palm Producers," *Forbes*, January 10, 2022. On the persistence of cosmetics as soft rejuvenation, see Stark, *The Cult of Youth*, 205–13.

Chapter Five

1. "Man Is Kidnapped; Gland Purloined," *Chicago Daily Tribune*, October 14, 1922.

2. "First Case of Gland Larceny in Windy City," *Los Angeles Times*, October 14, 1922; "Two More Lose Glands," *Chicago Daily Tribune*, October 15, 1922; "Man Is Kidnapped"; "Bought Stolen Glands for $100,000, Is Claim," *Washington Post*, November 25, 1922.

3. On the sexual rejuvenation craze of the 1920s, see McLaren, *Impotence*, 181–207; P. Cohen, *In Our Prime*, 60–79; Stark, *The Cult of Youth*, 24–67; Voronoff, *Rejuvenation by Grafting*, 6.

4. Lister, *A Curious History of Sex*, 124. See also Berliner, "Mephistopheles and Monkeys," 306–25; "Voronoff's Conclusions on Testicular Grafting Questioned," *Journal of the American Medical Association* 90 (1928): 1489. The most recent Brinkley biography is R. A. Lee, *The Bizarre Careers of John R. Brinkley*.

5. Stoff, "Verjüngungsrummel"; Pettit, "Becoming Glandular," 1058–59.

6. Foucault, "Technologies of the Self," 18

7. Grant, *The Passing of the Great Race*, 56. Useful studies of the eugenics movement in the United States are Lombardo, *A Century of Eugenics in America*; Stern, *Eugenic Nation*; Leonhardt, *Illiberal Reformers*.

8. Pound, *Make It New*.

9. Irving Fisher to his wife Margaret, September 2, 1927, box 6, Irving Fisher Papers, Yale University Library; on Mussolini's pronatalist policies, see Cassata, *Building the New Man*, 135–37.

10. "Memorandum from the International Federation of Eugenic Organizations to His Excellency Benito Mussolini," September 1927, box 73, Charles Benedict Davenport Papers, American Philosophical Society.

11. On the place of eugenics in the interwar right, see Kühl, *The Nazi Connection*. Fisher's illness and work in health reform is covered in Bouk, *How Our Days Became Numbered*, 114–40.

12. Fisher to William D. Eliot, December 6, 1909, box 3, Irving Fisher Papers; "National Society to Conserve Life," *New York Times*, December 30, 1913; T. Roosevelt, The New Nationalism, 22.

13. Fisher and Fisk, *How to Live*, xxv–xxxvi, 5–6, 293.

14. Quotes are from Fisher and Fisk, *How to Live*, 6; Fisher, "The Fight for Public Health," 25. On the elite's attempts to project fitness by appropriating working-class manhood, see Murphy, *Political Manhood*.

15. Fisk, "On Prolonging Human Life"; Veit, "'Why Do People Die?'"

16. Fisk, "On Prolonging Human Life," 58–59.

17. Fisher and Fisk, *How to Live*, 286–92; Freeman, *Social Decay and Regeneration*, 287; "Man Devoured by His Machines," *New York Times*, October 2, 1921; Fisher, "The Importance of Hygiene for Eugenics," 473; Fisk, "The Relationship of Alcohol to Society and to Citizenship." Willard is quoted in Tyrrell, *Reforming the World*, 172.

18. Stoddard, *The Rising Tide of Color*, 190; Grant, *The Passing of the Great Race*, 2nd ed., 74.

19. On Better Baby and Fitter Family contests, see Bender, *American Abyss*, 161–90. For the influence of agricultural breeders on the eugenics movement, see Rosenberg, "No Scrubs: Livestock Breeding, Eugenics, and the State in the Early Twentieth-Century United States."

20. See McLaren, *Impotence*, 188. On the controversy surrounding *Black Oxen*, see Prebel, "Engineering Womanhood."

21. Voronoff, *Life*, vi. Benjamin is quoted in McLaren, *Impotence*, 202.

22. On Lydston, see McLaren, *Impotence*, 200–202; L. L. Stanley, *Men at Their Worst*, 110; Blue, "The Strange Career of Leo Stanley."

23. "Want More Babies in Best Families," *New York Times*, September 25, 1921.

24. Hughes, "Rejuvenation through Joy," 73, 91–92, 94–98.

25. Hughes, *I Wonder as I Wander*, 69–190. Hughes wrote extensively about his trip to the Soviet Union in his autobiography.

26. Hughes, "Jazz as Communication"; Hughes, "The Negro Artist and the Racial Mountain"; Marian Dooley to Hughes, December 18, 1934, box 221, folder 3690, Langston Hughes Papers, Beinecke Rare Books and Manuscript Library.

27. See Bender, *American Abyss*, 161–90; J. H. Jackson, *Making Jazz French*, 71–103.

28. Lemke, *Primitivist Modernism*, esp. 10–58.

29. A. Locke, "The New Negro," 3; A. Locke, "Negro Youth Speaks," 48, 50; A. Locke, "Fire: A Negro Magazine," 563.

30. J. A. Rogers, "Jazz at Home," 217, 223–24. On the spread of jazz during the 1920s, see Ogren, *The Jazz Revolution*.

31. "Grin jungle joys" is a phrase from Hughes's 1926 poem "*Harlem Night Club*"; Mencken, "The Aframerican: New Style," 255. On Hughes and Winold Reiss, see Mehring, "Portraying Transnational America," 184–85.

32. On the relationship of jazz and organized crime, see English, *Dangerous Rhythms*.

33. Hughes, "Rejuvenation through Joy," 93. See also Chinitz, "Rejuvenation through Joy: Langston Hughes, Primitivism, and Jazz."

34. "Prominent and Respected Race Members Restored to Younger Days," *Negro World*, May 17, 1924; "Another Mail-Order Rejuvenating Concern Declared a Fraud," *Journal of the American Medical Association* 85, no. 9 (August 1925): 694–95. On Black beauty contests, see Peiss, *Hope in a Jar*, 213–15.

35. Fisher is quoted in BSA, *The National and World Jamborees in Pictures*, 130–31; Ray O. Wyland, "Prepared for Freedom," March 5, 1940, 3, box 6, Harold J. Homann Papers, Wisconsin Historical Society. On the 1937 national jamboree, see also Honeck, *Our Frontier Is the World*, 184–86.

36. Lenin is quoted in Neumann, "'Youth, It's Your Turn!'" 274.

37. For a broad overview, see Gorsuch, *Youth in Revolutionary Russia*; on fears of communist influence on 1920s youth, see Ryan, *Red War on the Family*.

38. Rosenberg, "Rebellion der Jugend," 53. On the fascist youth cult, see Ponzio, *Shaping the New Man*; Mosse, *The Image of Man*, 155–80.

39. "Miss Ilma, Back from Europe, Says New Spirit Prevails There," *New York Times*, December 10, 1933; Poling, *Youth Marches*, 6; Davis, *The Lost Generation*, 5–6.

40. Rauchway, *The Great Depression and the New Deal*, 38–55; F. D. Roosevelt, "First Inaugural Address," 15.

41. On Roosevelt's disability, see Houck and Kiewe, *FDR's Body Politics*, esp. 77–92.

42. On the CCC, see Maher, *Nature's New Deal*. For a comparative perspective, see Patel, *Soldiers of Labor*.

43. Karl Kidd and John E. Hussey are quoted in Salmond, *The Civilian Conservation Corps*, 132–33.

44. Henry Luce is quoted in Katznelson, *Fear Itself*, 244; F. D. Roosevelt, "October 5, 1937: Quarantine Speech."

45. See Melosh, *Engendering Culture*.

46. Katznelson, *When Affirmative Action Was White*. On the CCC's treatment of women and minorities, see Patel, *Soldiers of Labor*, 165–73.

47. Roy Wilkins to James E. West, June 4, 1937, box I C:269, NAACP Papers, Discrimination, Boy Scouts, Library of Congress, Manuscript Division. See also Honeck, *Our Frontier Is the World*, 159.

48. On Lothrop Stoddard, Harry Laughlin, and Nazi Germany, see E. Black, *War against the Weak*, 261–318. The German population scientist Friedrich Burgdörfer popularized the phrase "people without youth" in his book *Volk ohne Jugend*.

49. Hughes, "Ballad of Roosevelt," 9.

Chapter Six

1. US Senate, *Military Situation in the Far East*, 312. On MacArthur's 1951 Senate testimony, see also James, "Command Crisis: MacArthur and the Korean War."

2. Ludwig, *How to Treat the Germans*, 76.

3. Luce, "The American Century."

4. See William Cohen's classic piece "The Colonized as Child." On the intersections of gender, race, and childhood, see Paisley, "Childhood and Race." "Little brown brothers" was a term coined by William Howard Taft to refer to Filipinos.

5. I make a similar point in Honeck, "Rubble and Rebirth."

6. For accounts, see Goedde, *GIs and Germans*; Hagemann and Michel, *Gender and the Long Postwar*.

7. Goedde, *GIs and Germans*, 128–29.

8. Keppler, "A Trifle Embarrassed."

9. On the shifting visual semantics of Uncle Sam, see Schäfer, *Yankee Yarns*; Louis Dalrymple, "School Begins."

10. Dalrymple, "The Idol of the Aunties"; Kipling, "The White Man's Burden."

11. Bartholomew, "The Old Pupil Turns Out to Be the Worst One in Class"; Dalrymple, "School Begins."

12. Taft, "The Duty of Americans in the Philippines"; Miles, "Major General Nelson Miles's Proclamation (July 28, 1898)," 195; Rossiter, *"Right Forward, Fours Right, March!"* 8. Thomas is quoted in Niedermeier, "Colonial Self-Positioning," 126.

13. See Immerwahr, *How to Hide an Empire*, 96–103. For a fuller account of the Moro Boy Scouts, see Honeck, *Our Frontier Is the World*, 135–37.

14. Theodore Roosevelt Jr. to James E. West, December 4, 1937, box 30, Theodore Roosevelt Jr. Papers, Library of Congress, Manuscript Division.

15. Zahra, *The Lost Children*, 9.

16. Catherine Filene Shouse, Travel Diary, June 20, 1950, box 3, The Papers of Catherine Filene Shouse, Schlesinger Library, Harvard Radcliffe Institute.

17. Shouse, Travel Diary, June 29, 1950.

18. Carruthers, *The Good Occupation*, 6; see also Höhn, *GIs and Fräuleins*.

19. See also Wertheim, *Tomorrow, the World*, 5; Lippmann, *The Cold War*.

20. Fay, *Theaters of Occupation*, 3–4, 18–19; Brickner, *Is Germany Incurable?* 8; Erikson, *Childhood and Society*; Ponten, "Die Identität des Feindes," 74.

21. See also Fay, *Theaters of Occupation*, 4–12.

22. A copy of the poster is preserved as part of Record Group 260, Office of Military Government, Bavaria (hereafter OMGUS Bavaria), Education & Cultural Relations, Group Activities, Branch, box 43, National Archives and Records Administration (NARA) II; "Interview with General Clay," *Stars and Stripes*, October 24, 1946. On the GYA's role in reeducation, see also Goedde, *GIs and Germans*, 127–65.

23. US Army photograph, "Youth Discuss World Peace in Nuremberg," December 20, 1948, box 91, The Papers of Catherine Filene Shouse.

24. See Goedde, *GIs and Germans*, 155; US State Department, *Young Germany*, 77; Simpich, "Uncle Sam Bends a Twig in Germany," 538.

25. Goedde, *GIs and Germans*, 157–58, 160; Simpich, "Uncle Sam Bends a Twig in Germany," 535–36.

26. Potter, *People of Plenty*; Blaustein, *Nightmare Envy and Other Stories*, 3–4.

27. US Senate, *Military Situation in the Far East*, 313.

28. "Basic Factors Affecting Democratization and Decentralization of the Bavarian Government," May 19, 1947, Record Group 260, OMGUS Bavaria, Civil Administration Division, Cultural Exchange Program, 1946–1949, box 202. Knöringen is quoted in Elliott, "Democratization of Germany," February 4, 1948, OMGUS Bavaria, Civil Administration Division, Cultural Exchange Program, 1946–1949, box 207.

29. Rivet, "New Sub-Title for Reorientation Program," December 13, 1948, box 11, OMGUS Bavaria, Records of the Education and Cultural Relations Division, Administrative Records of the Director's Office, 1945–1949; Füssl, "Between Elitism and Educational Reform," 410.

30. Interdivisional Reorientation Committee, "Report No. 3—Reorientation Program," August 16, 1949, box 205, OMGUS Bavaria, Civil Administration Division, Cultural Exchange Program, 1946–1949; Roger H. Wells to Civil Administration Division, August 27, 1949, box 206, OMGUS Bavaria, Civil Administration Division, Cultural Exchange Program, 1946–1949.

31. "Memorandum: German Expert Returning from the United States," September 6, 1949, box 11OMGUS Bavaria, Records of the Education and Cultural Relations Division, Administrative Records of the Director's Office, 1945–1949.

32. Muhlen, "America and American Occupation in German Eyes," 53.

33. Grabbe, "Konrad Adenauer, John Foster Dulles, and West German-American Relations," 113–14.

34. MacArthur, "VJ Day Broadcast, September 2, 1945, USS Missouri, Tokyo Bay."

35. Gulick, *The American Japanese Problem*, 213. On anti-Asian racism, see Kurashige, *Two Faces of Exclusion*, 86–138.

36. Eaton is quoted in Horne, *Race War*, 14–15.

37. On the links between US colonialism in the Philippines and the occupation of Japan, see Schueller, *Campaigns of Knowledge*; Angulo, *Empire and Education*, 91.

38. Shibusawa, *America's Geisha Ally*, 13–53. On women and sex labor in postwar Japan, see Kramm, *Sanitized Sex*; Angulo, *Empire and Education*, 115–22.

39. "The First Lesson," *Pittsburgh Post-Gazette*, September 8, 1945.

40. Bhabha introduced hybridity and mimicry as key concepts of postcolonial analysis in his seminal *The Location of Culture*. On childhood as a site of transpacific reconciliation, see Jacobs, "Attacking Children with Nuclear Weapons."

41. See Kitamura, *Screening Enlightenment*, 54–57.

42. See May, *Homeward Bound*. On the moral panics about youth in the 1950s, see Medovoi, *Rebels*. A transnational perspective is provided in Poiger, *Jazz, Rock, and Rebels*.

43. See Karsunke, "Kilroy Was Here/Kilroy war hier," an English-language translation of Karsunke's poem, published in 1967 in the *New Left Review*.

Chapter Seven

1. Gemie, *The Hippie Trail*, 1–10. See also Jobs, *Backpack Ambassadors*, 214–18.

2. "The Hippies," *Time Magazine*, July 7, 1967; MacLean, *Magic Bus*, 6.

3. Roszak, *The Making of a Counter Culture*. On Roszak's critics, see Braunstein and Doyle, *Imagine Nation*, 5–14.

4. "Growing Pains at UC," *San Francisco Chronicle*, November 15, 1964; De Schweinitz, "The Proper Age for Suffrage"; R. N. Butler, "Age-Ism"; Stevens, "The Counterculture," 310.

5. Marcuse, *One-Dimensional Man*. For an informed discussion of the significance of age as a category for analyzing the 1960s, see also Scott, *Younger than Now*.

6. Braunstein, "Forever Young," 243–74.

7. Kupferberg, "The Love of Politics and the Politics of Love," 4–5.

8. The phrase "sweet scenes of childhood" appears in Coleridge, "Sonnet: To the River Otter (1793)." On Timothy Leary and the rise of LSD, see Stevens, *Storming Heaven*.

9. The term "youthquake" was coined in 1965 by *Vogue* to refer to new trends in fashion and pop culture. See also Marwick, "The Cultural Revolution of the Long Sixties," 782.

10. Mailer, "The White Negro: Superficial Reflections on the Hipster"; J. Baldwin, "The Black Boy Looks at the White Boy," 277–78; 284–85.

11. Mailer, "The White Negro," 283; 291–92.

12. Ellison, "Ralph Ellison to Albert Murray, September 4, 1958," 534.

13. Students for a Democratic Society (hereafter SDS), "The Port Huron Statement." On the SDS's connections to the West German student movement, see Klimke, *The Other Alliance*.

14. On the free speech movement, see Schrecker, *The Lost Promise*; Lana Taylor is quoted in R. Cohen, *Howard Zinn's Southern Diary*, 6.

15. See Schrecker, *The Lost Promise*, 85–116.

16. SDS, "Port Huron Statement," 243; Harrington is quoted in J. Miller, *Democracy Is in the Streets*, 115.

17. SDS, *SDS Work-Ins*, 21.

18. SDS, *SDS Work-Ins*, 2–3, 24; Kuhn, *The Hardhat Riot*. On the "fascist labor" charge, see Rarick, "Man's Hope for Peace—A Weapon of War," 17964.

19. On the symbiotic relationship between peaceful protest and armed resistance, see Wendt, *The Spirit and the Shotgun*.

20. Carmichael and Thelwell, *Ready for Revolution*, 396; Stokely Carmichael, "Black Power."

21. Rhodes, *Framing the Black Panthers*, 188–18; Fernandez, *The Young Lords*.

22. Cleaver, *Soul on Ice*, 189; Willis, "Radical Feminism and Feminist Radicalism," 94.

23. See, for example, Estepa, "Taking the White Gloves Off"; and Plant, *Mom*, 146–78.

24. Comfort, *The Joy of Sex*, 224; Morgan, "No More Miss America!"; Paris, "The Sexual Clock," 924.

25. Arnold, *Sister Gin*, 196–205, 199. On aging in queer literature in the United States after 1945, see also Hess, *Queer Aging in North American Fiction*.

26. Buckley, "The World of LSD."

27. Buckley, "The World of LSD."

28. R. Stanley, *The Psychedelic Sixties*, 109; Kesey, *One Flew over the Cuckoo's Nest*.

29. "The Beats Are Cool—and Hot," *Los Angeles Times*, August 2, 1994. On the Beatniks and their influence on the counterculture and youth travel, see Jobs, *Backpack Ambassadors*, 138–40; Burroughs, "Academy 21: A Deconditioning," 21.

30. Braunstein, "Forever Young," 253; Huxley, "Aldous Huxley to Humphrey Osmond, September 16, 1954," 126.

31. See, for example, "Millbrook Summer School: Psychedelic Training Courses (August 19–28, 1966)," Timothy Leary Papers, Series IV: 1960–1976, Castalia Foundation and Millbrook (1964–1968), New York Public Library Archives; Braunstein, "Forever Young," 254; Huxley, "Wanted, A New Pleasure (1931)," 262.

32. Hayden is quoted in Small, *Antiwarriors*, 80; Cleaver is quoted in Flynn, *A Conservative History of the American Left*, 309–10.

33. Whether Nixon really called Leary "the most dangerous man in America" remains controversial, although he certainly wanted him behind bars. See Wierzbicki, *When Music Mattered*, 217. Buckley, "The World of LSD."

34. Lewis, *The American Adam*, 1, 26.

35. Braunstein, "Forever Young," 253. See also T. Miller, *The 60s Communes*, 183–86.

36. T. Miller, *The 60s Communes*, 185. Gaston is quoted in J. Hall, *Is This the Future*, 12–14.

37. Shé is quoted in "Free Love, Flower Power, and Fallouts: How Kids Cope with Communes," *The Guardian*, June 22, 2018. For more critical testimonies, see Cain, *Wild Child*.

38. "Changes," *San Francisco Oracle* 1, no. 7 (February 1967), 30.

39. Bryant, *The Anita Bryant Story*, 24; "Gay Law Foes to Plan Vote Drive," *Miami Herald*, January 26, 1977.

40. Unpublished paper by Eckelmann-Berghel, "'Young Stalwarts of Immobility.'" On Bryant's "Save Our Children" campaign and conservative grassroots mobilization in the 1970s, see Frank, "'The Civil Rights of Parents.'"

41. Agnew and Peale are quoted in Mintz, *Huck's Raft*, 318.

42. "Transcript of Acceptance Speeches by Nixon and Agnew to the G.O.P. Convention," *New York Times*, August 9, 1968; Blumenthal, "New Nixon and Youth Politics, 1968."

43. McGirr, *Suburban Warriors*; Nickerson, *Mothers of Conservatism*; Brückmann, *Massive Resistance and Southern Womanhood*; Schlafly, "The Precious Rights ERA Will Take Away from Wives," 1.

44. Delmont, *Why Busing Failed*, 34.

45. On the complex interplay of white supremacy, reproductive politics, and antiabortion activism, see Holland, *Tiny You*; Reagan, "Republican National Convention Acceptance Speech, July 17, 1980."

46. Scott, *Younger than Now*, 2.

Chapter Eight

1. For a collection of photographs of the 1984 "Brigade Run" in West Berlin, see Deutsche Digitale Bibliothek. "Brigade Run." On the US Army's "Be All You Can Be" recruitment campaign, see Ghilani, "'The Army Just Sees Green,'" 145–61.

2. Fonda, *Jane Fonda's Workout Book*, 24; "The Fitness Craze: America Shapes Up," *Time Magazine*, November 2, 1981.

3. "The Fitness Craze: America Shapes Up," 95; Gurin and Harris, "Taking Charge: The Happy Health Confidents," 53.

4. Tom Wolfe, "The 'Me' Decade"; Sennett, *The Fall of Public Man*, 259, 337; Lasch, *The Culture of Narcissism*.

5. Martschukat, *The Age of Fitness*, 3; see also Petrzela, "Thanks, Gender! An Intellectual History of the Gym," 86–104.

6. On the Turners (German for gymnasts), see Honeck, "Men of Principle." On Sandow and Macfadden, see J. Black, *Making the American Body*, 11–30. The dictum "weakness is a crime" appeared in the first issue of *Physical Culture* in 1899.

7. Cooper, *Aerobics*, 84.

8. US Senate, *Select Committee on Nutrition and Human Needs, Dietary Goals for the United States*, xiii. On low fat as ideology, see LaBerge, "How the Ideology of Low Fat Conquered America."

9. Jacques, "Death and the Mid-Life Crisis." On women shaping the midlife-crisis discourse since the 1970s, see Schmidt, *Midlife Crisis*.

10. Lasch, *Culture of Narcissism*, 5.

11. "Mrs. King Defeats Riggs 6–4, 6–3, 6–4, amid a Circus Atmosphere"; "Bobby Riggs," *The Tonight Show Starring Johnny Carson*.

12. On King's pre-match interview on ABC, see "Tennis Battle of the Sexes Special."

13. Gulick is quoted in Buckler, *Wo-He-Lo*, 22–23.

14. See, for example, Verbrugge, "Gender, Science, and Fitness"; G. S. Hall, *Adolescence*, vol. 1, 213.

15. On the popularity of swimming in interwar America, see Stieglitz, "Swimming the Crawl to Educate the Modern Body"; H. Macfadden, "Business Girls Should Swim for Better Posture," *Physical Culture*.

16. Steinem, "The Politics of Muscle," 93–94. Actor Jane Powell released her aerobics video *Fight Back with Fitness* in 1986; Fonda, *Jane Fonda's Workout Book*, 47; Lee, "Women's Liberation and Sixties Armed Resistance," 25.

17. Friedan, *The Feminine Mystique*. While not addressing fitness directly, Friedan takes aim at the "cult of beauty, clothing, cosmetics, perfumes, hairdos, diet, and exercise" (190); Sontag, "Double Standard of Aging," 34–35, 38.

18. On Missett and the invention of Jazzercise, see Petrzela, *Fit Nation*, 179–82; and J. Black, *Making the American Body*, 81–82.

19. Missett is quoted in Petrzela, *Fit Nation*, 137; Friedman, *Let's Get Physical*, 162, 216.

20. On the significance of fitness in gay culture, see Alvarez, *Muscle Boys*, 93–111.

21. On white women, suburbanization, and crime in the 1970s, see Borstelmann, *The 1970s*, 76–95, 162–74; Missett, *More Jazzercise*.

22. Petrzela, *Fit Nation*, 182; Morrison, *The Bluest Eye*, 122.

23. On the Progressive Era roots of organized exercise for African American women, see Purkiss, *Fit Citizens*. The complex history of fast food, health, and African American politics is explored in Chatelain, *Franchise*. On the New Right's welfare-queen rhetoric, see Kohler-Hausmann, "Welfare Crises, Penal Solutions and the Origins of the 'Welfare Queen.'"

24. Berk is quoted in Petrzela, *Fit Nation*, 184. See Missett, "Jazzercise 1982 Original Workout 80's Video," for the lascivious moves and language in the early 1980s; Newton-John, "Physical."

25. "New Product of General Foods: The Physically Fit Employee," *New York Times*, May 30, 1974; H. F. Waters, "Keeping Fit," 79. On Hollywood in the age of Reagan, see, for example, Kendrick, *Hollywood Bloodshed*.

26. Brown is quoted in Kaplan, "Exercise: The New High," 250. Nixon is quoted in Snider, "Exercise Not Always Beneficial," 53.

27. "The McDonald's Executive: 7 Special Ingredients," *Black Enterprise*, April 1978, 36; "Fast Food and Quick Bucks," *Black Enterprise*, April 1978, 28.

28. Chatelain, *Franchise*, 3–6.

29. Engel, *Fat Nation*, 83–84; "Why Do I Make Myself Fat?" *Seventeen*, March 1973. On the November 1973 "Fit, Fat, and Forty One" episode of the *Bob Newhart Show*, see Zimdars, *Watching Our Weights*, 38.

30. On early modern ideas about fasting and rejuvenation, see Schwartz, *Never Satisfied*, 15–24; Cullather, "The Foreign Policy of the Calory."

31. On Kellogg and food reform, see Wilson, *Dr. John Harvey Kellogg and the Religion of Biologic Living*, 62–81; S. Bennett, *Old Age, Its Cause and Prevention*, 28; B. Macfadden, *Vitality Supreme*, xi, 134–35.

32. A useful investigation of the 1950s obesity scare is Rasmussen, *Fat in the Fifties*.

33. Jean Nidetch recounted how Weight Watchers began in her memoir *The Story of Weight Watchers*; "15,000 Weight Watchers Cheer Svelte Founder and Other Stars," *New York Times*, June 12, 1973; Associated Press, "Former Fat People Picnic at Madison Square Garden to Herald Weight-Watchers 10th Anniversary Show."

34. "The End of The Rainbow May Be Tragic—Scandal of the Diet Pills," *Life Magazine*, January 26, 1968, 28; "Slim and Strong: The Perfect Diet," *Men's Health*, October 1986.

35. Rather, "Wellness." On Oprah Winfrey's wellness ambassadorship, see Baker, *Wellness Culture*, 105–6. On Johnson and Johnson's "Live for Life" program, see US Department of Health and Human Services, *Report on the 1984 National Conference for Youth on Drinking and Driving*, vi-6–vi-8.

36. On Carpenter's death, see Saukko, *The Anorexic Self*, 62; Levin, "Jane Fonda," 24–28.

37. McRuer, "Compulsory Able-Bodiedness and Queer/Disabled Existence"; Louderback, *Fat Power*, 17; Freespirit and Aldebaran, "Fat Liberation Manifesto, November 1973."

38. Freespirit and Aldebaran, "Fat Liberation Manifesto, November 1973," 342; Putnam, *Bowling Alone*.

39. Jung, "Die Lebenswende," 441–60. On Jung's renaissance in the 1980s and influence on US psychology, see Steinberg, "Depression."

40. Erikson, *Childhood and Society*, 247–74; Mintz, *Huck's Raft*, 276–82; Cross, *Men to Boys*, 61–62.

41. Desmond is quoted in P. Cohen, *In Our Prime*, 100.

42. Jacques, "Death and the Mid-Life Crisis," 502–14; Sheehy, *Passages*; Levinson, *The Seasons of a Man's Life*, 270.

43. On Brim, see P. Cohen, *In Our Prime*, 124–26; Hirschman and Holbrook, "Hedonic Consumption."

44. Lasch, "Aging in a Culture without a Future," 42, 44; Lasch, *The Culture of Narcissism*, 209–10.

45. Lasch, *The Culture of Narcissism*, 193, 210, 217.

46. Sontag, "The Double Standard of Aging," 31; Paris, "The Sexual Clock," 922.

47. Blake, "Interview with Jane Fonda"; Woitas, *"We Become What We Do,"* 173–75.

48. Fitzgerald, *The Great Gatsby*, 218.

49. Friedan, *The Fountain of Age*, 36, 39.

Chapter Nine

1. Regalado, "Meet Altos Labs, Silicon Valley's Latest Wild Bet on Living Forever."

2. Altos Labs, "Alto Labs Launches"; Steele, "A Drug to Treat Aging May Not Be a Pipe Dream"; Delbert, "Jeff Bezos Is Paying for a Way to Make Humans Immortal."

3. Useful cultural histories of modern-day Silicon Valley are Daub, *What Tech Calls Thinking,* and O'Mara, *The Code.*

4. "If They Could Turn Back Time: How Tech Billionaires Are Trying to Reverse the Aging Process," *The Guardian,* February 17, 2022; Maya Kossof, "Peter Thiel Wants to Inject Himself with Young People's Blood," *Vanity Fair,* August 1, 2016; HBO, "The Blood Boy," season 4, episode 5, *Silicon Valley,* 2017.

5. Daub, *What Tech Calls Thinking,* 57–76; Stanford Medicine News Center, "Old Human Cells Rejuvenation with Stem Cell Technology," press release, March 24, 2020, https://med.stanford.edu/news/all-news/2020/03/old-human-cells-rejuvenated -with-stem-cell-technology.html. For a critical history, see Rasko and Power, *Flesh Made New.*

6. O'Connell, *To Be a Machine,* 8; More, "A Letter to Mother Nature."

7. See, for instance, Ciurria, "Transhumanism Is Eugenics for Educated White Liberals."

8. Coen and Coen, *The Big Lebowski.*

9. Frodeman, *Transhumanism, Nature, and the End of Science,* 63; Boyle, *A Free Enquiry into the Vulgarly Received Notion of Nature,* 125, 135. See also Kang, "From the Machine-Man to the Automaton-Man."

10. See also Krementsov, *Revolutionary Experiments;* Muri, *The Enlightenment Cyborg,* 1–5; Tomas, "Reimagining the Human Body in the Age of the Cyborg."

11. J. Huxley, "Transhumanism," 3–17.

12. World Transhumanist Association (hereafter WTA), *Transhumanist Declaration.* WTA is now also known as Humanity+.

13. WTA, *Transhumanist Declaration;* Hauskeller, "How to Become a Post-Dog," 29; Transhumanist Party, *Transhumanist Bill of Rights.*

14. Bostrom, "A History of Transhumanist Thought," 12; Zuckerberg is quoted in Daub, *What Tech Calls Thinking,* 23.

15. Marinetti, "The Futurist Manifesto," 13–14.

16. Eveleth, "When Futurism Led to Fascism—and Why It Could Happen Again"; Bostrom, "The Vulnerable World Hypothesis," 455; Raffi Khatchadourian, "The Doomsday Invention."

17. Kurzweil, "The Church-Turing Thesis"; Kurzweil, *The Age of Spiritual Machines,* 61; WTA, *Transhumanist Declaration,* 69. On Turing's forecasts, see Krüger, *Virtual Immortality,* 144–45.

18. Kurzweil, *The Age of Spiritual Machines.*

19. Sandberg and McKenna are featured in a 2006 documentary by the Belgian filmmaker Frank Theys, *TechnoCalyps.* Sandberg's transhumanist prayer is also vividly captured in the introduction of O'Connell, *To Be a Machine.*

20. Alex Moshakis, "How to Live Forever: Meet the Extreme Life-Extensionists," *The Guardian,* June 23, 2019.

21. De Grey, "Rejuvenation Biotechnology—Will 'Age' Soon Cease to Be 'Aging'?"

22. For an inside report of the 2018 RAADfest in San Diego, see Winny, "Für immer jung: Ein Wochenende unter Menschen, die sich weigern zu sterben"; Kurzweil and Grossman, *Fantastic Voyage*.

23. Hayflick made this critical remark for the 2014 documentary by Jason Sussberg and David Alvarado, *The Immortalists*. Kaeberlein is quoted in Andrew Zaleski, "Is There Any Truth to Antiaging Schemes?"

24. Fukuyama, "Transhumanism"; Fukuyama, *Our Posthuman Future*.

25. Goldstein, "What Follows the End of History? Identity Politics"; Fukuyama, *Our Posthuman Future*, 15.

26. Bostrom, "In Defense of Posthuman Dignity."

27. Ayyadi, "The Latest Conspiracy Trend: Transhumanism."

28. For an interview with Elon Musk, including his views on underpopulation, see Döpfner, "Musk Discusses the War in Ukraine and the Importance of Nuclear Power."

29. "Meet the 'Elite' Couples Breeding to Save Mankind," *The Telegraph*, April 19, 2023; Simone Collins is quoted in J. Black, "Billionaires Like Elon Musk Want to Save Civilization by Having Tons of Genetically Superior Kids."

30. Kirsch, "Bryan Johnson, Tech Mogul Trying to Stop Aging"; Wong, "I Went to a Rave with the 46-Year-Old-Millionaire Who Claims to Have the Body of a Teenager."

31. Torres, "How Elon Musk Sees the Future"; Shulman and Bostrom, "Embryo Selection for Cognitive Enhancement"; Musk (@elonmusk), "Watch the opening scene of Idiocracy."

32. Fincher, *The Curious Case of Benjamin Button* (film); Fitzgerald, "The Curious Case of Benjamin Button," 224.

33. Fitzgerald, "The Curious Case of Benjamin Button," 212.

34. D. Thomas, "Do Not Go Gentle into That Good Night," 122. On childhood as a "vanishing act," see Maza, "'The Kids Aren't All Right,'" 1271.

35. See Xi Jinping, "Forging Ahead to Open a New Chapter on China-Russia Friendship." On Russia's abduction of Ukrainian children, see, for example, UN Human Rights Council, *Report of the Independent International Commission of Inquiry on Ukraine*, 17–18.

36. Istvan, "The Current State of Transhumanism."

Bibliography

Archival Collections

American Philosophical Society, Philadelphia
    Charles Benedict Davenport Papers
Bancroft Library, University of California, Berkeley
    Gertrude Franklin Horn Atherton Papers
Beinecke Rare Books and Manuscript Library, Yale University, New Haven, CT
    Langston Hughes Papers
Brooks Memorial Library, Brattleboro, VT
    Starr Willard Cutting, unpublished typescript on Robert Wesselhöft
Indiana Historical Society, Indianapolis
    Madam C. J. Walker Papers, 1911-2005
Library of Congress, Manuscript Division, Washington, DC
    NAACP Papers
    Theodore Roosevelt Jr. Papers
Library of Congress, Prints and Photographs Division, Washington DC
National Archives and Records Administration (NARA) II, College Park, MD
    Office of Military Government (OMGUS), Record Group 260
New York Public Library Archives
    Timothy Leary Papers
Schlesinger Library, Harvard Radcliffe Institute, Cambridge, MA
    Beecher-Stowe Family Papers
    The Papers of Catherine Filene Shouse
Wisconsin Historical Society, Madison, WI
    Harold J. Homann Papers
Yale University Library, New Haven, CT
    Irving Fisher Papers
    William Kent Family Papers

Newspapers and Periodicals

GREAT BRITAIN

The Guardian

UNITED STATES

American Museum, or, Universal Magazine
Black Enterprise
Boston Daily Globe
Business Insider
Chicago Daily Tribune
Chicago Tribune
Companion & Weekly Miscellany
Daily Scioto Gazette

Florida Health Notes
Forbes
Harper's Bazaar
Journal of the American Medical Association
Ladies' Home Journal
Lantern
Liberator
Life Magazine
Los Angeles Times
*Massachusetts Magazine, or, Monthly
    Magazine of Knowledge & Rational
    Entertainment*
Medical Intelligencer
Men's Health
Miami Herald
Negro World
New York Amsterdam News
New York Daily Times
New York Daily Tribune
New York Herald
New York Magazine
New York Times

New York Times Magazine
Newsweek
Pennsylvania Magazine
Physical Culture
Pittsburgh Post-Gazette
Portage Weekly Democrat
Punch Magazine
Raleigh Register
Royal Magazine
San Francisco Chronicle
San Francisco Oracle
Seventeen
The Telegraph
Time Magazine
United States Magazine and Democratic Review
Vanity Fair
Vice
Vogue
Washington Post
Water-Cure Journal
Yankee-Notions
Youth's Temperance Advocate

Media

Alvarado, David, and Jason Sussberg. *The Immortalists*. Structure Films, 2014.
Associated Press. "Former Fat People Picnic at Madison Square Garden to Herald
    Weight-Watchers 10th Anniversary Show." AP Archive video, May 18, 1973, https://www
    .youtube.com/watch?v=AK7aGbs9fpU.
Blake, Barry R. "Interview with Jane Fonda." *Inside Entertainment*, 1990. YouTube, 7:21.
    https://www.youtube.com/watch?v=cpmAOonSAOc.
"Bobby Riggs Talks about His Upcoming Tennis Match with Billie Jean King." *The Tonight
    Show Starring Johnny Carson*, August 9, 1973. YouTube, 11:35. https://www.youtube.com
    /watch?app=desktop&v=vJdk-VE-Zuo.
Buckley, William F., Jr. "The World of LSD." Episode 053, *Firing Line with William
    Buckley Jr.*, originally broadcast April 10, 1967. YouTube, 48:27. https://www.youtube
    .com/watch?v=BnoCHlybAnU.
Coen, Joel, and Ethan Coen. *The Big Lebowski*. Working Title Films, 1998.
De Grey, Aubrey. "Rejuvenation Biotechnology—Will 'Age' Soon Cease to Be 'Aging'?"
    Centre for Effective Altruism, August 29, 2019. YouTube, 29:00. https://www.youtube
    .com/watch?v=YgkA9D_cKnE&list=PLwp9xeoX5p8MqGMKBZK7k O8dTysnJ-Pzq
    &index=13&t=42s.
Fincher, David. *The Curious Case of Benjamin Button*. Paramount Pictures, 2008.
Istvan, Zoltan. "The Current State of Transhumanism: Interview with Zoltan Istvan."
    Singularity University, March 5, 2023. YouTube, 55:24. https://www.youtube.com
    /watch?v=ITv70KSv21w.

————. "Revolutionary Politics Are Necessary for Transhumanism to Succeed," Vice, November 3, 2016. https://www.vice.com/en/article/ezpqba/revolutionary-politics -are-necessary-for-transhumanism-to-succeed.

Lemmons, Kasi, and DeMane Davis. *Self Made: Inspired by the Life of Madam C. J. Walker*. SpringHill Company, 2020.

Missett, Judi Sheppard. "Jazzercise 1982 Original Workout 80's Video." YouTube, 2:42– 3:40. https://www.youtube.com/watch?v=LD1xSc70RRk. Accessed March 30, 2023.

————. *More Jazzercise*. MCA Records, MCA-5375. Vinyl, 1982.

"Mrs. King Defeats Riggs 6–4, 6–3, 6–4, amid a Circus Atmosphere." *New York Times*, September 21, 1973.

Musk, Elon (@elonmusk). "Watch the opening scene of Idiocracy." X/Twitter, June 18, 2022, 3:26 A.M. https://twitter.com/elonmusk/status/1537970070307020808?lang=de.

Newton-John, Olivia. "Physical." MCA, Music Video, 1981.

Powell, Jane. *Fight Back with Fitness*. Karl-Lorimar Video, 1986.

Red Hot Chili Peppers. *Californication*. Warner Bros. Records, 1999.

"Tennis Battle of the Sexes Special." September 20, 1973. YouTube, 11:00–13:30. https:// www.youtube.com/watch?v=qqB3yi8MVbQ.

Theys, Frank. *TechnoCalyps*. Votnik, 2006.

Primary Sources

PRINTED

Abbot, W. W., ed. *The Papers of George Washington, Confederation Series*, vol. 6. Charlottesville: University Press of Virginia, 1997.

Adams, Abigail. "Abigail Adams to John Adams, March 31, 1776." In *The Adams Papers: Adams Family Correspondence*, edited by L.H. Butterfield, Wendell D. Garrett, and Marjorie Sprague, vol. 1, 370. Cambridge, MA: Harvard University Press, 1963.

Adams, John. "John Adams to Philip Mazzei, December 15, 1785." In *The Adams Papers*, edited by Gregg L. Lint, Sara Martin, C. James Taylor, Sara Georgini, Hobson Woodward, Sara B. Sikes, and Amanda M. Norton, vol. 18, 45–50. Cambridge, MA: Harvard University Press, 2016.

Anonymous. *The Female Advocate, Written by a Lady*. New Haven, CT: T. Green, 1801.

Anonymous. *The Metropolis of the Water Cure, or Records of a Water Patient in Malvern*. London: Simpkin, Marshall, 1858.

Arden, Elizabeth. *The Elizabeth Arden Exercises for Health and Beauty*. London: Elizabeth Arden Inc., 1924.

Arnold, June. *Sister Gin*. New York: Daughters, 1975.

Atlantic and Gulf Railroad. *Guide to Southern Georgia and Florida, Containing a Brief Description of Points of Interest to the Tourist, Invalid or Emigrant, and How to Reach Them*. Savannah, GA: General Passenger Department, Atlantic and Gulf Railroad, 1879.

Austin, George Lowell. *The Life and Times of Wendell Phillips*. Boston: Lee & Shepard, 1888.

Baldwin, James. "The Black Boy Looks at the White Boy." In *The Price of the Ticket: Collected Nonfiction, 1948–1985*. New York: St. Martin's/Marek, 1985.

Baldwin, James A. "East River, Downtown: Postscript to a Letter from Harlem." In *Nobody Knows My Name: More Notes of a Native Son*, 72–82. New York: Delta 1961.

Bartholomew, Charles L. "The Old Pupil Turns Out to Be the Worst One in Class." *Minneapolis Journal*, October 7, 1898.

Barton, William. *Observations on the Progress of Population, And the Probabilities of the Duration of Human Life, in the United States of America.* Philadelphia: American Philosophical Society, 1791.

Beard, Daniel Carter. *Hardly a Man Is Now Alive: The Autobiography of Dan Beard.* New York: Doubleday, 1939.

Beard, George Miller. *American Nervousness.* New York: G. P. Putnam's Sons, 1881.

Bennett, Sanford. *Old Age, Its Cause and Prevention: The Story of an Old Body and Face Made Young.* New York: Physical Culture, 1912.

Black, Julia. "Billionaires Like Elon Musk Want to Save Civilization by Having Tons of Genetically Superior Kids." *Business Insider*, November 18, 2022.

Blumenbach, Johann Friedrich. *Über den Bildungstrieb und das Zeugungsgeschäfte.* Göttingen: Dieterich, 1781.

Boyle, Robert. *A Free Enquiry into the Vulgarly Received Notion of Nature.* London: H. Clark, 1686.

Brickner, Richard. *Is Germany Incurable?* Philadelphia: J. B. Lippincott, 1943.

Brooks, Van Wyck, ed. *Poor Richard: The Almanacs for the Years 1733–1758.* New York: Heritage Club, 1964.

Bryant, Anita. *The Anita Bryant Story.* Old Tappan, NJ: Fleming H. Revell, 1977.

BSA. *The National and World Jamborees in Pictures.* New York: Boy Scouts of America, 1937.

Bullock, Fanny, and William Hunter Workman. *Algerian Memories: A Bicycle Tour over the Atlas to the Sahara.* London: T. Fisher Unwin, 1895.

Burgdörfer, Friedrich. *Volk ohne Jugend: Geburtenschwund und Überalterung des deutschen Volkskörpers.* Berlin: Vowinckel Verlag, 1932.

Burroughs, William S. "Academy 21: A Deconditioning." *San Francisco Oracle* 1, no. 10 (1967): 21.

Butler, Robert N. "Age-Ism: Another Form of Bigotry." *Gerontologist* 9, no. 4 (Winter 1969): 243–46.

Butterfield, L. H., ed. *The Adams Papers, Diary and Autobiography of John Adams, 1755–1770*, vol. 1. Cambridge, MA: Harvard University Press, 1961.

Cleaver, Eldridge. *Soul on Ice.* New York: Ramparts Press, 1968.

Cohausen, Johann Heinrich. *Hermippus Redivivus: The Sage's Triumph over Old Age and the Grave.* London: J. Nourse, 1749.

Cold Water Army. *New Jersey Juvenile Temperance Band: True Likeness.* n.d. [c. 1840].

Coleridge, Samuel Taylor. "Sonnet: To the River Otter (1793)." In *The Complete Poetical Works of Samuel Taylor Coleridge*, edited by Ernest Hartley Coleridge, 48. Oxford: Clarendon Press, 1912.

Comfort, Alex. *The Joy of Sex: A Cordon Bleu Guide to Lovemaking.* New York: Crown/Simon & Schuster, 1972.

Cook, Mark. "Camp Lou." *Harper's Monthly Magazine* 62 (1880–81): 865.

Cooper, Kenneth H. *Aerobics.* New York: M. Evan, 1968.

Currier, Nathaniel. *The Drunkard's Progress: From the First Glass to the Grave.* New York: N. Currier, 1846.

Davis, Maxine. *The Lost Generation: A Portrait of American Youth Today*. New York: Macmillan, 1936.

De Leon, Edwin. *The Position and Duties of "Young America."* Columbia, SC: A. S. Johnston, 1845.

De Pauw, Cornelius. *A General History of the Americans, of their Customs, Manners, and Colors*. Translated by Daniel Webb. Rochdale, UK: T. Wood, 1806.

Douglass, Frederick. *My Bondage and My Freedom*. New York: Miller, Orton & Mulligan, 1855.

———. *Narrative of the Life of Frederick Douglass, An American Slave, Written By Himself*. Boston: Anti-Slavery Office, 1846.

Edwards, William A., and Beatrice Harraden. *Two Health-Seekers in Southern California*. Philadelphia: J. P. Lippincott, 1897.

Ellison, Ralph. "Ralph Ellison to Albert Murray, September 4, 1958." In *The Selected Letters of Ralph Ellison*, edited by John F. Callahan and Marc C. Conner, 534. New York: Random House, 2019.

Erikson, Erik H. *Childhood and Society*. New York: W. W. Norton, 1950.

Eveleth, Rose. "When Futurism Led to Fascism—and Why It Could Happen Again." *Wired*, April 18, 2019.

Fishbein, Morris. *Fads and Quackery in Healing*. New York: Covici Friede, 1932.

Fisher, Irving. "The Fight for Public Health." *The Humanitarian* 11, no. 8 (1916): 25.

———. "The Importance of Hygiene for Eugenics." In *Proceedings of the First National Conference on Race Betterment*, 472–76. Battle Creek, MI: Gage Printing Company, 1914.

Fisher, Irving, and Eugene L. Fisk. *How to Live: Rules for Healthy Living Based on Modern Science*. New York: Funk & Wagnalls, 1915.

Fisk, Eugene L. "On Prolonging Human Life." *North American Review* 776 (July 1920): 51–62.

———. "The Relationship of Alcohol to Society and to Citizenship." *Annals of the American Academy of Political and Social Sciences* 109 (September 1923): 1–14.

Fitzgerald, F. Scott. "The Curious Case of Benjamin Button." In *Tales of the Jazz Age*, 192–224. New York: Charles Scribner's Sons, 1922.

———. *The Great Gatsby*. New York: Charles Scribner's Sons, 1925.

Fonda, Jane. *Jane Fonda's Workout Book*. New York: Simon & Schuster, 1981.

Franklin, Benjamin. *Observations Concerning the Increase of Mankind, Peopling of Countries, &c*. Boston: S. Kneeland, 1755.

Freeman, R. Austin. *Social Decay and Regeneration*. London: Constable, 1921.

Freespirit, Judy, and Aldebaran. "Fat Liberation Manifesto, November 1973." In *The Fat Studies Reader*, edited by Esther Rothblum and Sondra Solovay, 341–42. New York: New York University Press, 2009.

Freneau, Philip. "The Rising Glory of America." In *The Poems of Philip Freneau: Written Chiefly During the Late War*, 42–58. Philadelphia: Francis Bailey, 1786.

Friedan, Betty. *The Feminine Mystique*. New York: W. W. Norton, 1963.

———. *The Fountain of Age*. New York: Simon & Schuster, 1993.

Garvey, Marcus. "The Black Woman." In *The Poetical Works of Marcus Garvey*, edited by Tony Martin, 44–45. Dover, MA: Majority Press, 1983.

———. "W. E. Burghardt Du Bois as a Hater of Dark People." In *Philosophy and Opinions of Marcus Garvey*, vol. 2, edited by Amy Jacques Garvey, 310–20. Paterson, NJ: Frank Cass, 1925.

Gothwaite, Everett D. *Trade in Philippine Copra and Coconut Oil.* Washington, DC: US Government Printing Office, 1925.

Graham, Stephen. *In Quest of El Dorado.* New York: D. Appleton, 1923.

Grant, Madison. *The Passing of the Great Race: Or, the Racial Basis of European History,* 1st and 2nd ed. New York: Charles Scribner's Sons, 1916, 1919.

Gulick, Sidney L. *The American Japanese Problem: A Study of the Racial Relations of the East and the West.* New York: Charles Scribner's Sons, 1914.

Hall, Granville Stanley. *Adolescence: Its Psychology and Its Relations to Physiology, Anthropology, Sociology, Sex, Crime, Religion, and Education,* 2 vols. New York: Appleton, 1904.

Hamilton, Alexander. "The Federalist No. 11, November 24, 1787." In *The Papers of Alexander Hamilton, January 1787–May 1788,* edited by Harold C. Syrett, vol. 4, 339–46. New York: Columbia University Press, 1962.

Hart, Oliver. *America's Remembrancer . . . A Sermon Delivered in Hopewell, New Jersey.* Philadelphia: T. Dobson, 1791.

Hawthorne, Nathaniel. *The Blithedale Romance.* Boston: Ticknor, Reed & Fields, 1852.

———. "Dr. Heidegger's Experiment." In *Twice-Told Tales,* 319–34. Boston: American Stationers Co., 1837.

———. "Rappacini's Daughter." In *Mosses from an Old Manse,* 107–48. Boston: Houghton, Mifflin, 1883.

Hufeland, C. W. *The Art of Prolonging Life.* London: Bell, 1797.

Hughes, Langston. "Ballad of Roosevelt." *New Republic* 31, November 14, 1934.

———. *I Wonder as I Wander: An Autobiographical Journey.* New York: Hill & Wang, 1956.

———. "Jazz as Communication." In *The Langston Hughes Reader,* 492–94. New York: George Braziller, 1958.

———. "The Negro Artist and the Racial Mountain." *The Nation,* June 23, 1926, 692–93.

———. "Rejuvenation through Joy." In *The Ways of White Folks,* repr., 69–98. New York: Knopf, 1934.

———. *The Weary Blues.* New York. Alfred A. Knopf, 1926.

Huxley, Aldous. "Aldous Huxley to Humphrey Osmond, September 16, 1954." In *Psychedelic Prophets: The Letters of Aldous Huxley and Humphry Osmond,* edited by Cynthia Carson, Paul Bisbee, Erika Dyck, Patrick Farrell, James Sexton, and James W. Spisak, 126. Montreal: McGill-Queen's University Press, 2018.

———. "Wanted, A New Pleasure (1931)." In *Aldous Huxley: Complete Essays,* vol. 3, edited by Robert S. Baker and James Sexton, 260–64. Chicago: Ivan R. Dee, 2001.

Huxley, Julian. "Transhumanism." In *Julian Huxley. New Bottles for New Wine,* 13–17. London: Chatto & Windus, 1957.

Jacques, Elliot. "Death and the Mid-Life Crisis." *International Journal of Psychoanalysis* 46 (1965): 502–14.

Jefferson, Thomas. "Jefferson to Edward Bancroft, January 26, 1789." In *The Papers of Thomas Jefferson,* vol. 14, edited by Julian P. Boyd, 492–94. Princeton, NJ: University of Princeton Press, 1958.

———. "Jefferson to St. George Tucker, August 28, 1797." In *The Papers of Thomas Jefferson,* vol. 29, edited by Barbara B. Oberg, 519–20. Princeton, NJ: Princeton University Press, 2002.

———. *Notes on the State of Virginia*. Philadelphia: R. T. Rawle, 1801.

———. "Thomas Jefferson's Anecdotes of Benjamin Franklin, December 4, 1818." In *The Papers of Thomas Jefferson, Retirement Series*, vol. 13, edited by J. Jefferson Looney, 462–65. Princeton, NJ: Princeton University Press, 2016.

Jung, Carl Gustav. "Die Lebenswende." In *Gesammelte Werke*, vol. 8 ("Die Dynamik des Unbewußten"), 441–60. Olten: Walter Verlag, 1989.

Kalm, Pehr. *Travels into North America: Containing Its Natural History*. London: Fleet-Street, 1771.

Kaplan, Janice. "Exercise: The New High." *Glamour* (May 1978): 250.

Karsunke, Yaak. "Kilroy was here/Kilroy war hier." *New Left Review* 1, no. 43 (May/June 1967).

Kenworthy, Charles J. *Climatology of Florida*. Savannah, GA: Morning News Steam Printing House, 1880.

Keppler, Joseph Jr. "A Trifle Embarrassed." *Puck Magazine*, August 3, 1898.

Kesey, Ken. *One Flew over the Cuckoo's Nest*. New York: Viking Press & Signet Books, 1962.

King, Dan. *Quackery Unmasked*. Boston: David Clapp, 1858.

Kipling, Rudyard. "The White Man's Burden." *McClure's Magazine* 12, no. 4 (February 1899): 290–91.

Kupferberg, Tuli. "The Love of Politics and the Politics of Love." *East Village Other* (May 1967): 4–5.

Kurzweil, Ray. *The Age of Spiritual Machines: When Computers Exceed Human Intelligence*. New York: Viking Press, 1998.

Lasch, Christopher. "Aging in a Culture without a Future." *Hastings Center Report* 7, no. 4 (August 1977): 42–44.

———, Christopher. *The Culture of Narcissism: American Life in an Age of Diminishing Expectations*. New York: Norton, 1979.

Lawrence, D. H. *Studies in Classic American Literature*. London: Martin Secker, 1920.

Levinson, Daniel J. *The Seasons of a Man's Life*. New York: Alfred A. Knopf, 1979.

Levis, Richard J. *Diary of a Spring Holiday in Cuba*. Philadelphia: Porter & Coates, 1872.

Lewis, R. W. B. *The American Adam: Innocence, Tragedy, and Tradition in the Nineteenth Century*. Chicago: University of Chicago Press, 1955.

Lincoln, Abraham. "Address Before the Young Men's Lyceum in Springfield, Illinois, January 27, 1838." In *Collected Works of Abraham Lincoln*, vol. 1, edited by Roy P. Basler, 108–15. New Brunswick, NJ: Rutgers University Press, 1953.

———. "Address Delivered at the Dedication of the Cemetery at Gettysburg, November 19, 1863." In *Collected Works of Abraham Lincoln*, vol. 7, edited by Roy P. Basler, 22–23. New Brunswick, NJ: Rutgers University Press, 1953.

———. "Speech at Lewistown, Illinois, August 17, 1858." In *Collected Works of Abraham Lincoln*, vol. 2, edited by Roy P. Basler, 546–47. New Brunswick, NJ: Rutgers University Press, 1953.

Lippmann, Walter. *The Cold War: A Study in Foreign Relations*. New York: Harper, 1947.

Locke, Alain. "Fire: A Negro Magazine." *The Survey* (August–September 1927): 563.

———. "Negro Youth Speaks." In *The New Negro: An Interpretation*, 47–56. New York: Albert and Charles Boni, 1925.

———. "The New Negro." In *The New Negro: An Interpretation*, 3–18. New York: Albert and Charles Boni, 1925.

Locke, John. *Two Treatises of Government*. London: Black Swan, 1689.

London, Jack. *Jack London's Tales of Adventure*. Edited by Irving Shepard. Garden City, NY: Hanover House, 1956.

———. "A Piece of Steak." In *The Chinago and Other Stories*, 277–319. New York: Leslie Judge Co., 1911.

———. *A Son of the Sun*. Garden City, NY: Doubleday, 1912.

Louderback, Lew. *Fat Power*. New York: Hawthorn Books, 1970.

Love, Nat. *The Life and Adventures of Nat Love*. Los Angeles: Nat Love, 1907.

Luce, Henry R. "The American Century." *Life*, February 17, 1941.

Ludwig, Emil. *How to Treat the Germans*. New York: Willard, 1943.

MacArthur, Douglas. "VJ Day Broadcast, September 2, 1945, USS Missouri, Tokyo Bay." In *General MacArthur: Speeches and Reports, 1908–1964*, edited by Edward T. Imparato, 136–38. Nashville, TN: Turner Publishing, 2000.

Macfadden, Bernarr. *Vitality Supreme*. New York: Physical Culture Publishing, 1915.

Macfadden, Helen. "Business Girls Should Swim for Better Posture." *Physical Culture* (July 1937): 46–47.

———. *Help Yourself to Beauty*. New York: Macfadden Book, 1939.

MacLean, Rory. *Magic Bus: On the Hippie Trail from Istanbul to India*. New York: Viking Press, 2006.

Madison, James. "The Federalist No. 10." In *The Papers of James Madison*, edited by Robert A. Rutland, Charles F. Hobson, William M. E. Rachal, and Frederika J. Teute, vol. 10, 263–70. Chicago: University of Chicago Press, 1977.

Mailer, Norman. "The White Negro: Superficial Reflections on the Hipster." *Dissent* (Fall 1957): 276–93.

Malthus, Thomas Robert. *An Essay on the Principle of Population*. London: St. Paul's Churchyard, 1798.

Marcuse, Herbert. *One-Dimensional Man: Studies in the Ideology of Advanced Industrial Society*. Boston: Beacon Press, 1964.

Marinetti, Filippo Tommaso. "The Futurist Manifesto." In *F. T. Marinetti: Critical Writings*, edited by Günter Berghaus, 11–17. New York: Farrar, Straus and Giroux, 2006.

McKivigan, John R., Julie Husband, and Heather L. Kaufman, eds. *The Speeches of Frederick Douglass: A Critical Edition*. New Haven, CT: Yale University Press, 2018.

Mencken, H. L. "The Aframerican: New Style." *American Mercury* 7 (February 1926): 255.

Merchant, Ben, ed. *My Dear Wister: The Frederic Remington-Owen Wister Letters*. Palo Alto, CA: American West, 1972.

Merrill, Walter M., ed. *The Letters of William Lloyd Garrison*, vol. 3. Cambridge, MA: Harvard University Press, 1973.

Miles, Nelson. "Major General Nelson Miles's Proclamation (July 28, 1898)." In *The Spanish-American War: A Documentary History with Commentaries*, edited by Brad K. Berner, 194–95. Lanham, MD: Fairleigh Dickinson University Press, 2014.

Mitchell, Silas Weir. *Wear and Tear, or Hints for the Overworked*. Philadelphia: J. B. Lippincott, 1871.

Morrison, Toni. *The Bluest Eye*. New York: Holt, Rinehart and Winston, 1970.

Morse, Jedidiah. *The American Geography, or, A View of the Present Situation of the United States of America*. Elizabethtown, NJ: Shepard Kollock, 1789.

Muhlen, Norbert. "America and American Occupation in German Eyes." *Annals of the American Academy of Political and Social Sciences* 295 (September 1954): 52–61.

Muir, John. *Our National Parks*. Boston: Houghton Mifflin, 1901.

Murray, William H. H. *Adventures in the Wilderness; or, Camp-Life in the Adirondacks*. Boston: Fields, Osgood, 1869.

Nascher, I. L. *Geriatrics: The Diseases of Old Age and Their Treatment*. Philadelphia: P. Blakiston's Son & Co., 1914.

Nidetch, Jean. *The Story of Weight Watchers*. New York: WW Twentyfirst Corporation/ World Publishing, 1970.

O'Connell, Mark. "600-Hundred Miles in a Coffin-Shaped Bus, Campaigning against Death Itself." *New York Times Magazine*, February 9, 2017.

———. *To Be a Machine: Adventures among Cyborgs, Utopians, Hackers, and the Futurists Solving the Modest Problem of Death*. New York: Doubleday, 2017.

Ontario Division of Industrial Hygiene. *Health Confessions of Business Women*. Ontario: C. W. James, 1923.

Paine, Thomas. *Common Sense: Addressed to the Inhabitants of America*. Philadelphia: R. Bell, 1776.

Palmolive Company. *A Day in the Palmolive Factory*. Milwaukee: Palmolive, 1925.

Perkins Gilman, Charlotte. *Women and Economics*. Boston: Small, Maynard & Co., 1898.

Peterson, Merrill D., ed. *Thomas Jefferson: Writings*. New York: Library of America, 1984.

Poling, Daniel A. *Youth Marches*. Philadelphia: Judson Press, 1937.

Potter, David M. *People of Plenty: Economic Abundance and the American Character*. Chicago: University of Chicago Press, 1956.

Pound, Ezra. *Make It New*. New Haven, CT: Yale University Press, 1935.

Rarick, John R., Hon. (Louisiana). "Man's Hope for Peace—A Weapon of War." *Congressional Record*, 91st Congress, vol. 116/13 (June 2, 1970): 17964.

Regalado, Antonio. "Meet Altos Labs, Silicon Valley's Latest Wild Bet on Living Forever." *MIT Technology Review*, September 4, 2021.

Remondino, Peter C. *The Mediterranean Shores of America. Southern California: Climatic, Physical, and Meteorological Conditions*. Philadelphia: F. A. David, 1892.

Reynolds, Charles B. *The Landing of Ponce de Leon: A Historical Review*. Mountain Lakes, NJ: Reynolds, 1934.

Rogers, J. A. "Jazz at Home." In *The New Negro: An Interpretation*, edited by Alain Locke, 216–25. New York: Albert and Charles Boni, 1925.

Roosevelt, Franklin D. "First Inaugural Address." In *The Public Papers and Addresses of Franklin D. Roosevelt*, vol. 2, edited by Samuel I. Rosenman, 269–73. New York: Random House, 1938.

Roosevelt, Theodore. *African Game Trails*. New York: Charles Scribner's Sons, 1910.

———. *The New Nationalism*. New York: The Outlook Company, 1910.

Rosenberg, Alfred. "Rebellion der Jugend." *Nationalsozialistische Monatshefte* 1 (1930): 50–59.

Rossiter, Emanuel. *"Right Forward, Fours Right, March!" A Little Story of Company I, Third Wisconsin Volunteers, First Brigade, First Division, First Corps*. Superior, WI, 1900.

Roszak, Theodore. *The Making of a Counter Culture: Reflections on the Technocratic Society and Its Youthful Opposition.* New York: Doubleday, 1969.

Rubinstein, Helena. *Beauty in the Making.* New York: Helena Rubenstein Inc., 1930.

Rush, Benjamin. "On Old Age [1789]." In *The Selected Writings of Benjamin Rush*, edited by Dagobert D. Runes, 342–57. New York: Philosophical Library, 1947.

Savage, Edward. *Liberty in the Form of the Goddess of Youth: Giving Support to the Bald Eagle.* Philadelphia: E. Savage, 1796.

Schlafly, Phyllis. "The Precious Rights ERA Will Take Away from Wives." *The Phyllis Schlafly Report* (August 1973): 1.

Schurz, Carl. "Carl Schurz to his wife Margarethe, August 16, 1860." In *Intimate Letters of Carl Schurz, 1841–1869*, edited and translated by Joseph Schafer, 218. Madison: State Historical Society of Wisconsin, 1928.

———. "True Americanism." In *Speeches, Correspondence, and Political Papers of Carl Schurz*, vol. 1, edited by Frederic Bancroft, 48–71. New York: G. P. Putnam's Sons, 1913.

Schuyler, George. *Black No More.* New York: Macaulay Company, 1931.

———. "Unnecessary Negroes." *Messenger* 8 (1926): 307.

Sennett, Richard. *The Fall of Public Man.* New York: Penguin, 1977.

Seton, Ernest Thompson. *The Birch-Bark Roll of the Woodcraft Indians.* New York: Doubleday, 1907.

Sheehy, Gail. *Passages: Predictable Crises of Adult Life.* New York: E. P. Dutton, 1976.

Simpich, Frederick. "Uncle Sam Bends a Twig in Germany." *National Geographic Magazine* (October 1948): 529–50.

Smith, Adelaide, and Reuben Rockwood. *Modern Beauty Culture.* New York: Prentice-Hall, 1935.

Snider, A. J. "Exercise Not Always Beneficial." *Science Digest* (March 1973): 53.

Snodgrass, Katherine. *Copra and Coconut Oil.* Stanford, CA: Food Research Institute Stanford University, 1928.

Sontag, Susan. "The Double Standard of Aging." *Saturday Review*, September 23, 1972, 29–38.

Stanley, Leo L. *Men at Their Worst.* New York: Appleton Century, 1940.

Steinem, Gloria. "The Politics of Muscle." In *Moving beyond Words: Age, Rage, Sex, Power, Money, Muscles*, 93–97. New York: Touchstone, 1995.

St. John de Crèvecoeur, Hector. *Letters from an American Farmer*, repr. New York: Fox, Duffield, 1904.

Stoddard, Lothrop. *The Rising Tide of Color against White World-Supremacy.* New York: Charles Scribner's Sons, 1920.

Stowe, Charles Edward. *Life of Harriet Beecher Stowe: Compiled from Her Letters and Journals.* Boston: Houghton & Mifflin, 1889.

Stowe, Harriet. *Palmetto Leaves.* Boston: James R. Osgood, 1873.

Stratemeyer, Edward, and Charles Copeland, *American Boys' Life of Theodore Roosevelt.* Boston: Lee & Shepard, 1904.

Strunsky, Anna. "Memoirs of Jack London." *The Masses* 9 (July 1917).

Students for a Democratic Society. "The Port Huron Statement." In *The Port Huron Statement: Sources and Legacies of the New Left's Founding Manifesto*, edited by Richard Flacks and Nelson Lichtenstein, 239–40. Philadelphia: University of Pennsylvania Press, 2015.

Students for a Democratic Society. *SDS Work-Ins: Towards a Worker-Student Alliance.* Chicago: Students for a Democratic Society, 1969.

Taft, William Howard. "The Duty of Americans in the Philippines." *Official Gazette (Supplement)*, December 23, 1903.

Thomas, Dylan. "Do Not Go Gentle into That Good Night." In *Selected Poems: 1934–1952*, 122. New York: J. M. Dent & Sons, 1953.

Thoreau, Henry David. *Walden: Or, Life in the Woods.* Boston: Ticknor and Fields, 1854.

Train, George Francis. *Spread-Eagleism.* London: Sampson Low, Son & Co., 1860.

Turner, Frederick J. "The Significance of the Frontier in American History." *Annual Report of the American Historical Association* (1893): 197–227.

US Department of Health and Human Services. *Report on the 1984 National Conference for Youth on Drinking and Driving.* Rockville, MD: National Institute on Alcohol Abuse and Alcoholism, 1984.

US Senate. *Military Situation in the Far East: Hearings before the Committee on Armed Services and the Committee on Foreign Relations*, part I. Washington, DC: Government Printing Office, 1951.

US Senate. *Select Committee on Nutrition and Human Needs, Dietary Goals for the United States*, 2nd ed. Washington, DC: Government Printing Office, 1977.

US State Department. *The Seal of the United States: How It Was Developed and Adopted.* Washington, DC: US Department of State, 1892.

US State Department. *Young Germany: Apprentice to Democracy.* Washington, DC: US Government Printing Office, 1951.

Voronoff, Serge. *Life: A Study of the Means of Restoring Vital Energy and Prolonging Life.* New York: E. P. Dutton, 1920.

———. *Rejuvenation by Grafting.* New York: Adelphi, 1925.

Warren, Mercy Otis. *History of the Rise, Progress, and Termination of the American Revolution*, vol. 3. Boston: Manning and Loring, 1805.

Waters, H. F. "Keeping Fit." *Newsweek*, May 23, 1977, 79.

Whitman, Walt. "Song of Myself." In *Leaves of Grass*, 29–78. Boston: Small, Maynard, 1897. First published 1855.

Wister, Owen. *Lady Baltimore.* New York: Macmillan, 1906.

Wright, Henry Clark. *Six Months at Graefenberg.* London: Charles Gilpin, 1845.

Wolfe, Tom. "The 'Me' Decade: Reports on America's New Great Awakening." *New York Magazine*, August 23, 1976.

Wong, Matteo. "I Went to a Rave with the 46-Year-Old-Millionaire Who Claims to Have the Body of a Teenager," *The Atlantic*, February 22, 2024.

World Transhumanist Association. *Transhumanist Declaration.* Los Angeles: WTA, 1998.

ONLINE

Adams, Johan. "Adams to Elbridge Gerry, April 17, 1813." *Founders Online*, National Archives. https://founders.archives.gov/documents/Adams/99-02-02-6000.

Advertisement for Madam C. J. Walker Products. "From a Slave Cabin to Riches and a Benefactress to Her Race," (ca. 1928). Collection of the Smithsonian National Museum of African American History and Culture. https://nmaahc.si.edu/object/nmaahc_2013 .153.11.2. Accessed January 3, 2023.

Alto Labs. "Altos Labs Launches with the Goal to Transform Medicine through Cellular Rejuvenation Programming," press release, January 19, 2022. https://www.prnewswire.com/news-releases/altos-labs-launches-with-the-goal-to-transform-medicine-through-cellular-rejuvenation-programming-301463541.html.

Anonymous. "Young America denims." Photograph, Library of Congress, n.d. [c. 1858]. https://www.loc.gov/item/96516004/. Accessed March 14, 2021.

Ayyadi, Kira. "The Latest Conspiracy Trend: Transhumanism." *Bell Tower News*, December 14, 2022. https://www.belltower.news/the-end-of-humanity-the-latest-conspiracy-trend-transhumanism-144273/.

Blumenthal, Seth. "New Nixon and Youth Politics, 1968." *Process: A Blog for American History*, December 20, 2018. https://www.processhistory.org/blumenthal-1968/.

Carmichael, Stokely. "Black Power, October 29, 1966." *BlackPast*, July 13, 2010. https://www.blackpast.org/african-american-history/speeches-african-american-history/1966-stokely-carmichael-black-power/.

Cosmetics and Skin. n.d. "Stories from the History and Science of Cosmetics, Skin-Care and Early Beauty Culture." https://www.cosmeticsandskin.com, accessed January 3, 2023.

Ciurria, Mich. "Transhumanism Is Eugenics for Educated White Liberals." *Biopolitical Philosophy*, January 19, 2023. https://biopoliticalphilosophy.com/2023/01/19/transhumanism-is-eugenics-for-educated-white-liberals.

Deutsche Digitale Bibliothek. "Brigade Run in West Berlin." https://www.deutsche-digitale-bibliothek.de/item/L2GZIPBMQYQYNB7GBSZFJ343ZUMXCC4P. Accessed March 21, 2023.

Döpfner, Mathias. "Elon Musk Discusses the War in Ukraine and the Importance of Nuclear Power—and Why Benjamin Franklin Would Be 'the Most Fun at Dinner.'" Interview, *Business Insider*, March 26, 2022. https://www.businessinsider.com/elon-musk-interview-axel-springer-tesla-war-in-ukraine-2022-3.

Jefferson, Thomas. "Thomas Jefferson to Benjamin Chambers, December 28, 1805." *Founders Online*, National Archives. https://founders.archives.gov/documents/Jefferson/99-01-02-2910. Accessed September 18, 2019.

Kahler, Herbert. "Herbert Kahler to Verne Chatelain, January 18, 1934." In "Proposed Fountain of Youth Natl. Monument, Florida," File No. 0–35, US Department of the Interior. http://www.npshistory.com/publications/proposed-parks/fl-fountain-of-youth-nm.pdf. Accessed March 14, 2023.

Kirsch, Noah. "Bryan Johnson, Tech Mogul Trying to Stop Aging, Wants His Own Nation-State," *Daily Beast*, March 19, 2024. https://www.thedailybeast.com/bryan-johnson-blueprint-tech-mogul-trying-to-stop-aging-wants-his-own-nation-state.

Kurzweil, Ray. "The Church-Turing Thesis." *Kurzweil Library + collections*, August 6, 2001. https://www.kurzweilai.net/the-paradigms-and-paradoxes-of-intelligence-part-2-the-church-turing-thesis.

Lilienthal, C. H. *Young America*. C. H. Lilienthal, N.Y./Lith. Of Sarony, Major & Knapp, 449 Broadway, N. York. Photograph, Library of Congress, n.d. [c. 1860]. https://www.loc.gov/item/2003689286/. Accessed December 2, 2019.

More, Max. "A Letter to Mother Nature." *Max More's Strategic Philosophy* (blog), August 1999; revised May 2009. http://strategicphilosophy.blogspot.com/2009/05/its-about-ten-years-since-i-wrote.html.

Morgan, Robin. "No More Miss America!" *Redstockings*, New York Radical Women, press release, August 22, 1968, plank 6. http://www.redstockings.org/index.php/no-more-miss-america.

Rather, Dan. "Wellness." *60 Seconds*. CBS News video, originally broadcast November 1979. https://danratherjournalist.org/investigative-journalist/60-minutes/60-minutes-additional-videos/video-wellness. Accessed April 2, 2023.

Reagan, Ronald. "Republican National Convention Acceptance Speech, July 17, 1980." Ronald Reagan Presidential Library and Museum. https://www.reaganlibrary.gov/archives/speech/republican-national-convention-acceptance-speech-1980.

Roosevelt, Franklin D. "October 5, 1937: Quarantine Speech," audio and transcript, The Miller Center, University of Virginia. https://millercenter.org/the-presidency/presidential-speeches/october-5-1937-quarantine-speech. Accessed February 13, 2023.

Rubinstein, Helena. "The War Face," advertisement, c. 1917. *Mary Evans Picture Library*. https://www.prints-online.com/helena-rubinstein-ad-war-face-ww1-14143246.html. Accessed January 4, 2013.

Stanford Medicine News Center, "Old Human Cells Rejuvenation with Stem Cell Technology," press release, March 24, 2020. https://med.stanford.edu/news/all-news/2020/03/old-human-cells-rejuvenated-with-stem-cell-technology.html.

Tranhumanist Party. *Transhumanist Bill of Rights*. Version 3.0. Adopted via electronic vote on December 2–9, 2018. https://transhumanist-party.org/tbr-3/. Accessed April 17, 2023.

Travelguide. Schomburg Center for Research in Black Culture, Jean Blackwell Hutson Research and Reference Division, The New York Public Library. https://digitalcollections.nypl.org/search/index?utf8=%E2%9C%93&keywords=Travelguide. Accessed December 28, 2021.

Toll, Roger. "Roger Toll to National Park Service, April 8, 1935." In "Proposed Fountain of Youth Natl. Monument, Florida," File No. 0–35, US Department of the Interior. http://www.npshistory.com/publications/proposed-parks/fl-fountain-of-youth-nm.pdf.

Torres, Emile P. "How Elon Musk Sees the Future: His Bizarre Sci-Fi Vision Should Concern Us All." *Salon*, July 17, 2022.

UN Human Rights Council. *Report of the Independent International Commission of Inquiry on Ukraine*, February 26–April 5, 2024. https://www.ohchr.org/sites/default/files/documents/hrbodies/hrcouncil/coiukraine/a-hrc-55-66-aev.pdf.

US Department of the Interior. "Proposed Fountain of Youth Natl. Monument, Florida," File No. 0–35 (May 1929). http://www.npshistory.com/publications/proposed-parks/fl-fountain-of-youth-nm.pdf.

Walker, Madam C. J. "From a Slave Cabin to Riches and a Benefactress of Her Race. " Collection of the Smithsonian National Museum of African American History and Culture, n.d. [c. 1928]. https://nmaahc.si.edu/object/nmaahc_2013.153.11.2. Accessed January 3, 2023.

Winny, Annalies. "Für immer jung: Ein Wochenende unter Menschen, die sich weigern zu sterben." The Burnout and Escapism Issue, *Vice*, February 7, 2019. https://www.vice.com/de/article/mbybpb/immortalisten-konferenz-raadfest-ein-wochenende-unter-menschen-die-sich-weigern-zu-sterben.

Xi, Jinping. "Forging Ahead to Open a New Chapter on China-Russia Friendship."
Ministry of Foreign Affairs of the People's Republic of China, March 20, 2023. https://
www.fmprc.gov.cn/mfa_eng/zxxx_662805/202303/t20230320_11044359.html.

Secondary Literature

Alonso, Harriet Hyman. *Growing Up Abolitionist: The Story of the Garrison Children.*
Amherst: University of Massachusetts Press, 2002.

Alvarez, Erick. *Muscle Boys: Gay Gym Culture.* New York: Routledge, 2010.

Angulo, A. J. *Empire and Education: A History of Greed and Goodwill from the War of 1898 to
the War on Terror.* New York: Palgrave Macmillan, 2012.

Appleby, Joyce. *Inheriting the Revolution: The First Generation of Americans.* Cambridge,
MA: Harvard University Press, 2000.

Aron, Cindy S. *Working at Play: A History of Vacations in the United States.* New York:
Oxford University Press, 1999.

Baker, Stephanie Alice. *Wellness Culture: How the Wellness Movement Has Been Used to
Empower, Profit and Misinform.* Bingley, UK: Emerald Publishing, 2022.

Baldwin, Alice M. *The New England Clergy and the American Revolution.* Durham, NC:
Duke University Press, 1928.

Banta, Martha. *Barbaric Intercourse: Caricature and the Culture of Conduct.* Chicago:
University of Chicago Press, 2003.

Bartlett, Irving H. *Wendell Phillips: Brahmin Radical.* Westport, CN: Greenwood Press,
1973.

Bauernkämper, Arnd. "Der Neue Mensch." *Docupedia Zeitgeschichte,* July 4, 2017. https://
docupedia.de/zg/Bauerkaemper_neue_mensch_v1_de_2017.

Baumann, Zygmunt. *Mortality, Immortality and Other Life Strategies.* Cambridge, MA:
Polity Press, 1992.

Bederman, Gail. *Manliness and Civilization: A Cultural History of Race and Gender in the
United States, 1880–1917.* Chicago: University of Chicago Press, 1996.

Beerbohm, Max. *A Defense of Cosmetics.* New York: Dodd, Mead, 1922.

Bell, J. L. "From Saucy Boys to Sons of Liberty: Politicizing Youth in Pre-Revolutionary
Boston." In *Children in Colonial America,* edited by James Marten, 204–16. New York:
New York University Press, 2007.

Bender, Daniel E. *American Abyss: Savagery and Civilization in the Age of Industry.* Ithaca,
NY: Cornell University Press, 2009.

Berghoff, Hartmut, and Thomas Kühne, eds. *Globalizing Beauty: Consumerism and Body
Aesthetics in the Twentieth Century.* Basingstoke: Palgrave, 2013.

Berliner, Brett A. "Mephistopheles and Monkeys: Rejuvenation, Race, and Sexuality in
Popular Culture in Interwar France." *Journal of the History of Sexuality* 13, no. 3
(July 2004): 206–325.

Berry, Daina Ramy. *The Price for Their Pound of Flesh: The Value of the Enslaved, from
Womb to Grave, in the Building of a Nation.* Boston: Beacon Press, 2017.

Bhabha, Homi K. *The Location of Culture.* New York: Routledge, 1994.

Bird, Ayana D., and Lori L. Tharps. *Hair Story: Untangling the Roots of Black Hair in
America.* New York: St. Martin's Press, 2014.

Black, Edwin. *War against the Weak: Eugenics and America's Campaign to Create a Master Race*. Washington, DC: Dialog Press, 2012.

Black, Jonathan. *Making the American Body: The Remarkable Saga of Men and Women Whose Feats, Feuds, and Passions Shaped Fitness History*. Omaha: University of Nebraska Press, 2013.

Blaustein, George. *Nightmare Envy and Other Stories: American Culture and European Reconstruction*. New York: Oxford University Press, 2018.

Blight, David W. *Race and Reunion: The Civil War in American Memory*. New Haven, CT: Yale University Press, 2001.

Blue, Ethan. "The Strange Career of Leo Stanley: Remaking Manhood and Medicine at San Quentin State Penitentiary, 1913–1951." *Pacific Historical Review* 78, no. 2 (May 2009): 210–41.

Bold, Christine. *The Frontier Club: Popular Westerns and Cultural Power, 1880–1924*. New York: Oxford University Press, 2013.

Borstelmann, Thomas. *The 1970s: A New Global History from Civil Rights to Economic Inequality*. Princeton, NJ: Princeton University Press, 2012.

Bostrom, Nick. "In Defense of Posthuman Dignity." *Bioethics* 19, no. 3 (2005): 202–14.

———. "A History of Transhumanist Thought." *Journal of Evolution and Technology* 14, no. 1 (April 2005): 1–25.

———. "The Vulnerable World Hypothesis." *Global Policy* 10, no. 4 (November 2019): 455–76.

Bouk, Dan. *How Our Days Became Numbered: Risk and the Rise of the Statistical Individual*. Chicago: University of Chicago Press, 2015.

Boyer Lewis, Charlene M. *Ladies and Gentlemen on Display: Planter Society at the Virginia Springs, 1790–1860*. Charlottesville: University of Virginia Press, 2001.

Bradley, Ian. *Water: A Spiritual History*. London: Bloomsbury, 2012.

Brandenburg, David J. "A French Aristocrat Looks at American Farming: La Rochefoucauld-Liancourt's Voyage dans les États-Unis." *Agricultural History* 32, no. 3 (1958): 163.

Braunstein, Peter. "Forever Young: Insurgent Youth and the Sixties Culture of Rejuvenation." In *Imagine Nation: The American Counterculture of the 1960s and '70s*, edited by Peter Braunstein and Michael William Doyle, 243–74. New York: Routledge, 2002.

Braunstein, Peter, and Michael William Doyle, eds. *Imagine Nation: The American Counterculture of the 1960s and '70s*. New York: Routledge, 2002.

Brückmann, Rebecca. *Massive Resistance and Southern Womanhood: White Women, Class, and Segregation*. Athens: University of Georgia Press, 2021.

Brückner, Martin. *The Geographic Revolution in Early America: Maps, Literacy and National Identity*. Chapel Hill: The University of North Carolina Press, 2006.

Brumberg, Joan Jacob. *The Body Project: An Intimate History of American Girls*. New York: Random House, 1997.

Buckler, Helen. *Wo-He-Lo: The Story of the Camp Fire Girls, 1910–1960*. New York: Holt, Rinehart and Winston, 1961.

Bumgarner, John Reed. *The Health of the Presidents: The 41 US Presidents through 1993 from a Physician's Point of View*. Jefferson, NC: MacFarland, 1994.

Bundles, A'Lelia. *On Her Own Ground: The Life and Times of Madam C. J. Walker.* New York: Scribner, 2001.

Butler, Judith. *Gender Trouble: Feminism and the Subversion of Identity.* New York: Routledge, 1990.

Cain, Chelsea, ed. *Wild Child: Girlhoods in the Counterculture.* Emeryville, CA: Seal Press, 1999.

Cardon, Nathan. "Fanny Bullock Workman, Transimperial Mobility, and Fantasies of 'Anglo-Saxon' Subjectivity in the Gilded Age." Unpublished paper, 2023.

Carmichael, Stokely, and Ekwueme Michael Thelwell. *Ready for Revolution: The Life and Struggles of Stokely Carmichael (Kwame Ture).* New York: Scribner, 2005.

Carruthers, Susan L. *The Good Occupation: American Soldiers and the Hazards of Peace.* Cambridge, MA: Havard University Press, 2016.

Cassata, Francesco. *Building the New Man: Eugenics, Racial Science and Genetics in Twentieth-Century Italy.* Translated by Erin O' Loughlin. Budapest: Central European University Press, 2011.

Cayleff, Susan E. *Wash and Be Healed: The Water-Cure Movement and Women's Health.* Philadelphia: Temple University Press, 1987.

Chappel, James. *Golden Years: How Americans Invented and Reinvented Old Age.* New York: Basic Books, 2024.

Chatelain, Marcia. *Franchise: The Golden Arches of Black America.* New York: Liveright, 2020.

Chauncey, George. *Gay New York: Gender, Urban Culture, and the Making of the Gay Male World.* New York: Basic Books, 1994.

Chen, Yinghong. *Creating the New Man: From Enlightenment Ideals to Socialist Realities.* Honolulu: University of Hawai'i Press, 2009.

Chernow, Ron. *Washington: A Life.* New York: Penguin, 2010.

Chinitz, David. "Rejuvenation through Joy: Langston Hughes, Primitivism, and Jazz." *American Literary History* 9, no. 1 (Spring 1997): 60–78.

Cocks, Catherine. *Tropical Whites: The Rise of the Tourist South in the Americas.* Philadelphia: University of Pennsylvania Press, 2013.

Cohen, Patricia. *In Our Prime: The Fascinating History and Promising Future of Middle Age.* New York: Scribner, 2012.

Cohen, Robert. *Howard Zinn's Southern Diary: Sit-Ins, Civil Rights, and Black Women's Student Activism.* Athens: University of Georgia Press, 2018.

Cohen, William "The Colonized as Child: British and French Colonial Rule." *African Historical Studies* 3, no. 2 (1970): 427–31.

Cole, Thomas R. *The Journey of Life: A Cultural History of Aging in America.* New York: Cambridge University Press, 1992.

Conn, Steven. *Americans against the City: Anti-Urbanism in the Twentieth Century.* New York: Oxford University Press, 2014.

Cordell, Ryan C. "Alcohol and Temperance." In *The Early Republic and Antebellum America: An Encyclopedia of Social, Political, Cultural, and Economic History*, edited by Christopher G. Bates, 72–75. New York: Routledge, 2015.

Courtwright, David T. *Violent Land: Single Men and Social Disorder from the Frontier to the Inner City.* Cambridge, MA: Harvard University Press, 1996.

Cross, Gary. *Men to Boys: The Making of Modern Immaturity*. New York: Columbia University Press, 2008.

Cullather, Nick. "The Foreign Policy of the Calory." *American Historical Review* 112, no. 2 (April 2007): 337–64.

Culver, Lawrence. *The Frontier of Leisure: Southern California and the Shaping of Modern America*. New York: Oxford University Press, 2010.

Dalrymple, Louis. "The Idol of the Aunties." *Puck Magazine*, May 10, 1899.

———. "School Begins." *Puck Magazine*, January 25, 1899.

Dalton, Kathleen. *Roosevelt: A Strenuous Life*. New York: Vintage Books, 2004.

Daub, Adrian. *What Tech Calls Thinking: An Inquiry into the Intellectual Bedrock of Silicon Valley*. New York: Macmillan, 2020.

De Schweinitz, Rebecca. "The Proper Age for Suffrage: Vote 18 and the Politics of Age from World War II to the Age of Aquarius." In *Age in America: From the Colonial Era to the Present*, edited by Corinne T. Field and Nicholas Syrett, 209–36. New York: New York University Press, 2015.

Delbert, Caroline. "Jeff Bezos Is Paying for a Way to Make Humans Immortal." *Popular Mechanics*, January 26, 2022.

Delmont, Matthew F. *Why Busing Failed: Race, Media, and the National Resistance to School Desegregation*. Oakland: University of California Press, 2016.

Deloria, Philip J. *Playing Indian*. New Haven, CT: Yale University Press, 1998.

Dixon, Juliet. "Saving Your Face from Sunburn." *Delineator* 99, no. 2 (September 1921): 34.

Dorman, Jacob S. "Skin Bleach and Civilization: The Racial Formation of Blackness in 1920s Harlem." *Journal of Pan-African Studies* 4, no. 4 (June 2011): 47–80.

Droessler, Holger. *Coconut Colonialism: Workers and the Globalization of Samoa*. Cambridge, MA: Havard University Press, 2022.

Du Bois, W. E. B. "Back to Africa." *Century* 150 (February 1923): 539–48.

Duane, Anna Mae. *Suffering Childhood in Early America: Violence, Race, and the Making of the Child Victim*. Athens: University of Georgia Press, 2010.

Dugatkin, Lee Alan. *Mr. Jefferson and the Giant Moose: Natural History in Early America*. Chicago: University of Chicago Press, 2009.

Dunaway, Wilma A. *The African-American Family in Slavery and Emancipation*. New York: Cambridge University Press, 2003.

Eckelmann-Berghel, Susan. "'Young Stalwarts of Immobility': Anti-Civil Rights Youth and the Defense of White Childhood." Unpublished paper, 2023.

Engel, Jonathan. *Fat Nation: A History of Obesity in America*. Lanham, MD: Rowman & Littlefield, 2018.

English, T. J. *Dangerous Rhythms: Jazz and the Underworld*. New York: William Morrow, 2022.

Estepa, Andrea. "Taking the White Gloves Off: Women Strike for Peace and 'the Movement,' 1967–73." In *Feminist Coalitions: Historical Perspectives on Second-Wave Feminism in the United States*, edited by Stephanie Gilmore, 84–112. Urbana: University of Illinois Press, 2008.

Eyal, Yonatan. *The Young America Movement and the Transformation of the Democratic Party, 1828–1861*. New York: Cambridge University Press, 2007.

Faderman, Lillian, and Stuart Timmons. *Gay L.A.: A History of Sexual Outlaws, Power Politics, and Lipstick Lesbians*. Berkeley, CA: Basic Books, 2006.

Faust, Drew Gilpin. *This Republic of Suffering: Death and the American Civil War*. New York: Alfred A. Knopf, 2008.

Fay, Jennifer. *Theaters of Occupation: Hollywood and the Reeducation of Germany*. Minneapolis: University of Minnesota Press, 2008.

Fernandez, Johanna. *The Young Lords: A Radical History*. Chapel Hill: The University of North Carolina Press, 2019.

Field, Corinne T. *The Struggle for Equal Adulthood: Gender, Race, Age, and the Fight for Citizenship in Antebellum America*. Chapel Hill: The University of North Carolina Press, 2014.

Field, Corinne T., and Nicholas Syrett, eds. *Age in America: From the Colonial Era to the Present*. New York: New York University Press, 2015.

Fischer, Kirsten. "Vitalism in America: Elihu Palmer's Radical Religion in the Early Republic." *William and Mary Quarterly* 73, no. 3 (July 2016): 501–30.

Fitoussi, Michele. *Helena Rubinstein: The Woman Who Invented Beauty*. London: Gallic Books, 2013.

Flynn, Daniel J. *A Conservative History of the American Left*. New York: Crown Forum, 2008.

Foner, Eric. *Reconstruction: America's Unfinished Revolution, 1863–1877*. New York: Harper and Row, 1988.

Forth, Christopher E. "Corpulence, Modernity, and Transcendence in the Early Twentieth Century." In *The Body in History, Culture, and the Arts*, edited by Justyna Jajszczok and Aleksandra Musial, 69–81. New York: Routledge.

Foucault, Michel. "Technologies of the Self." In *Technologies of the Self: A Seminar with Michel Foucault*, edited by Luther H. Martin, Huck Gutman, and Patrick H. Hutton, 16–49. Amherst: University of Massachusetts Press, 1988.

Frank, Gillian. "'The Civil Rights of Parents:' Race and Conservative Politics in Anita Bryant's Campaign against Gay Rights in 1970s Florida." *Journal of the History of Sexuality* 22, no. 1 (January 2013): 126–60.

Friedman, Danielle. *Let's Get Physical: How Women Discovered Exercise and Reshaped the World*. New York, G.P. Putnam's Sons, 2022.

Frodeman, Robert. *Transhumanism, Nature, and the End of Science*. New York: Routledge, 2019.

Fukuyama, Francis. *Our Posthuman Future: Consequences of the Biotechnological Revolution*. New York: Farrar Straus & Giroux, 2002.

———. "Transhumanism." *Foreign Policy* 114 (September–October 2004): 42–43.

Füssl, Karl-Heinz. "Between Elitism and Educational Reform: German American Exchange Programs, 1945–1970." In *The United States and Germany in the Era of the Cold War, 1945–1990: A Handbook*, Vol. 1: 1945–1968, edited by Detlef Junker, 409–16. New York: Cambridge University Press, 2004.

Gemie, Sharif. *The Hippie Trail: A History*. Manchester: Manchester University Press, 2017.

Gemme, Paola. *Domesticating Foreign Struggles: The Italian Risorgimento and Antebellum American Identity*. Athens: University of Georgia Press, 2005.

Ghilani, Jessica L. "'The Army Just Sees Green': Utopian Meritocracy, Diversity, and the United States Army Recruitment in the 1970s." In *Propaganda and Public Relations in Military Recruitment: Promoting Military Service in the Twentieth and Twenty-First*

Centuries, edited by Brendan Maartens and Thomas Bivins, 146–60. London: Routledge, 2021.

Gill, Tiffany M. *Beauty Shop Politics: African American Women's Activism in the Beauty Industry*. Urbana: University of Illinois Press, 2010.

Glauser, Wayne. "Three Approaches to Locke and the Slave Trade." *Journal of the History of Ideas* 51, no.2 (April–June 1990): 199–216.

Gobat, Michel. *Empire by Invitation: William Walker and Manifest Destiny in Central America*. Cambridge, MA: Harvard University Press, 2018.

Goedde, Petra. *GIs and Germans: Culture, Gender, and Foreign Relations*. New Haven, CT: Yale University Press, 2003.

Goldstein, Evan. "What Follows the End of History? Identity Politics." *The Chronicle of Higher Education*, August 27, 2018.

Gollner, Adam Leith. *The Book of Immortality: The Science, Belief, and Magic Behind Living Forever*. New York: Scribner, 2013.

Goodheart, Adam. *1861: Civil War Awakening*. New York: Vintage Books, 2011.

Gorsuch, Anne E. *Youth in Revolutionary Russia: Enthusiasts, Bohemians, Delinquents*. Bloomington: Indiana University Press, 2000.

Grabbe, Hans-Jürgen. "Konrad Adenauer, John Foster Dulles, and West German-American Relations." In *John Foster Dulles and the Diplomacy of the Cold War*, edited by Richard H. Immerman, 109–32. Princeton, NJ: Princeton University Press, 1990.

Greenberg, Amy. *Manifest Manhood and the Antebellum American Empire*. New York: Cambridge University Press, 2005.

Grinspan, Jon. "A Birthday Like None Other: Turning Twenty-One in the Age of Popular Politics." In *Age in America: From the Colonial Era to the Present*, edited by Corinne T. Field and Nicholas Syrett, 86–102. New York: New York University Press, 2015.

———. *The Virgin Vote: How Young Americans Made Democracy Social, Politics Personal, and Voting Popular in the Nineteenth Century*. Chapel Hill: The University of North Carolina Press, 2016.

———. "'Young Men for War': The Wide Awakes and Lincoln's 1860 Presidential Campaign." *Journal of American History* 96, no. 2 (2009): 357–78.

Gurin, Joel, and T. George Harris. "Taking Charge: The Happy Health Confidents." *American Health* (March 1987): 53.

Haber, Caroline, and Brian Gratton, *Old Age and the Search for Security: An American Social History*. Bloomington: Indiana University Press, 1994.

Hagemann, Karen, and Sonya Michel, eds. *Gender and the Long Postwar: The United States and the Two Germanys*. Baltimore: Johns Hopkins University Press, 2014.

Hahn, Steven. *A Nation without Borders: The United States and Its World in an Age of Civil Wars, 1830–1910*. New York: Viking, 2016.

Haidarali, Laila. *Brown Beauty: Color, Sex, and Race from the Harlem Renaissance to World War II*. New York: New York University Press, 2018.

Haiven, Max. *Palm Oil: The Grease of Empire*. London: Pluto Press, 2022.

Hall, Josephine. *Is This the Future? An Investigation into Communal Living*. London: Lulu Press, 2011.

Harrison, Robert Pogue. *Juvenescence: A Cultural History of Our Age*. Chicago: University of Chicago Press, 2014.

Hauskeller, Michael. "How to Become a Post-Dog: Animals in Transhumanism." *Between the Species* 20, no. 1 (2017): 25–37.

Haynes, April R. *Riotous Flesh: Women, Psychology, and Solitary Vice in Nineteenth-Century America*. Chicago: University of Chicago Press, 2015.

Hedrick, Joan D. *Harriet Beecher Stowe: A Life*. New York: Oxford University Press, 1994.

Hess, Linda M. *Queer Aging in North American Fiction*. New York: Palgrave Macmillan, 2019.

Hirschman, Elizabeth C., and Morris B. Holbrook. "Hedonic Consumption: Emerging Concepts, Methods, and Propositions." *Journal of Marketing* 46, no. 3 (Summer 1982): 92–101.

Hobsbawm, Eric. *The Age of Extremes: The Short Twentieth Century, 1914–1991*. London: Michael Joseph, 1994.

Hodges, Graham Russell Gao. *David Ruggles: A Radical Black Abolitionist and the Underground Railroad in New York City*. Chapel Hill: The University of North Carolina Press, 2010.

Hoff, Derek. *The State and the Stork: The Population Debate and Policy Making in US History*. Chicago: University of Chicago Press, 2012.

Hoganson, Kristin L. *Consumer's Imperium: The Global Production of American Domesticity*. Chapel Hill: The University of North Carolina Press, 2007.

Höhn, Maria. *GIs and Fräuleins: The German-American Encounter in 1950s West Germany*. Chapel Hill: The University of North Carolina Press, 2002.

Holland, Jennifer. *Tiny You: A Western History of the Anti-Abortion Movement*. Oakland: University of California Press, 2020.

Holt, Michael F. *The Rise and Fall of the American Whig Party: Jacksonian Politics and the Onset of the Civil War*. New York: Oxford University Press, 1999.

Honeck, Mischa. "Men of Principle: Gender and the German American War for the Union." *Journal of the Civil War Era* 5, no. 1 (March 2015): 43–47.

———. *Our Frontier Is the World: The Boy Scouts in the Age of American Ascendancy*. Ithaca, NY: Cornell University Press, 2018.

———. "Rubble and Rebirth: Postwar Rejuvenation and the Erasure of History." *Journal of Social History* 53, no. 4 (Summer 2020): 889–905.

———. *We Are the Revolutionists: German-Speaking Immigrants and American Abolitionists after 1848*. Athens: University of Georgia Press, 2011.

Honeck, Mischa, Kristine Alexander, and Isabel Richter. "Mapping Modern Rejuvenation." Special issue, *Journal of Social History* 53, no. 4 (Summer 2020): 875–88.

Horne, Gerald. *Race War: White Supremacy and the Attack on the British Empire*. New York: New York University Press, 2004.

Houck, Davis W., and Amos Kiewe. *FDR's Body Politics: The Rhetoric of Disability*. College Station: Texas A & M University Press, 2003.

Hultkranz, Åke. "The Immortality of the Soul among North American Indians." *Zeitschrift für Ethnologie* 121, no. 2 (1996): 221–43.

Hünemörder, Markus. *The Society of the Cincinnati: Conspiracy and Distrust in Early America*. New York: Berghahn Books, 2006.

Immerwahr, Daniel. *How to Hide an Empire: A History of the Greater United States*. New York: Farrar, Straus & Giroux, 2019.

Isenberg, Nancy. *White Trash: The 400-Year Untold History of Class in America*. New York: Viking, 2016.

Jackson, Jeffrey H. *Making Jazz French: Music and Modern Life in Interwar Paris*. Durham, NC: Duke University Press, 2003.

Jackson, Maurice, and Jacqueline Bacon, eds. *African Americans and the Haitian Revolutions: Selected Essays and Historical Documents*. New York: Routledge, 2010.

Jacobs, Robert. "Attacking Children with Nuclear Weapons: The Centrality of Children in American Understandings of the Bombings of Hiroshima and Nagasaki." In *War and Childhood in the Era of the Two World Wars*, edited by Mischa Honeck and James Marten, 267–82. New York: Cambridge University Press 2019.

James, D. Clayton. "Command Crisis: MacArthur and the Korean War." In *MacArthur and the American Century: A Reader*, edited by William M. Leary, 384–98. Lincoln: University of Nebraska Press, 2001.

Jefferson, Alison Rose. *Living the California Dream: African American Leisure Sites during the Jim Crow Era*. Lincoln: University of Nebraska Press, 2020.

Jennings, Eric T. *Curing the Colonizers: Hydrotherapy, Climatology, and French Colonial Spas*. Durham, NC: Duke University Press, 2006.

Jha, Meeta Rani. *The Global Beauty Industry: Colorism, Racism, and the National Body*. London: Routledge, 2016.

Jobs, Richard Ivan. *Backpack Ambassadors: How Youth Travel Integrated Europe*. Chicago: University of Chicago Press, 2017.

Johnson, Louise Claire. *Behind the Red Door: How Elizabeth Arden's Legacy Inspired My Coming-of-Age-Story in the Beauty Industry*. Columbus, OH: Gatekeeper Press, 2021.

Johnson, Walter. "Time and Revolution in African America: Temporality in the History of Atlantic Slavery." In *Rethinking American History in a Global Age*, edited by Thomas Bender, 148–67. Berkeley: University of California Press, 2002.

Jones, Geoffrey. *Beauty Imagined: A History of the Global Beauty Industry*. New York: Oxford University Press, 2010.

Kang, Minsoo. "From the Machine-Man to the Automaton-Man: The Enlightenment Origins of the Mechanistic Imagery of Humanity." In *Vital Matters: Eighteenth-Century Views of Conception, Life, and Death*, edited by Helen Deutsch and Mary Terrall, 148–73. Toronto: University of Toronto Press, 2012.

Katznelson, Ira. *Fear Itself: The New Deal and the Origins of Our Time*. New York: Liveright Publishing, 2013.

———. *When Affirmative Action Was White: An Untold History of Racial Equality in Twentieth-Century America*. New York: W. W. Norton, 2005.

Kemper, Steve. *A Splendid Savage: The Restless Life of Frederick Russell Burnham*. New York: W. W. Norton, 2016.

Kendrick, James. *Hollywood Bloodshed: Violence in 1980s American Cinema*. Carbondale: Southern Illinois University Press, 2009.

Kerber, Linda. "The Republican Mother: Women and the Enlightenment: An American Perspective." *American Quarterly* 28, no. 2 (Summer 1976): 187–205.

Kerkvliet, Benedict J. *Peasant Rebellion in the Philippines: The Origins and Growth of HMB*. Madison: University of Wisconsin Press, 1972.

Khatchadourian, Raffi. "The Doomsday Invention." *The New Yorker*, November 23, 2015.

Kilby, Rick. *Finding the Fountain of Youth: Ponce de Leon and Florida's Magical Waters.* Gainesville: University of Florida Press, 2013.

Kimmel, Michael S. *The History of Men: Essays in the History of American and British Masculinities.* Albany: State University of New York Press, 2005.

———. *Manhood in America: A Cultural History.* New York: Free Press, 1996.

Kitamura, Hiroshi. *Screening Enlightenment: Hollywood and the Cultural Reconstruction of Defeated Japan.* Ithaca, NY: Cornell University Press, 2010.

Klein, Herbert S. *The Atlantic Slave Trade.* New York: Cambridge University Press, 1999.

———. *A Population History of the United States.* New York: Cambridge University Press, 2012.

Klepp, Susan E. "Revolutionary Bodies: Woman and the Fertility Transition in the Mid-Atlantic Region, 1760–1820." *Journal of American History* 85, no. 3 (December 1998): 910–45.

———. *Revolutionary Conceptions: Women, Fertility, and Family Limitation in America, 1760–1820.* Chapel Hill: The University of North Carolina Press, 2009.

Klimke, Martin. *The Other Alliance: Student Protest in West Germany and the United States in the Global Sixties.* Princeton, NJ: Princeton University Press, 2010.

Knight Lozano, Henry. "U.S. Settler Colonial Climates: Southern California, Hawai'i, and the Healthful Tropics." *American Nineteenth Century History* 20, no. 2 (2019): 183–204.

Kohler-Hausmann, Julilly. "Welfare Crises, Penal Solutions and the Origins of the 'Welfare Queen.'" *Journal of Urban History* 4, no. 5 (2015): 756–71.

Kramer, Paul A. *The Blood of Government: Race, Empire, the United States, and the Philippines.* Chapel Hill: The University of North Carolina Press, 2006.

Kramm, Robert. *Sanitized Sex: Regulating Prostitution, Venereal Disease, and Intimacy in Occupied Japan.* Oakland: University of California Press, 2017.

Krementsov, Nikolai. *Revolutionary Experiments: The Quest for Immortality in Bolshevik Science and Fiction.* New York: Oxford University Press, 2014.

Krüger, Oliver. *Virtual Immortality: God, Evolution, and Singularity in Post- and Transhumanism.* Bielefeld: transcript Verlag, 2021.

Kühl, Stefan. *The Nazi Connection: Eugenics, American Racism, and German National Socialism.* New York: Oxford University Press, 1994.

Kuhn, David Paul. *The Hardhat Riot: Nixon, New York City, and the Dawn of the White Working-Class Revolution.* New York: Oxford University Press, 2020.

Kupperman, Karen Ordahl. "International at the Creation: Early Modern American History." In *Rethinking American History in a Global Age*, edited by Thomas Bender, 103–22. Berkeley: University of California Press, 2002.

———. *Roanoke: The Abandoned Colony.* Totowa, NJ: Rowman & Littlefield, 1984.

Kurashige, Lon. *Two Faces of Exclusion: The Untold History of Anti-Asian Racism in the United States.* Chapel Hill: The University of North Carolina Press, 2016.

Kurzweil, Ray, and Terry Grossman, *Fantastic Voyage: Live Long Enough to Live Forever.* Emmaus, PA: Penguin Publishing Group, 2004.

LaBerge, Ann F. "How the Ideology of Low Fat Conquered America." *Journal of the History of Medicine and Allied Sciences* 63, no. 2 (April 2008): 139–77.

Lause, Mark A. *Young America: Land, Labor, and the Republican Community.* Urbana: University of Illinois Press, 2005.

Lee, Choonib. "Women's Liberation and Sixties Armed Resistance." *Journal of the Study of Radicalism* 11, no. 1 (Spring 2017): 25–52.

Lee, R. Alton. *The Bizarre Careers of John R. Brinkley*. Lexington: University Press of Kentucky, 2022.

Lemke, Sieglinde. *Primitivist Modernism: Black Culture and the Origins of Transatlantic Modernism*. New York: Oxford University Press, 1998.

Leonhardt, Thomas C. *Illiberal Reformers: Race, Eugenics, and American Economics in the Progressive Era*. Princeton, NJ: Princeton University Press, 2017.

Levin, Susanna. "Jane Fonda: From Barbarella to Barbells." *Women's Sports and Fitness* 9, no. 12 (1987): 24–28.

Linker, Beth. *War's Waste: Rehabilitation in World War I America*. Chicago: University of Chicago Press, 2011.

Lister, Kate. *A Curious History of Sex*. London: Unbound, 2020.

Lombardo, Paul A., ed. *A Century of Eugenics in America: From the Indiana Experiment to the Human Genome Era*. Bloomington: Indiana University Press, 2011.

Lynn, Martin. *Commerce and Economic Change in West Africa: The Palm Oil Trade in the Nineteenth Century*. New York: Cambridge University Press, 1997.

Maat, Harro. "Agriculture and Food Production." In *The Routledge Handbook on the History of Development*, edited by Corinna R. Unger, Iris Borowy, and Corinne A. Pernet, 190–203. New York: Routledge, 2022.

Maher, Neil M. *Nature's New Deal: The Civilian Conservation Corps and the Roots of the American Environmental Movement*. New York: Oxford University Press, 2008.

Martschukat, Jürgen. *The Age of Fitness: How the Body Came to Symbolize Success and Achievement*. Translated by Alex Skinner. Cambridge: Polity Press, 2021.

Marwick, Arthur. "The Cultural Revolution of the Long Sixties: Voices of Reaction, Protest, and Permeation." *American Historical Review* 27, no. 4 (December 2005): 780–806.

Matthews, Jean. *The Rise of the New Woman: The Woman's Movement in America, 1875–1930*. Chicago: Ivan R. Dee, 2003.

May, Elaine Tyler. *Homeward Bound: American Families in the Cold War*. New York: Basic Books, 1988.

May, Robert E. *Manifest Destiny's Underworld: Filibustering in Antebellum America*. Chapel Hill: The University of North Carolina Press, 2002.

Maza, Sarah. "'The Kids Aren't All Right': Historians and the Problem of Childhood." *American Historical Review* 125, no. 4 (October 2020): 1261–85.

McDaniel, W. Caleb. "The Fourth and the First: Abolitionist Holidays, Respectability, and Radical Interracial Reform." *American Quarterly* 57, no. 1 (March 2005): 129–51.

———. *The Problem of Democracy in the Age of Slavery: Garrisonian Abolitionists and Transatlantic Reform*. Baton Rouge: Louisiana State University Press, 2013.

McGirr, Lisa. *Suburban Warriors: The Origins of the New American Right*. Princeton, NJ: Princeton University Press, 2001.

McLaren, Angus. *Impotence: A Cultural History*. Chicago: University of Chicago Press, 2007.

McRuer, Robert. "Compulsory Able-Bodiedness and Queer/Disabled Existence." In *The Disability Studies Reader*, 3rd ed., edited by Lennard J. Davis, 383–92. New York: Routledge, 2010.

Medovoi, Leerom. *Rebels: Youth and the Cold War Origins of Identity*. Durham, NC: Duke University Press, 2005.

Mehlman Petrzela, Natalia. *Fit Nation: The Gains and Pains of America's Exercise Obsession*. Chicago: University of Chicago Press, 2023.

———. "Thanks, Gender! An Intellectual History of the Gym." In *American Labyrinth: Intellectual History for Complicated Times*, edited by Raymond Haberski Jr. and Andrew Hartman, 86–104. Ithaca, NY: Cornell University Press, 2018.

Mehring, Frank. "Portraying Transnational America: Aesthetic and Political Dimensions in Winold Reiss's 'Plea for Color.'" In *Re-Framing the Transnational Turn in American Studies*, edited by Winfried Fluck, Donald E. Pease, and John Carlos Rowe, 164–92. Hanover, NH: Dartmouth College Press, 2011.

Melosh, Barbara. *Engendering Culture: Manhood and Womanhood in New Deal Public Art*. Washington, DC: Smithsonian Institution Scholarly Press, 1991.

Merrill, Dennis. *Negotiating Paradise: US Tourism and Empire in Twentieth-Century Latin America*. Chapel Hill: The University of North Carolina Press, 2009.

Miller, Brian Craig. *Empty Sleeves: Amputation in the Civil War South*. Athens: University of Georgia Press, 2015.

Miller, James. *Democracy Is in the Streets: From Port Huron to the Siege of Chicago*. Cambridge, MA: Havard University Press, 1987.

Miller, Timothy. *The 60s Communes: Hippies and Beyond*. Syracuse, NY: Syracuse University Press, 1999.

Mintz, Steven. *Huck's Raft: A History of American Childhood*. Cambridge, MA: Harvard University Press, 2004.

———. "Reflections on Age as a Category of Historical Analysis." *Journal of the History of Childhood and Youth* 1, no. 1 (2008): 91–94.

Mosse, George L. *The Image of Man: The Creation of Modern Masculinity*. New York: Oxford University Press, 1996.

Muri, Allison. *The Enlightenment Cyborg: A History of Communications and Control in the Human Machine, 1660–1830*. Toronto: University of Toronto Press, 2007.

Murphy, Kevin P. *Political Manhood: Red Bloods, Mollycoddles, and the Politics of Progressive Era Reform*. New York: Columbia University Press, 2010.

Neumann, Matthias. "'Youth, It's Your Turn!': Generations and the Fate of the Russian Revolution (1917–1932)." *Journal of Social History* 46, no. 2 (Winter 2012): 273–304.

Nicholas, Jane, and Michelle Smith. "Soft Rejuvenation: Cosmetics, Idealized White Femininity, and Young Women's Bodies, 1880–1930." *Journal of Social History* 53, no. 4 (Summer 2020): 906–21.

Nickerson, Michelle. *Mothers of Conservatism: Women and the Postwar Right*. Princeton, NJ: Princeton University Press, 2012.

Niedermeier, Silvan. "Colonial Self-Positioning: Approaching the Snapshots of an American Woman in the Philippines (1900–1902)." In *New Perspectives on the History of Gender and Empire: Comparative and Global Approaches*, edited by Ulrike Lindner and Dörte Lerp, 115–48. London: Bloomsbury Academic, 2018.

Nigg, Joseph. *The Phoenix: An Unnatural Biography of a Mythical Beast*. Chicago: University of Chicago Press, 2016.

O'Brien, Karen. *Narratives of Enlightenment: Cosmopolitan History from Voltaire to Gibbon.* New York: Cambridge University Press, 1997.

O'Mara, Margaret. *The Code: Silicon Valley and the Remaking of America.* New York: Penguin Books, 2019.

Offenburger, Andrew. *Frontiers in the Gilded Age: Adventure, Capitalism & Dispossession from Southern Africa to the U.S.-Mexican Borderlands, 1880–1917.* New Haven, CT: Yale University Press, 2019.

Ogren, Kathy J. *The Jazz Revolution: Twenties America and the Meaning of Jazz.* New York: Oxford University Press, 1989.

Olson, Lester C. *Benjamin Franklin's Vision of Community: A Study in Rhetorical Iconology.* Columbia: University of South Carolina Press, 2004.

Onuf, Peter. *Jefferson's Empire: The Language of American Nationhood.* Charlottesville: University of Virginia Press, 2000.

Osterhammel, Jürgen. *The Transformation of the World: A Global History of the Nineteenth Century.* Princeton, NJ: Princeton University Press, 2014.

Painter, Nell Irvin. *The History of White People.* New York, 2010.

Paisley, Fiona. "Childhood and Race: Growing Up in the Empire." In *Gender and Empire,* edited by Philippa Levine, 240–59. New York: Oxford University Press, 2004.

Paris, Leslie. *Children's Nature: The Rise of the American Summer Camp.* New York: New York University Press, 2008.

———. "The Sexual Clock: Middle-Aged American Women and Sexual Vitality in the 1960s and 1970s." *Journal of Social History* 53/4 (2020): 922–38.

Patel, Kiran Klaus. *Soldiers of Labor: Labor Service in Nazi Germany and New Deal America.* New York: Cambridge University Press, 2005.

Patterson, Gordon. "The Trials and Tribulations of Amos Quito: The Creation of the Florida Anti-Mosquito Association." In *Paradise Lost? The Environmental History of Florida,* edited by Jack E. Davis and Raymond Arsenault, 160–76. Gainesville: University Press of Florida, 2005.

Peiss, Kathy. *Hope in a Jar: The Making of America's Beauty Culture.* Philadelphia: University of Pennsylvania Press, 2011.

Pettit, Michael. "Becoming Glandular: Endocrinology, Mass Culture, and Experimental Lives in the Interwar Age." *American Historical Review* 118, no. 4 (October 2013): 1052–76.

Phillips, Rod. *Alcohol: A History.* Chapel Hill: The University of North Carolina Press, 2014.

Phillips, Wendell. "Public Opinion." In *Selections from the Works of Wendell Phillips,* edited by A. D. Hall, 21–35. Boston: H. M. Caldwell, 1902.

Plant, Rebecca Jo. *Mom: The Transformation of Motherhood in Modern America.* Chicago: University of Chicago Press, 2010.

Poiger, Uta. G. *Jazz, Rock, and Rebels: Cold War Politics and American Culture in a Divided Germany.* Oakland: University of California Press, 2000.

Pomfret, David M. "Imperial Rejuvenations: Youth, Empire and the Problem of Accelerated Aging in 'Tropical' Colonies, c. 1800–1914." *Journal of Social History* 53, no 4. (Summer 2020): 939–62.

Ponten, Frederic. "Die Identität des Feindes: Erik H. Erikson, Margaret Mead und die Erfindung der Reeducation." *Zeitschrift für Kulturwissenschaften* 2 (2020): 67–95.

Ponzio, Alessio. *Shaping the New Man: Youth Training Regimes in Fascist Italy and Nazi Germany.* Madison: University of Wisconsin Press, 2015.

Power Smith, Mark. *Young America: The Transformation of Nationalism before the Civil War.* Charlottesville, VA: University of Virginia Press, 2022.

Prebel, Julie. "Engineering Womanhood: The Politics of Rejuvenation in Gertrude Atherton's Black Oxen." *American Literature* 76, no. 2 (2004): 307–37.

Purkiss, Ava. *Fit Citizens: A History of Black Women's Exercise from Post-Reconstruction to Postwar America.* Chapel Hill: The University of North Carolina Press, 2023.

Putnam, Robert D. *Bowling Alone: The Collapse and Revival of American Community.* New York: Touchstone Books by Simon & Schuster, 2000.

Ramsbrock, Annelie. *The Science of Beauty: Culture and Cosmetics in Modern Germany.* New York: Palgrave Macmillan, 2015.

Rasko, John, and Carl Power, *Flesh Made New: The Unnatural History and Broken Promise of Stem Cells.* Sidney: ABC Books, 2021.

Rasmussen, Nicolas. *Fat in the Fifties: America's First Obesity Crisis.* Baltimore: Johns Hopkins University Press, 2019.

Rauchway, Eric. *The Great Depression and the New Deal: A Very Short Introduction.* New York: Oxford University Press, 2008.

Rhodes, Jane. *Framing the Black Panthers: The Spectacular Rise of a Black Power Icon.* Urbana: University of Illinois Press, 2017.

Roberts, Timothy Mason. *Distant Revolutions: 1848 and the Challenge to American Exceptionalism.* Charlottesville: University of Virginia Press, 2009.

Robins, Jonathan E. *Oil Palm: A Global History.* Chapel Hill: The University of North Carolina Press, 2021.

Rooks, Noliwe M. *Hair Raising: Beauty, Culture, and African American Women.* New Brunswick, NJ: Rutgers University Press, 2000.

Rosa, Hartmut. *Social Acceleration: A New Theory of Modernity.* New York: Columbia University Press, 2013.

Rosenberg, Gabriel N. "No Scrubs: Livestock Breeding, Eugenics, and the State in the Early Twentieth-Century United States." *Journal of American History* 107, no. 2 (September 2020): 362–87.

Ryan, Erica J. *Red War on the Family: Sex, Gender, and Americanism during the First Red Scare.* Philadelphia: Temple University Press, 2015.

Salmond, John A. *The Civilian Conservation Corps, 1933–1942: A New Deal Case Study.* Durham, NC: Duke University Press, 1967.

Saukko, Paula. *The Anorexic Self: A Personal, Political Analysis of a Diagnostic Discourse.* Albany: State University of New York Press, 2008.

Schäfer, Stefanie. *Yankee Yarns: Storytelling and the Invention of the National Body in Nineteenth-Century American Culture.* Edinburgh: Edinburgh University Press, 2022.

Schaffner, Anna Katharina. *Exhaustion: A History.* New York: Columbia University Press, 2016.

Scharnhorst, Gary. *Owen Wister and the West.* Norman: University of Oklahoma Press, 2015.

Schmidt, Susanne. *Midlife Crisis: The Feminist Origins of a Chauvinist Cliché*. Chicago: University of Chicago Press, 2020.

Schrecker, Ellen. *The Lost Promise: American Universities in the 1960s*. Chicago: University of Chicago Press, 2021.

Schueller, Malini Johar. *Campaigns of Knowledge: US Pedagogies of Colonialism and Occupation in the Philippines and Japan*. Philadelphia: Temple University Press, 2019.

Schwartz, Hillel. *Never Satisfied: A Cultural History of Diets, Fantasies, and Fats*. New York: Free Press, 1986.

Scott, Holly V. *Younger than Now: The Politics of Age in the 1960s*. Amherst: University of Massachusetts Press, 2016.

Segrave, Kerry. *Baldness: A Social History*. Jefferson, NC: MacFarland, 1996.

Shibusawa, Naoko. *America's Geisha Ally: Reimagining the Japanese Enemy*. Cambridge, MA: Harvard University Press, 2006.

Shprintzen, Adam D. *The Vegetarian Crusade: The Rise of an American Reform Movement, 1817–1921*. Chapel Hill: The University of North Carolina Press, 2013.

Shulman, Carl, and Nick Bostrom, "Embryo Selection for Cognitive Enhancement: Curiosity or Game Changer?" *Global Policy* 5, no. 1 (2014): 85–92.

Silber, Nina. *The Romance of Reunion: White Northerners and the South, 1865–1900*. Chapel Hill: The University of North Carolina Press, 1993.

Sinha, Manisha. *The Slave's Cause: A History of Abolition*. New Haven, CT: Yale University Press, 2017.

Sklar, Kathrin Kish. "All Hail to Pure Cold Water!" *American Heritage* 26 (December 1974): 64–70.

Skwiot, Christine. *The Purpose of Paradise: U.S. Tourism and Empire in Cuba and Hawai'i*. Philadelphia: University of Pennsylvania Press, 2010.

Slotkin, Richard. *Gunfighter Nation: The Myth of the Frontier in Twentieth-Century America*. Norman: University of Oklahoma Press, 1998.

Small, Melvin. *Antiwarriors: The Vietnam War and the Battle for America's Hearts and Minds*. Lanham, MD: Rowman & Littlefield, 2002.

Stanley, Richard. *The Psychedelic Sixties: A Social History of the United States, 1960–1969*. Bloomington, IN: iUniverse, 2013.

Stark, James F. *The Cult of Youth: Anti-Ageing in Modern Britain*. Cambridge, New York: Cambridge University Press, 2020.

Steele, Andrew. "A Drug to Treat Aging May Not Be a Pipe Dream." *Wired*, January 1, 2023.

Steinberg, W. "Depression: A Discussion of Jung's Ideas." *Journal of Analytical Psychology* 34, no. 4 (October 1989): 339–52.

Stern, Alexandra Minna. *Eugenic Nation: Faults and Frontiers of Better Breeding in Modern America*. Berkeley: University of California Press, 2016.

Stevens, Jay. "The Counterculture." In *The Social Fabric: American Life from the Civil War to the Present*, vol. 2, edited by John H. Cary, Julius Weinberg, and Thomas L. Hartshorne, 309–27. New York: Harper Collins, 1991.

———. *Storming Heaven: LSD and the American Dream*. New York: Atlantic Monthly Press/Little, Brown, 1987.

Stewart, James Brewer. "Heroes, Villains, Liberty, and License: The Abolitionist Vision of Wendell Phillips." In *Antislavery Reconsidered: New Perspectives on the Abolitionists,* edited by Lewis Perry and Michael Fellman, 168–91. Baton Rouge: Louisiana State University Press, 1979.

Stieglitz, Olaf. "Swimming the Crawl to Educate the Modern Body: Visual Material and the Expanding Market for Participatory Sports in the USA, 1890s–1930s." In *Body, Capital, and Screens: Visual Media and the Healthy Self in the 20th Century*, edited by Christian Bonah and Anja Laukötter, 159–80. Amsterdam: Amsterdam University Press, 2020.

Stoff, Heiko. *Ewige Jugend: Konzepte der Verjüngung vom späten 19. Jahrhundert bis ins Dritte Reich*. Cologne: Böhlau, 2004.

———."Verjüngungsrummel: Der Kampf um Wissenschaftlichkeit in den 1920er Jahren." In *Pseudo-Wissenschaft: Konzeptionen von Nichtwissenschaftlichkeit in der Wissenschaftsgeschichte*, edited by Dirk Rupnow, Veronika Lipphardt, Jens Thiel, and Christina Wessely, 194–222. Frankfurt/Main: Suhrkamp, 2008.

Sullivan, Robert B. "Sanguine Practices: A Historical and Historiographic Reconsideration of Heroic Therapy in the Age of Rush." *Bulletin of the History of Medicine* 68, no. 2 (Summer 1994): 211–34.

Syrett Nicholas L., and David M. Pomfret. "Concepts of Youth." In *A Cultural History of Youth in the Modern Age*, vol. 6, edited by Kristine Alexander and Simon Sleight, 19–40. London: Bloomsbury Academic, 2023.

Thomas, Lynn M. *Beneath the Surface: A Transnational History of Skin Lighteners*. Durham, NC: Duke University Press, 2020.

Thomson, Keith. *Jefferson's Shadow: The Story of His Science*. New Haven, CT: Yale University Press, 2012.

Tomas, David. "Reimagining the Human Body in the Age of the Cyborg." *Body & Society* 1/3, no. 4 (1995): 21–43.

Trimmer, Eric. *Rejuvenation: The History of an Idea*. London: Hale, 1967.

Turner, Terrence. "The Social Skin." In *Beyond the Body Proper*, edited by Judith Farquhar and Margaret Lock, 83–103. Durham, NC: Duke University Press, 2007.

Tyrrell, Ian. *Reforming the World: The Creation of America's Moral Empire*. Princeton, NJ: Princeton University Press, 2010.

Varon, Elizabeth R. *We Mean to Be Counted: White Women and Politics in Antebellum Virginia*. Chapel Hill: The University of North Carolina Press, 1998.

Veit, Helen Zoe. "'Why Do People Die?' Rising Live Expectancy, Aging, and Personal Responsibility." *Journal of Social History* 45, no. 4 (Summer 2012): 1026–48.

Verbrugge, Martha H. "Gender, Science, and Fitness: Perspectives on Women's Exercise in the United States in the 20th Century." *Health and History* 4, no. 1 (2002): 52–72.

Viktorin, Carolin, Jessica C. E. Gienow-Hecht, Annika Estner, and Marcel K. Will, eds. *Nation Branding in Modern History*. New York: Berghahn Books, 2018.

Wallach, Glen. *Obedient Sons: The Discourse of Youth and Generations in American Culture, 1630–1860*. Amherst: University of Massachusetts Press, 1997.

Washington, Margaret. *Sojourner Truth's America*. Urbana: University of Illinois Press, 2009.

Wegs, J. R. "Working-Class Adolescence in Austria, 1890–1930." *Journal of Family History* 17, no. 4 (1992): 439–50.

Weinbaum, Alys Eve, Lynn M. Thomas, Priti Ramamurthy, Uta G. Poiger, Madeleine Yue Dong, and Tani E. Barlow, eds. *The Modern Girl around the World: Consumption, Modernity, and Globalization*. Durham, NC: Duke University Press, 2008.

Wendt, Simon. *The Spirit and the Shotgun: Armed Resistance and the Struggle for Civil Rights*. Gainesville: University Press of Florida, 2007.

Wertheim, Stephen. *Tomorrow, the World: The Birth of US Global Supremacy*. Cambridge, MA: Belknap Press of Harvard University Press, 2020.

Widmer, Edward L. *Young America: The Flowering of Democracy in New York City*. New York: Oxford University Press, 1999.

Wierzbicki, James. *When Music Mattered: American Music in the Sixties*. New York: Palgrave Macmillan, 2022.

Willis, Ellen. "Radical Feminism and Feminist Radicalism." *Social Text* 9/10 (1984): 91–118.

Wilson, Brian C. *Dr. John Harvey Kellogg and the Religion of Biologic Living*. Bloomington: Indiana University Press, 2014.

Windon, Nathaniel. "Superannuated: Old Age on the Antebellum Plantation." *American Quarterly* 71, no. 3 (September 2019): 767–87.

Woitas, Melanie. *"We Become What We Do," Eine Geschichte der Aerobics in den USA*. PhD diss., Universität Erfurt, 2019.

Woodhead, Lindy. *War Paint: Elizabeth Arden and Helena Rubinstein*. London: Virago Press, 2003.

Woodson, Thomas. "Doctor Wesselhoeft and Doctor Rappacini." *Nathaniel Hawthorne Review* 28 (Spring & Fall 2002): 1–28.

Woodward, C. Vann. "The Aging of America." *American Historical Review* 82, no. 3 (June 1977): 583–94.

Wrobel, David M. *Global West, American Frontier: Travel, Empire, and Exceptionalism from Manifest Destiny to the Great Depression*. Albuquerque: University of New Mexico Press, 2013.

Zahra, Tara. *The Lost Children: Reconstructing Europe's Families after World War II*. Cambridge, MA: Havard University Press, 2011.

Zaleski, Andrew. "Is There Any Truth to Anti-Aging Schemes?" *Popular Science*, June 12, 2018.

Zimdars, Melissa. *Watching Our Weights: The Contradictions of Televising Fatness in the 'Obesity Epidemic'*. New Brunswick, NJ: Rutgers University Press, 2019.